Leigh & Sylvia,
I hear that you appreciate
a drink; that's eminently
sensible. Let's hope this helps
you to navigate the Spanish
wine scene. Graeme Chesters.

THE WINES

OF

SPAIN

GW00599631

by

Graeme Chesters

SURVIVAL BOOKS • LONDON • ENGLAND

First published 2001

Survival Books Limited, 1st Floor, 60 St. James's Street,
London SW1A 1ZN, United Kingdom
☎ +44 (0)20-7493 4244, ⊠ +44 (0)20-7491 0605
⊠ info@survivalbooks.net
🖳 www.survivalbooks.net

British Library Cataloguing in Publication Data.
A CIP record for this book is available from the British Library.
ISBN 1 901130 91 6

Printed and bound in Finland by WS Bookwell Ltd.

To Louise, my ultimate drinking partner,
for patience, support, love and manicures.

ACKNOWLEDGEMENTS

First of all I would like to thank Peter Read, whose idea this book was and who recognised the potential in my writing and helped and encouraged me with this, my first non-fiction book. Thanks also to my newspaper (*The Entertainer*) for providing me with a regular outlet for my writing and to my friends at Birdie Vinos in Fuengirola (Spain) for providing me with the opportunity to run wine courses. My study of Spanish wine has been made much more enjoyable by the shared enthusiasm of five people: Louise, Patrick, Steve, Sue and Wicki. Our numerous tastings over the years have contributed to many of the reviews in this book and long may they continue. Also many thanks to my parents and in-laws for patience, support and for being nice people.

I am also indebted to Jim Watson (for the superb cover design, illustrations and maps), Paul Nurme for the cover photograph, Joe & Kerry Laredo for their excellent work in designing the book's layout and preparing the manuscript, Joaquín Núñez and Carmen Perera (Instituto de Comercio Exterior) for providing the colour photographs, and to anyone else who helped in any way whom I have failed to mention.

CONTENTS

ABOUT THE AUTHOR

Graeme Chesters was born in 1963 in the north-west of England and graduated from Bristol University in 1985 with a BA (Hons) in philosophy. He worked for Lloyd's brokers in the City of London for ten years, during a time of lively corporate entertainment and generous expense accounts in London's financial sector. Graeme quickly developed an interest in the wines drunk at these occasions and began to study the subject in depth. He also began writing in his spare time and after having articles published in Britain decided to relocate to Spain in 1995 to pursue a career as a writer. In addition to writing a weekly wine page for a Spanish and Portuguese newspaper (*The Entertainer*) and contributing to the British wine magazine *Decanter*, he also writes children's novels and about travel.

By the same publisher

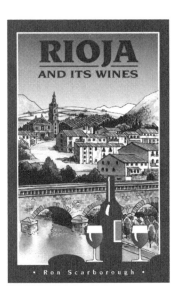

See **page 335** for details.

INTRODUCTION

Until 20 to 25 years ago, the Spanish wine scene was easy to characterise: Spain was generally known only for its sherry and some excellent reds from Rioja. Along with these (and a few other exceptions) it was mainly a producer of cheap and cheerful plonk – often mixed with lemonade and served in Sangría – consumed largely by holidaymakers in the country's myriad coastal resorts. This was an over-simplification of Spain's wines, but not so far from the truth. How things have changed in the last two decades, during which the Spanish wine industry has been transformed out of all recognition.

The country now offers so much more than Rioja, sherry and cheap sweet table wines, with a selection of quality wines as varied and exciting as you'll find anywhere. Although they aren't always as well known as those from other countries, the quality and choice of wines is increasing annually and many offer outstanding value for money. However, there remains a paucity of information available about Spanish wine, which usually rates just a few pages is most general wine books. This book is designed to redress the balance and is the most comprehensive and up-to-date book dedicated to Spanish wine published in English, and is essential reading for every wine lover.

Inside you'll discover Spain's many diverse wine regions, including their history; geography, soil and climate; and future developments. Included is a selection of each region's bodegas (wine producers), chosen on the basis of quality or because they make wines representative of their region, with reviews of their leading wines (over 2,000). Wines are categorised as expensive, inexpensive or excellent value for money, in relation to regional or national price averages. Invariably not all of a bodega's wines are reviewed, but those chosen are generally the best or those offering particularly good value for money. Reviews aren't vintage-specific but are based on a wine's average performance and characteristics over the past five years.

These are exciting times to be studying and drinking Spanish wines. Spain now makes as many styles of wine as anywhere – probably more – and both quality and variety have increased dramatically in recent years. The country's best wines can compete with those from anywhere in the world and in just about any style. So fill your glass, relax and allow yourself to be transported to a country with 'everything under the sun' – including some of the world's finest wines.

Salud!

Graeme Chesters
August 2001

1.

OVERVIEW

Wine production in the Iberian peninsula stretches back at least to the time of the Phoenicians – who arrived before 1,000 BC – and was continued by the Greeks, the Romans and, in some regions, even by the Moors, despite Islam's strictures against alcohol. A hundred years after the Moors were finally expelled at the end of the 15th century, Spain found an important foreign market (Britain) for one of its most famous and historic wines: sherry. Thus began a long, close wine association, although it started as a result of an act of hostility: Sir Francis Drake's raid on Cádiz in 1587, which led to the seizure of large quantities of sherry wines. These subsequently became popular in Britain and even today the country is sherry's biggest export market.

The modern Spanish wine industry began to take shape from the latter 18th century, when British merchants moved to the sherry region to set up businesses to capitalise on the wine's popularity in Britain. The arrival of French wine makers and merchants in Rioja in the mid-19th century – in search of wine when phylloxera was ravaging Bordeaux's vineyards – began the modern Spanish table wine industry, the French bringing new ideas and techniques (including ageing in oak barrels).

But the current Spanish wine industry only really developed and came to international prominence as recently as the '80s and '90s. Until then much of the country was restrained by outdated equipment and ideas, an absence of co-ordinated wine regulations and quality control, lack of investment and local or national crises. Nearly four decades of relative isolation during the rule of General Franco – which ended with his death in 1975 – did not help.

Throughout the '60s and '70s, the growing numbers of tourists visiting Spain increased the demand for decent wines, as did a burgeoning Spanish middle class, but what really kick-started the wine industry was joining the European Union (EU) in 1986. This provided the decisive spur to build on the improvements that had been gradually taking place, the resulting EU grants funding modernisation and new development. The opening up of the country's frontiers to free trade also exposed Spain to fresh ideas and competition.

The influence of the New World must also be taken into account. The '70s and '80s saw the arrival in Europe of well made, cleverly marketed wines from California and southern hemisphere countries led by Australia. These producers avoided fustiness, wine snobbery and elitism, and their varietally named, imaginatively labelled, fruity, commercial wines rapidly gained legions of fans. Producers in Spain and other Old World countries quickly realised that they would have to look to their laurels because the whiff of competition was in the air.

The attack came at all levels: Spain's bulk producers were threatened by well made, well presented, inexpensive, everyday wines, while in the middle and top end of the market the likes of Rioja found that tastes were changing, with the concentrated, fruity styles from the New World luring their customers away. Spain saw that survival was at stake and that change was inevitable: quality would have to improve while over-attachment to volume production and anachronistic thinking would have to end.

Fortunately, the country is well suited to quality wine production and also has more land devoted to vines than elsewhere, although lower yields – about a third of those of France and a mere fifth of Germany's vast crops – make it the world's third-largest wine producer, behind France and Italy. Spain's strength is diversity: it has such a variety of terrain that the country resembles a mini-continent and a range of different wines to match. At one extreme is Galicia in the north-west, which is cool, damp and cloudy, with a landscape reminiscent of southern Ireland; while at the other is the desert-like south-east, similar to North Africa and one of the driest parts of Europe. There is also everything in between: high mountains, rolling hills, Mediterranean lowlands, elevated plains and fertile river valleys. This results in a wide range of climates, micro-climates and, crucially, altitudes. Large areas of Spain have hot summers, but the high altitude of many vine growing regions – up to 900m (2,952ft) above sea level on the mainland and up to 1,750m (5,741ft) in the Canaries – means that grapes enjoy cool nights in which to recover after the torrid days and thus retain their all-important acidity, aromas and flavours.

This, allied to poor soils and lack of water – better grapes are often produced in trying environments – as well as a reasonable range of good quality indigenous grape varieties and the full sweep of foreigners, means that Spain can produce large quantities of decent quality grapes. Improved technology and advances in vine growing and wine making have helped the country to capitalise on its abundant natural advantages and there has been an important new openness to modern ideas, which has coincided with the rise to prominence of younger wine makers.

The last two decades have seen Spain's wine landscape change and improve rapidly. There are now around ten high quality red wine regions, with several others making progress, and half a dozen producing excellent whites, with general standards very much on the increase. In addition, many good rosés, sparkling and fortified wines are produced.

Wine Regions

Spain has 55 denominated wine regions (shown on the map inside the front cover), with more in the offing, plus a number of others producing the Spanish equivalent of table wine. The 55 regions are classified as Denominación de Origen (D.O.), which signifies an official wine region whose boundaries, permitted grape varieties, vineyard management techniques, quality levels and other characteristics are decided by the local governing body (Consejo Regulador). A further classification, Denominación de Origen Calificada (D.O.Ca), was introduced in 1991 and is reserved for wines of the very highest quality. To date only Rioja enjoys this honour, although it is expected to be awarded to a few other regions in the near future.

For the purposes of this book, Spain's wine regions have been grouped into 13 areas (most containing a number of D.O.s), listed below and described in chapters 2 to 14:

- Andalucía and Estremadura

- Aragón

- The Balearics

- The Basque Country

- The Canary Islands

- Castilla-La Mancha

- Castilla-León

- Catalonia

- Cava

- Galicia

- The Levante

- Navarra

- Rioja

Each region uses a number of grape varieties, including indigenous and foreign grapes, which must be approved by the Consejo Regulador. These are described in the following section.

Grape Varieties

This section describes the principal grape varieties used to make Spain's wines, one of the best indicators of what they are like. Some are considered globally, which will help to relate them to their Spanish equivalents.

Black grape varieties indigenous to Spain

Bobal: This grape is grown mainly in the hot south-east of the country, which was until recently an area renowned for big, strong, headache-inducing reds. Bobal was never guilty of making these, producing light-bodied wines with refreshing acidity and lowish alcohol. It is associated particularly with D.O. Utiel-Requena, and as well as reds, it makes characterful rosés.

Cariñena: The name 'Cariñena' comes from a town in Aragón in north-east Spain and the grape is most commonly grown in Catalonia, Rioja and, of course, Aragón. It is often blended with Garnacha, contributing acidity and resistance to oxidation. In France, Cariñena is called Carignan and is by far that country's most common grape; it is also grown in California and North Africa. The grape has generally been seen as more of a workhorse than a distinguished performer, although Cariñena grapes from old vines also feature in some of the top wines of D.O. Priorato in Catalonia.

Garnacha Peluda: This is a mutation of Garnacha Tinta (below) and is, to all intents and purposes, the same thing.

Garnacha Tinta: This warm-weather grape is the world's most widely grown black variety. It enjoys this distinction mainly because of its vast plantings in Spain and southern France, where it is known as Grenache, although it is also found in California, Australia and several other Mediterranean countries. It makes strong, pale, fruity reds – which sometimes verge on the jammy – and characterful rosés. Garnacha is grown in many areas of Spain and is particularly important in Rioja, where it is often blended with Tempranillo to add juice and body to the latter's lean, structured qualities. In Navarra it makes the majority of the region's good quality, reasonably priced rosés, but its most noble appearance is in the imposing, dark, complex wines of Priorato in Catalonia, often blended with Cariñena. Red wines made solely from Garnacha have traditionally not been suitable for long ageing because of their susceptibility to oxidation, but wines such as Rioja producer Martínez-Bujanda's Garnacha are beginning to challenge this view.

❦ **Graciano:** Arguably Spain's best native black grape, Graciano has colour, aroma, flavour and style. It was once grown fairly widely in Rioja but almost died out because its low yields were deemed uneconomic. Thankfully it is making a small comeback, with the wines it produces almost always reassuringly expensive. The grape is also found in southern France, California and Argentina.

❦ **Mencía:** This is grown in parts of Galicia and Castilla-León in north-west Spain. It is of good quality and makes light, aromatic red wines, sometimes low in tannin and thus lacking the structure for long ageing unless blended with other varieties. Some think the grape has similarities to Cabernet Franc.

❦ **Monastrell:** Because of its popularity in south-east Spain, this is the country's second most common black grape. It favours warm weather – appropriate in large areas of Spain – and can make good quality, dark, tasty, alcoholic wines. In France it is called Mourvèdre and is grown mainly in the south of the country, and it is increasing in popularity in Australia and California. Monastrell used to be seen as a rough-and-ready variety, but it has been re-evaluated recently and modern methods have shown that it can make very good wines.

❦ **Tempranillo:** This is Spain's most widely distributed, high quality, indigenous black grape variety. Rather confusingly, it is known by different names in different parts of the country and because these sometimes appear on wine labels it is useful to know them: in Rioja, Navarra, Somontano and the Levante region of the south-east, it is thankfully called Tempranillo, but in Catalonia it is known (in Catalan) as Ull de Llebre or, in Castilian, as Ojo de Liebre (hare's eye). In Ribera del Duero it becomes Tinto Fino or Tinta del País, in La Mancha and Valdepeñas it is Cencibel, in Toro it is unimaginatively called Tinto de Toro and in the region surrounding the capital it is likewise called Tinto de Madrid.

Tempranillo is pale, fine and tannic, and is often blended with other grape varieties. In Rioja its main partner is Garnacha, while in Catalonia and Navarra it is frequently twinned with Cabernet Sauvignon. The resultant wines can be very long-lived, with the Tempranillo contributing savoury, strawberry flavours, structure and a strong affinity with oak ageing. Most of the classic wines of Ribera del Duero are Tempranillo-based.

The grape is also grown in Portugal where it goes by yet more names: Tinta Roriz in the Dão and Douro, while in Alentejo it is confusingly named Aragonez. Apart from Iberia, Tempranillo is only grown seriously in Argentina and Mexico, and there are small plantings in France and Australia.

Foreign black grape varieties used in Spain

❦ **Cabernet Franc:** Cabernet Franc is the least acclaimed of the three main varieties blended to make the celebrated red wines of Bordeaux in western France. This is unfair because it is a characterful grape, aromatic, fruity and herbaceous. Cabernet

Franc is also grown in France's Loire Valley, north-east Italy, Australia, California and South Africa. In Spain its cultivation is mostly restricted to Castilla-León and Galicia.

❧ **Cabernet Sauvignon:** This, the world's most famous black grape, is eagerly grown throughout the world. It is an important constituent of many of Bordeaux's red wines, which are still the model many wine makers aspire to, hence their desire to use the grape. Cabernet is a classy performer, herby, spicy and tannic, with a distinctive aroma of blackcurrants. When aged in oak, which it often is, it takes on notes of cedar and tobacco, and can make wines capable of long ageing. Cabernet Sauvignon is often at its best when blended with other grape varieties.

It makes superb wines in Italy – notably the so-called Supertuscans – and is very important in central and eastern Europe, although to date these wines are quite primitively made. Across the Atlantic, California has made great Cabernet Sauvignons, some with distinctive minty hints and capable of long ageing, and Chile is making fruity wines with the grape.

South Africa's best reds have generally been made from Cabernet Sauvignon, and Australia – the world's most innovative wine making country of the last 30 years – has unsurprisingly made some great examples. Most famous are the wines produced on the distinctive terra rossa soil of Coonawarra in the south-east, and the country has also had notable success blending Cabernet Sauvignon with Shiraz.

Some of the first Cabernet Sauvignon in Spain was planted in the 19th century, at the famous Vega Sicilia estate in Ribera del Duero. One or two Rioja bodegas with French contacts planted the grape at around the same time – most famously Marqués de Riscal – but for many years after it was little seen in Spain. Indeed there was hostility in certain quarters to what was seen as a foreign interloper which would irrevocably change the character of Spain's wines.

In the 21st century attitudes have changed and Cabernet is now particularly important in Catalonia, Navarra and Somontano, either on its own or blended with other varieties; Tempranillo and Cabernet Sauvignon are particularly good bed-fellows. It is also grown in many other parts of the country, even Rioja, where it is making its presence felt in some of the top wines; feelings in the region are, however, still ambivalent about the grape. Cabernet is also a constituent of some of the great wines of Ribera del Duero – although Tempranillo is still dominant in the region – and it has an increasing presence in Priorato. Some of Spain's best varietal Cabernets come from non-D.O. parts of Castilla-La Mancha: see the entries for Dehesa del Carrizal and Marqués de Griñón on page 130.

❧ **Merlot:** Along with the two Cabernets – Franc and Sauvignon – this is the third of the three most prevalent grapes used in Bordeaux. It is blended with the other two in some of Bordeaux's reds, but also shines on its own, or with small additions, in certain wines of the Bordeaux sub-regions of St.-Emilion and Pomerol, which are some of the world's most lauded and expensive, capable of long ageing.

Merlot can also make smooth, fragrant, plummy wines that mature quickly for early drinking; these are popular in today's 'want-it-now' world, which partly explains the grape's success in many parts of the world. North-east Italy makes plump wines with Merlot and several eastern European nations are growing increasing amounts. California and Washington state produce notable Merlot wines, while Chile is making delicious, fruity examples. South Africa has enjoyed success, although Merlot is not yet as important in Australia and New Zealand as other black grapes.

In Spain, Merlot is seen by some as an 'acceptable' foreign black grape variety because of its smooth, sweet tannins and more mellow personality than the beefier Cabernet Sauvignon. To date it is mainly grown in Catalonia and Somontano – and the wines produced by the likes of Jean León, Miguel Torres and Viñas del Vero are of high quality – but if its world-wide popularity grows we may see more widespread plantings.

❦ **Negramoll:** Spain's Negramoll is thought to be identical to the more famous and quaintly titled Tinta Negra Mole, a respectable rather than remarkable black grape that became popular on the island of Madeira from the 19th century. In Spain, it is most important in the Canary Islands, where it is used to make decent reds in the light and fruity style, although it has the potential to impart a lot of colour and tannin to its wines.

❦ **Pinot Noir:** The great black grape of Burgundy and Champagne is capable of producing marvellous wines, but often fails to do so and has thus gained a reputation for being temperamental. When young, Burgundy reds can recall raspberries, strawberries and cherries, which as the wines age, evolve deliciously into flavours of liquorice and savoury foods. If good, they are astounding, but picking the right bottle of Burgundy is something of a lottery.

It used to be thought that Pinot Noir would never produce good wines outside France, but successes elsewhere – notably in the New World – have disproved this old chestnut; cooler parts of California, Oregon, Chile, Australia and New Zealand have all made good Pinots. Italy, Germany, Austria and Switzerland are making progress with Pinot Noir, although the large quantities made in Romania are generally of low quality, unrepresentative of this characterful grape. Spain does not grow it extensively, but decent Pinot Noir is now made in Catalonia and Somontano, and there are promising plantings in other regions.

❦ **Shiraz/Syrah:** This grape goes by two names: Syrah in France and invariably Shiraz in the New World. It is the leading variety of the northern Rhône in south-east France, where it makes heavy, deep-coloured, peppery, tannic wines which can age superbly. Syrah is also grown extensively in the southern Rhône, where it is one of the constituent grapes in wines like the internationally popular, although sometimes overrated, Châteauneuf-du-Pape, and is making progress in the Midi.

California and Washington state are increasingly keen on the grape, but outside France it is most important in South Africa and Australia. Here it is known as Shiraz and often produces wines which are bigger and riper than the average French example. Australia is the New World king or queen of the grape, its most planted variety and producer of a range of styles in different parts of the country. Penfold's Grange is Australia's highest expression of Shiraz and the country's greatest red wine – a global classic.

As can be gathered from the places where it is most successful, Shiraz is a warmer climate grape and hence suitable for many parts of Spain. It has made most strides in the south-eastern D.O. of Jumilla, either on its own or blended with Monastrell, and a notable example is produced in the non-D.O. area of the Montes de Toledo. Catalonia's D.O.s are also beginning to make worthy wines from the grape. Logic dictates that there will be further plantings in Spain, although logic, as we know, does not always out.

White grape varieties indigenous to Spain

❦ **Airén:** Owing to the huge areas covered by this grape in the vast hinterland of La Mancha, it is the world's most planted variety. Until recently it produced bland, often badly constructed white wines, or was added to the region's reds to beef up their acidity, but modern technology means that it can now be made into fresh, crisp whites for drinking young, while the practice of adding it to reds is falling out of favour. It will never, however, make great wines and its position as the world's most planted grape may eventually be threatened as growers increasingly replace it with better quality varieties.

❦ **Albariño:** This is Spain's most characterful native white grape, brimful of complex fruit flavours and capable of producing aromatic, elegant, refreshing wines of great quality and ever higher prices. It is grown primarily in Galicia in the cool, damp, north-west of the country and also across the border in northern Portugal, where it is known as Alvarinho and is used in many of the better Vinho Verde wines.

❦ **Garnacha Blanca:** This is grown in several parts of Spain, notably the Catalan D.O.s of Tarragona and Terra Alta, and also in Rioja. It produces wines which tend to be full and high in alcohol, although sometimes low in acidity. However, with careful wine making it can yield good results, including barrel-fermented examples of some complexity. The grape is also grown extensively throughout southern France, where it is known as Grenache Blanc.

❦ **Godello:** Godello hails from the Valdeorras D.O. in Galicia and is a tangy grape which can produce tasty, attractively bitter wines.

❦ **Macabeo/Viura:** This is another grape with more than one name, a common variety in the north of Spain. As Viura, it is the primary grape of Rioja's white wines, which, as we will discuss in the section on that region, are not Rioja's strength, while as Macabeo it is one of the three traditional grapes used to make Catalan Cava. It is of medium quality, resistant to oxidation and tends to produce lightish, refreshing wines with floral touches.

❦ **Moscatel:** The various types of Moscatel – which are often difficult to distinguish from each other – are cultivated primarily in the east of Spain and around Cádiz and Málaga in the south. They produce various styles of dry and sweet wines, which are often 'grapey' – unlike most varieties – and can be very sweet indeed. At its best, with wood ageing, Moscatel makes complex, dark wines, characterised by the best of the Málaga region.

❦ **Palomino:** This is the sherry grape, providing excellent raw material for fortified wines, although making bland, instantly forgettable table wines in the region. It is also grown in parts of northern Spain, where it produces light wines with bitter almond touches. Elsewhere, it is called Listan de Jerez in France, where it is of little consequence, and Perrum in Portugal. Palomino also appears in California, Australia and Chile, and is important in South Africa as a bulk blending grape.

- **Parellada:** This is the best of the three varieties traditionally used to make Catalan Cava and also appears in a fair number of Catalan table wines, most famously Viña Sol. It has decent acidity, lowish alcohol and fruity flavours, but on its own is unsuitable for long ageing.

- **Pedro-Ximénez:** This is invariably shortened to 'PX' and is grown extensively throughout southern Spain. It is the primary grape of D.O. Montilla-Moriles near Córdoba, which makes sherry-like fortified wines, although the locals will give you a frosty reception if you compare them with those of their rivals from down river. It is also grown in sherry country itself and is often blended with Palomino to make Málaga's sweet wines. Outside Spain, it is planted in California, South America, Australia and South Africa.

- **Treixadura:** Grown mainly in the Ribeiro area of Galicia, Treixadura has been described as a poor man's Albariño, although to be compared with that noble variety is no bad thing. It is a floral, appley grape, sometimes blended with Albariño, although not grown extensively.

- **Verdejo:** This is primarily the grape of D.O. Rueda – and parts of Castilla-León – and is of good quality with nutty touches and an attractive, bitter bite. It was formerly used to make Rueda's fortified wines, but these days forms the backbone of many of the region's successful, young, fruity table wines. It also responds well to oak ageing and can be blended with other grapes, including Sauvignon Blanc.

- **Xarel-lo:** One of the three primary Catalan Cava grapes, Xarel-lo is also used to produce table wines. It is of medium quality, modern technology allowing it to make fresh, fruity, characterful wines for drinking young. Experiments with oak ageing are yielding good results and might increase its repertoire.

Foreign white grape varieties used in Spain

- **Chardonnay:** The great white grape of both Burgundy and Champagne is an inveterate traveller, probably second only to Cabernet Sauvignon in terms of world-wide distribution, although neither covers as much vineyard hectareage as many less noble varieties. It makes the famous white wines of the eastern French region of Burgundy, with names such as Chablis, Pouilly-Fuissé, Montrachet and Corton-Charlemagne; some of these different styles of Chardonnay are considered to be the best dry whites in the world. In the Champagne region of the north-east, Chardonnay is one of three varieties – along with Pinot Noir and Pinot Meunier – which form the backbone of the region's famous sparkling wines. The grape is also grown quite extensively in other parts of the country.

  However, it is Chardonnay's expansion to, and influence in, other parts of the world which have been something of a phenomenon over the last 30 years. Indeed, so successful has it been, that 'white wine' and 'Chardonnay' have become almost synonymous in many people's minds. This situation has arisen because of Chardonnay's bountiful attributes: it is easy both to grow and to vinify, can make a wide variety of wine styles and responds better than any other white grape to oak ageing, and oak flavours are popular. As to Chardonnay's distinguishing characteristics, these are difficult to pin down: the grape is something of a chameleon, able to pick up the stamp of the climate, soil and ageing techniques that it has been exposed to. Thus, certain Chablis wines are redolent of nuts, minerals and green apples, while New World Chardonnays can be big mouthfuls of tropical fruit and new oak.

California has taken to the grape like the proverbial duck to water, producing both commercial, vaguely sweet styles and also classy wines sometimes in the mould of the better Burgundies. Australian Chardonnay is white wine to some drinkers, the country's fruity, oaky wines proving enormously popular. As with California, favoured Australian vineyards have also proved capable of making much more elegant, subtle wines from the grape. New Zealand is famous for Sauvignon Blanc, but actually produces more Chardonnay and some of these wines are noted for their elegant acidity. South Africa, Chile and Argentina have also taken up the baton and all are making progress with this grape.

Moving back to the Old World, many European countries produce Chardonnay, although if we discussed the continent's output in any detail it would fill this book. Indeed, such is the grape's profile, that aspiring wine makers everywhere see the creation of an acceptable example as something of a rite of passage. But there is danger in all this: that of homogeneity. This is especially so with a flexible grape like Chardonnay, a fairly neutral base upon which the wine maker can imprint his stamp. And if Chardonnay is made in the same way – with the barrel-fermented style over-used – it tastes much the same wherever in the world it is made. Added to this is the fact that because of its commercial success, Chardonnay has often been grown instead of local grape varieties, again at the expense of variety.

Spain has come later to the gravy train than some countries. In fact, general cultivation of Chardonnay did not begin until the '80s and while the grape is now grown in most parts of the peninsula, it is of central importance only in Navarra, Somontano and the Catalan D.O.s. These regions are well suited to its production and are making increasingly distinguished wines from the grape. However, looking at Spain's overall white wine profile, it seems unlikely that Chardonnay will stifle the use of other grapes and variety should be maintained.

- **Gewürztraminer:** This particularly characterful grape is renowned as the most difficult to pronounce and to spell. It produces deep-coloured wines with distinctive aromas of spices, petals, grapefruit and lychees. Gewürztraminer is at its best in the Alsace region of north-east France and can also be good in Germany, Washington state, Oregon, New Zealand and parts of northern Italy. As can be seen, it favours coolish locations, ripening too quickly in warm climates and becoming bitter and oily. Therefore it will never be a widespread variety in Spain and its growth is currently restricted to fresh, high parts of Catalonia and Somontano.

- **Riesling:** Pronounced 'reece-ling', this is one of the world's best white grapes, unfairly overlooked in the wake of the modishness of other varieties, notably the ubiquitous Chardonnay. This is a shame because Riesling has much going for it: distinctive flowery aromas, a range of interesting flavours, lowish alcohol, an ability to make both dry and sweet wines, good fruit acidity and the facility to age for many years in bottle while developing subtle, oily qualities. Germany and Alsace in France are the classic growers of the grape and it also does well in parts of Austria, South Africa, the west coast of the USA. and Australia. As with Gewürztraminer, Riesling favours a cooler climate and in Spain it is grown mainly in the higher parts of Catalonia and Somontano.

Sauvignon Blanc: Sauvignon enjoys the fabulous distinction of having had its aroma compared with cat's pee on a gooseberry bush.' It doesn't really smell like this of course; if it did, nobody would turn it into wine. However, it does have a distinctive, sharp nose which can include gooseberries, grass, asparagus and nettles.

It is the grape of the upper Loire in western France, most famously in such wines as Sancerre and Pouilly-Fumé, the best of which are attractively flinty and austere. Sauvignon is also a constituent grape in some of the much lauded sweet white wines of Sauternes in Bordeaux, although it is a junior partner to Sémillon in the blend. Elsewhere in Europe, parts of Austria and north-east Italy also specialise in the grape.

However, one has to travel across the globe to reach the country which over the last couple of decades has excelled with it: New Zealand. The Kiwis produce exhilarating, pungent, herbaceous wines with hints of tropical fruits, which have snatched the Sauvignon limelight from the none-too-pleased French. Other New World wine makers are trying to replicate this success, although Australia is generally too warm for the grape.

Sauvignon Blanc in Spain is very much associated with D.O. Rueda, where it makes wines ideal for the hot Spanish summer: young, vibrant, fruity and flavoursome. The higher regions of Catalonia can also make good Sauvignon.

View of Jerez including palm trees,
now so prevalent in Andalucía

2.

ANDALUCÍA & ESTREMADURA

Andalucía, a large southern province, is the source of many people's picture postcard image of Spain, with its frequently blue skies, sunshine, sandy beaches, white hill villages and flamenco glamour. The dense holiday developments of the Costa del Sol are the region's main attraction for many visitors, the coast boasting mainland Europe's best climate. But Andalucía is much more than beach-heaven, with a long, complex history, stunning landscapes and – in Córdoba, Granada and Seville – some of Europe's most beautiful cities, each with stunning relics of its Moorish past.

Andalucía also has a long tradition of viticulture, with the wines of Jerez and Málaga among Spain's most historic. The province currently has four D.O.s – Condado de Huelva, Jerez, Málaga and Montilla-Moriles – and this section is divided accordingly.

D.O. Condado de Huelva

In Brief: *A low-profile region producing sherry-like fortified wines and everyday, white table wines.*

At the beginning of the 21st century, Condado de Huelva – which lies in the far south-west of Spain – has a non-existent national and international profile. This was not always the case, with fortified wines from the region among the first Spanish wines to be drunk in northern Europe; they receive a mention in Chaucer's *Pardoner's Tale*.

Since the 16th century, however, the region has been overshadowed by its neighbour Jerez and Condado de Huelva's sherry-like wines (produced on similar chalky soils to those of Jerez) might be better known but for the fact that for many years a lot were sent to Jerez for blending. This practice was outlawed when Condado de Huelva was made a D.O. in 1964.

It now covers around 6,000 hectares of vineyards, has over 4,000 growers and 15 bottling bodegas, with more who do not bottle their wines. A fair amount of the region's output is consumed locally – with small producers supplying bars, hotels and restaurants – while the larger ones still send a lot of their output to other regions for blending or distillation.

Authorised grape varieties are:

- **White:** Garrido Fino, Listán de Huelva, Moscatel de Alejandría, Palomino, Pedro Ximénez and Zalema, the last accounting for over three-quarters of all plantings. However, there are moves to replace it with the other varieties.

Condado de Huelva's sherry-like wines are divided into two basic types:

- *Condado Pálido:* these are aged for at least two years under *flor* (a yeast which forms on fino sherry – see page 27 for further details) and are similar to fino sherries, although more full-bodied and less subtle. They contain between 14 and 17 per cent alcohol.

◆ *Condado Viejo:* similar to oloroso sherry (see page 27 for further details), these are aged for at least two years, can be dry or sweet and contain between 15 and 23 per cent alcohol. Quality varies, with some of the wines complex and interesting, while others are bland and one-dimensional.

Production of white table wines was stepped up in the '80s when modern technology (notably cold fermentation) made it easier to make them in this hot part of the world. However, it can still be a struggle and grapes must be picked early before they become 'cooked' and lose their aroma, freshness and acidity. The Zalema grape can also be a problem, because if not treated gently during picking and transportation it has a tendency to brown. This is one of the factors behind moves to replace it with other varieties. Condado de Huelva's table whites are of acceptable and decent quality rather than outstanding.

Geography, Soil and Climate

Lying in the far south-west of Spain – on the Atlantic coast and close to Portugal – Condado de Huelva has a Mediterranean climate with Atlantic influences. Winters are short and mild, while summers are long and sunny, with temperatures moderated by westerly ocean breezes. At 550mm (21in) per year, rainfall is modest, although higher than along most of Spain's southern Mediterranean coast.

Future Development

Condado de Huelva is primarily a producer of wines for the local market and for bulk transportation to other regions for blending or distillation. It is now looking to raise its profile and supply more wines to the rest of Spain. Initial emphasis is on its fresh, simple table whites and the authorities are experimenting with ten white and ten black grape varieties to see if they are suitable for inclusion under the D.O.'s authorised list. This will offer more diversity to the table wine style, which as yet is rather monotonously straightforward, although fresh and easy to drink.

The region's sherry-like generosos suffer from the daunting reputation of the wines of Jerez in both the domestic and international markets, but Condado de Huelva's producers can actually learn a valuable lesson from their counterparts in Jerez: that fortified wines need to be marketed and perhaps even re-branded to appeal to younger, 'modern' drinkers. The producers of Jerez are doing this and those of Condado de Huelva would be well advised to follow suit.

Selected Bodegas

Andrade (☎ 959 410 106) Founded in 1942, Andrade produces a variety of wines, including:

◆ *Puente del Rey (white):* A light, simple wine with green fruit and refreshment value.

- *Murallas de Niebla (white):* Quite a thick wine, with some bite, but rather flabby and unstructured.

- *Doceañero Oloroso (oloroso):* This is a dark amber colour with a full nose of mature fruit with medicinal hints and a powerful palate with bittersweet touches and finish. A satisfying wine.

- *Doceañero Cream (generoso):* A superior wine – one of the region's best – with a complex, caramelly nose and a bittersweet, toasty palate. Recommended.

Díaz (☎ 959 410 340) Founded in 1955, some of this producer's sherry-like wines are worth sampling, including:

- *La Concha (fino):* A characterful wine with bitter bite and herbaceous flavours.

- *Solera 1955 (oloroso):* A dryish wine, aromatic and flavoursome.

Oliveros (☎ 959 410 057) Founded in 1940, this operation's white table wines are not its strength and are best avoided, while the following fortified wine is worth tasting:

- *La Bolita Pálida (generoso):* A dry wine with attractive bittersweet flavours.

Vinícola del Condado Sociedad Cooperativa Andaluza (☎ 959 410 261) Founded in 1956, this large co-operative makes a range of adequate and decent wines, including:

- *Privilegio del Condado (white):* A light, pale, inexpensive wine, which is refreshing but lacks real interest.

- *Mioro Pálido (fino):* A tasty wine with pungent bite. Recommended.

D.O. Jerez

In Brief: *The source of some of Spain's most historic, highest quality, best value, most ignored wines. There is a range of styles, from light finos to dark, dense wines of great complexity and depth, both sweet and dry.*

Sherry country ('sherry' being the anglicised version of 'Jerez') lies in the south-west of Spain. It forms a triangle of land between the three towns of Jerez de la Frontera, Sanlúcar de Barrameda and Puerto de Santa María, and for many people its wines are those most synonymous with Spain.

This is perhaps because they have the longest history of any Spanish wines and were already well known in Roman times, having been developed by the Greeks or even the Carthaginians. They have also been some of the most exported of Spain's wines and have enjoyed a long and fruitful association with Great Britain, which in turn carried them throughout the world via its empire.

Although sherries had been known in Britain from earlier, the English really developed a taste for them following the influx of wines seized by Sir Francis Drake during his 1587 raid on Cádiz. During the 17th, 18th and 19th centuries British merchants moved to Jerez to build on this association and run their sherry operations, and their names survive in some of today's firms, e.g. Garvey, Osborne and Sandeman. The association continues to this day, with Britain still sherry's largest export market (The Netherlands is a close second) and the British consuming more sherry than the Spanish.

Other Spanish regions – Condado de Huelva, Montilla-Moriles and Rueda – make similar wines, but none can compete with the best of Jerez. The wine's special character comes from the local climate and soils (more of which later) and also the method of production.

Unlike standard table wines, sherry is matured with access to air. This might be expected to lead to rapid oxidation and spoilage, but sherry's secret is that it naturally develops a protective covering of white yeasts called *flor* ('flower'). This unpleasant-sounding yet magical substance controls the access of air to the must, kills damaging bacteria and imparts aroma and flavour. The quantity of *flor* varies according to the type of wine. It is thick on *finos*, even thicker on *manzanillas* (a particularly saline, maritime *fino* produced at Sanlúcar de Barremeda) and less thick on *olorosos*.

Sherry's other great 'secret' is the *solera* system of ageing, which involves the blending of older and younger wines to maintain the same style of wine year after year. It works thus: the *solera* comprises rows of oak butts (usually of 500 litres and made from American oak) which are set out in tiers. Each tier (or 'scale') of butts contains wine of the same variety but of different age. When wine is required, it is taken from the butts on the lowest tier which contain the oldest wine. These butts are then replenished from the next oldest scale and so on throughout the system. By this method, bodegas maintain the same colour, aromas and flavours year after year, meaning that, with very few exceptions, there are no sherry vintages and the wines carry the same style and qualities year after year. Fino soleras generally consist of around five scales, olorosos less, while manzanillas can have close to twenty.

The wine styles of Jerez are as follows:

- **Fino:** this is the driest, lightest sherry, a pale, greenish-yellow colour and fortified to 15 to 15.5 per cent alcohol, with pungent, tangy aromas and flavours.

- **Manzanilla:** made only in Sanlúcar de Barrameda, this is a type of fino with an especially pronounced salty, maritime tang garnered from the coastal position.

- **Amontillado:** a dry, amber wine with flavours of nuts and dried fruits. It is so-called after a style of wine originally made in Montilla. A genuine amontillado (as opposed to those made by mixing fino and oloroso) is a fino which has been aged further after the flor has died or been removed and refortified to between 16 and 18 per cent.

- **Oloroso:** the darkest sherry, fragrant, nutty, pruny and full, with between 16 and around 20 per cent alcohol. It is matured without flor and can be either dry or semi-sweet, although 'authentic' ones are bone dry.

- **Palo Cortado:** a cross between an amontillado and an oloroso.

- **Raya:** a rare type of oloroso.

- **Cream:** inexpensive oloroso blended with Pedro Ximénez.

- **Sweet fortified dessert:** the region also makes this style of wine, from Pedro Ximénez and Moscatel, and examples can be very good indeed.

Only three grape varieties are authorised in Jerez, Moscatel and Pedro Ximénez each accounting for around five per cent of plantings, while Palomino – the sherry grape par excellence – dominates all, with 90 per cent. Palomino invariably makes bland table wines, but is transformed in Jerez, being used for all the types of sherry and pretty much exclusively for the finos. Pedro Ximénez is usually used to make dessert wines, while Moscatel is employed for sweet sherries.

Jerez D.O. covers around 10,500 hectares of vines (slightly more than its rival Montilla-Moriles), with 2,800 growers and 62 bodegas. Exports are crucial, accounting for 80 per cent of sales, with only 20 per cent of production sold to the domestic market (this is in stark contrast to Montilla, where the figures are reversed). Of Jerez's exports, around 30 per cent is medium sherry, 27 per cent fino and 22 per cent cream sherry. In Spain things are very different, with manzanilla accounting for nearly 60 per cent of sales.

Geography, Soil and Climate

Jerez's climate is Mediterranean with Atlantic influences. Winters are short and mild, while summers are long, hot and dry, with temperatures away from the coast sometimes exceeding 38°C (100°F). However, prevailing westerly winds soften the climate and also bring humidity. Annual rainfall varies between 550 and 600mm (22 and 24in), higher than much of central and eastern Spain, but still modest. The oft discussed soils of Jerez are split into three types:

▲ **Albariza:** this is the best soil, bright white in colour and containing up to 40 per cent chalk, with the balance comprising sand and clay. It has good water retentive qualities, important in a region where summers are long and hot.

▲ **Arena:** the least favoured soil, sandy and containing 10 per cent chalk, it is mainly used to grow Moscatel.

▲ **Barro:** this is the medium quality soil, a clay with around 10 per cent chalk.

Future Development

The '90s was not a good decade for fortified wines, with many drinkers looking for lighter, lower-alcohol wines. Sherry suffered, along with many other fortifieds, but sales are picking up again. The messages from consumers are mixed: on the one hand, they have veered away from fortifieds to table wines, concerned about their alcohol intake; on the other, the alcohol levels in many table wines have been on the increase, with a lot of New World-style Chardonnays and 'spicy blockbuster' red wines containing between 13.5 and 15 per cent alcohol, the latter similar to the fino sherry level.

So all is far from lost and the problem is not one of alcohol levels or flavour (blind tastings show that the sherries – especially finos and manzanillas – are popular with a wide range of consumers) but that of image. In northern Europe and North America, sherry is still seen by many as a drink for bibulous clerics and old ladies. Thus González-Byass (one of the big three sherry concerns, along with Allied-Domecq and José Medina) has marked the early 21st century by re-branding its Tío Pepe fino as a vibrant, fashionable drink for the thrusting young thing. The bottle has been redesigned (to mimic a New World table wine bottle) and the name Tío Pepe is writ large on a separate shoulder label, while the word' sherry' itself is underplayed and quite hard to locate on the main label.

Finos are at the forefront of the region's marketing drive – both in Spain and abroad (with northern Europe a particular target) – because new, younger drinkers are keen on them, especially manzanillas. Jerez is marketing them hard to maintain and then increase market share, and will subsequently look to its amontillados and olorosos, which also have a ready market as is shown by the recent upsurge of sales of those other fortified glories, Madeira and Port.

Sherries surely have a long future and some of them are rightly regarded as among the world's great wines and also as under-priced, all the more so considering that they are expensive to make. And sherry is a very flexible wine. Served chilled in a *copita* (a tallish sherry glass, filled to no more than a quarter to a third full and narrow at the rim to hold aromas) fino, manzanilla and some of the lighter amontillados are *the* warm weather drinks and ideal accompaniments to a range of foods, which is often overlooked. The other sherries provide a wide range of drinking styles, ideal with some cheeses, desserts and for after dinner sipping.

Selected Bodegas

A.R. Valdespino, S.A. (☎ 956 331 450) Founded in 1837, this is one of the few sherry firms that remains family owned. Methods are traditional, with wines still fermented in oak butts as opposed to the temperature-controlled, stainless steel tanks used by many others. Its range includes:

🌢 *Inocente (fino):* A well made, dry, bitter, pungent fino.

🌢 *Don Gonzalo (oloroso):* A decent quality, mahogany wine, with toasty, caramel, bittersweet flavours. Perhaps too sweet for purists.

🌢 *Pedro Ximénez (sweet):* An enjoyable, mahogany wine with sweet, raisiny, toasty flavours.

Antonio Barbadillo, S.A. (☎ 956 360 241) Founded in 1821, and still family owned, Barbadillo is one of the largest operations in Sanlúcar de Barrameda and is particularly associated with excellent manzanillas, although its other sherries are well worth tasting. Many consumers along the Costa del Sol know the firm for Castillo de San Diego, a neutral white wine made outside the D.O.. Barbadillo's range includes:

🌢 *Muy Fina (manzanilla):* A light, dry wine, easy to drink but not especially characterful.

🌢 *Eva (manzanilla):* A more satisfying, potent wine than the Muy Fina, with delicious, pungent, tangy flavours. Good.

🌢 *Solear (manzanilla):* A well known, popular manzanilla, Solear is light, fresh and commercial but still characterful.

🌢 *Príncipe (amontillado):* An aromatic, amber wine with a full, lively palate of dry flavours and hints of sweetness. Recommended, but a touch expensive compared with some other wines of similar quality.

- *Cuco (oloroso):* A powerful, mahogany wine with long, dry flavours. Good.

- *Eva Cream (sweet):* A dark gold, this wine has smooth, attractive, long, honeyed flavours.

- *Jerez Dulce Pedro Ximénez (sweet):* This mahogany wine has a powerful nose of honeyed raisins and nuts, and a full, sweet palate with length. Moreish and recommended.

Barón, S.A. (☎ 956 383 000) Founded in 1871, this modest-size operation is strongest on manzanillas. Its range includes:

- *Atalaya (manzanilla):* Not the most aromatic wine, but very drinkable, with attractive salty, bitter touches.

- *Atalaya (amontillado):* A dark golden wine with powerful dry flavours.

- *Vino Viejo (oloroso):* An aromatic wine in the bittersweet style with flavour and length.

Croft Jerez, S.A. (☎ 956 319 600) Long associated with Port, but only involved with sherry since 1970 (and hence the owner of one of the most modern installations), Croft has garnered a high reputation for its wines – especially the oloroso and palo cortado – and has a prominent international profile because the vast majority of its produce is exported. Certain people object to the 'international' style of some of the wines, thinking them not authentically Spanish, but none can deny that Croft has done much to take sherry to an international audience. Its range includes:

- *Croft Delicado (fino):* A light, refreshing wine with some tangy character.

- *Croft Original Pale Cream Sherry (sweet):* Croft's biggest seller, and singled out for criticism by those who don't favour the 'international' style, this is a well made wine with quite a complex, herbaceous, tangy nose and a tasty, mouthfilling palate, sweet but not overly so.

- *Croft Palo Cortado (palo cortado):* A lovely wine with balance, flavour, aroma, pungence, dryish flavours and length. Rightly lauded.

- *Rancho Croft (oloroso):* Expensive and over a quarter of a century old, this can be stunning, full, complex and balanced with delicious, integrated, bittersweet flavours. One of the region's better wines.

Delgado Zuleta, S.A. (☎ 956 360 543) Founded back in 1744, this modest-size firm is best known for manzanilla, with the following one of the best examples of this attractive style of fino:

- *La Goya (manzanilla):* A pungently aromatic wine, this has a mouthfilling, tasty palate with saline touches. Highly recommended.

Emilio Hidalgo, S.A. (☎ 956 341 078) Founded in 1874, this operation makes a range of good and very good wines at competitive prices, including:

● *Charito (manzanilla)*: A tasty, easy-drinking wine with some character.

● *Gobernador (oloroso)*: A mahogany wine with lots of straightforward, dryish, bittersweet flavours. Not a bad introduction to the style.

● *Privilegio Pedro Ximénez (sweet)*: This mahogany wine has a toasty nose and a mouthfilling palate with some very sweet flavours.

Emilio Lustau, S.A. (☎ 956 341 597) Founded in 1896, this firm produces a wide range of wines (some of them at higher prices than the regional average) and is also known for *almacenista* sherries. Almacenistas are small producers who do not sell their wines direct to the public but to the large concerns. Emilio Lustau has enjoyed success bottling and shipping them for sale, with top *almacenista* wines much sought-after. Lustau's range includes:

● *Lustau Solera Reserva Jarana (fino)*: A well made, light, tasty, dry wine, more expensive than many.

● *Lustau Solera Reserva Papirusa (manzanilla)*: A light, understated wine, eminently drinkable but could do with more punch, and as with the fino, quite expensive.

● *Single Cask (amontillado)*: An amber wine with a tasty, bittersweet palate. It is commercial rather than for the purist, which is not a criticism.

● *Lustau Solera Reserva Moscatel Superior Emilín (sweet)*: A mahogany wine with lots of fruity, raisiny, toasty flavours. Moreish.

● *Lustau Almacenista 1/50 Vides Single Cask (palo cortado)*: Amber-coloured, this is a tasty, bittersweet wine, well made rather than outstanding, and quite expensive.

Federico Paternina, S.A. (☎ 956 186 112) Founded in 1810, this operation makes a wide range of wines, with the following two among the best:

● *Imperial (fino)*: A dark fino, golden in colour, with a powerful, pungent palate, integrated and suitably aged. Interesting, as it should be for the price.

● *Victoria Regina (oloroso)*: A dark wine with a complex nose of nuts, honey and oak, and a powerful palate with lots of flavour, more dry than sweet.

Garvey, S.A. (☎ 956 319 650) Founded by an Irishman in 1780, Garvey is a famous old sherry name and, like many of the Jerez bodegas, has passed through several pairs of hands. Quality seems to have been unaffected and Garvey produces a solid range of good to excellent wines, including:

● *San Patricio (fino)*: One of the better finos, pale, light and elegant as well as flavoursome and salty. Good.

● *La Lidia (manzanilla)*: A fresh, understated wine, decent rather than distinguished.

● *Oñana (amontillado)*: This is very good, with a complex, balanced nose and palate of bitter nut, oak and sweet touches. Recommended.

◆ *Puerta Real (oloroso):* Another very good wine, with complex, powerful, flavours which are both dry and bittersweet.

◆ *Jauna (palo cortado):* One of the better examples of this style of wine, this has complexity, power and balance, and is dry, sweet and toasty at the same time. Highly recommended.

◆ *Gran Orden Pedro Ximénez (sweet):* Yet another fine wine, with a complex, chocolatey, toasty nose and a big, powerful palate with great length and bittersweet balance. An engaging bottle.

González-Byass, S.A. (☎ 956 357 000) Founded in 1835, and now one of the largest sherry firms, González-Byass is also the name that many consumers, both in Spain and abroad, associate with sherry production. The company's size and fame are matched by the quality of its wines, which is high across a wide range of styles. Its Tío Pepe fino is Spain's and the world's most famous sherry, recently repackaged and re-launched as a drink for the 21st century. González-Byass is also a notable producer of brandy, including Soberano, one of Spain's biggest sellers. Its range of sherries includes:

◆ *Tío Pepe (fino):* The world's best selling fino is also one of the best, dry, elegant, powerful and well judged. Highly recommended and the logical starting point for those wanting to become acquainted with fino.

◆ *El Rocío (manzanilla):* Cheaper than Tío Pepe (manzanilla is usually less expensive than fino) this is a smooth, tasty wine with attractive bitterness.

◆ *Del Duque (amontillado):* A superior wine, powerful, complex and long with bitterness and a touch of sweetness well contrasted. Recommended.

◆ *Matusalem Dulce (oloroso):* Made from 84 per cent Palomino and 16 per cent Pedro Ximénez, this mahogany wine has a complex nose of toast, figs, vanilla and cinnamon, and a mouthfilling palate with lots of toasty flavour and bitterness and sweetness working well together. Recommended.

◆ *González-Byass 'Añada' (oloroso):* This 30-year-old wine is often regarded as one of Jerez's and Spain's top bottles and carries a high price tag accordingly. It has everything: power, complexity, length, balance and style. One of the ultimate sherry experiences.

◆ *Noé Pedro Ximénez (sweet):* Another of the bodega's top wines, at a third of the price of the above, this dark wine has powerful, persistent aromas and flavours of bittersweet chocolate and sweet pastry. Delicious.

Herederos de Argüeso, S.A. (☎ 956 360 112) Founded in 1822, this firm is most noted for its range of very good, competitively priced manzanillas. The wines include:

◆ *Argüeso (manzanilla):* A well made, inexpensive, light, 'maritime' wine.

◆ *Las Medallas de Argüeso (manzanilla):* Better than the above, powerful, long and attractively bitter.

◆ *San León (manzanilla):* One of the best manzanillas, this is both notably smooth and elegant as well as pungent. Highly recommended.

◆ *Argüeso Amontillado Viejo (amontillado):* The colour of old gold, this has a toasty, woody nose and a powerful, dry, tangy palate with length. A good, 'authentic', dry wine.

Hijos de Rainiera Pérez-Martín, S.A. (☎ 956 319 564) Founded in the early 19th century, this Sanlúcar de Barrameda firm is renowned for producing one of the best known and most popular manzanillas – La Guita, a local term for cash.

◆ *La Guita (manzanilla):* A regional classic, this is a smooth, tasty, easy-drinking wine with bite. Compulsory.

Infantes de Orleans-Borbón, S.A.E. (☎ 956 360 241) Originally founded in the later 19th century, this firm produces a range of good quality, competitively priced wines, including:

◆ *Álvaro (fino):* Good, reasonably priced wine, dry and pungently flavoursome.

◆ *Torre Breva (manzanilla):* Rather lightweight in comparison with the above.

◆ *El Botánico (amontillado):* An aromatic, dry wine of complexity and balance at an affordable price.

◆ *Carla Pedro Ximénez (sweet):* A mahogany wine with a powerful, up-front palate of bittersweet flavours. It is a good, straightforward, reasonably priced introduction to this style of wine.

John Harvey, B.V. (☎ 956 346 000) One of the great old names of Jerez, this Bristol company was originally founded in 1796 and became a famous shipper and blender of sherries (most notably Bristol Cream and Bristol Milk) before buying its own vineyards in 1970. It produces a worthy range of wines and the following is sometimes the world's biggest selling sherry and a wine which has done much to spread the word about the region to northern Europe and the USA.:

◆ *Bristol Cream (sweet):* This famous blend of 80 per cent Palomino and 20 per cent Pedro Ximénez is sometimes sneered at by purists as commercial juice for the masses. That is unfair since it is a decent wine, an old gold colour with a sweet, toasty, vanilla nose and a balanced, tasty palate with bittersweet flavours.

José de Soto, S.A. (☎ 956 319 650) Founded in the 19th century, this firm is famous as the first to produce *ponche*, a blend of brandy and herbs. It also makes a range of good and very good sherries, including:

◆ *Campero (fino):* A dry, tasty, nicely bitter wine.

◆ *Don José María (fino):* A dry, pungent wine, more up-front and less subtle than the above.

◆ *Don José María (amontillado):* A dark golden wine with a tasty, dry palate offering bittersweet touches and length. Good.

◆ *Don José María (oloroso):* Mahogany-coloured, this has a nose of vanilla, old wood and furniture, and a tasty, long, mouthfilling palate. Recommended.

La Cigarrera (☎ 956 381 285) Founded in 1758, this small Sanlúcar de Barrameda firm makes one of the best manzanillas:

◆ *La Cigarrera (manzanilla):* A quite powerful, complex, elegant nose and a tasty, long, saline and bitter palate make this one of the best manzanillas. Highly recommended.

Luis Caballero, S.A. (☎ 956 851 810) Founded in the 18th century, and perhaps best known as the producer of the best selling *ponche*, Caballero also makes a small range of sherries, including:

◆ *Pavón (fino):* A good fino, fresh, tangy and dry.

◆ *Lerchundi Moscatel (sweet):* This mahogany wine is not the most subtle around but it offers honest, tasty, toasty, fruity flavours.

Manuel de Argüeso, S.A. (☎ 956 331 450) Founded in 1822, this operation makes a small range of good and very good wines, including:

◆ *Señorita (manzanilla):* Good manzanilla, refreshing and tangy.

◆ *Oloroso Viejo (oloroso):* A mahogany colour with a nose of old wood, this is a flavoursome, aged wine, still with a hint of sweetness.

◆ *Candado Pedro Ximénez (sweet):* A dark mahogany wine, this has an engaging nose of toasted caramel and honey, and a complex palate with depth and interest.

Marqués del Real Tesoro (☎ 956 321 004) Founded in 1897, this operation makes a range of good and excellent wines, including:

◆ *La Bailaora (manzanilla):* An inexpensive manzanilla, lightish and nicely bitter.

◆ *Tío Mateo (fino):* The producer's flagship wine, this is superior fino, aromatic, pungent and long. Recommended.

◆ *Coleccionista Real Tesoro (amontillado):* A dark wine with a sweet, woody, toasty nose and a notably dry palate with power and length. Superior and expensive.

◆ *Coleccionista Pedro Ximénez (sweet):* This dark wine is notably good value, offering a full, tasty palate with sweet dates, toast and chocolate for little money. Good.

Osborne y Cía, S.A. (☎ 956 852 183) Founded in 1772, this is another great old Jerez name, now the owner of one of the most modern wineries and the bull insignia trademark seen throughout Spain. It also makes large amounts of spirits, but is best known for its wide range of high quality sherries, including:

◆ *Fino Quinta (fino):* One of the best finos, powerfully aromatic, pungent, dry and long. Highly recommended.

◆ *Coquinero (amontillado):* This offers high quality for a modest price, a golden wine with a tangy, woody nose and a long, nutty, flavoursome palate.

- *10 RF (oloroso):* An affordable, approachable, mahogany wine with bittersweet, toasty flavours.

- *Bailén (oloroso):* A slightly more expensive, drier oloroso, toasty, tasty and balanced.

- *Solera India (oloroso):* A superb wine and one of the region's very best. A dark mahogany, this has a powerful, complex nose, toasty, fruity and caramelised, while the palate is full, balanced, compelling and complex. Break the law to secure a bottle of this, several times if necessary.

- *Solera Pap (palo cortado):* A dark gold, this powerful wine balances sweetness and bitterness very well and offers flavour and length. Good.

- *Pedro Ximénez 1827 (sweet):* This mahogany wine has a sweet, toasty nose and while it does not always have the most complex palate, it is powerful and flavoursome. A lot of wine for the money.

- *Rare Sherry Pedro Ximénez (sweet):* Generally regarded as one of Spain's best sweet wines, this very dark PX has a concentrated, chocolatey nose and a powerful, deep palate with great length and balance between the bitter and sweet elements. Very good indeed.

Pedro Domecq, S.A. (☎ 956 151 500) Founded way back in 1730, Domecq is one of the oldest and most respected sherry bodegas, with a range of very good and superb wines, one of Jerez's finest. The range includes:

- *La Ina (fino):* Regarded by some purists as the best fino, this has salty olives on the nose and a powerful, pungent, complex palate with great length. A must.

- *Maruja (manzanilla):* A very good manzanilla with lots of 'maritime' personality. Recommended.

- *Amontillado 51 Viejísimo (amontillado):* A top quality, expensive, dark amber wine, aromatic, tasty, powerful, dry and long. Recommended.

- *Sibarita (oloroso):* Another top quality, expensive wine, mahogany-coloured and with a powerful nose of fruits, coffee and toasted nuts. The palate offers mouthfilling, bittersweet flavours of same and length. Recommended.

- *Río Viejo (oloroso):* Another pricey treat, this dark wine has a sweet, nutty, toasty nose and a full, balanced palate with interest and length. Recommended.

- *Capuchino (palo cortado):* Yet another top sherry, an aromatic, mahogany wine with a tasty palate, dry with bittersweet touches and notably long. Very good.

- *Venerable Pedro Ximénez (sweet):* One of Spain's very best sweet wines – on a par with Osborne's Rare Sherry PX – this is chocolate-coloured with a concentrated nose of dates and chocolate, and a full, deep palate with unctuous, toasty, chocolatey flavours and great length. Highly recommended.

Pedro Romero, S.A. (☎ 956 360 736) Founded in 1860, this small operation makes a range of decent and good quality wines, at both the lower and upper ends of the regional price scale. The wines include:

◆ *Pedro Romero (manzanilla):* Not the most aromatic manzanilla, but powerfully tasty and long. Good.

◆ *Aurora (manzanilla):* More expensive and aromatic, but gentler on the palate. The Pedro Romero is probably more consistent.

◆ *Don Pedro Romero (amontillado):* This dark golden wine has a powerful, bitter, long palate, engaging but a touch unsubtle. It is priced at the same level as the region's best but lacks their complexity and finesse.

◆ *Viña El Álamo (oloroso seco):* An inexpensive, mahogany wine with good, honest, dry, bitter flavours rather than deep complexity.

◆ *Viña El Álamo Cream (sweet):* A dark, sweet wine at a competitive price with lots of flavour and attractive toasty, bitter touches. It is a good place to start for investigating this type of wine.

Sánchez Romate Hermanos, S.A. (☎ 956 182 212) Founded in 1781, this firm is well known as the producer of Cardenal Mendoza, one of Jerez's best brandies, and also for its range of good and excellent sherries and sweet wines, including:

◆ *Marismeño (fino):* Not especially aromatic, the palate is dry, flavoursome and persistent.

◆ *N.P.U. (amontillado):* This amber wine has a bittersweet, toasty nose and a tasty, dry palate. Good value.

◆ *La Sacristía de Romate (amontillado):* Twice the price of the above and a jump in quality, this is a powerful, flavoursome, dry wine with some sweet contrast.

◆ *Don José (oloroso):* A mahogany wine, powerful, tasty and both dry and bittersweet, but not the most subtle.

◆ *Cardenal Cisneros Pedro Ximénez (sweet):* This excellent, chocolate-coloured wine has a complex nose of caramel, jam and chocolate and a powerful, mouthfilling, tasty palate with the bitter and sweet elements working beautifully together. Recommended.

◆ *La Sacristía de Romate Pedro Ximénez (sweet):* Another chocolatey wine with a raisiny, chocolatey nose and a sweet, powerful palate with lots of flavour, length and interest.

Sandeman Coprimar, S.A. (☎ 956 301 100) Founded in 1790 by a Scotsman, Sandeman has long been famous for its Port and sherry, and also for the firm's insignia that appears on its labels: a black silhouette of a figure in a cape and a wide-brimmed hat. The range of good and excellent wines includes:

◆ *Soléo (fino):* Not especially representative of its type and quite 'wine-like', without much pungent kick, but mouthfilling and oaky.

◆ *Don Fino (fino):* A superior fino, dry, pungent, maritime and tasty.

◆ *Character (amontillado):* This affordable, amber wine has a bittersweet, toasty nose and a palate of the same, with length. A good 'newcomer's' wine.

◆ *Royal Esmeralda (amontillado):* A big jump in price (around four times), this is classy, engaging wine. It has a powerful, bittersweet nose of old wood and a mouthfilling palate with lots of dry flavour and length.

◆ *Armada (oloroso):* A good value wine, mahogany-coloured and with a sweet vanilla nose, the palate is a well managed blend of bitter and sweet flavours. Good.

◆ *Royal Corregidor (oloroso):* Four times the price of the above, this superior, dark wine has a complex, concentrated nose and a flavoursome, bittersweet palate, confident and notably persistent.

◆ *Royal Ambrosante Pedro Ximénez (sweet):* A high quality sweet wine, pricey by Jerez standards, although modest on a global scale. It is a dark chocolate colour with a nose of caramel, chocolate and dates, while the palate is full and flavoursome with toasty, fruity flavours and great length. Very good.

Vinícola Hidalgo y Cía, S.A. (☎ 956 385 304) Founded in 1792, this bodega is famous for its La Gitana manzanilla, a great favourite both in Spain and abroad, although it also makes a wide range of wines of good to very good quality, including:

◆ *La Gitana (manzanilla):* A superior manzanilla, maritime and flavoursome. Recommended.

◆ *Napoleón (amontillado):* A mid-amber colour, this is an enjoyable wine with a nutty nose and a tasty, mouthfilling palate with length. Good value.

◆ *Hidalgo Amontillado Viejo (amontillado):* The producer's top amontillado, this amber wine has a potent, woody, pungent nose and a palate with complex, nutty, oaky flavours.

◆ *Jerez Cortado Hidalgo (palo cortado):* A golden wine with a nutty nose and a dry, flavoursome palate with bitter bite. Recommended.

Williams and Humbert (☎ 956 331 300) Founded in 1877, this large firm has long been an important name in the region and its wide range of good and excellent wines includes:

◆ *Pando (fino):* An aromatic wine with lots of maritime personality and length. Good.

◆ *Alegría (manzanilla):* One of the best manzanillas, tasty, refreshing and characterful, with an air of elegant class. The presentation could do with a makeover.

◆ *Jalifa (amontillado):* A golden amber wine with a powerful, pungent, oaky nose and a long, dry, characterful palate. Recommended.

◆ *Dry Sack (oloroso):* A famous name offering quite a lot of personality for a modest price, this amber wine is bittersweet, flavoursome and persistent. Notable value for money.

◆ *Canasta Cream (sweet):* This mahogany wine has quite a complex, toasty nose and a sweet, powerful, toasty palate. Good and reasonably priced.

◆ *Don Zoilo Pedro Ximénez (sweet):* A dark wine with a honeyed nose and a concentrated, mouthfilling, sweet palate with contrasting old wood. Recommended.

D.O. Málaga

In Brief: The source of a variety of wine styles (many of them sweet), some of which offer complexity and high quality, while others are over-sweet and one-dimensional.

The sweet wines of Málaga have been famous since Roman times, both in Spain and elsewhere. By the 18th century, they were more popular in the important British market than sherry and by the early years of the 19th century production was around 20 million litres per year, with North America the largest export market.

In the early 21st century, production is little more than a tenth of that. Like many sweet dessert wines, Málaga's popularity has dwindled as drinkers look for dry wines and are concerned about their alcohol intake. The province of Málaga's rapid urban growth during the last 30 years of the 20th century also meant that there was great competition for land, with the tourist hotels and apartment complexes of the Costa del Sol often winning over vineyards. Now, only two producers of any size survive: Larios and López Hermanos.

D.O. Málaga has four different production zones: two are on the coast – one centred on the city of Málaga, the other on the resort town of Estepona – and two are inland – one to the north of Málaga city, the other to the north-east in a hilly region called the Axarquia. Prior to 1876, when phylloxera hit the region (it was one of the first in Spain to be affected) many grape varieties were grown, but since then the number has been drastically reduced. Pedro Ximénez and Moscatel are dominant (indeed they are the only varieties authorised by the D.O. for new plantings) with Doradilla, Lairén and Rome also permitted.

There are several styles of Málaga wine, going by a variety of names, a rather confusing state of affairs. This does not help the consumer, especially at a time when the wine's popularity has been in decline and clarity would be an asset. Moves are afoot to try to simplify things and the following are the six most commonly used categories:

● **Málaga Joven:** A young, unaged white wine with between 10 and 15 per cent alcohol.

● **Málaga Pálido:** An unaged white.

● **Málaga:** A wine aged for between 6 and 24 months.

● **Málaga Noble:** A wine aged for between two and three years.

● **Málaga Añejo:** A wine aged for between three and five years. – Málaga Trasañejo: wines aged for over five years.

Unfortunately, things are not this straightforward, with wines also characterised according to their sweetness and you will also find the following terms used:

- **Blanco Seco:** As the name implies, these wines are dry. Made from Pedro Ximénez they are light or dark yellow according to age and can resemble both Montillas and amontillados. Alcohol levels vary between 15 and 22 per cent.

- **Dulce Color:** This is the style of wine most associated with the name of Málaga, a dark amber colour, high in sugar and treacly. Its alcohol levels range between 14 and 23 per cent.

- **Lágrima:** This literally means 'tear' and refers to the best wines, made from juice derived from natural pressure of the grapes above and involving no pressing. They are golden, aromatic, sweet and long, with alcohol at between 14 and 23 per cent.

- **Moscatel:** a style made using Moscatel grapes from the Axarquia, these wines vary in colour from yellow to golden brown (depending on age) and are characterised by a typically fruity Moscatel nose and sweetness. Alcohol varies between 15 and 20 per cent.

- **Mountain Wine:** the term used for Málaga wines during the 18th and 19th centuries and you might also see them referred to as 'Lady's Wine'.

- **Pajarete:** a semi-dry or dry wine, dark in colour, containing between 15 and 20 per cent alcohol.

- **Pedro Ximénez:** wines made from the grape of the same name produced in the northern part of the D.O. Aged versions are dark, aromatic and have a tangy finish. Alcohol varies between 16 and 20 per cent.

- **Rome:** refers to wines made from this grape.

- **Semidulce:** although this means semi-sweet, it refers to one of the drier styles of Málaga, often dark yellow with a long, dry finish. Alcohol varies between 16 and 23 per cent.

As the above demonstrates, the traditional picture of Málaga wine as one type of dark, sweet, dessert wine is inaccurate; there are in fact many styles, strengths, colours and levels of sweetness. As to how they are all made, if we covered the methods in detail the description would run to several chapters. In the most common method grapes are dried in the sun prior to pressing to raise sugar levels and are then fermented in wooden vats with wine alcohol added when required to stop fermentation. This is traditionally done at the site where the grapes are grown and the wine is then taken to the city of Málaga to be aged in wooden barrels or a *solera* system (see page 27 for details) and blended, as required by D.O. law.

Geography, Soil and Climate

Climatic conditions vary across the D.O.. Coastal Andalucía has a very mild, sub-tropical climate, with mid-winter temperatures averaging around 17°C (63°F), rising to 30°C (86°F) in summer. Inland, conditions are more continental, with cold, sometimes frosty winters and short, very hot summers, with temperatures reaching 40°C (104°F) and more. Rainfall is concentrated in the winter and across the region varies between 400 and 500mm (16 and 20in) per year. The long months of uninterrupted, warm sunshine are ideal for ripening grapes and increasing sugar levels, desirable for the production of dessert wines.

Future Development

The future looked bleak in the '90s when Málaga's best producer – Scholtz Hermanos – closed, having been in business since 1807. Some thought that its demise would have a knock-on effect and speed the cessation of wine making in the area, especially with the land pressures to build yet more tourist accommodation.

However, production has stabilised and López Hermanos is picking up the Scholtz Hermanos baton. There are even new vineyard plantings, despite the competition for land from the apartment and hotel crowd. Málaga currently has around 1,050 hectares of vineyards, 300 growers, 9 agers of wine and 5 producers. It cannot afford to lose any more but there are positive signs for the future – although 21st century drinkers are meant to be looking for dry table wines, the popularity of Port and Madeira (probably Málaga's nearest equivalent) shows that there is a market for high-alcohol, fortified and dessert wines. And the better Málaga wines make for excellent after-dinner drinking – it is just a question of convincing enough people of this. Some sherry producers are looking to repackage their products and sell them to a younger market and maybe Málaga could do something similar if it wants to be more than an anachronistic, regional curiosity.

Selected Bodegas

Gomara, S.L. (☎ 952 342 075) Founded in 1994, this small operation makes a wide range of wines, with the following a selection of its decent, inexpensive bottles:

◆ *Gomara Fino (fino):* Made from Pedro Ximénez, this inexpensive wine is dry and has bittersweet hints and light, tangy flavours. Not a bad attempt, but the folks of Jerez will not be too worried.

◆ *Gomara Moscatel Málaga (sweet):* This golden wine has a characteristic Moscatel nose and the palate is sweet, tasty and perfumed. Good.

◆ *Gomara Málaga Dulce (sweet):* Made from Pedro Ximénez, this dark wine has a toasty nose with caramel and is sweet, dense and raisiny.

Hijos Suárez (Bodegas Quitapenas) (☎ 952 290 129) Founded in 1880, this small operation makes some laudable wines, including:

◆ *Oro Viejo Trasañejo 5 Años (sweet):* This mahogany wine has a thick, sweet, toasty nose and a palate with similar characteristics. A good representative of its type and recommended.

◆ *Viejo Abuelo 10 Años Trasañejo (sweet):* This is also a deep mahogany colour and has a powerful, complex nose of raisins, wood and sweet fruits, while the palate is deep, mouthfilling, toasty, flavoursome and complex. Delicious and ably demonstrates what the region is capable of.

Larios, S.A. (☎ 952 247 056) Founded in the 19th century, Larios is a household name in Spain for its gin and is also a manufacturer of brandy. It produces a fair quantity of Málaga wine, much of it destined for the export market. The following is a well known, decent, inexpensive example:

🌢 *Málaga Larios Crianza en Madera (sweet):* A blend of 90 per cent Pedro Ximénez and 10 per cent Moscatel, this mahogany wine has a toasty nose with caramel and a similar, sweet palate.

López Hermanos, S.A. (☎ 952 319 454) Founded in 1885, and Málaga's biggest producer by a huge margin, this operation is leading the way in terms of quality as well as quantity. From its extensive range, try the following:

🌢 *Trajinero Dry (oloroso):* This inexpensive, dark golden wine has a complex, toasty nose and a flavoursome, balanced, bittersweet palate. Recommended.

🌢 *Málaga Virgen Pedro Ximénez (sweet):* This mahogany wine has a sweet, toasty nose and the palate offers dense, soundly constructed, generous flavours of the same. A satisfying wine.

🌢 *Don Juan Pedro Ximénez (sweet):* Generally regarded as the region's best (and very costly) example of the grape. It has a complex nose of fruits, caramel and fruit preserves, and a powerful palate of sweet flavours and oak, while the finish is remarkably long. This is Málaga at its best and worth the expense.

Pedro A. López (☎ 952 433 789) Founded in the '40s, this modest operation buys in grapes and wines, and while its output is of mixed quality, the following is invariably good:

🌢 *Málaga del Abuelo (sweet):* A dark mahogany wine with a sweet, toasty nose and a concentrated palate of mature fruit and toast. Recommended.

Tierras de Molina, S.A. (☎ 952 740 100) Founded in 1977, this operation makes wines primarily for the local market that to some outside tastes might appear rather one-dimensional sweet and heavy. However, the following is popular and worthy:

🌢 *Carpe Diem Málaga Añejo (sweet):* A dark caramel colour with a nose of mature fruit, raisins and toast, the palate is thick, sweet and mature.

D.O. Montilla-Moriles

In Brief: A source of good value, sherry-like wines, especially of the fino type.

Montilla-Moriles lies to the south of the city of Córdoba in northern Andalucía, in one of the sunniest, hottest parts of Spain. Wine making in the region dates back at least to Roman times and Montilla's *tinajas* (earthenware containers in which the wine was traditionally fermented, now usually replaced by steel tanks) are direct descendants of Roman amphorae.

Montilla-Moriles makes white table wines but is best known for wines that resemble those of Jerez. They are made in a similar way to sherry (although from the Pedro Ximénez grape not the Palomino) but require less or no grape spirit to fortify them because the grapes become especially ripe in this hot, sunny region and thus develop more sugar to turn into alcohol. Like sherry, the wines are then aged in *solera* (see page 27 for details) although sometimes for a shorter period. Montilla's best soil – the chalky *albero* – is also similar to the *albariza* of Jerez.

Montilla's wines tend to be a touch higher in alcohol than those of Jerez and are sometimes described as poor man's sherries. This is unfair, and while not too many equal sherry for quality, a lot *are* good and offer excellent value. Indeed, Montilla-Moriles sells nearly as much wine in Spain as Jerez, although rather less abroad, where it has long been in the shadow of the sherry name.

Indeed, until Montilla was made a D.O. in 1945, a fair amount of its output was sent to Jerez for blending, but this practice is now outlawed, although some Montilla wine is still packed off to the distillery or is sold in bulk for blending. But do not let this put you off the region. Montilla's best known wines – light, flor-growing, dry finos made from the first pressing of the grapes – are worthy, tasty and reasonably priced.

As with many fortified wines, Montilla has suffered a decline in sales in recent years. The region's vineyard hectareage has been reduced, with some of the land turned over to other crops, most notably the noble olive. The number of bodegas has declined accordingly. Montilla-Moriles D.O. currently covers just over 10,000 hectares of vines, has 4,300 growers and around 70 bodegas.

Authorised grape varieties are:

- **White:** Baladí, Layrén, Moscatel, Pedro Ximénez and Torrontés. Pedro Ximénez is dominant, covering around 75 per cent of the vineyards.

Geography, Soil and Climate

Montilla-Moriles' climate is semi-continental Mediterranean, which, in English, means that it is Mediterranean with slight – as opposed to pronounced – continental influences. Summers are long, dry and very hot, while winters are short but can have cold snaps and frosts sometimes reduce harvests. The region has a notable 3,000 hours of sunshine per year (which means an average of 8.2 hours per day, comparable with some desert regions) and this contributes to the grape's high alcohol levels.

Future Development

To compensate for the global slowdown in the demand for fortified wines, some Montilla producers have been making young, fruity, white table wines to offer consumers wines that are fashionable. This is a brave attempt to latch onto market trends, but it is difficult to see it being a big success given the region's torrid climate, which is not ideal for dry whites. Montilla-Moriles' whites are often simple creatures, lacking acidity and needing to be drunk quickly, before they lose their freshness.

As for the fortified wines, Jerez producers are trying to 're-brand' fino as a fashionable drink for the thrusting young thing and Montilla might look to latch onto this and stress the same, while also emphasising Montilla's decent quality and particularly good value. The foreign market could also be targeted. Sales lag far behind those of sherry (Montilla exports around 15 per cent of its production while Jerez manages a massive 80 per cent) although the message seems to be getting across that Montilla wines are worthy, with Britain and Holland important markets. One last point: folks in Montilla-Moriles are adamant that, because their wines are rarely artificially fortified, they do not give you a hangover, unlike the wines of Jerez. Without wishing to be negative, the author's experience is that this is pushing things a bit. Still, it is a possible marketing ploy.

Selected Bodegas

Alvear, S.A. (☎ 957 650 100) Founded in 1929, Alvear is the largest and one of the best of the region's bodegas and the logical starting point for investigating Montilla-Moriles' wines. The firm produces around 8 million litres per year and makes a wide variety of wines, including:

🍷 *Marqués de la Sierra (white):* This is Alvear's young, dry table wine, a bit thin on the nose, but better on the palate, easy to drink and with hints of bite. A reasonable, everyday white, but nothing to shout about.

🍷 *C.B. (fino):* This popular, inexpensive wine is dry, tangy, flavoursome and long. Recommended.

🍷 *Capataz (fino):* Slightly pricier than the C.B., this is also more powerful, with length and delicious olive-bitter flavours. Very good.

🍷 *Festival Pale Cream (sweet):* A powerful, pungent, sweet wine. Good, and inexpensive.

🍷 *Pelayo (oloroso):* The colour of old gold, this is another very good, inexpensive wine, mouthfilling, bittersweet and toasty with some complexity. Recommended.

🍷 *Pedro Ximénez 1927 (sweet):* A step up in price, although still not expensive, this mahogany wine has attractive fruit and dried fruit on the nose, and a sweet, oaky palate with some complexity. Very good.

🍷 *Pedro Ximénez 1830 (sweet):* Regarded by some as the region's best wine, this is several times more expensive than the priciest of the foregoing. It is a dark wine with a powerful, very complex nose and a similar palate, offering lots of sweet flavours of honey, figs and raisins. Utterly delicious and one of Spain's very best of its type, although naturally you pay for the privilege.

Aragón y Cia, S.A. (☎ 957 500 046) Founded in 1946, this firm makes around half the amount of wine as Alvear and produces a range of decent and good wines, including:

🍷 *Moriles 47 (fino):* A decent, light, inexpensive, flavoursome, everyday fino.

🍷 *Moriles P.G. (fino):* Better than the above with dry, pungent flavours and length.

- *Pilycrim Pale Cream (sweet):* A light, sweet wine with some flavour.

- *Araceli Pedro Ximénez (sweet):* A mahogany wine with lots of very sweet, concentrated flavours and length. Good.

Compañía Vinícola del Sur (☎ 957 650 235) Founded in 1925, this large operation produces a range of wines, with the internationally known Monte Cristo perhaps the most famous. Its wines include:

- *Verbenera (fino):* A tasty, aromatic wine with nutty, salty flavours. Recommended.

- *Monte Corto Pale Cream (sweet):* A sweet, up-front wine, with honest flavours.

Conde de la Cortina, S.A. (☎ 957 650 100) Founded in 1973, and run by regional big boys Alvear, this operation makes good quality, reasonably priced wines, including:

- *Moriles Monumental (fino):* A dry, enjoyably bitter, inexpensive wine.

- *Fino C.C. (fino):* A better version of the above, with nice salty touches. Good.

- *Moscatel (sweet):* A mahogany wine with lots of heady fruit and personality. Recommended and reasonably priced.

Crismona, S.A. (☎ 957 695 514) Founded in 1904, this firm's Viejo Oloroso ably demonstrates the quality that Montilla is capable of with this style of wine. The bodega's range includes:

- *Los Cabales (fino):* A lightish wine that sometimes lacks fino personality.

- *Crismona Viejo Oloroso (oloroso):* This wine has an elegant, toasty nose but comes into its own on the palate with complex flavours of dried fruits, bitterness and sweetness well contrasted and combined. An appealing, moreish wine.

Cruz Conde (Promeks Industrial) (☎ 957 652 000) Founded in 1902, this is another long established, solid Montilla firm producing a range of wines, including:

- *Donerre (fino):* A decent, tasty fino with a nice tang.

- *Cruz Conde Moscatel (sweet):* A tasty, dark wine, full of Moscatel personality.

Delgado, S.L. (☎ 957 600 085) Founded in 1874, this operation's output is of mixed quality, with the following the most reliable wines:

- *Lagar de Benazola (white):* An inexpensive, fruity young white with some bite. Better than the regional average.

- *F.E.O. (fino):* The acronym is perhaps unfortunate (feo means 'ugly' in Spanish), but this is quite full-bodied, tasty fino.

Gracia Hermanos, S.A. (☎ 957 650 162) Founded in 1962, this firm makes a range of good and very good wines at competitive prices, including:

♦ *Viña Verde Afrutado (white):* A light, fresh, everyday young white with good acidity. Better than the average Montilla white.

♦ *Gracia Pale Cream (semi-sweet):* A tasty, refreshing, sweet wine at a modest price. *María del Valle (fino):* An aromatic wine with flavour, bite and length.

♦ *Montearruit (amontillado):* A golden wine with a powerful nose and a full, dry palate. Good and reasonably priced.

♦ *Gracia Pedro Ximénez (sweet):* A mahogany wine with a toasty nose and a palate with bittersweet balance and length. Recommended.

Marín, S.L. (☎ 957 380 110) Founded in 1895, this is another solid producer of decent wines, including:

♦ *Los Marinos (fino):* A tasty, unctuous fino. Good.

♦ *Periquito (fino):* A refreshing fino with good bitterness.

♦ *Marín Pedro Ximénez (sweet):* A mahogany wine with attractive toasty, caramel flavours.

Mora Chacón (☎ 957 502 211) This small producer makes a mixed range of wines, with the best being very good. It includes:

♦ *Solera (fino):* Quite full-bodied, everyday fino, not the most subtle.

♦ *Santogo (fino):* An aromatic, pungent wine with attractive bitterness and length. Good.

♦ *Don Santogo (amontillado):* A dark golden colour, this has a complex, nutty nose and a powerful palate with pungent bittersweet flavours and length. Recommended.

Navarro, S.A. (☎ 957 650 644) Founded in 1830, this bodega makes a mixed quality range of wines, including:

♦ *Andalucía (fino):* An elegant, dry, bitter wine. Good.

♦ *Navarro (amontillado):* A powerful, tasty, dry wine with bitter touches and finish. Recommended.

Navisa-Industrial Vinícola Española, S.A. (☎ 957 650 450) Founded in 1950, this large operation is one of Montilla-Moriles' more prominent producers, with 'Cobos' one of the region's best known names . It makes a wide selection of wines, with quality varying from passable to very good. The following are some of the better wines, with the finos and Tres Pasas Pedro Ximénez particularly recommended:

♦ *Vega María (white):* A light, drinkable, young white with some bitter almond character.

♦ *Viña Carrerón Semi-seco (white):* An aromatic, sweetish, inexpensive wine with some character and flavour.

● *Cobos (fino):* A dry, tasty, characterful fino.

● *Montebello (fino):* As above and sometimes more powerful.

● *Montulia (fino):* Similar to Cobos, with a bittersweet tang.

● *Pompeyo (fino):* Lighter than the above and thus a good introduction to this style of wine.

● *Dos Pasas Pedro Ximénez (sweet):* A deep mahogany colour, this is a straightforward though pleasing wine, sweet, toasty and enjoyable.

● *Tres Pasas Pedro Ximénez (sweet):* One of the region's best examples of the style, this dark wine has a quite complex nose of toasty, sweet things and a full, powerful, tasty palate with concentrated, sweet, chocolatey flavours and bitter bite. Recommended.

Pérez Barquero, S.A. (☎ 957 650 500) Founded in 1905, this large operation is one of the region's best. Its range of good and excellent wines includes:

● *Viña Amalia (white):* A light, fresh, well made, inexpensive everyday white wine. One of Montilla's better table whites.

● *Gran Barquero (fino):* A light, elegant, tasty, dry wine. Good.

● *Gran Barquero (amontillado):* The colour of aged gold, this has a powerful, complex nose of wood and dried fruits, while the palate offers lots of long, powerful, bittersweet flavours. Rather delicious and inexpensive.

● *Gran Barquero (oloroso):* As worthy as the above, with balance and attractive bittersweet flavours.

● *Gran Barquero Pedro Ximénez (sweet):* A much praised, modestly priced wine, this dark PX has a toasty, caramel nose and a concentrated, toasty, sweet palate with balance and lots of flavour. Delicious.

Robles, S.A. (☎ 957 650 063) Founded in 1927, this is a solid producer of a wide range of decent quality, reasonably priced wines, with the finos notable for offering good quality at low prices. The range includes:

● *Castillo de Montilla (white):* A light, gently flavoursome, dry wine.

● *Patachula (fino):* A tasty, gently bitter wine, easy to drink and inexpensive.

● *Robles Copeo (fino):* A tasty, unctuous, modestly priced wine.

● *Selección de Robles (fino):* Another well made, characterful, inexpensive wine. Good.

● *Robles Abuelo Pepe (oloroso):* A dark wine with a complex nose of caramel and sweet dough and a long, bittersweet palate. Good, and competitively priced.

● *Robles Pedro Ximénez (sweet):* A mahogany wine with a sweet, flavoursome palate of toast and caramel flavours. Well priced and a good introduction to the style.

Toro Albalá, S.A. (☎ 957 660 046) Founded in 1922, this is one of Montilla-Montiles' most venerable producers, with an excellent range of wines, one of which is notable for being one of Spain's most expensive. The range includes:

● *Joven Eléctrico (white):* So called because the bodega is on the site of a power station, this young table white is one of the region's better and more expensive examples. It is light, fruity, herbaceous and has some bite.

● *Fino Eléctrico (fino):* A pungent, bittersweet, persistent wine with the maritime hints associated with manzanilla. Recommended.

● *Fino del Lagar (fino):* Pungent, dry, bittersweet and unctuous, this is a good fino but expensive.

● *Don PX (sweet):* A superior mahogany wine, with a complex, fruity, honeyed nose and a palate with concentrated, sweet flavours and character. Very good.

● *Don PX Bacchus (sweet):* This is the remarkably expensive wine referred to in the introduction, retailing in the region of GB£300 (US$450) per bottle. It is as aromatic, complex, concentrated and balanced as it could be. Certainly one of Spain's very best dessert wines.

Torres Burgos, S.A. (☎ 957 501 062) An old firm, dating back to the 19th century, this small operation produces a modest range of wines of which the following two stand out and are well worth investigating:

● *Moriles T.B. Etiqueta Negra (fino):* One of the best Montilla finos, this inexpensive wine is aromatic, powerful, dry and has a manzanilla-like hint of maritime saltiness. Recommended.

● *Moriles 1980 (amontillado):* This excellent wine has a complex nose of toast and nuts, and a complex, toasty, bittersweet palate with good length. Not cheap, but worth the price.

Selected non-D.O. Bodegas

Bodegas Las Monjas (☎ 952 114 124) Founded in 1992, this bodega is situated in the Ronda mountains, inland from the upmarket Costa del Sol resort of Marbella. It was founded by one of Marbella's more famous residents, Prince Alfonso Hohenlohe, who gave his name to the wines. Prices are competitive and quality is good, although production is limited.

● *Príncipe Alfonso Colección Personal (rosé):* Made from 80 per cent Tempranillo and 20 per cent Syrah, this is enjoyable, robust rosé, tasty and persistent.

● *Príncipe Alfonso Reserva Privada (red):* A blend of many varieties – mainly Cabernet Sauvignon and Tempranillo, but also Petit Verdot, Syrah and Merlot – this is an engaging oak-aged wine, integrated and juicily flavoursome from a part of the world rarely associated with reds. The bodega also makes a younger red, but this one is more interesting.

Estremadura, lying in the landlocked south-west centre of Spain, is a sparsely populated, trying environment, baking hot in the summer and with infertile soils. It is most associated in Spanish minds with three things: as the birthplace of Cortés, Pizarro and many other conquistadors, who reeked so much havoc in Central and South America; as home to the majority of Spain's cork trees; and as the source of excellent (and sometimes vastly expensive) air-dried Serrano ham. But it is rarely associated with wine.

However, Estremadura, like so many parts of Spain, has a long and sometimes distinguished viticultural history, and in the Middle Ages its wines were actively sought by various European monarchs. It was renowned for *Montánchez*, a red wine made from the Garnacha, Monastrell and Bején grape varieties, unique because it grows a *flor*, like sherry. Over the last hundred years or so, Estremadura's reputation for wine has faded, although in the early 21st century its situation looks more promising, with the one D.O. – Ribera del Guadiana – the focus of the region's hopes for the future.

D.O. Ribera del Guadiana

In Brief: As yet, primarily a producer of volume, everyday wines – mainly white – but improvements are underway and it might become a region to watch for full-bodied, inexpensive reds.

Designated a D.O. only in 1997, Ribera del Guadiana covers what were previously five Vinos de la Tierra (see **Appendix A** for details of the term Vino de la Tierra). It covers nearly 10,000 hectares of vineyards, has 1,400 growers, nearly 90 bodegas and is split into six sub-zones (see **Geography, Soil & Climate** below).

The full list of authorised grape varieties in Ribera del Guadiana is extensive:

- **White:** Alarije, Borba, Cayetana Blanca, Chelva (or Montua), Cigüente, Chardonnay, Eva, Macabeo, Malvar, Moscatel, Pardina, Parellada, Pedro Ximénez, Perruno, Sauvignon Blanc and Verdejo.

- **Black:** Bobal, Cabernet Sauvignon, Garnacha Tinta, Graciano, Jaén, Mazuela, Merlot, Monastrell, Pinot Noir, Syrah and Tempranillo.

It is difficult to generalise about the region's wine styles in view of its wide variety of both environments and grape varieties. However, we can say that the better whites are confident, flavoursome wines, as opposed to shy little things. The rosés are noted for their fruitiness and can be quite alcoholic, while Ribera del Guadiana's red wines are strong and redolent of mature fruit.

The majority of the region's wines are white, predominantly from the Cayetana Blanca grape, which has notably high yields and makes rather plain, low-acid wines. Ribera del Guadiana is still seen as primarily a bulk producer, with a fair proportion of its produce sent to Jerez and northern Spain for blending or destined for the distillery. However, it is trying to change this image and while quality is still mixed and the region does not make any outstanding wines, it has only been a D.O. since 1997. With the changes envisaged below, Ribera del Guadiana may begin to surprise a few people and capitalise on the improving quality and value being offered by some of its wines. Finally, although the D.O. encompasses around 10,000 hectares of vineyards,

Extremadura as a whole has nearly 90,000, with a lot of everyday wines produced, although little of interest.

Geography, Soil and Climate

Ribera del Guadiana is split into six sub-zones, encompassing a variety of altitudes and grape growing environments:

▲ **Cañamero**: Lying in the south-east of the province of Cáceres, Cañamero's vineyards lie between 600 and 850m (1,968 and 2,788ft) above sea level in an area with a fairly mild, stable climate and annual rainfall of 800mm (31in). The principal grape variety is the white Alarije, which covers around 70 per cent of the vineyards.

▲ **Matanegra**: This also has a relatively equable climate (considering its inland location) and its vineyards lie at around 600m (1,968ft) above sea level. Bega and Montúa are the dominant white grape varieties, while Cabernet Sauvignon, Garnacha and Tempranillo are the pre-eminent black grapes.

▲ **Montánchez**: This hilly sub-zone has a variety of altitudes and aspects, with an average vineyard height of 600m (1,968ft) above sea level. The climate is continental, with hot summers, cold winters and annual rainfall of around 550mm (22in). The white grape Borba covers 60 per cent of the vineyards.

▲ **Ribera Alta**: This also has a continental climate and its vineyards lie at between 400 and 450m (1,312 and 1,476ft) above sea level. Alarije and Borba are the most favoured white grape varieties, while Garnacha and Tempranillo are the dominant black grapes.

▲ **Ribera Baja**: As the name suggests (baja means 'low'), this sub-zone's vineyards are *not* at altitude, averaging 280m (918ft) above sea level. The climate is continental with moderating maritime influences and the dominant white grapes are Cayetana Blanca and Pardina, while the favoured black variety is Tempranillo.

▲ **Tierra de Barros**: This is the biggest sub-zone, covering some 4,500 hectares, noted for the fertility of its soils. Vines lie at 500m (1,640ft) above sea level, annual rainfall is low (between 350 and 450mm/14 and 18in) and Cayetana Blanca and Pardina are the most important white grapes, while Cabernet Sauvignon, Garnacha and Tempranillo are the dominant black grapes.

Future Development

As mentioned above, the D.O. is looking to move away from its image as a producer of large amounts of bland, everyday wine. Resistance to change and lack of investment have held it back, but there are definite signs of improvement. The starting point is grape varieties and in this land of predominantly white ones (mainly the high-yielding, uninteresting Cayetana Blanca), there are moves to reduce the proportion of whites, plant more black grapes and concentrate on quality varieties, primarily Pardina for white wines and blends of Garnacha and Tempranillo for reds. Moscatel, Pinot Noir and Sauvignon Blanc are also yielding good results and there may be more emphasis on these in the future.

Selected Bodegas

Casimiro Toribio Boraita (☎ 924 551 235) Founded in 1953, this smallish operation makes quite a wide range of inexpensive wines, with the following red worth trying:

♦ *Viña Puebla Joven (red)*: This young Tempranillo has an exuberant nose and palate of mature fruit, a decent, tasty, everyday red.

Castelar, S.A. (☎ 924 533 073) Founded in 1963, this producer makes a modest range of respectable and good quality, inexpensive wines, including:

♦ *Castelar Blanco (white)*: A blend of Cayetana, Macabeo and Pardina, this is a decent, inexpensive, everyday wine, with straightforward fruity and herby flavours.

♦ *Castelar Tinto (red)*: Mainly Tempranillo, with some Garnacha, this is an aromatic young red, fruity, tasty and with some interest. Recommended and inexpensive.

Cooperativa San Marcos de Almendralejo (☎ 924 670 410) Founded in 1980, this large co-operative controls over 3,000 hectares of vines and makes a wide selection of inexpensive, everyday wines, with the red crianzas the most interesting. Its range includes:

♦ *Campobarro Blanco (white)*: This inexpensive blend of 90 per cent Pardina and 10 per cent Cayetana is aromatic, fruity and has a slight bitter kick. Rather good for the price.

♦ *Campobarro Macabeo (white)*: A well made, low-priced wine with lots of honest fruit flavours.

♦ *Campobarro Tinto (red)*: Made from 80 per cent Tempranillo and 20 per cent Garnacha, this well made, inexpensive, young red is aromatic, fruity and balanced. Good.

♦ *Valdegracia Crianza (red)*: A decent, reasonably priced, oaked Tempranillo, powerfully fruity with smooth tannins. It is representative of the solid, everyday quality that the region is capable of with this style of wine.

Inviosa (☎ 924 671 235) Founded in 1980, this is one of the region's better and better known producers, with an eye on the international market. Its wines are produced from both Spanish and foreign varieties, not all made under the D.O.. Its range includes:

♦ *Lar de Barros Macabeo (white)*: A well made, light, fruity, young white wine for not much money.

♦ *Lar de Oro Fermentado en Barrica (white)*: This barrel-fermented Chardonnay is made outside the D.O. and is a creditable, reasonably priced wine, with a powerful nose and tasty, unctuous palate.

◆ *Lar de Barros Tinto (red)*: A Tempranillo, Garnacha and Graciano crianza, this notably inexpensive wine is a well made blend of spicy fruit and oak. Superior, everyday, slightly rustic drinking.

◆ *Lar de Oro Cabernet Sauvignon (red)*: Another wine made outside the D.O., this crianza is tasty and fruity, not too heavy on the oak. As above, it is superior, everyday drinking, although more expensive than the Lar de Barros.

Martinez Payva, S.A.T. (☎ 924 671 130) Founded in 1979, this small operation makes some of the region's better, more characterful wines and while not all of its efforts succeed, it is obviously looking to expand the variety of the region's styles and appeal to international tastes. Its range includes:

◆ *Doña Francisquita Blanco (white)*: A blend of Cayetana Blanca and Pardina, this young white is light, straightforward and inexpensive with some herby character.

◆ *De Payva Chardonnay (white)*: This inexpensive young Chardonnay offers a fair amount of fruit and herb flavours, and is typical of the region in being powerful and confident. It doesn't scream 'Chardonnay' at you but is a tasty, interesting wine. Recommended.

◆ *De Payva Fermentado en Barrica (white)*: This barrel-fermented Cayetana Blanca suffers from excessive oak and is thus tiring to drink.

◆ *Doña Francisquita Tinto (red)*: A well made, inexpensive crianza made from 80 per cent Tempranillo and 20 per cent Garnacha, this is powerful and mouthfilling with mature fruit and smooth tannins. Good.

Romale, S.L. Antonia Ortiz Ciprián (☎ 924 665 877) Founded in 1989, this large operation makes a small range of wines, of which the crianza red is the best. It includes:

◆ *Viña Romale Blanco (white)*: This young, inexpensive blend of Cayetana Blanca and Macabeo has characterful fruit and some length.

◆ *Viña Romale Tinto (red)*: Made from 85 per cent Tempranillo and 15 per cent Garnacha, this young red has decent fruit and flavour but is rather aggressive, astringent even.

◆ *Privilegio de Romale Crianza (red)*: This inexpensive Tempranillo crianza is much better than the young red, with spicy fruit and oak well integrated and persistence. Good.

Sociedad Cooperativa Agrícola Vinícola Extremeña San José (☎ 924 524 417) Founded in 1963, this very large co-operative (with 4,500 hectares of vines) produces a wide range of well made, inexpensive, everyday wines, including:

◆ *Viña Canchal Blanco (white)*: An aromatic, fruity wine with balance and bite. Rather good for the price.

◆ *Viña Canchal Rosado (rosé)*: A light, refreshing, fruity Tempranillo. Good.

● *Viña Canchal Tinto (red):* A tasty, mouthfilling young Tempranillo with some interest. Recommended.

● *Viña Canchal Crianza (red):* A well made, straightforward, commercial blend of Tempranillo and oak at a low price. Superior everyday wine.

Sociedad Cooperativa Montevirgen (☎ 924 685 025) Founded in 1962, this large co-operative draws from 3,000 hectares of vines and makes a small range of respectable, inexpensive, everyday wines, including:

● *Marqués de Villalba Blanco (white):* A light, gently fruity, uncomplicated wine.

● *Señorío de Villalba (rosé):* Made from 80 per cent Tempranillo and 20 per cent Pardina, this is decent, fruity pink wine for easy drinking.

● *Marqués de Villalba Tinto (red):* A competent, quite powerful Tempranillo, but it could do with more interest.

Sociedad Cooperativa San Isidro de Villafranca (☎ 924 524 136) Founded in 1960, this is another large co-operative (although half the size of the foregoing) with the following white and red offering good value:

● *Valdequemao Blanco (white):* A well made, everyday Macabeo with a fair amount of fruit and some length.

● *Valdequemao Tinto (red):* A fruity young Tempranillo with personality and bite. Good.

Somontano vineyards in the foothills of the Pyrenees

3.

ARAGÓN

Wine making in Aragón dates back at least to the time of the ancient Mediterranean's most extensive empire, Rome. Indeed, one of the region's D.O.s – Cariñena – is named after the Roman town of Carae and history records that in the 3rd century B.C. its people drank wine mixed with honey; this sounds awful, although never having tried it, I should not venture an opinion.

For much of its history, Aragón was known for powerful, dark red wines, some containing as much as 18 per cent alcohol. The wines were so potent because the hot summers produced very sweet grapes with a lot of sugar to turn into alcohol. Modern wine makers tackle this by picking grapes earlier, before they build up high sugar levels. Historically, Aragón's wines were often destined for blending with weaker wines from other regions, but they could also be of good quality and when the phylloxera epidemic raged in France, French firms set up operations in Aragón to send wines back to France.

The last quarter of the 20th century has seen the region begin to transform itself – especially D.O. Somontano – into a modern, dynamic wine making area, with technologically advanced co-operatives and innovative, quality-seeking private operations. Aragón's four D.O.s now make many styles of wine, ranging from robust, 'Spanish' wines (although considerably lighter than in earlier times) to modern, sophisticated, fruit-driven, 'international' ones.

D.O. Calatayud

In Brief: To date, primarily a source of decent, inexpensive, everyday rosés and Garnacha reds, but it has the potential to make more distinguished wines.

Situated halfway down Aragón's western border, Calatayud has been a D.O. since 1989, although the region has been making wines for much longer than this: there are literary references to them dating from the 1st century and mention of grape production going back to the 5th century B.C. Calatayud D.O. currently has 7,500 hectares of vineyards, nearly 2,500 grape producers and around 12 bodegas (most are co-operatives), producing increasing amounts of well made, inexpensive wines with notable price/quality ratios. This has been heeded abroad, with 75 per cent of the region's bottled wines exported, Britain being the largest market.

Authorised and/or employed grape varieties are:

- **White:** Chardonnay, Garnacha Blanca, Macabeo, Malvasía and Moscatel de Alejandría.

- **Black:** Cabernet Sauvignon, Garnacha Tinta, Mazuela, Merlot, Monastrell, Syrah and Tempranillo.

For now, the region's whites are generally fresh and fruity rather than complex or distinguished, while rosés – still Calatayud's signature wines and made primarily from Garnacha – are clean, aromatic and flavoursome, and offer good value. As for reds, the region's traditional Garnacha wines are increasingly being blended with other varieties to mitigate against Garnacha's tendency towards oxidation and also to add body and structure in order to make wines which will respond better to ageing. The D.O. is also conscious that other regions (notably Priorato in Catalonia) are producing high quality, complex wines for long ageing from grapes produced by old Garnacha vines. It is encouraging grape growers and wine makers to try to make similar use of Calatayud's aged Garnacha vines.

Geography, Soil and Climate

Calatayud's vineyards are located between 550 and 880m (1,804 and 2,887ft) above sea level on limestone-based soils lying over loam, quartzite and sandstone. The climate is continental with some maritime influences and arid, with annual rainfall of between 300 and 550mm (12 and 22in). Calatayud is subject to frosts for up to half of the year, which can affect grape yields.

Future Development

Plantings of foreign, mainly black, grape varieties and the stress on improving and expanding the range of the region's Garnacha reds, show that Calatayud is aiming to become known as a red wine region. Its harsh climate and high altitude vineyards provide the marginal conditions which in other parts of Spain, e.g. Ribera del Duero, have lead to success. Currently, all of Calatayud's wines are in the 'inexpensive' category, and, such is the way of things, producing some more expensive examples would improve the region's image.

Selected Bodegas

Bodegas y Viñedos del Jalón, S.A./Castillo de Maluenda (☎ 976 893 027) Originally founded in the '40s, this large co-operative was reorganised in 1999 and produces a range of mainly rosé and red wines. The rosés are fresh, attractive and notably inexpensive, and of the reds, the following are the best:

◆ *Castillo de Maluenda Tinto (red):* A fresh, aromatic, flavour-filled Tempranillo for a modest price.

◆ *Castillo de Maluenda Garnacha Selección (red):* A smooth, full-bodied, flavoursome wine with some interest. Recommended.

◆ *Castillo de Maluenda Crianza (red):* A blend of Garnacha and Tempranillo, this inexpensive, well made crianza is smooth and tasty.

Cooperativa San Gregorio (☎ 976 899 206) Founded in 1965, this co-operative has 1,000 hectares of its own vines and its strongest suit is its red wines, including:

◆ *Monte Armantes Tinto (red):* A young, aromatic wine with lots of fruity flavours.

◆ *Viña Fuerte Garnacha (red):* Well balanced, characterful, flavoursome and persistent.

Cooperativa Virgen de la Sierra (☎ 976 899 015) Founded in the mid-'50s, this small co-operative produces a range of wines with an attractive price/quality ratio, including:

◆ *Monte Maguillo Rosado (rosé):* A well made, aromatic rosé with lots of flavour. Recommended.

◆ *Monte Maguillo Tinto (red):* A blend of Garnacha and Tempranillo, this young wine is aromatic and has lots of fruity flavours.

Cooperativa Virgen del Mar y de la Cuesta (☎ 976 895 071) Founded in 1965, this small co-operative makes a range of notably inexpensive wines, the following red being the best:

◆ *La Olmedilla Tinto (red):* A blend of Garnacha and Tempranillo, this young wine has lots of characterful, tasty fruit for a price that seems uneconomically low from the producer's point of view.

Sociedad Cooperativa del Campo San Alejandro (☎ 976 892 205) This is another producer of decent, everyday wines at notably low prices, including:

◆ *Viñas de Miedes Blanco (white):* A young yet full-bodied and flavoursome wine.

◆ *Viñas de Miedes Rosado (rosé):* A balanced, tasty rosé for a low price.

◆ *Viñas de Miede Tinto (red):* A blend of Garnacha and Tempranillo, this is a well made, straightforward, everyday red wine.

◆ *Marqués de Nombrevilla (red):* A blend of 50 per cent Garnacha and 50 per cent Tempranillo, this young red has lots of lively fruity flavours for a modest price. It responds well to a slight chilling.

D.O. Campo de Borja

In Brief: Still mainly a source of everyday wines, but it is garnering a reputation for tasty, characterful young and crianza reds at competitive prices.

Situated north of D.O. Calatayud and just to the south of D.O. Navarra, Campo de Borja has been a D.O. since 1977. It has around 6,300 hectares of vineyards, 2,500 grape growers and 13 bodegas. The region's traditional wines were big, alcoholic reds, often Aragón's strongest, many of which were sent to other regions and countries for blending, but Campo de Borja is now showing its ability to make the lighter wines which appeal to modern drinkers. This has been appreciated abroad and exports account for 50 per cent of production (Denmark and Sweden being the most important markets) and are increasing.

Authorised grape varieties are:

- **White:** Macabeo and Moscatel, with Chardonnay and Garnacha Blanca due soon.

- **Black:** Cabernet Sauvignon, Garnacha, Mazuela and Tempranillo, with Merlot and Syrah to follow.

The region's white wines are light, fruity and straightforward, while the rosés are of good quality with attractive freshness and flavour. Garnacha is the dominant grape for reds, accounting for 75 per cent of plantings. Young examples are aromatic and flavoursome, the crianzas can be smooth and finely structured, while the reservas are sometimes rustic with hints of oxidation. Blends of black varieties are yielding the most exciting results, producing characterful, inexpensive wines.

Geography, Soil and Climate

Campo de Borja's vineyards lie on undulating plains at between 350 and 700m (1,148 and 2,296ft) above sea level in a region with a continental climate, sometimes subject to Atlantic influences. Winters are cold and summers are hot and dry, while annual precipitation is low, ranging from 350 to 450mm (14 to 18in). Campo de Borja is prey to 'el cierzo', a dry, cold, north-westerly wind.

Future Development

With wines like Borsao Tinto and Borsao Crianza, Campo de Borja has shown itself capable of making good quality young and crianza red wines at competitive prices. They have garnered a lot of positive attention in the Spanish press (and begun to penetrate the northern European markets, including the influential British one) and their success will raise the region's profile and encourage other producers to aim for quality. Considering its geographical position – to the south of the noted regions of Rioja and Navarra – Campo de Borja has little excuse for not becoming a successful wine region.

Selected Bodegas

Bodegas Aragonesas, S.A. (☎ 976 862 153) Founded in 1984, and with 3,500 hectares of its own vines, this large co-operative makes a wide range of respectable and decent wines for low prices (with reds its strong suit, most from Garnacha), including the following:

- *Coto de Hayas Blanco (white):* A simple, fruity, everyday white wine.

- *Coto de Hayas Blanco Fermentado en Barrica (white):* A well made, straightforward, barrel-fermented wine.

- *Coto de Hayas Rosado (rosé):* Competent, refreshing pink wine.

- *Viña Tito Tinto (red):* A well made, straightforward, fruity, young red wine.

- *Coto de Hayas Tinto (red):* As above.

- *Coto de Hayas Garnacha Centenaria (red):* Made from grapes from old Garnacha vines and spending four months on American oak, this is a ripe, medium-bodied wine with balance, lively tannins and bite. Recommended.

- *Coto de Hayas Tinto Crianza (red):* Made from 60 per cent Garnacha, 25 per cent Tempranillo and 15 per cent Cabernet Sauvignon, this is quite a one-dimensional blend of fruit and oak, sometimes a little rough around the edges.

- *Coto de Hayas Tinto Reserva (red):* A rounded, easy-drinking reserva with a rustic feel. This is not a criticism and for the price it is probably as good as it could be.

- *Duque de Sevilla Reserva (red):* A concentrated, tannic mouthful which needs food, at its best at eight or nine years old.

Bodegas Bordejé, S.A.T. (☎ 976 868 080) This small, family-run firm was founded in 1770 and owns around 50 hectares of its own vineyards. Of its modest range of respectable, sometimes characterful wines, the following has the best price/quality ratio:

- *Abuelo Nicolás (red):* The name means 'Uncle Nicholas' and is a superior young red wine with lots of fresh fruit for drinking lightly chilled on a hot day. Recommended.

Bodegas Borsao Borja (☎ 976 867 116) Founded in 1958, Borsao is a co-operative with 1,450 hectares of its own vines and a technologically advanced winery. It has shown that Campo de Borja is eminently capable of producing wines of good quality at low prices and has been instrumental in bringing the D.O.'s name to wider prominence; its style and approach have been much mimicked in the region. Try the following for an appreciation of what Campo de Borja has to offer:

- *Borsao Tinto (red):* Made from a blend of 50 per cent Garnacha, 30 per cent Tempranillo and 20 per cent Cabernet Sauvignon – although the percentages vary from year to year – this is generally regarded as one of the better Spanish reds in its (low) price band. It is a young wine with rich flavours, structure and fruity interest. Highly recommended.

- *Borsao Crianza (red):* A superior crianza for a notably low price, this has power, body, lots of flavour and persistence. Recommended.

Cooperativa Santa Ana (☎ 976 862 841) Founded in 1959, this co-operative has a small range of wines, with the following showing the quality of which it is capable:

- *El Tenor Crianza (red):* A well made, characterful crianza with lots of flavour.

Crianzas y Viñedos Santo Cristo Sociedad Cooperativa (☎ 976 868 096) Founded in 1955, this co-operative makes a large range of wines of decent quality at modest prices, including:

- *Moscatel Ainzón (sweet white):* A superior, aromatic, flavoursome, sweet wine with around 15 per cent alcohol. Competitively priced and recommended. An interesting weapon in Campo de Borja's armoury.

- *Viña Collado Rosado (rosé)*: Decent, tasty pink wine from Garnacha for a low price, although quality can be variable.

- *Viña Collado Tinto (red)*: A blend of Garnacha and Tempranillo, this is tasty, straightforward, everyday, young red wine, although as with the rosé, quality can be variable.

- *Viña Ainzón Tinto Crianza (red)*: This blend of 60 per cent Tempranillo and 40 per cent Garnacha is a well made, honest, flavoursome crianza for a competitive price.

Ruberte Hermanos (☎ 976 858 063) Founded in 1982 and family owned, this operation's wines are of mixed quality but there are signs of potential for the future with the following worth trying:

- *Muzo Alcoraz (red)*: This young blend of Garnacha and Tempranillo has lots of tasty fruit.

- *Ruberte Crianza (red)*: A straightforward, aromatic, tasty blend of Cabernet Sauvignon, Garnacha and Tempranillo, quite heavy on the oak.

D.O. Cariñena

In Brief: A source of good, everyday red wines with character and strength.

Cariñena is the name of both a wine region lying to the east of D.O. Calatayud and also of a black grape variety. It might be expected that the Cariñena grape would monopolise the region's vineyards, but that would be too logical and predictable, and it is actually Garnacha that is the dominant grape in D.O. Cariñena. The Cariñena grape variety is more common in Catalonia, where in its most noble form it contributes to some of the 'designer' wines of Priorato.

The wine region of Cariñena was famous during Roman times for the quality of its wines and continued to be Aragón's most important wine area until recently; it has now been replaced by Somontano, certainly at the high quality end of the market. However, Cariñena still has more hectares under vine than any of the other Aragón D.O.s (seven times as many as Somontano) and makes more decent quality, everyday wine than the others.

Currently, Cariñena has nearly 18,000 hectares of vines, 3,500 grape growers, and around 50 bodegas, 25 of which now bottle their wines, a sign of the region's drive to improve quality – in the not-too-distant past much of Aragón's wine was sold in bulk. Authorised and/or utilised grape varieties are:

- **White:** Garnacha Blanca, Macabeo, Moscatel Romano and Parellada.

- **Black:** Cabernet Sauvignon, Garnacha Tinta, Juan Ibañez, Mazuela (Cariñena), Monastrell and Tempranillo.

The region's limited number of white wines are simple and fruity, while the rosés are competent and flavoursome. But it is the robust reds that the region is known for: the young ones are purple in colour and full of flavour with a tang on the finish; the crianzas are more polished versions of this with fruit and wood well integrated. Reds made from 100 per cent Garnacha have traditionally not aged well over extended periods because they have been subject to oxidation, a situation also found in other Spanish regions.

Geography, Soil and Climate

Cariñena's climate is continental with some maritime influences. Summers can be very hot while winters are often severe. This is one of the most arid parts of Spain and as well as scanty rainfall, the region is subject to the dry 'cierzo' wind, which further lowers humidity levels. Vines are sited at between 400 and 800m (1,312 and 2,624ft) above sea level on poor soils weak in organic material and thus ideal for growing vines.

Future Development

Garnacha's ageing problems have already been mentioned and Cariñena's better reds are increasingly blends of Garnacha with other varieties, generally Cabernet Sauvignon, Tempranillo and Mazuelo. These wines age better and have more structure than those made 100 per cent from Garnacha. In the near future the authorities will probably also authorise the use of Merlot and Syrah as alternatives. With these changes the region should begin to produce more good crianzas and reservas, which will sell at higher prices than Cariñena's wines can generally command at present.

Selected Bodegas

Bodegas Ignacio Marín, S.L. (☎ 976 621 129) Founded in 1903, and with 77 hectares of its own vines, this operation makes a fairly wide range of wines. Quality is mixed, with the whites (excluding the Moscatel) best avoided for now and some of the reds insubstantial although pleasant. The following are worth tasting:

◆ *Barón de Lajoyosa Moscatel (sweet white):* A characterful example of the personality-filled Moscatel grape, this shows that Cariñena can make good examples of this type of wine.

◆ *Duque de Medina Reserva (red):* A 'commercial' reserva red with fruit and oak correctly assembled and a sweetness running through it.

Bodegas San Valero (☎ 976 620 400) Founded in 1945, this large operation is one of Cariñena's best known wine makers and produces a range of competent, popular wines found in many Spanish supermarkets, including:

◆ *Monte Ducay Blanco (white):* Respectable, inexpensive white wine with some character. Has its off years.

◆ *Monte Ducay Rosado (rosé):* Well made, fruity pink wine.

◆ *Monte Ducay Tinto (red):* A powerful, fruity, decent, young red.

◆ *Monte Ducay Crianza (red):* A competent, easy-drinking blend of fruit and oak.

◆ *Monte Ducay Reserva (red):* Well made, flavoursome and rather stylish.

Bodegas Virgen del Águila Sociedad Cooperativa (☎ 976 622 748) Founded in 1953, this co-operative has over 2,000 hectares of its own vines and produces low-priced wines of reasonable quality, especially:

◆ *Val de Paniza Rosado (rosé):* Simple, fruity pink wine from the Garnacha grape.

◆ *Señorío del Águila Tinto Crianza (red):* A blend of Cabernet Sauvignon, Garnacha and Tempranillo, this is a smooth, well made, straightforward crianza for a competitive price.

◆ Señorío del Águila Tinto Reserva (red): A blend of the same grapes as the crianza, this is a smooth, balanced, appealing reserva for a low price.

Covinca Sociedad Cooperativa (☎ 976 142 653) Founded in 1988, this large co-operative has 3,000 hectares of its own vines and produces a range of wines which have varied in quality from poor to good, but standards are improving and the following are worth investigating:

◆ Torrelongares Rosado (rosé): A light, fresh, inexpensive blend of Garnacha and Tempranillo.

◆ Torrelongares Tinto (red): A blend of Garnacha and Tempranillo, this is superior, inexpensive young wine with lots of fruit flavours and a good finish. Recommended.

Grandes Vinos y Viñedos, S.A. (☎ 976 621 261) Founded in 1997, this large operation has over 5,000 hectares of its own vines and produces an extensive range of wines, giving it a notable presence in Spanish supermarkets. Quality is variable and perhaps the range could be trimmed, although the following are all worthy and demonstrate that Grandes Vinos can make good wines and has the capability to improve:

◆ *Monasterio de las Viñas Blanco (white):* A well made, straightforward, everyday white wine from the Macabeo grape.

◆ *Monasterio de las Viñas Rosado (rosé):* This 100 per cent Garnacha is aromatic, flavoursome and satisfying.

◆ *Corona de Aragón Rosado (rosé):* A blend of Cabernet Sauvignon and Garnacha (mainly the latter), this is quite elegant, classy pink wine.

◆ *Monasterio de las Viñas Tinto (red):* A blend of Garnacha, Mazuelo and Tempranillo, this is a soundly constructed, characterful, young red for not much money.

◆ *Monasterio de las Viñas Cabernet Sauvignon (red):* A full-bodied, concentrated, young wine, with a touch of class for a low price.

◆ *Monasterio de las Viñas Tinto Crianza (red):* A blend of Garnacha, Mazuelo and Tempranillo, this is an integrated, easy-to-drink, fruity/oaky wine at a competitive price. With less Garnacha it would have a more elegant structure and a longer life.

◆ *Monasterio de las Viñas Tinto Gran Reserva (red):* The same blend as the crianza, but with less Garnacha, this is a smooth, straightforward wine with decent flavour, although it is not for mulling over.

◆ *Corona de Aragón Tinto (red):* A blend of Cariñena, Garnacha and Tempranillo, this young wine has lots of full-bodied flavour for a modest price.

◆ *Corona de Aragón Tinto Crianza (red):* A blend of Cabernet Sauvignon, Cariñena, Garnacha and Tempranillo (the last being dominant), this is a professionally made, characterful fruity/oaky wine for a low price. Recommended.

◆ *Corona de Aragón Cabernet Sauvignon (red):* A tasty, characterful, well made, young wine.

◆ *Corona de Aragón Tinto Reserva (red):* A blend of Cabernet Sauvignon, Cariñena and Tempranillo (with Tempranillo dominant), this has power, elegance and fruit/oak integration for a modest price. It is the type of wine which Cariñena D.O. makes well and will secure commercial success both domestically and abroad.

Manuel Moneva e Hijos, S.L. (☎ 976 627 020) Founded in 1900, and with 40 hectares of its own vines, this family firm makes a small range of competitively priced wines which are improving. Look for the younger examples, including:

◆ *Viña Vadina Blanco (white):* An inexpensive, fruity, refreshing, young Macabeo. Good value.

◆ *Viña Vadina Tinto (red):* A blend of Cabernet Sauvignon, Garnacha and Tempranillo (with the last dominant), this young red is both mouthfilling and easy to drink.

◆ *Viña Vadina Tinto Reserva (red):* Drink the most recent available for a modestly-priced wine with attractive, rounded, spicy fruit.

Solar de Urbezo, S.L. (☎ 976 621 968) Founded in 1995, this small operation only makes a handful of wines but they are of good quality and at competitive prices, a positive sign for the region's future. It is at the forefront of the drive to raise Cariñena's profile.

◆ *Urbezo Chardonnay (white):* Chardonnay is a rarity in Cariñena and this aromatic, unctuous, balanced example spends a month in oak. Impressive, as is the low price.

◆ *Viña Urbezo Tinto (red):* A blend of Tempranillo, Syrah and Garnacha, this young red wine is moreishly attractive, with a lovely nose and lots of mouthfilling fruit and length for a low price. Recommended and the type of bottle to win the region new converts.

◆ *Solar de Urbezo Crianza (red):* This blend of 40 per cent Cabernet Sauvignon, 40 per cent Tempranillo and 20 per cent Merlot has attracted a lot of plaudits and garnered a lot of attention for the bodega. It has balance and soundly constructed, concentrated flavours, with a smoothness and style which have surprised those who thought the region incapable of making such wines. Recommended.

Tosos Ecológica (☎ 976 147 045) Founded in 1995, this small operation has 20 hectares of its own vines and produces increasingly good wines at prices slightly higher than Cariñena's typically low levels, including:

◆ *Lágrima Virgen Blanco (white):* An attractive, fruity, dry wine for drinking young from the Macabeo grape.

◆ *Lágrima Virgen Rosado (rosé):* A light, fruity, Garnacha pink wine, perhaps a touch expensive and can have its off years.

◆ Lágrima Virgen Tinto (red): A blend of Garnacha, Mazuelo and Tempranillo (with Garnacha dominant), this smooth, concentrated, fruity, aromatic wine is one of the region's better reds and a positive sign. Recommended.

D.O. Somontano

In Brief: An important, cool-climate region, making high quality white and red wines, sometimes 'international' in style.

This small region, lying in the Pyrenean foothills of north-east Aragón, is one of Spain's successes, both domestically and abroad, producing wines unlike those of Aragón's other D.O.s. Its wines were first recorded in around 500 B.C. and have enjoyed a good reputation in France for over 200 years. Indeed there is a century-old tradition of French firms setting up shop on the Spanish side of the Pyrenees.

Somontano became a D.O. in 1984 and a combination of the perceptive growth and blending of international and local grape varieties with supportive investment by the Aragonese authorities and financial institutions has brought success. Since the mid-'90s, Somontano wines have received plaudits from Spanish and foreign wine critics (and an impressive number of prizes and awards at wine fairs and trade tastings) and enjoyed a profile and success which belie the region's modest size and output. It has only around 2,400 hectares of vines, 400 grape growers and 10 bodegas.

Somontano's success has had beneficial consequences for Aragón's other D.O.s because it has focused attention on the entire region. It has also shown what the province is capable of and should encourage interest and investment within and beyond Somontano's boundaries. Three producers – Bodega Pirineos, Viñas del Vero and Viñedos y Crianzas del Alto Aragón, S.A., the last thankfully often known by the brand name of its wines, Enate – are the dominant forces in Somontano. Some see their rivalry (and sometime co-operation) as healthy competition which has spurred each to perform to its best potential; others regard it as divisive and something that has hindered Somontano from presenting a united front against its competitors. The truth is probably somewhere in the middle, although the D.O.'s success seems to favour those who see the situation as positive.

Authorised grape varieties are:

● **White:** Alcañón, Chardonnay, Garnacha Blanca, Gewürztraminer and Macabeo.

- **Black:** Cabernet Sauvignon, Garnacha, Merlot, Moristel, Parraleta, Pinot Noir and Tempranillo.

Somontano is known for its clever use of grapes, growing them in favourable locations and making full use of local, national and international varieties. The latter were first introduced by a French family called Lalanne (see the bodega of the same name on page 68) in the 19th century.

Somontano's whites made from Macabeo are generally fruity, everyday bottles. One or two examples show that the grape can also produce wines with more complexity. The region's Chardonnays, made in a variety of styles, are some of Spain's better examples from this ubiquitous grape variety. Rosés are as we would want: light, fruity, tasty and refreshing, with one – Enate's Cabernet Sauvignon rosé – sometimes rated as Spain's best pink wine.

As for reds, those made from Moristel and Tempranillo are the most 'traditional': fruity and quite powerful, and thus most like the wines from Aragón's other D.O.s. Somontano's most successful reds are blends of local and national varieties with foreign ones, or blends of foreign varieties. They are elegant, structured wines, often benefiting from further bottle ageing, with lots of fruit and a clever, understated use of oak. Not all are recognisably Spanish in style or flavours, understandable given Somontano's proximity to France and its extensive use of French grape varieties.

Geography, Soil and Climate

Somontano means 'under the mountain', apposite for an area situated in the Pyrenean foothills. Its vineyards lie at between 350 and 650m (1,148 and 2,132ft) above sea level in a cool climate region. The mountains protect Somontano from the worst ravages of winter winds, while its latitude and altitude moderate summer temperatures. This is a region with four defined seasons, giving pronounced temperature increases at the end of spring and decreases at the end of the autumn. Throughout the year there is a marked diurnal temperature range, with large differences between daytime highs and night-time lows. Precipitation is a modest 500 to 550mm (20 to 22in) per year, but abundant mountain streams ensure that Somontano rarely has the parched look of many Spanish wine regions.

Future Development

Somontano's cool, sometimes unpredictable climate is suited, in good years, to the aristocratic, 'difficult' Pinot Noir grape, still little grown in Spain. Viñas del Vero has enjoyed success with it and others will probably try to follow. Chenin Blanc and Gewürztraminer, even rarer in Spain than Pinot Noir, have also enjoyed success. Somontano may prove to be one of the few Spanish regions suited to them and should continue to be one of Spain's most successful D.O.s for wines based on foreign varieties, of good quality/value, and popular in both export and domestic markets.

Selected Bodegas

Bodega Pirineos (☎ 974 311 289) Re-equipped and re-launched in 1993, this large operation produces Somontano's widest range of wines. Quality varies from fairly good to excellent, with most of the wines having a notable price/quality ratio. The range includes:

◆ *Montesierra Blanco (white):* A superior, young Macabeo, aromatic, well made and characterful.

◆ *Montesierra Macabeo Vendimia Tardia (white):* This golden wine is aromatic and offers a powerful, structured mouthful of delicious flavours for a modest price. Recommended.

◆ *Montesierra Chardonnay Fermentado en Barrica (white):* A professionally made barrel-fermented Chardonnay at a reasonable price, with more complexity in some years than others.

◆ *Alquézar Rosado (rosé):* A blend of Macabeo and Tempranillo, this is competent pink wine at the correct price.

◆ *Montesierra Tinto (red):* A blend of Cabernet Sauvignon, Moristel and Tempranillo, this popular wine is a superior young red with lots of fruit, bite and characterful flavours for a modest price.

◆ *Alquézar Tinto (red):* Another superior young red, this 100 per cent Tempranillo offers mouthfilling, flavoursome fruit.

◆ *Montesierra Crianza (red):* A blend of Moristel, Tempranillo and Cabernet Sauvignon, this is a well made, powerful blend of fruit and oak flavours with well judged tannins. One of the better Spanish reds in its price range and newly and attractively labelled.

◆ *Montesierra Cabernet Sauvignon/Tempranillo Crianza (red):* An excellent crianza, balanced, flavoursome and moreish with an attractive finish.

◆ *Bodega Pirineos Merlot-Cabernet Crianza (red):* A smooth, characterful, quite complex wine for a modest price. Recommended.

◆ *Señorío de Lazán Reserva (red):* A delicious blend of dark, spicy fruit flavours with well judged oak and tannins, this has power, persistence and some complexity. Recommended.

◆ *Montesierra Parraleta (red):* This unusual, flavoursome wine, the bodega's most expensive, has attractive 'rustic' touches. Rather expensive.

Bodegas Borruel, S.A.T. (☎ 974 319 175) This small operation was founded in 1903 and has a modest 20 hectares of its own vineyards. Quality is mixed, with the following the best wines:

◆ *Osca Chardonnay (white):* An inexpensive, barrel-fermented Chardonnay, straightforward and good for the price. Quality varies from year to year.

◆ *Osca Rosado (rosé):* Aromatic, fruity, drinkable pink wine from the Tempranillo grape.

◆ *Castillo de l'Ainsa Tinto Crianza (red):* A well made, modestly-priced blend of fruit and oak, satisfying and easy to drink.

◆ *Osca Gran Eroles Reserva (red):* A blend of Moristel and Tempranillo, this is smooth, aromatic and tasty. A well made, satisfying wine.

Bodegas Lalanne, S.A. (☎ 974 310 689) Founded in 1843 by a French family (see page 66), this small operation has around 40 hectares of its own vines. Its everyday wines are respectable, but the following are the bodega's more interesting bottles:

◆ *Lalanne Cabernet/Merlot (red):* A very tasty young wine with tannic backbone and length. Recommended.

◆ *Lalanne Crianza (red):* A blend of Cabernet Sauvignon and Merlot, with the former dominant, this is a well made, straightforward crianza with lots of fruit flavours and, in some years, complexity.

◆ *Lalanne Reserva (red):* The same blend as above, this is near the top end of the price scale for Somontano wines and is a flavoursome wine, perhaps overpriced.

Viñas del Vero (☎ 974 302 216) Founded in 1986, this is one of Somontano's best producers – and one of Spain's more forward-looking – its wines winning numerous awards both domestically and internationally. It boasts an ultra-modern winery and 550 hectares of vineyards spread over a range of micro-climates, producing a wide selection of stylishly presented wines, some of the reds with a claret-like feel, from local and international varieties. Quality is generally very high, as is value for money. The range includes:

◆ *Viñas del Vero Blanco (white):* The bodega's simplest wine, a well made, easy-drinking blend of Chardonnay and Macabeo.

◆ *Viñas del Vero Chardonnay (white):* An unctuous, flavoursome, satisfying Chardonnay.

◆ *Viñas del Vero Chardonnay Fermentado en Barrica (white):* A powerful example of this popular style of wine. As is often the case with these wines, it is at its best at two, preferably three, years old.

◆ *Viñas del Vero Gewürztraminer (white):* Spanish examples of this grape are not quite as rare as a straight-talking politician, but they are thin on the ground. This is a satisfying, unctuous, refreshing wine, redolent of the variety's perfumed, fruity qualities.

◆ *Viñas del Vero Clarión (white):* Regularly voted as one of Spain's better whites, this is a blend of Chardonnay with small proportions of Chenin Blanc and Gewürztraminer, although the back label is reticent about revealing which varieties are used. It is a subtle, classy, elegant and flavoursome wine. Recommended.

◆ *Viñas del Vero Tempranillo (red):* A characterful, zippy, young wine with fruit and bite.

◆ *Viñas del Vero Duque de Azara Crianza (red):* A blend of Cabernet Sauvignon, Moristel and Tempranillo, this is a superior crianza for a competitive price, tasty, integrated and quite complex.

◆ *Viñas del Vero Merlot (red):* This is one of Spain's better Merlots in its price range, aromatic, concentrated and satisfying with attractive eucalyptus touches. Recommended.

◆ *Viñas del Vero Pinot Noir (red):* A good example of this 'difficult' grape, with an appealing mid-weight palate of elegant red fruits and some bite. Unfortunately, its production is being phased out to devote the Pinot grapes to other wines, notably Gran Vos.

◆ *Viñas del Vero Cabernet Sauvignon (red):* An aromatic, full, complex wine which should not be drunk too young. The winner of several prizes. Recommended.

◆ *Viñas del Vero Val de Vos Reserva (red):* A blend of Cabernet Sauvignon and Merlot, Val de Vos has a complex nose, power, structure and delicious flavours of fruit and oak in harmony. An elegant, satisfying wine, best from around five years old. Its production will cease shortly to allow the bodega to concentrate on Gran Vos.

◆ *Viñas del Vero Gran Vos Reserva (red):* Before the release of Blecua, this blend of Cabernet Sauvignon, Merlot and Pinot Noir was the bodega's flagship wine. It has a classy, claret-like feel, depth, power, complexity and harmony. Thoroughly recommended.

◆ *Blecua (red):* A recent release, this is by far the bodega's most expensive wine, designed to compete with the country's best. It boasts a deep, complex nose and a powerful, tannic palate with lots of flavour and length. As yet, it is too early to tell how it will develop in bottle.

Viñedos y Crianzas del Alto Aragón, S.A. (☎ 974 302 323) Founded in 1991, and thankfully known as Enate (after the wine's brand name), this operation is Viñas del Vero's main rival for the title of 'best of Somontano.' As with Vero, quality is generally very high across Enate's range of modern, fruit-driven wines, although while Vero's labels are subtle and elegant, Enate's are decorated with lively, distinctive, increasingly famous, modern artwork. The range includes:

◆ *Enate Chardonnay 234 (white):* A superior young Chardonnay, fruity, powerful, balanced and flavoursome with bite. Recommended.

◆ *Enate Chardonnay Fermentado en Barrica (white):* One of Spain's best white wines, this is powerful, complex and classy. Delicious and recommended.

◆ *Enate Gewürztraminer (white):* Very aromatic, flavoursome and unctuous, this will surprise those who might assume that Spain would struggle with the grape.

◆ *Enate Cabernet Sauvignon Rosado (rosé):* Often voted one of Spain's best pink wines (it is also one of the most expensive), this has a distinctive Cabernet nose and more power, flavour and interest than most of its competitors. Recommended.

◆ *Enate Tinto Cabernet-Sauvignon-Merlot (red):* Aromatic, powerful, characterful and inexpensive, this combines the feel of a young and crianza wine, with lively fruit and toasty oak. Recommended.

- *Enate Crianza (red):* A blend of Cabernet Sauvignon and Tempranillo, with the latter dominant, this shows how well these two grapes sit together, along with oak. Balanced, structured, flavoursome and long. Recommended.

- *Enate Cabernet Sauvignon Reserva (red):* One of Spain's best expressions of this noble grape, this is perfectly structured with lots of style, flavour and interest, as well as being easy to drink. Recommended, and, for what it offers, very reasonably priced.

- *Enate Merlot-Merlot (red):* So good they named it twice? Yes, according to many. A new release, this is already being bracketed with Spain's best wines, and in view of that is very reasonably priced. It has a toasty nose with mature fruit and some depth, while the palate has great personality, beautiful balance and bite. Highly recommended, although let's see how it develops in bottle before calling it the best thing since sliced bread.

- *Enate Reserva Especial (red):* This blend of 50 per cent Cabernet Sauvignon and 50 per cent Merlot was first released in 1998. It is the bodega's most expensive bottle, with a powerful, complex nose and an energetic, flavoursome, expressive palate with well judged tannins. Very good indeed.

Selected non-D.O. Bodega

Venta D'Aubert (☎ 978 769 021) Founded in 1987, situated in Teruel province and Swiss-owned, this small, high quality operation has attracted a lot of attention, especially for its Domus red wine. Its range includes:

- *Venta D'Aubert (white):* A blend of Chardonnay, Garnacha Blanca and Viognier (the latter a real rarity in Spain), this superior white wine has attractive tropical fruit flavours, elegance, bite and some complexity.

- *Domus (red):* A blend of Cabernet Sauvignon and Garnacha, sometimes with small additions of other grapes, this is an aromatic wine with lots of deep, concentrated flavours and length. Increasingly expensive but very good.

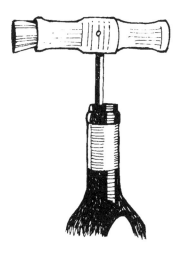

Most noted for beach holidays, the Balearics also have a long wine making history

4.

THE BALEARICS

Binissalem

Mallorca

Pla i Llevant

The history of the Balearics' wine industry is mainly that of the largest island, Majorca. Although now strongly associated with the holiday industry and not infrequently with the excesses of the package end of that business, Majorca has a long history of wine making. It stretches back at least to the Roman occupation, with the classical scholar Pliny writing admiringly about the island's wines. Production continued after the Romans departed and during the Middle Ages, the island's sweet wines made from the Malvasía grape were popular on the mainland.

Majorca next came to wine prominence in the later 19th century, when the phylloxera louse devastated the majority of Europe's vines. It hit the island later than most of the continent and before it did the Majorcans planted large areas with vines to profit from the wine shortage caused by the disease. They enjoyed success for a short time, even sending their wines to France, but when phylloxera finally arrived in 1891 it obliterated the island's vines as it had in most of the rest of Europe.

Majorca's wine industry has never since regained its former level of prominence, and today there are only 1,300 hectares under vine, compared with a maximum of around 30,000 in the late 19th century. To put this in perspective, the massive D.O. La Mancha has nearly 190,000 hectares, Rioja has around 50,000 and Penedés in Catalonia covers 27,000.

Of Majorca's 1,300 hectares of vines, around 600 are to be found in the island's two D.O.s. Binissalem, the focus of Balearics' wine production, covers 390 hectares north-east of the capital, Palma, in the centre of the northern part of the island. The recently created D.O. Pla i Llevant de Mallorca was previously a Vinos de la Tierra covering 700 hectares of vines; the D.O. covers around 210 hectares on the east of the island. Majorca's other vineyards are spread over small wine areas, with Banyalbufar notable both for its attempts to reintroduce the now neglected Malvasía grape and also because the actor Michael Douglas owns a vineyard there.

As has been said, Majorca is very much the leader of the Balearics' wine industry, both historically and currently, but wine is also made on other islands.

Ibiza, better known for its hedonistic, party crowd, has around 100 hectares of vines, with the Monastrell and Moscatel grapes popular. Most of the wine produced is for local consumption, quite a lot of it by the families who make it, or it is sold to the bulk market. However, there are stirrings of progress and two small bodegas have formed the Ibiza Vinos de la Tierra Association. The island of Formentera has a modest 40 hectares of vines, spread over diminutive plantations. Plans are afoot for a bodega making wines from Cabernet Sauvignon, Merlot and Tempranillo grapes.

The majority of the Balearic Islands' vineyards are given over to indigenous grapes, although foreign varieties are of increasing importance. Those wishing to try the full range of the wines are best advised to visit the islands, particularly Majorca. With their huge influx of tourists, the Balearics consume more wine than they produce and exports are limited. Some 95 per cent of Binissalem's output is drunk domestically, most of it on Majorca itself, although more Balearic wines are now available on the mainland than a few years ago; those looking for them abroad will have to search long and hard.

At least three-quarters of Majorca's wines are red, many made from the Manto Negro grape. It is flexible, able to make agreeable wines either for drinking young or for oak-ageing. They are characterised by a deep colour, fruity feel and good balance, although they can lack acidity. Whites and rosés vary according to the grape variety used.

D.O. Binissalem

In Brief: Most noted as a source of characterful, young red wines and has also shown that it can produce good quality, aged reds.

Binissalem is a growing D.O. and now covers 390 hectares of vineyards, with 120 growers and six bodegas; further expansion is expected in the near future.
The following grape varieties are authorised:

* **White:** Chardonnay, Macabeo, Moll (also called Prensal Blanc), Moscatel and Parellada.

* **Black:** Cabernet Sauvignon, Callet, Monastrell, Manto Negro and Tempranillo. Manto Negro is the dominant grape, covering 225 hectares.

Binissalem's white wines have attractive fruit and herb characteristics, with some of the wines made from Prensal displaying character and complexity. Rosés can be quite full-bodied and sometimes lack acidity, but reds are the region's signature wines, accounting for around 70 per cent of production. The majority are made in the 'young' style from Manto Negro and display balance, mature fruit and length.

Geography, Soil and Climate

Binissalem has a classic Mediterranean climate, with hot, dry summers and short, mild winters; annual rainfall is around 550mm (22in). The Sierra de Tramuntana hills protect the vineyards from potentially damaging north winds which sometimes blow the island's way. Soils are mainly ferruginous clays and the vineyards are situated between 75 and 200m (246 and 656ft) above sea level; this is sometimes lower than is necessary to have nights cool enough to allow grapes to recover and preserve their acidity after the day's heat.

Future Development

This is difficult to predict: tourism has dominated the island for some decades now and landowners have found it more profitable and less unpredictable to devote their land to holiday developments and related enterprises than to cultivate vines. There has also been a pronounced drift of people away from agriculture to work in the tourist resorts. Majorca's vine hectareage diminished during the 20th century from around 3,000 after the phylloxera devastation to today's 1,300 hectares. This has meant that the island no longer produces a lot of wine; hence, its profile is low and so is general customer interest and enthusiasm. Increased production is therefore required to attract attention and thus stimulate further growth: something of a chicken-and-egg situation. However, there are signs of better times ahead: the late 20th century saw a resurgence in the popularity of 'Mediterranean' wines, with obvious benefits for Binissalem, and the early years of this century have seen the D.O. growing, with signs of yet further development.

As will be seen in the wine reviews, Binissalem has proved capable of making good wines – with the focus on reds – and the odd great one and there is no reason why this cannot be built on, especially in well sited, higher vineyards. As for whites, Prensal is yielding some interesting results and more emphasis on the superior foreign varieties might generate further progress.

Selected Bodegas

Antonio Nadal (☎ 971 724 518) Founded in 1960, this bodega has nearly 30 hectares of its own vines and an annual production of around 100,000 litres. Wines include:

● *Blanc de Moll (white):* This blend of Moll and Macabeo is refreshing and tasty, characterised by appley fruit and good acidity.

● *Tres Uvas (red):* A flavoursome Manto Negro-based wine, sometimes lacking acidity. It can be very alcoholic: 14 per cent plus.

Hereus de Ribas (☎ 971 622 673) Originally founded in 1711 and revamped in 1986, this bodega has 40 hectares of its own vines and produces around 100,000 litres per year. The white and rosé are recommended, as is the following red:

● *Hereus de Ribas Crianza (red):* A successful blend of Cabernet Sauvignon, Manto Negro, Syrah and Tempranillo, this is smooth, fruity and drinkable. Recommended, but perhaps over-priced.

Jaume de Puntiró (☎ 971 620 023) Founded in the early '80s, this bodega makes a wide range of wines, generally of good quality, with the whites its strength. The following are the most reliable:

● *Jaume de Puntiró (white):* Made from Prensal Blanc, this is fruity, balanced, tasty and persistent.

● *Jaume de Puntiró Fermentado en Barrica (white):* This barrel-fermented Prensal Blanc is unctuous and flavoursome, with creamy, nutty oak slightly dominating the fruit.

● *Jaume de Puntiró Buc Crianza (red):* This blend of 65 per cent Manto Negro, 20 per cent Cabernet Sauvignon and 15 per cent Callet has an attractive peppery nose and a smooth, integrated, flavoursome palate. Recommended, although it is expensive and in some years can lack acidity.

José L. Ferrer/Franca Roja (☎ 971 511 050) Founded in 1931, this bodega has 80 hectares of its own vines and an annual production of over 500,000 litres. Its reputation is rising, along with the quality of its wines, which include:

● *Blanc de Blancs (white):* A blend of 95 per cent Moll and 5 per cent Parellada, this is a flavoursome, herby, spicy, everyday wine.

● *Viña Veritas (white):* A well conceived, fruity, toasty, barrel-fermented blend of mainly Moll with some Parellada, this is tasty and balanced. It is best drunk when it is a couple of years old.

● *José L. Ferrer Rosado (rosé):* Mainly Manto Negro, this is quite full-bodied, fruity and mouthfilling, although it sometimes lacks acidity.

● *Viña Veritas Crianza (red):* A blend of 75 per cent Manto Negro, 15 per cent Tempranillo and 10 per cent Cabernet Sauvignon, this is tasty and smooth although it can lack acidity.

● *José L. Ferrer Crianza (red):* This is made from 85 per cent Manto Negro, 10 per cent Tempranillo and 5 per cent Cabernet Sauvignon, and is a straightforward, herby, flavoursome, balanced wine, but again lack of acidity can be a problem. Well priced.

● *José L. Ferrer Reserva (red):* Made primarily from Manto Negro, with Tempranillo, Cabernet Sauvignon and Callet, this has a spicy nose and a smooth, suitably aged palate with some class. Recommended.

Macià Batle, S.A. (☎ 971 140 014) Founded in 1998, this small bodega has already shown that it is capable of producing good quality wines, including:

● *Macià Batle Blanc de Blancs (white):* Made from Prensal, this is a good white wine, flavoursome, mouthfilling and balanced with a long finish. Recommended.

● *Macià Batle Rosado (rosé):* A blend of 85 per cent Manto Negro and 15 per cent Callet, this is fruity, refreshing and persistent. Good pink wine.

● *Macià Batle Tinto (red):* Primarily Manto Negro, with Callet and Cabernet Sauvignon, this varies in quality from year to year. It can be fruity and characterful, or it can be flat and lacking acidity.

● *Macià Batle Crianza (red):* Made from 85 per cent Manto Negro and 15 per cent Callet, this is a decent, straightforward blend of mature fruit and oak.

D.O. Pla i Llevant

In Brief: *A source of wines of mixed quality, although it has shown that it can make good whites and reds. General standards should improve and this is one to watch.*

The newest D.O., Pla i Llevant lies in the east of Majorca and as yet covers a modest 210 hectares of vineyards, with 65 growers and 8 bodegas.
  Authorised grape varieties are:

● **White:** Chardonnay, Macabeo, Moscatel, Parellada and Prensal Blanc.

- **Black:** Cabernet Sauvignon, Callet – the most common variety – Fogoneu, Manto Negro, Merlot, Monastrell, Syrah and Tempranillo.

Geography, Soil and Climate

Pla i Llevant has a Mediterranean climate, with long, hot, dry summers and short, mild winters. Summer temperatures are moderated by sea breezes, while winters can be prey to short cold snaps if the wind blows from the north. Annual rainfall is a modest 500mm (20in), with autumn the rainiest season.

Future Development

Prior to its very recent investiture as a D.O., the region had a long wine making history and has shown itself to be capable of making good wines. As yet, many of its better ones contain a proportion of the international favourites Chardonnay and Cabernet Sauvignon. These impart personality, although inevitably of an international flavour and the D.O. will probably garner more attention by concentrating on local varieties, especially Callet, Manto Negro and Prensal, either as varietals or blended with foreign grapes.

Selected Bodegas

Jaume Mesquida (☎ 971 647 106) Founded in 1945, this bodega makes a wide range of wines, with quality ranging from acceptable to good. The following are worth investigating:

- *Jaume Mesquida Blanco (white):* This blend of 75 per cent Prensal Blanc and 25 per cent Chardonnay varies in quality. It can be mouthfilling, tasty, unctuous and well balanced, or it can demonstrate faults.

- *Jaume Mesquida Cabernet Sauvignon (red):* This again varies in quality, although much less radically than the above, and has some complexity on the nose while the palate is smooth, tasty and suitably aged.

- *Vinya Esther Crianza (red):* A blend of 90 per cent Merlot and 10 per cent Callet, this is an aromatic wine with smooth, integrated flavours, although a little expensive.

Pere Seda (☎ 971 605 087) This producer has a solid rather than remarkable range of wines, with some of them rather characterless. The following are the most reliable:

- *Pere Seda Novell Blanco (white):* A blend of 60 per cent Prensal and 40 per cent Macabeo, this is a crisp, refreshing, everyday wine.

- *Pere Seda Chardonnay (white):* A fresh, tasty, characterful young wine, possibly slightly overpriced.

- *L'Arxiduc Rosado (rosé):* Made from 50 per cent Merlot and 50 per cent Tempranillo, this is characterful, fruity pink wine.

◆ *Pere Seda Tinto (red):* Drink the most recent release for a light, smooth, everyday red.

Vins Can Majoral (☎ 971 125 516) This tiny bodega was founded in 1985 and makes a good white wine from the Catalan grape Xarel-lo:

◆ *Can Majoral Xarel-lo (white):* A refreshing, herby, mouthfilling wine. Drink the latest release.

Vinyes i Bodegas Miquel Oliver (☎ 971 561 117) Founded in 1912, this bodega has ten hectares of its own vines and produces 175,000 litres per year. Wines include:

◆ *Celler Son Caló Blanc de Blancs (white):* A blend of Prensal and Macabeo, this is well made, herby, fruity, everyday wine.

◆ *Miquel Oliver Muscat (white):* A dry wine with a full nose and attractive bitter touches; it could sometimes do with more acidity.

◆ *Ses Ferritges Reserva (red):* A blend of Cabernet Sauvignon and Merlot, this is a smooth, tasty wine with some complexity. Recommended.

Selected Non-D.O. Majorcan Bodegas

Ánima Negra, often known as A.N. (☎ 971 581 031) Founded as recently as 1994, this bodega has quickly become a star and demonstrates the high quality which Majorca is capable of producing. It has around ten hectares of its own vines and produces only 10,000 to 20,000 litres per year, over half of which is exported so foreigners have a fighting chance of securing a bottle. It is quite possible that this exclusive bodega will choose not to increase volume.

◆ *Ánima Negra (red):* This was originally a blend of Cabernet Sauvignon and Callet, but the proportion of the latter is increasing with every vintage and the wine may become a Callet varietal, or the blend may be modified again. It has great body, structure, complexity and flavour. A.N. is probably the Balearics' best wine and is up there with the top Mediterranean reds. Sell your house for a bottle.

Finca San Bordil's (☎ 971 182 200) Founded in 1998, this small bodega produces a range of good and very good wines, indicative of what Majorca is capable of.

◆ *Finca San Bordil's Muscat (white):* This aromatic wine is soundly constructed, smooth and characterful with attractive bittersweet touches. Good.

◆ *Finca San Bordil's Chardonnay (white):* Flavoursome, unctuous, refreshing and persistent. Good Chardonnay.

◆ *San Bordil's Negre (red):* This blend of Merlot, Manto Negro, Cabernet Sauvignon, Callet and Syrah has a powerful, deep nose and a big, mouthfilling, tasty, complex palate with fruit and oak working well. Recommended.

Florianópolis (☎ 971 235 413) Founded in 1985, this bodega has 60 hectares of its own vines and produces 250,000 litres annually. Wines include:

- *Santa Catarina Chardonnay (white)*: A respectably fruity, tasty example of this popular grape.

- *Santa Catarina Merlot Crianza (red)*: Spicy, toasty and structured, this well made wine is flavoursome and mouthfilling with some bite. Good.

- *Santa Catarina Cabernet Sauvignon Reserva (red)*: Well priced, mouthfilling, warm-climate Cabernet. Good.

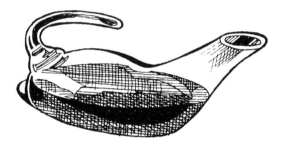

The Guggenheim Museum at Bilbao, symbol of the modern Basque Country

5.

THE BASQUE COUNTRY

The Basque country (*País Vasco* in Castilian Spanish) lies in the north-west of Spain's Atlantic coastal region. It is a beautiful part of the country, with a thin, green coastal strip giving way to mountains rising just back from the sea. The Basque country has long been

Bizkaiko Getariako
Txakolina Txakolina

isolated, both geographically and culturally. Indeed its language, which scholars cannot link conclusively with any other linguistic group, is now thought to be a relic of a prehistoric western European tongue, which has survived in this remote enclave.

In modern Spain the Basque region is unfortunately first and foremost associated with its violent struggle for independence, but more positively it is also increasingly noted for its culture and cuisine. The relatively new Guggenheim museum in Bilbao has attracted a lot of publicity – more perhaps for its radical architecture than for its contents – while Basque cuisine is generally recognised as being Spain's finest.

Wine and food are rightly seen as each other's natural partners and the success of the region's cuisine has focused some attention on Basque wines. The region's traditional produce is 'Txacoli' (pronounced 'Chacolí' and we will call it thus from now on), a young, 'green', acidic (some would say aggressively acidic), low alcohol (between 9 and 11.5 per cent), slightly sparkling white, often compared with northern Portugal's Vinhos Verdes. Small amounts of red wine are also made and while some people regard Basque wines as thin, bland and too astringent, others point to the better examples' fruity flavours, refreshing acidity, attractive pétillance (naturally occurring bubbles, giving a prickle of gas) and suitability as partners for the region's excellent seafood.

Basque white wine is called Txacolín Gorri and is made from the Ondarrubi Zuri grape, while the red is known as Txacolín Zuri and is made from Ondarrubi Beltza. Production methods are traditional, with vines grown high on trellises (as in parts of Galicia) to protect them from frost, expose them to the sun and keep them off the often damp ground. Tending them used to be labour-intensive, but modern technology and mechanisation have been introduced where possible.

Chacolí used to be made all along the Basque coast and there are documents attesting to its production dating back to the 8th century. But its very existence was threatened in the 19th century when vine pests and diseases greatly reduced the number of vineyards. Phylloxera, however, was not a problem, because the region's high rainfall leads to flooding of the vineyards in winter which kills the bug. Thus the vines grown today are generally ungrafted. By the '80s, vineyard hectareage was tiny and Chacolí was again in real danger of extinction. Indeed, instigating the Basque country's two D.O.s was seen as a radical way of saving it.

D.O. Bizkaiko Txacolina

In Brief: The source of small amounts of acidic wines, mainly white. Many have only local appeal but some are strangely enjoyable.

Located in the province of Vizcaya, this was the second Basque region to be designated a D.O.. Initially, it covered only around 60 hectares of vineyards, but this has grown to

120 hectares, with 215 growers and over 60 bodegas. Around 85 per cent of production is white wine, 10 per cent rosé and 5 per cent red. As has always been the case with Basque wine, the vast majority of this – 90 per cent – is consumed locally, with much of the balance sold to Barcelona and Madrid, mainly to Basque 'émigrés' and restaurants.

Authorised grape varieties are:

- **White:** Folle Blanche and Ondarrubi (or Hondarrabi) Zuri.

- **Black:** Ondarrubi (or Hondarrabi) Beltza.

The region's dominant white wines are quite aromatic, with flowers and fruit on the nose. On the palate they are light, with an 'arresting' quality due to their high acidity. Local rosés are also light and fresh, again with high acidity. The tiny amounts of red wine are something of a jolt, once again because of high acid levels.

Geography, Soil and Climate

The climate is strongly maritime, with coolish summers, mild winters and high rainfall, between 1,000 and 1,300mm (39 and 51in) per year. Soils are clay-based with a relatively high organic content.

Future Direction

This is perhaps the more forward-thinking of the two Basque D.O.s because unlike its neighbour, Bizkaiko Txacolina is looking to experiment with foreign grape varieties to offer more quality and variety. It also wants to increase its volume of production, improve its image and move beyond being a producer of what are essentially wines for local tastes and consumption. Experiments are being carried out with Chardonnay (inevitably), La Petit Mansen del Jurançon, Riesling and Sauvignon Blanc, and in the medium to long term the authorities may authorise up to 25 per cent of these foreigners in local wines.

The selection of bodegas is very limited owing to the tiny amounts of wine produced by most and the difficulty of securing them.

Selected Bodegas

Aretxondo, S.A.T. (☎ 946 742 706) Founded in 1995, this is one of the region's largest producers, although tiny by national standards. Its wines display attention to detail and are good representatives of the local grape varieties' somewhat limited charms. The range includes:

- *Aretxondo Bion-Etxea Mahastia (white):* A fresh, soundly constructed, quite fruity wine.

- *Marko (white):* A decent, straightforward white wine, fresh, clean and redolent of green fruit.

Doniene-Gorrondona, S.A. (☎ 946 194 795) This is another of the region's largest producers and the following two wines, one white and one red, show the best of local wine making:

◆ *Doniene Blanco (white):* This is one of the region's best whites, with herbs on the nose and a fruity, refreshing palate with some interest and bite. It is quite expensive but well worth trying, especially if you have previously thought that the region's wines are only good for cleaning silver.

◆ *Gorrondona (red):* This young red has lots of fruit on the nose and attractive, astringent fruit on the palate. Strangely appealing and, as above, quite expensive for what it is, but worth trying.

D.O. Getariako Txacolina

In Brief: *The source of the Basque country's best white wines, some of which defy their image as bland and too acidic by offering interesting fruit flavours and character.*

This was the first Basque D.O. and when it was founded in 1990, it comprised a mere 47 hectares. It now covers 125, will increase in size in the future and has 37 growers and 17 bodegas. White wines account for 85 per cent of production and reds 15 per cent. Some 98 per cent of its wines are consumed in Spain, the vast majority locally, with a mere 2 per cent exported.
    Authorised grape varieties are:

● **White:** Hondarrabi Zuri.

● **Black:** Hondarrabi Beltza.

Whites are dominant and are the only wines reviewed here. They are noted for their fruity, floral nose and on the palate are invigoratingly fresh with an agreeable spritz of gas. The region is reckoned to make the Basque country's best Chacolí wines.

Geography, Soil and Climate

Getariako Txacolina's climate is strongly maritime, with coolish summers, mild winters and high rainfall of 1,600mm (63in) per year.

Future Development

Unlike its neighbour Bizkaiko Txakolina, Getariako is not looking to experiment with foreign grape varieties. It does not need to because the overall standard of its wines is better than Bizkaiko's. The region's future will consist of expanding its vineyard hectareage, raising its profile and trying to sell more wines outside the province.

Selected Bodegas

Txacoli Rezabal (☎ 943 580 899) Founded in 1996, this forward-thinking operation is notable for fair quality and its barrel-fermented wine.

- *Rezabal (white):* A decent, fruity wine, respectable but nothing remarkable.

- *Rezabal Fermentado en Barrica (white):* More successful than might be imagined, with Hondarrabi Zuri's gentle fruit still evident and not overwhelmed by the oak. Interesting and recommended.

Txacoli Ulacia (☎ 943 140 893) The following wine is both reasonably priced and characterful, representative of these whites at their best:

- *Ulacia (white):* A blend of primarily Hondarrabi Zuri with Beltza, this fruitily aromatic wine has lots of fruity flavour and a hint of class. Recommended.

Txomin Etxaniz (☎ 943 140 702) Founded in 1989, this is the largest and one of the best of the Basque region's producers.

- *Txomin Etxaniz (white):* This has quite a complex, fruity nose and offers an unctuous mouthful of fruity, refreshing flavours. A rather good wine.

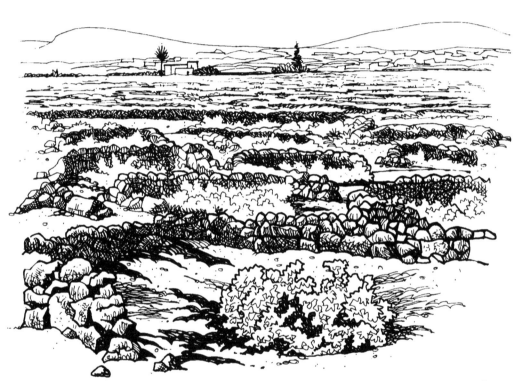

Vines on Lanzarote growing in pits to protect them from the wind

6.

THE CANARY ISLANDS

L ittle is known about the history of the Canary Islands prior to the 15th century. However, soon after they were annexed by Castille, the islands' sweet wines made from the Malvasía (or Malmsey) grape became popular. It appears that vines were brought by the mainland conquerors,

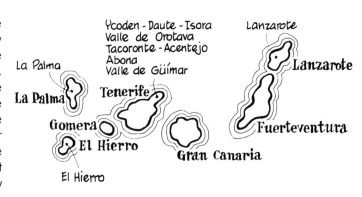

since there is no evidence as yet that the islands' original inhabitants – the mysterious Guanches – cultivated them. The Canaries' Malvasía wines are famously mentioned by Shakespeare in two of his plays, referred to as both 'sack' and 'marvellous searching wines'. Britain was a significant market, importing nearly 700,000 gallons per year by the early decades of the 19th century, after which the wine's style declined in popularity.

As with the Balearics, the 21st century finds the Canaries strongly identified with the holiday industry, especially the winter sun and timeshare markets. And lying at a latitude of between 27 and 29 degrees north, many people believe them to be too hot for wine production. However, the close proximity of the Portuguese island of Madeira, maker of world-renowned wines, should banish this misconception and as we will see over the following pages, there are currently eight D.O.s in the Canary Islands, actively concerned with the production of a wide range of wine styles. Hence this section is split into eight, with each D.O. considered separately.

Those wishing to try the islands' wines will encounter the same obstacle as with Balearics' wines: exports are limited because the islands' constant stream of tourists – along of course with the locals – provides a ready market and prices in the Canaries are higher than those which could be achieved on the mainland or abroad.

D.O. Abona

In Brief: A source of decent, dry, everyday white wines.

A D.O. only since 1996, Abona lies at the southern tip of the island of Tenerife. It has grown quickly and now has 1,800 hectares of vines, 1,200 grape growers and 7 bodegas.

Authorised grape varieties are:

- **White:** Bermejuelo, Listán Blanco, Malvasía, Sabro and Verdello.

- **Black:** Listán Negro and Negramoll.

White wines are dominant, representing 80 per cent of production, with Listán Blanco the pre-eminent grape. At present, whites are dry, fruity and balanced, rosés are light and fresh, and reds are light.

Geography, Soil and Climate

The Canaries have warm winters and hot summers at sea level, with temperatures moderated by trade winds. However, generalisations are difficult because the individual islands have a variety of micro-climates, often the result of altitude and aspect. This is so with Abona, which experiences a diversity of weather conditions because vineyards are sited across a wide range of altitudes, from 300 to 1,750m (984 to 5,741ft) above sea level, including some of Europe's highest plantings. The dominant climatic feature is light, this being the sunniest part of an already sunny island. Rainfall varies between 350 and 550mm (14 and 22in) per year. Again, it is difficult to generalise about soils, but those at the lower levels tend to be sandy and calcareous, while soils in the higher parts of the region are volcanic.

Future Development

This fledgling D.O. has, by Canary Island standards, a better than average potential to make good wines and needs to experiment with alternative grape varieties and to do so in each of its various environments to find out what does best where. New barrel-fermented whites made from Listán Blanco are of increasing quality and could lead to a higher profile for the D.O.'s wines.

Selected Bodegas

Cooperativa Cumbres de Abona (☎ 922 768 604) Founded in 1989 this co-operative has a modest 3 hectares of its own vines and produces 300,000 litres per year. Wines include:

● *Cumbres de Abona (white):* 100 per cent Listán Blanco, this fresh, fruity, everyday wine has attractive touches of herbs.

● *Flor de Chasna (white):* This Listán Blanco varies in quality from year to year. It can be a well made, unctuous, persistent wine, or a bland, uninteresting mouthful. More consistency please.

● *Viña Peraza Ecológico (white):* This Listán Blanco is fresh, with herby flavours, good acidity and persistence. Recommended.

● *Cumbres de Abona (rosé):* Made from Listán Negro, this varies in quality too, either a clean, quaffable rosado with mature fruit or a bit of a plain mouthful.

La Ortigosa, S.L. (☎ 922 161 147) This bodega was founded in 1994 and has 2.8 hectares of its own vines producing around 40,000 litres annually. The following is its most interesting wine by far:

● *Leña Blanca Fermentado en Barrica (white):* A well made, persistent barrel-fermented Listán Blanco, with integrated fruit and oak. Better in some years than others.

D.O. El Hierro

In Brief: A source of some fresh, fruity white wines.

A D.O. since 1994, El Hierro is on – and named after – the smallest of the Canary Islands. It has 270 hectares of vineyards, 350 grape growers and 18 wine makers, two of which bottle their wines.
Authorised grape varieties are:

● **White:** Baboso, Bermejuelo, Güal, Listán Blanca, Moscatel, Pedro Ximénez and Verijadiego.

● **Black:** Baboso Negro, Listán Negro, Negramoll and Vijariego Negro.

As in Abona, whites are of primary importance, accounting for 70 per cent of production, with Verijadiego responsible for 80 per cent of the wines. For now, the island's whites are fresh and fruity, sometimes with attractive tropical touches. The rosés are clean and fresh, while the reds have decent body and fruit.

Geography, Soil and Climate

El Hierro has three climatic zones but, overall, the island is known for particularly mild weather, with low rainfall and an increase in humidity with altitude. Its volcanic soils have a high capacity for water retention and vines are planted at altitudes ranging from 175 to 600m (574 to 1,968ft) above sea level.

Future Development

One large concern – Cooperativa Del Campo Frontera – dominates the island and its interest in and use of modern techniques and technology bode well for the future. A possible improvement would be to site vineyards at higher altitudes.

Selected Bodegas

Cooperativa del Campo Frontera (☎ 922 556 016) No wines were available for review at the time of writing.

Fleitas (☎ 922 559 078) No wines were available for review at the time of writing.

D.O. La Palma

In Brief: Produces respectable dry white and rosé wines, although it is probably strongest on sweet whites.

Sitting in the north-west of the Canaries, the island of La Palma makes some interesting wines from its 1,175 hectares of vines. It has almost 1,500 grape growers and 14 bodegas.

Authorised grape varieties are many and varied, so please brace yourselves:

- **White:** Albillo, the beautifully named Bastardo Blanco, Bermejuela, Bujariego, Burra Blanca, Forastera Blanca, Güal, Listán Blanco, Malvasía, Moscatel, Pedro Ximénez, Sabro, Torrontés and Verdello.

- **Black:** Almuñeco/Listán Negro, Bastardo Negro, Malvasía Rosada, Moscatel Negro, Negramoll and Tintilla.

Currently, the D.O.'s wines can be characterised as follows, with whites and rosés its strongest suit: whites: the dry wines are noted for their fruitiness, sometimes with attractive minerally touches; the sweet Malvasía wines have herby flavours and complexity; rosés are light and delicate; while reds are light and fresh.

Geography, Soil and Climate

The island has the highest land in relation to surface area of all the Canaries and this obviously has a large influence on climate. It leads to a broad range of grape-growing environments, part of the reason for the island's extensive and interesting selection of wine styles. The vines are grown at altitudes ranging from 200 to 1,400m (656 to 4,593ft) above sea level, on mainly volcanic soils.

Future Development

The island is already successfully using a variety of techniques and grape-growing environments to make an interesting range of wines from a wide selection of grapes and should continue experimenting in this vein.

Selected Bodegas

Carballo, S.L. (☎ 922 444 130) Founded in 1990, this bodega has seven hectares of its own vines and makes a modest 15,000 litres per year. The following wines are worth seeking out:

- *Carballo Malvasía Dulce (white):* A high quality, golden, sweet wine which is mouthfilling, flavoursome and memorable. Recommended.

- *Carballo Negramoll (red):* Well made in the light and tasty style.

Eufrasina Pérez Rodríguez (☎ 922 400 447) Founded in 1997, this tiny bodega produces a modest range of wines, with the following standing out:

- *El Nispero (white):* This is an attractive white wine, fruity, balanced and with some interest, but it is expensive.

Llanovid, S. Cooperativa Ltda. (☎ 922 444 078) Founded in 1985, you are more likely to be able to secure a bottle from this bodega since it produces 450,000 litres per year. The following are the best of its wide range:

♦ *Teneguía Listán Blanco (white):* A fresh, aromatic, herbaceous wine at a low price. Good.

♦ *Teneguía Bujariego (white):* Light, tasty and refreshing, everything you could want from this type of wine.

♦ *Malvasía Dulce (white):* One of the island's signature sweet wines, with an unctuous, flavoursome palate and good length. Recommended.

S.A.T. El Hoyo (☎ 922 440 616) Founded in 1994 this bodega has 110 hectares of its own vines and makes 200,000 litres per year. Quality is mixed, with the following the most dependable wines:

♦ *Hoyo de Mazo (white):* This is a clean, flavoursome, unctuous Listán Blanco, a good everyday wine.

♦ *Hoyo de Mazo (rosé):* A tasty, refreshing Negramoll with decent acidity.

♦ *Mazegas (red):* Light, with flavoursome red fruit.

D.O. Lanzarote

In Brief: The source of some characterful sweet white wines.

Parts of this windswept, volcanic island look positively moon-like, not very promising wine making territory. In fact, Lanzarote makes some good quality wines from its 2,300 hectares of vines, notably sweet whites. It has around 1,700 grape growers, 15 bodegas.
　　Authorised grape varieties are:

● **White:** Breval, Burrablanca, Diego, Listán Blanco, Malvasía (the dominant variety), Moscatel and Pedro Ximénez.

● **Black:** Listán Negra and Negramoll.

Currently, the reds, pinks and dry whites, while certainly competent, are sometimes a touch heavy and overcooked. The sweet whites, at their best, are the island's strength: amber-coloured with nutty, minerally touches.

Geography, Soil and Climate

Lanzarote has a dry, sub-tropical climate, with rainfall of only 200mm (8in) per year. Hot, dusty winds from the Sahara sometimes act like a hair-drier to raise temperatures. Fortunately, the island's volcanic soils are ideal for conserving what little water there is.

Lanzarote is relatively flat, its maximum elevation being 670m (2,198ft), and vines are grown in depressions in the ground surrounded by low walls to protect them from the elements, especially wind. Rank upon rank of these, spread across the dark, volcanic soil, present an unusual sight and add to the island's otherworldly feel.

Future Development

Lanzarote can build on its reputation for sweet whites. The heat and wind are not generally conducive to the production of high quality dry whites, reds and rosés, although there are exceptions.

Selected Bodegas

Barreto (☎ 928 520 717) Founded in 1980, this bodega makes quite a wide range of wines from its 40 hectares of vines, the following being the best:

- *El Campesino Malvasía Seco (white):* An aromatic wine with mouthfilling fruit and personality. Recommended and competitively priced.

- *El Campesino Licor de Moscatel (sweet white):* An aromatic wine with a tasty, nutty, sweet palate. Well made and enjoyable.

El Grifo (☎ 928 800 586) El Grifo has a pedigree stretching back to 1775, plenty of time to have established itself as probably the island's best producer. The current winery was built in 1970 and the bodega has 40 hectares of its own vines and releases 500,000 litres per year. Wines include:

- *El Grifo Malvasía Seco (white):* Fresh, fruity and dry with an attractive bitterness. It demonstrates that it is sometimes possible to make this type of wine on Lanzarote.

- *El Grifo Malvasía Semidulce (white):* Well conceived and sweet, with fruity, herby touches.

- *El Grifo Fermentado en Barrica (white):* If drunk when two, preferably three, years old, this is a tasty, unctuous, barrel-fermented wine. However, compared with similar-style mainland competitors, it is expensive.

- *Moscatel de Ana 1881 (sweet white):* This is one of the Canary Islands' better wines, a superior, powerfully aromatic bottle, tasty, mouthfilling and full of interesting flavours. Recommended.

La Gería, S.L. (☎ 928 510 743) This bodega, founded in 1990, has ten hectares of its own vines and produces 350,000 litres annually. Wines are respectable rather than remarkable, with these bottles worth trying:

- *La Gería Semidulce (white):* A decent, semi-sweet wine with lots of flavour.

- *La Gería Dulce (sweet white):* A tasty, concentrated Malvasía with character. Good.

Mozaga (☎ 928 520 485) Founded in 1973, Mozaga produces over 250,000 litres per year. Quality is mixed but this sweet white is reliable:

◆ *Mozaga Malvasía Dulce (white):* This has an attractive nose, balance, flavour and, of course, sweetness.

Tinache (☎ 928 840 849) Founded in 1975, this bodega makes interesting wines, with the following recommended:

◆ *Tinache Moscatel Seco (white):* This varies in quality and in good years is an aromatic wine with bittersweet bite.

◆ *Tinache Fermentado en Barrica (red):* A reasonably priced, barrel-fermented Negramoll, this is an attractive, fruity, toasty wine. Recommended.

D.O. Tacoronte-Acentejo

In Brief: *The Canary Islands' most prominent D.O., best for its characterful, young red wines.*

Lying in the mountainous north of Tenerife, Tacoronte-Acentejo was the Canary Islands' first D.O., designated in 1992. The region has just over 1,600 hectares of vineyards, intensively cultivated with dense plantings of vines. It has 1,930 grape growers and 30 bottling bodegas.
Grape varieties authorised and/or used are:

● **White:** Forastera Blanca, Güal, Listán Blanco, Malvasía, Marmajuelo, Moscatel, Pedro Ximénez, Torrontés, Verdello and Vijariego.

● **Black:** Listán Negro, Malvasía Rosada, Moscatel Negro, Negramoll and Tintilla.

Black varieties dominate, accounting for 85 per cent of plantings. Currently, the region's whites and rosés are competent rather than remarkable, the reds holding most interest: fresh with concentrated fruit, sometimes with a 'rustic' feel.

Geography, Soil and Climate

This part of Tenerife enjoys a mild, agreeable climate, without significant weather variations throughout the year. Rainfall is scarce, although relative humidity is quite high. Soils are rich in organic materials and vines are cultivated across a wide range of altitudes up to 1,000m (3,280ft) above sea level.

Future Development

The D.O. has quietly but successfully raised its profile over the last few years and includes some of the islands' best known bodegas. Young reds have enjoyed the most success and the next step is to make aged examples. In order to do this it will be necessary to plant good quality foreign grape varieties, better suited to ageing than the presently authorised ones.

Selected Bodegas

Buten (☎ 922 572 512) Founded in 1997, this tiny operation, which exports half of its output, produces an expensive, notably good red wine:

◆ *Cráter (red):* It does not take a linguistic genius to work out that this is the Spanish for 'crater', a reference to the Canaries' volcanic origins. Made from 60 per cent Listán Negro and 40 per cent Negramoll, this expensive wine is cited as one of the best reds from the Canary Islands. It is a confident wine, with fruit and oak working well together and a raft of interesting flavours. The price *is* high, but so is the quality and it is well worth seeking out to see how good Tacoronte reds can be.

El Lomo (☎ 922 540 205) Founded in 1990, this is a forward-thinking, modern bodega producing small amounts of a range of wines, including:

◆ *El Lomo (white):* Made primarily from Listán Blanco, this is a fruity wine with flavour and bite. Good.

◆ *El Lomo Fermentado en Barrica (white):* Made from the same blend as the above, this tends to be dominated by oak. It is flavoursome but rather one-dimensional.

◆ *El Lomo (red):* Made primarily from Listán Negro, this can be a very good young red with lots of fruity character. Some years are rather better than others.

Flores (☎ 922 577 194) Dating from 1972, Flores has six hectares of its own vines, producing a modest 25,000 litres annually. Quality is respectable or decent:

◆ *Viña Flores (white):* In good years, this is a mouthfilling, tasty wine with hints of oak, in others, it is a bit directionless.

◆ *Viña Flores Madera (red):* Moderately oaky and flavoursome. A fair everyday wine.

Insulares Tenerife, S.A. (☎ 922 570 617) Founded in 1992 as a result of a government initiative, this large concern was formerly a co-operative. It was designed to provide local growers with a home where their grapes could be turned into good wines. The bodega has 500 hectares of vines and produces 500,000 litres annually, huge by Canary Island standards. High technology is employed, wine quality is good and the bodega's profile is improving on the mainland; size can help. The following is a selection of the wide range of wines:

◆ *Viña Norte (white):* A well made, lightish, young white wine from Listán Blanco.

◆ *Viña Norte Fermentado en Barrica (white):* A flavoursome, unctuous, barrel-fermented wine.

◆ *Viña Norte Tinto: (red):* Made from 95 per cent Listán Negro and 5 per cent Negramoll, this is fruitily flavoursome and easy to drink. That is not a criticism.

◆ *Viña Norte Maceración Carbónica (red):* Made from the same blend as the above, this is light, fruity and suitable for chilling, which is welcome on Tenerife.

◆ *Viña Norte 6 Meses en Barrica (red):* Smooth and integrated, light on the oak.

◆ *Viña Norte Crianza (red):* Tasty, with the all-important balance between fruit and oak successfully engineered. Good, although not inexpensive.

◆ *Humboldt Vino Dulce (red):* A highly thought-of sweet red wine, very flavoursome and persistent. Try hard to secure a bottle.

Monje, S.L. (☎ 922 585 027) This bodega was founded in 1956 and has 14 hectares of its own vines producing 80,000 litres per year. Quality is high, but so are prices. Wines include:

◆ *Monje Dragoblanco (white):* A well made, characterful wine from Listán Blanco with pronounced herbaceous touches and bite, but pricey.

◆ *Evento Fermentado en Barrica (white):* A well made, barrel-fermented wine, drinking well at five years old, with refreshing unctuous flavours that are not overwhelmed by the oak, but it is very expensive – more than some of Spain's very best whites, e.g. Torres' Milmanda Chardonnay.

◆ *Monje Tradicional (red):* Made from 80 per cent Listán Negro, 15 per cent Listán Blanco and 5 per cent Negramoll, this is a competent, aromatic, fruity red with touches of oak, but heavy on cost.

◆ *Monje de Autor Crianza (red):* The same blend as the above, this is a well made, tasty, oak-aged wine, but not remarkable enough for the very high price.

San Diego (☎ 922 577 636) Founded in 1980, San Diego produces 20,000 litres annually and has five hectares of its own vines. The following sweet red is worth trying:

◆ *San Diego Afrutado (red):* A dark, sweet, tasty wine with hints of menthol Interesting.

D.O. **Valle de Güimar**

In Brief: A source of decent, everyday, dry white wines and improving reds.

Situated halfway down the east coast of Tenerife, this D.O. has 685 hectares of vines spread across a wide range of altitudes, 780 growers and 12 bottling bodegas.
   Authorised grape varieties are:

● **White:** Güal, Listán Blanco, Malvasía, Moscatel and Vijariego.

● **Black:** Listán Negro and Negramoll.

White wines account for 80 per cent of production, with the Listán Blanco grape dominant. Currently, reds are light, dry and fruity, while whites are noted for their floral flavours and, sometimes, their complexity.

Geography, Soil and Climate

The D.O. has a whole host of micro-climates because of its great range of altitude. The better wines, from grapes cultivated in higher vineyards, benefit from a large diurnal temperature range, cool nights allowing the grapes to recover after the strong sunshine. Soils in these higher regions are volcanic.

Future Development

While white wines dominate for now, the region is certainly capable of making accomplished reds and might stimulate their development by planting foreign grapes. Variations in vintage are difficult to legislate against if due to the vagaries of climate, but vintage quality varies more than might be expected and more consistency would be desirable.

Selected Bodegas

Comarca Valle de Güimar (☎ 922 510 437) Founded in 1990, this is a fair-size operation with 80 hectares of its own vines and an annual production of 300,000 litres. Quality varies from year to year, with the wines sometimes rather bland, but the following white is usually reliable:

◆ *Pico Cho Marcial (white):* Made from Listán Blanco, this is herby, fruity and refreshing.

Fulgencia Román (☎ 922 528 247) This much smaller bodega was also founded in 1990 and has 15 hectares of its own vines, producing 25,000 litres per year. Wines include:

◆ *Viña Chagua Blanco (white):* Mouthfilling and fresh.

◆ *Viña Chagua Tinto (red):* A smooth, flavoursome wine with body, which is better in some years than others.

D.O. Valle de la Orotava

In Brief: A producer of decent, everyday dry white, rosé and young red wines.

This D.O. lies in northern Tenerife, near the imposing volcano Mount Teide. It has 650 hectares of vines, 740 growers and 20 bottling bodegas.
    Authorised grape varieties are:

- **White:** Bastardo Blanco, Forastera Blanca, Güal, Listán Blanco, Malvasía, Maramjuelo, Moscatel, Pedro Ximénez, Torrontés, Verdello and Vijariego.

- **Black:** Listán Negro and Negramoll.

Currently, the D.O.'s wines can be characterised as follows: whites: fresh, fruity and herbaceous; rosés: few in number, but notably fruity and drinkable; and reds: light, tasty and fresh.

Geography, Soil and Climate

The D.O.'s climate is strongly influenced by the Atlantic Ocean, which has a cooling effect on the lower regions and humidifies higher areas, important as rainfall is low. Soils are light, nutrient-rich and quite acidic, with vineyards situated between 250 and 700m (820 and 2,296ft) above sea level.

Future Development

The region has shown itself capable of making good white, rosé and red wines, and future development could involve further production of reds by carbonic maceration, a method particularly suited to the area's grapes.

Selected Bodegas

Casa Miranda (☎ 922 330 499) Founded only in 1998, it is early to judge this small bodega properly, but quality is, as yet, mixed. The following wines show promise:

- *Bodegas de Miranda Seco (white):* An aromatic Listán Blanco with bite.

- *Bodegas de Miranda Maceración Carbónica (red):* This is as it should be, given the mode of production, with lots of lively fruit. Good.

El Calvario (☎ 922 308 725) Founded in 1926, this bodega produces 65,000 litres per year. The following red is respectable:

- *Cariante (red):* Made from Listán Negro, this is usually flavoursome and smooth, although in some years it can lack personality.

El Ratiño (☎ 922 308 720) Founded in 1980, this tiny bodega makes consistently good wines, not always the case in the Islands, where standards can vary from year to year.

- *Tajinaste Semi-Seco (white):* A tasty, balanced, sweet wine from Listán Blanco.

- *Tajinaste (red):* A flavoursome, fruity, everyday young red wine.

- *Tajinaste Maceración Carbónica (red):* This has excellent fruit character and personality. Good.

Valleoro (☎ 922 308 600) The big boy of the D.O., founded in 1988, Valleoro has 120 hectares of its own vines and produces 700,000 litres per year. Most of the wines are worthwhile, especially the following:

- *Gran Tehyda (white):* Fruity and straightforward with a pleasing hint of bitterness.

- *Gran Tehyda Afrutado (white):* Herby, flavoursome and light.

- *Gran Tehyda Rosado (rosé):* Tasty and well made. Good.

- *Gran Tehyda Maceración Carbónica (red):* A fruity, floral red ideal for chilling.

- *Gran Tehyda Tinto (red):* Light, smooth, everyday red.

- *Gran Tehyda Crianza Tinto (red):* A respectable, fruity/oaky wine.

D.O. Ycoden-Daute-Isora

In Brief: A region that has shown itself capable of making decent, everyday rosés and young reds, although it is still best for dry and sweet whites.

Also near Mount Teide in northern Tenerife, Ycoden D.O. has 985 hectares of vines – though the entire region covers 2,000 – 1,400 growers and 31 bodegas.
   The extensive list of authorised grape varieties is:

- **White:** Bastardo Blanco, Bermejuela, Forastera Blanca, Güal, Listán Blanco, Malvasía, Moscatel, Pedro Ximénez, Sabro, Torrontés, Verdello and Vijariego.

- **Black:** Bastarda Negra, Listán Negro, Malvasía Rosada, Moscatel Negra, Negramoll, Tintilla and Vijariego Negra.

Currently, the region's wines are as follows:

- *Whites:* dry, semi-sweet and sweet examples are characterised by their freshness and interesting expression of the constituent grapes.

- *Rosés:* notably herbaceous.

- *Reds:* generally of the fresh and fruity variety, although there are moves towards increased depth and complexity.

Geography, Soil and Climate

Once again climate is influenced by latitude and aspect, and as in several areas of the islands, trade winds are important in bringing humidity to the vineyards. They are planted at altitudes ranging from 50 to 1,400m (164 to 4,593ft) above sea level, on primarily volcanic soils.

Future Development

The D.O. is making decent wines, especially whites, and potential future developments might involve the production of more barrel-fermented examples and the planting of good quality foreign grape varieties in favoured, higher vineyards.

Selected Bodegas

Cueva del Viento, S.L. (☎ 922 811 796) Founded in 1988, this bodega has 3.5 hectares of its own vines and produces 100,000 litres per year. Quality is mixed, with the following wines the most reliable:

⬥ *Cueva del Viento Semi-Seco (white):* This has decent sweet flavour contrasting well with acidic bite. Good.

⬥ *Cueva del Viento (red):* A light, easy wine, but it could do with more punch and interest.

Francisco Javier Gómez Pimentel (☎ 922 810 237) Founded in 1920, this bodega has a fair selection of decent wines. Try these:

⬥ *Aceviño Blanco (white):* Well made, herby and flavoursome.

⬥ *Aceviño Blanco Barrica (white):* Drink at two or three years old for a reasonably complex and refreshing barrel-fermented wine.

⬥ *Aceviño Semi-Seco Blanco (white):* Well constructed and fairly sweet with contrasting bite.

⬥ *Aceviño Rosado (rosé):* This can be fresh, tasty and refreshing, but in some years it is a bit bland.

⬥ *Aceviño Tinto (red):* A light, smooth wine which could do with more punch.

S.A.T. Tajinaste (☎ 922 122 395) Founded in 1993, this modest bodega's whites and rosé are unremarkable, but this red is decent:

⬥ *Viña Donia Tinto (red):* Fruity, flavoursome and easy to drink; perhaps a touch expensive.

Viñamonte (☎ 922 828 085) This small producer turns out consistently respectable wines:

⬥ *Viñamonte Blanco (white):* A herby, flavoursome, unctuous wine from Listán Blanco.

⬥ *Viñamonte Rosado (rosé):* Another good pink wine from the D.O.: tasty and mouthfilling.

Viñátigo (☎ 922 828 768) Founded in 1990, this is one of the D.O.'s more consistent performers with a good range of wines, including:

- *Viñátigo Seco (white):* Made from the ubiquitous Listán Blanco, this is a tasty, dry wine with hints of sweetness. Good.

- *Viñátigo Semi-Seco (white):* This well made wine has sweet flavour balanced by acidic bite.

- *Viñátigo (rosé):* Made from Listán Negra, this is a well made, refreshing wine with some character. Good.

Windmills overlooking La Mancha's flat, parched landscape

FINCA
VALPIEDRA

Bodegas y Viñedos

ALION

RIBERA DEL DUERO
Denominación de Origen

75 cl.   COSECHA 1996   13,5% Vol.
Embotellado en la propiedad

BODEGAS Y VIÑEDOS ALION, S.A. - PADILLA DE DUERO - PEÑAFIEL Valladolid (ESPAÑA)

Esta cosecha ha sido escogida para ser embotellada en 304.890 botellas bordelesas, 4.000 magnum y 384 doble-magnum.

El número de esta botella es el

N.º embotellador 6812-VA

ESTATE BOTTLED   SINGLE VINEYARD   PRODUCE OF SPAIN

CONTINO
RIOJA
DENOMINACION DE ORIGEN CALIFICADA
RESERVA
De esta cosecha de 1990 se han embotellado
250.618 botellas de 0'75 litros

13% Vol.
75 cl. e   BOT.   N.º 0156723
Embotellado en la propiedad
VIÑEDOS DEL CONTINO, S. A.
LAGUARDIA - LASERNA, ESPAÑA
R.E Nº 5212 VI

PAZO DE BARRANTES
ALBARIÑO

12,0 %vol.   75 cl.

RIAS BAIXAS
Denominación de Origen
PRODUCT   Embotellado en la propiedad por: WHITE
OF SPAIN   BODEGAS PAZO DE BARRANTES, S.A.   WINE
Barrantes - Pontevedra - ESPAÑA

1998

N.º R.E. 7140 - PO - L-998

A.N.

MAURO
Vendimia Seleccionada
1995
Viñedos Propios

Vino de Mesa de Castilla y León

BODEGAS MAURO, S.A. TUDELA DE DUERO
VALLADOLID - ESPAÑA

13,6% Alc/Vol.   Lote 04 R.E. 5776 - VA   750 Ml.

ANIMA NEGRA S.L. vinyes de SON NEGRE, any 1999

▲ *Wine aging in Rio*

Harvesting grapes in Jerez ▲
(Carlos Navajas)

▲ *Sierra de Cantabria in La R*
(Fernando Brior

◀ *Historic wine press in Tenerife*

Photographs courtesy of the Spanish Institute for Foreign Exchange (ICEX)

Rioja's rich gastromy ▲

Palomino grapes
▼ (Carlos Navajas)

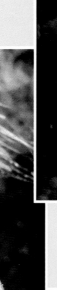

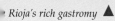

varran rosé wine ▲
(ix Lorrio)

▶

Barrels in Ribera del Duero
(Ignacio Muñoz-Seca)

Photographs courtesy of the Spanish Institute for Foreign Exchange (ICEX)

Vines on volcanic Lanzarote
(Piedad Sancho-Mata) ▼

▲ *Harvesting tempranillo grapes in La Ri*
(Carlos Navaj

▲ *Sherry tas*
(ACES/Fedeje

◄ *Traditional wine storage
vats in ValdePeñas*
(Ulrich Hartmann)

Photographs courtesy of the Spanish Institute for Foreign Exchange (ICEX)

7.

CASTILLA-LA MANCHA

The vast region of Castilla-La Mancha covers much of the southern half of Spain's central plateau. One of its most famous inhabitants was Miguel de Cervantes, the author of *Don Quixote*, who cleverly and memorably summed up the region's extreme climate by describing it as 'nine months of winter and three months of inferno.' This does not sound promising for any form of cultivation, but in fact La Mancha supplies around 40 per cent of Spain's wine from its six D.O.s and notable non-D.O. wine areas.

Cervantes was right about the climate because this is a region of stark extremes: summers are very hot, with temperatures of up to 45°C (113°F), while winters can be severe with several degrees of frost. Rainfall is unreliable and low, often coming from the violent thunderstorms which strike the region in spring and autumn. Indeed, the very name La Mancha comes from 'al-Manshah', the Arabic for 'dry land'.

La Mancha is flat, some would say monotonously so, and lies at between 500 and 750m (1,640 and 2,460ft) above sea level. It offers little to protect grapes from the elements and by far the most common variety grown is the white Airén, mainly because it can withstand the region's trying climate. Airén grows close to the ground and therefore its leaves shield the grapes from the worst of the sun, and the grapes themselves have thick skins which help to retain moisture. Its leaves also trap dew which helps to see the vines through the torrid summers. Unfortunately, despite its admirable hardiness, Airén is fairly characterless. It is *not* grown for its quality, but purely because it can withstand local conditions and gives decent yields.

Indeed, La Mancha is so large and Airén so dominant, that it is the most widely planted grape variety in the world. This is remarkable when you consider that the vast majority of it is grown in one region – La Mancha – of one country – Spain. As a result, up to 90 per cent of La Mancha's wine has been white, most of low quality, being thin, characterless and lacking acidity. White grapes have also traditionally been used in the blend for the region's reds, sometimes in large quantities, which has not improved their quality. Until recently, the reds of La Mancha (with the exception of some of the better wines of Valdepeñas), were invariably thin, bland and pale, with a negligible ability to age. And because the hot summers lead to very ripe grapes, they developed high levels of sugar – which subsequently turned into alcohol – meaning that the wines were often over-alcoholic.

But times, technology and techniques have changed, and the vast area of La Mancha is now seen as an upcoming region, mainly for red wines, but also for fresh, clean, honest whites for easy drinking. The '90s saw it slowly begin to demonstrate its potential to make both decent, reasonably priced everyday wines and also reds of some quality, the latter most notably in the non-D.O. Montes de Toledo region.

The introduction of cold fermentation has helped to maintain the Airén grape's gentle aromas and flavours, and earlier grape picking has avoided over-maturity and excessive sugar levels. Both have been important in the drive towards increased regional quality. So has vine replanting, mainly with Tempranillo – known as Cencibel in these parts. It has been a slow process to persuade growers to rip up the bland Airén and replant with better varieties. Airén is an easy option, giving high yields and well suited to La Mancha's trying environment. And La Mancha is a region still dominated by co-operatives, which tend to be conservative and resistant to new ideas, so change tends to be slow. This chapter is split into seven sections, covering the region's six D.O.s and significant non-D.O. wines.

D.O. Almansa

In Brief: A producer of a lot of bulk wine for blending and tiny amounts of bottled wine, mainly dark, strong, full-bodied and red.

Almansa lies in the transitional zone between Castilla-La Mancha and the Levante, and is sited just to the north of D.O.s Jumilla and Yecla. Designated a D.O. in 1975, Almansa has 7,600 hectares of vines, 750 growers and a mere 5 producers, only one of which – Bodegas Piqueras – bottles its wines. It thus has the same 'one-horse' feel as D.O. Yecla and, as with Yecla, it is legitimate to ask why it is a separate D.O. at all.

Garnacha and Monastrell are the most common grape varieties, with much of the wine produced sold in bulk for blending. The region's traditional style of red is dark, full-bodied and low in acid, with the Monastrell-based wines usually the best. Most of Almansa was unaffected by phylloxera and hence many of its vines are ungrafted.

Authorised grape varieties are:

- **White:** Airén.

- **Black:** Garnacha Tintorera, Monastrell and Tempranillo.

Geography, Soil and Climate

Almansa's climate is continental, but less extreme than the more central areas of Castilla-La Mancha. Rainfall is a low 350mm (14in) per year. Vines are grown at around 700m (2,296ft) above sea level on chalky soils low in organic material.

Future Development

Despite Bodegas Piqueras' success with red wines, no other Almansa producers have followed in its footsteps by bottling their own wines. The region has shown itself capable of making decent wines with Monastrell and Tempranillo, and experimental plantings of Cabernet Sauvignon, Merlot and Syrah show that the authorities are looking to the future. As things stand, however, the region's profile is low to non-existent and more bottling producers are needed to raise it.

Selected Bodegas

Bodegas Piqueras, S.A. (☎ 967 341 482) Founded in 1915, Almansa's only producer to bottle its wines shows that the region is capable of making characterful wines at competitive prices, mainly reds.

◆ *Castillo de Almansa Blanco (white):* A straightforward, inexpensive, fresh, white from Airén for drinking young.

◆ *Castillo de Almansa Rosado (rosé):* A light, competent, undemanding wine from Monastrell and Tempranillo.

◆ *Castillo de Almansa Tinto (red):* A respectable blend of Monastrell and Tempranillo with lively tannins.

◆ *Castillo de Almansa Tinto Crianza (red):* A decent, inexpensive crianza from Monastrell and Tempranillo, with fruit and oak well integrated.

◆ Castillo de Almansa Reserva (red): Another Monastrell/Tempranillo blend, this is the bodega's best wine, with balance, structure, flavour and some complexity for a modest price. Recommended.

D.O. La Mancha

In Brief: *The biggest wine region in Spain, producing large volumes of simple, clean, everyday white wines and increasing amounts of decent, characterful reds at competitive prices. La Mancha's best wines, some of them very good indeed, are made by producers operating outside the D.O.*

La Mancha is not only by far the largest D.O. in Spain, it is also the world's largest demarcated wine region, covering around 195,000 hectares and home to nearly 22,000 growers and over 290 producers. Its vinous history dates back at least to Roman times and during Spain's 'Golden Age' of Empire in the late Middle Ages, its wines were sufficiently prominent to appear in the works of great writers such as Cervantes, Lope de Vega and Tirso de Molina.

Although a D.O. only since 1976, it was in the '40s and '50s that production in the region was reinvigorated, with large amounts of everyday wine produced for a relieved and thirsty post-war world. Traditionally, the region focussed on bland, low-acid, alcoholic whites from the Airén grape (which still comprises around 70 per cent of La Mancha's vine-hectarage) and dark, alcoholic reds, often from Cencibel, the local name for Tempranillo. Most wine was made in co-operatives and large amounts were either sent for blending to regions with lower production levels or went for distillation.

In the '80s, the authorities realised that investment was needed to improve La Mancha's standards and standing, and they put money into the co-operatives and private bodegas in order to achieve this. White wines made from Airén can never be very good because the raw material is bland, but cold fermentation and improved picking and transportation have allowed the grape to make fresh, clean, low-priced whites for early drinking. The planting of more Tempranillo has also earned the region an improved reputation for decent, young reds with character at low prices.

Authorised grape varieties are:

● **White:** Airén, Chardonnay, Macabeo, Pardilla and Sauvignon Blanc.

● **Black:** Cabernet Sauvignon, Garnacha, Merlot, Moravia, Syrah and Tempranillo.

The region's whites from Airén are increasingly light, fresh and fruity for everyday drinking, the rosés light and respectable, but it is the reds that are showing most potential. La Mancha's young reds made from Tempranillo offer characterful, mouthfilling fruit at competitive prices, while the crianzas and reservas, although not yet hitting the heights, are improving and offer lots of flavour for modest prices.

Geography, Soil and Climate

La Mancha is a land of extremes, with summer temperatures sometimes exceeding 45°C (113°F), while winters can see the mercury fall to −15°C (5°F). Rainfall varies between 375 and 410mm (15 and 16in) per year, concentrated in the autumn and spring. Vineyards are situated at around 700m (2,296ft) above sea level on clay soils sitting on top of chalk.

Future Development

La Mancha's white Airéns are now probably as good as they can be and as an alternative, the superior Macabeo is being used to make wines with more character, body and ageing ability. The year 2000 also saw the authorisation of the top international varieties Chardonnay and Sauvignon Blanc and it will be interesting to see how they fare in La Mancha's challenging climate.

As for reds, some have compared La Mancha's potential with that of Australia. This might raise the hackles of the wine makers of Jumilla (which has been called the most Australian of Spain's wine regions because of its success with Syrah, Australia's signature black grape) and while it might be slightly premature to see La Mancha in quite this way, it is a sign of the interest in the area. And its young Tempranillos do offer interest and value, while the crianzas and reservas are improving all the time.

But Cabernet Sauvignon and the recently authorised Syrah are being seen as the way forward (and have probably attracted the Australian comparisons) and judging by the success that wine makers like the Marqués de Griñon have had with these grapes in non-D.O. areas of Castilla-La Mancha, the future could be very exciting indeed. And if further proof was needed, it is provided by the fact that distinguished Rioja and Ribera del Duero producers are setting up in La Mancha. This will be important for the region's push to improve quality because it needs more private wine makers to see the process through and ape the success of producers like the Marqués de Griñon. The co-operatives will always find it difficult to do so, because while the good ones are quality-conscious about the grapes they use, their fruit comes from various sources and it is inevitably difficult to control quality.

Selected Bodegas

Bodegas Ayuso (☎ 967 140 458) Founded in 1947, this large bodega is famous for its Estola range of wines, a staple of many a Spanish restaurant wine list and for sale in most supermarkets. The reds are better than the whites, the range including:

- *Viña Q (white):* A young, inexpensive white from Airén, which in better years is honestly fresh and drinkable, although it can be bland.

● *Estola Blanco (white):* A better version of the above.

● *Viña Q Rosado (rosé):* A blend of Garnacha and Tempranillo, this inexpensive rosé is light and straightforward.

● *Viña Q Tinto (red):* A blend of Garnacha and Tempranillo, this straightforward, young red is tasty and honest for a low price.

● *Estola Reserva (red):* A well made, flavoursome, structured wine for a low price, offering honest good value.

● *Estola Gran Reserva (red):* This is a lightish, rounded, tasty wine which makes for enjoyable drinking, but it isn't much like a gran reserva.

Centro Españolas, S.A. (☎ 926 505 653) Founded in 1991, this bodega has garnered good reviews for its Allozo range and is representative of what La Mancha is currently offering: decent, honest wines for competitive prices. The range includes:

● *Allozo Airén Blanco (white):* A tasty, drinkable young Airén for a low price. It is a decent representative of its type and La Mancha does make huge amounts of these wines.

● *Allozo Rosado (rosé):* A respectable, fresh pink wine from the Tempranillo grape.

● *Verdial Tinto (red):* A tasty, inexpensive, young Tempranillo with some character.

● *Allozo Tinto (red):* As above, with lively tannins and a punchy nose.

● *Rama Corta Tinto (red):* 75 per cent Tempranillo with 25 per cent Cabernet Sauvignon, this is aromatic, full-bodied and very tasty for a modest price. Good.

● *Allozo Crianza (red):* A well made, straightforward, easy-drinking crianza from the Tempranillo grape.

● *Allozo Reserva (red):* A flavoursome, mouthfilling Tempranillo with power, balance and a modest price tag. Recommended.

● *Allozo Gran Reserva (red):* This is quite a distinguished wine, with structure, personality and flavour. It is a fair representation of what La Mancha is capable of and, as with all the Allozo wines, is competitively priced.

Cooperativa Agraria Nuestra Señora de las Nieves (☎ 926 860 344) Founded in 1950, and with 750 hectares of its own vines, this co-operative makes respectable rather than remarkable wines, including:

● *Fúcares Blanco (white):* An old-fashioned La Mancha white, correctly made but without much interest.

● *Gran Fúcares Blanco (white):* This is rather better, with mouthfilling flavours and length.

● *Gran Fúcares Rosado (rosé):* Fresh and respectable, but lacking personality.

● *Fúcares Tinto (red):* A decent young red with tasty, characterful fruit.

Cooperativa Agrícola La Union (☎ 926 541 371) This large co-operative was founded in 1935 and has an impressive 5,000 hectares of vineyards. Its wines are respectable and inexpensive, including:

💧 *Muzaraque Blanco (white):* Light, fresh, easy-to-drink Airén.

💧 *Muzaraque Tinto (red):* A well made Tempranillo with decent fruity flavours.

Cooperativa Cristo de la Vega (☎ 926 530 388) Founded in 1955, this huge co-operative has 11,000 hectares of vines and makes a range of reasonable, everyday wines, including:

💧 *El Yugo Blanco (white):* A decent, fruity white.

💧 *El Yugo Rosado (rosé):* Fruity, characterful Tempranillo pink wine.

💧 *Cristo de la Vega Tempranillo (red):* A tasty, aromatic red for easy drinking.

Cooperativa del Campo Purísima Concepción (☎ 969 383 043) This co-operative dates back to 1958 and has 2,500 hectares of vineyards. It makes inexpensive, everyday wines, including:

💧 *Los Teatinos Tinto (red):* A well made, young Tempranillo.

💧 *Los Teatinos Tinto Crianza (red):* A tasty, straightforward crianza wine.

Cooperativa del Campo San Gines (☎ 969 382 037) Founded in 1956, this co-operative makes respectable wines from its 1,750 hectares of vines and can probably make the step up to produce more 'serious' ones. Its range includes:

💧 *Cinco Almudes Blanco (white):* Mainly Airén, with some Macabeo, this is fruity, everyday white wine.

💧 *Cinco Almudes Rosado (rosé):* Rather dull.

💧 *Cinco Almudes Tinto (red):* Mainly Tempranillo, with some Cabernet Sauvignon, this is attractively fruity young wine for a low price.

💧 *Cinco Almudes Tinto Crianza (red):* A tasty, balanced blend of fruit and oak for a modest price.

Cooperativa Jesús del Perdón (☎ 926 610 309) Founded in 1954 and with over 3,500 hectares of vines, this large co-operative makes the popular, reasonably priced Yuntero and Lazarillo wines:

💧 *Yuntero Blanco (white):* Tasty, inexpensive Macabeo with decent fruit.

💧 *Yuntero Blanco Crianza (white):* A brave attempt to give Airén the barrel-fermented treatment. Predictably, the wood wipes out the fruit in this thinnish wine.

💧 *Lazarillo Blanco (white):* Made outside D.O. control, this is a light, simple Airén white.

- *Yuntero Rosado (rosé):* Decent, tasty Tempranillo pink wine.

- *Lazarillo Tinto (red):* Again made outside the control of the D.O., this young Tempranillo is aromatic, tasty and refreshingly lively. Good.

- *Yuntero Crianza (red):* 75 per cent Tempranillo and 25 per cent Cabernet Sauvignon, this offers lots of flavour and decent fruit/oak integration for a modest price. Good.

- *Yuntero Reserva (red):* The same grapes as above, this is a competent, commercial, aged red with flavour and balance.

Cooperativa Nuestra Señora de la Cabeza (☎ 969 387 173) Founded in 1958, with 850 hectares of vineyards, this co-operative makes a modest range of wines of which the following is worth trying:

- *Casa Gualda Tinto Crianza (red):* An aromatic, mouthfilling crianza with some complexity at a competitive price.

Cooperativa Nuestra Señora de la Paz (☎ 925 190 269) Founded in 1965, this modest co-operative produces a small range of reasonable wines, including:

- *Altovela Blanco (white):* A competent, light, refreshing, everyday wine.

- *Matices Blanco (white):* An uncomplicated, respectable white.

- *Altovela Rosado (rosé):* A tasty, mouthfilling pink wine.

- *Altovela Tinto (red):* A fresh, tasty, tannic young red.

- *Matices Tinto (red):* An aromatic, concentrated, flavoursome young red.

- *Campo Amable Crianza (red):* An integrated crianza with flavour and body.

Cooperativa Nuestra Señora de los Remedios (☎ 925 380 322) Founded in 1967, this co-operative has 3,000 hectares of its own vines and makes a modest range of everyday wines, of which the following stand out:

- *Sanderuelo Blanco (white):* A light, tasty wine for a low price.

- *El Brosquil (red):* A well made, fruity young Tempranillo at a modest price.

Cooperativa Nuestra Señora de Manjavacas (☎ 967 180 025) This large co-operative was founded in 1948 and uses modern technology to produce a small range of decent wines, better than the La Mancha average, including:

- *Zagarrón Blanco (white):* A well made, aromatic, balanced white wine. Good.

- *Zagarrón Rosado (rosé):* A characterful, refreshing pink wine.

- *Zagarrón Tinto (red):* A lively, aromatic, flavoursome young red for everyday drinking.

Cooperativa Nuestra Señora del Espino (☎ 926 636 616) Founded in 1956, this co-operative makes good everyday wines at competitive prices, including:

◆ *Rezuelo Airén (white):* A straightforward, tasty, young white wine.

◆ *Rezuelo Tinto (red):* An aromatic, lively young Tempranillo.

Cooperativa Nuestra Señora del Rosario (☎ 967 166 066) This large co-operative was founded in 1950 and has almost 4,000 hectares of vines which produce a wide range of good quality, inexpensive wines that show the potential to become more than decent, everyday bottles. The range includes:

◆ *Canforrales Blanco (white):* A light, fresh wine with lively acidity from Macabeo for a notably low price.

◆ *Canforrales 100 Años (white):* A better than average Airén with some character at a low price.

◆ *Campos Reales Blanco (white):* This barrel-fermented wine is quite a good blend of fruit and oak, although perhaps overpriced.

◆ *Canforrales Rosado (rosé):* A tasty, aromatic rosé for a low price.

◆ *Canforrales Tinto (red):* An aromatic, mouthfilling young Tempranillo for a modest price.

◆ *Campos Reales Tinto Crianza (red):* This blend of Cabernet Sauvignon and Tempranillo is tasty and mouthfilling and at its best at four or five years old.

◆ *Campos Reales Reserva (red):* The same blend as above, this is competently made with a hefty dose of oak. Like the crianza, it is notably inexpensive.

Cooperativa Virgen de las Viñas (☎ 926 510 865) Founded in 1961, this is another large La Mancha co-operative producing a lot of decent, reasonably priced, everyday wine. The range includes:

◆ *Lorenzete Blanco (white):* A tasty, quite mouthfilling Airén for drinking young.

◆ *Tomillar Tinto (red):* Simple, tasty, young Tempranillo.

◆ *Tomillar Tinto Crianza (red):* A well made, flavoursome, straightforward blend of fruit and oak for a low price.

Cosecheros Embotelladores, S.A. (☎ 925 140 292) Founded in 1967, this is yet another producer of competent, everyday wines at low prices, notably:

◆ *Viña Donante Blanco (white):* A rather better than average young Airén, with decent flavour.

◆ *Viña Donante Tinto (red):* A lively, aromatic, tasty, young Tempranillo for a competitive price, a good example of a style of wine that La Mancha is renowned for.

◆ *Cuevas Reales Crianza (red)*: A blend of Cabernet Suvignon and Tempranillo, this wine is well made, quite powerful and tasty.

Enomar, S.L. (☎ 967 182 570) Founded in 1995, this is another producer of competent, straightforward wines that offer honest value for money but are not for mulling over. The range includes:

◆ *Benengeli Macabeo (white)*: Tasty and fruity for easy drinking.

◆ *Benengeli Garnacha (rosé)*: A decent, fresh rosé.

◆ *Benengeli Cencibel (red)*: An aromatic, lively young Tempranillo with lots of flavour. Good.

◆ *Benengeli Crianza (red)*: A fruity, tasty crianza.

Finca La Blanca (☎ 925 178 437) Founded only in 1996, this bodega is already showing signs that it is capable of making wines which rise above the level of the competent and everyday. Its range includes:

◆ *La Blanca (white)*: An aromatic, tasty young Macabeo, a cut above the standard La Mancha white.

◆ *La Blanca Tinto (red)*: A flavoursome, full-bodied young Tempranillo with an attractive nose. Good.

◆ *La Blanca Merlot (red)*: Interesting because Merlot is unusual in La Mancha, this is lightly tasty and undemanding. It could do with a bit more personality.

◆ *La Blanca Cabernet Sauvignon (red)*: Tasty and fruity but like some young Cabernets, the tannins can be rather aggressive.

◆ *Monte Don Lucio Crianza (red)*: A well made, fruity, spicy Cabernet at a competitive price. It shows that this bodega can make wines which appeal to the middle market as opposed to the respectable, everyday one.

J. Santos (☎ 925 195 120) Founded in 1900, this is another producer of reasonable, everyday wines which sometimes shows signs that it is capable of moving upmarket. Its range includes:

◆ *Julián Santos Tinto Crianza (red)*: A lightish, inexpensive Tempranillo crianza, this is pleasant but it could do with more body and personality.

◆ *Don Fadrique Tinto Reserva (red)*: A smooth, fruity reserva for a modest price.

◆ *Don Fadrique Gran Reserva (red)*: This modestly-priced, aged Tempranillo has balance and character, and hints at what the bodega is capable of.

Naranjo, S.L. (☎ 926 814 155) Founded in 1898, this small operation makes a modest range of drinkable wines at low La Mancha prices, including:

◆ *Viña Cuerva Blanco (white)*: Another light, fruity, everyday white wine for a low price.

♦ *Viña Cuerva Rosado (rosé):* A competent, undemanding pink wine from the Tempranillo grape.

♦ *Viña Cuerva Tinto Crianza (red):* A lightish, quite fruity crianza from Tempranillo, well made but unremarkable.

♦ *Viña Cuerva Reserva (red):* This can be a good, inexpensive red wine with lots of concentrated fruit flavours.

S.A.T. Santa Rita (☎ 967 180 071) Founded in the '70s, this small operation makes improving wines at modest prices and has the potential to move up the quality scale. Its range includes:

♦ *Verones Blanco (white):* This is not its best wine, but then it is made from the ubiquitous, limited quality Airén. That said, it is a respectable, fresh example at a low price.

♦ *Verones Blanco Macabeo (white):* A respectable, everyday wine with a bit of bite.

♦ *Verones Rosado (rosé):* A superior, aromatic rosé with some character.

♦ *Verones Tinto (red):* A rather good young Tempranillo with aroma, flavour and some length.

♦ *Verones Tinto Crianza (red):* A well made wine with balance and juicy flavour. Good.

Socieded Cooperativa La Magdalena (☎ 969 380 722) Founded in 1958, with around 1,500 hectares of its own vines, this is another co-operative making decent, everyday wines at attractive prices, including:

♦ *Vega Moragona Rosado (rosé):* An appetising, fruity rosé for drinking young.

♦ *Vega Moragona Tinto (red):* A mouthfilling, tasty young Tempranillo, offering youthful exuberance rather than mature depths.

♦ *Vega Moragona Tinto Crianza (red):* A tasty, balanced, integrated crianza for a modest outlay of money.

Vinícola de Castilla, S.A. (☎ 926 560 553) Founded in 1976, this large operation is one of La Mancha's most respected and boasts a well equipped bodega with all the latest technology. Its wide range of inexpensive wines is popular throughout Spain, with the following standing out:

♦ *Castillo de Alhambra Blanco (white):* A fresh, fruity young white from the Airén grape at a low price.

♦ *Señorío de Guadianeja Blanco (white):* A better version of the above for around the same price.

♦ *Castillo de Manzanares Blanco (white):* Not a bad attempt at oak-ageing the Viura/Macabeo grape. Inexpensive.

- *Blanco Selección Crianza (white):* This blend of Airén, Viura/Macabeo and Chardonnay has toasty, fruity flavours and some balance.

- *Castillo de Alhambra Rosado (rosé):* A fresh, flavoursome, low-priced Garnacha wine.

- *Castillo de Alhambra Tinto (red):* A well made, smooth, tasty young Tempranillo for a low price. Good.

- *Balada Cencibel Ecológico (red):* An aromatic, fruity, flavoursome young wine. Recommended.

- *Valle Hermoso Crianza (red):* A well made, mouthfilling wine from the Merlot grape. Recommended.

- *Señorío de Guadianeja Gran Reserva Cencibel (red):* This well known wine, along with the following Cabernet Sauvignon, is usually drunk at around 12 to 15 years old, and offers a round, smooth mouthful for a modest price.

- *Señorío de Guadianela Gran Reserva Cabernet Sauvignon (red):* A smooth, pleasing, easy-to-drink wine, usually superior to the Cencibel.

Vinícola de Tomelloso (☎ 926 513 004) Founded in 1986, this is regarded by some as La Mancha's best producer, making a range of good and high quality wines at competitive prices. The wines include:

- *Añil Blanco Macabeo (white):* A characterful, flavoursome white wine for a modest price.

- *Torre de Gazate Blanco (white):* A decent, fresh, young Airén wine, better than the average.

- *Torre de Gazate Sauvignon Blanc (white):* Not really representative of this distinctive variety, but a pleasant, fruity wine.

- *Torre de Gazate Rosado (rosé):* One of La Mancha's best rosés, made from Cabernet Sauvignon, with powerful, mouthfilling flavours. Recommended.

- *Torre de Gazate Tinto (red):* An aromatic, tasty Tempranillo with lively tannins at a modest price.

- *Torre de Gazate Tinto Crianza (red):* A blend of Cabernet Sauvignon and Tempranillo, this inexpensive crianza is characterful, integrated and flavoursome. Recommended.

- *Torre de Gazate Reserva (red):* This wine has one of the better price/quality ratios of any La Mancha red. It has a lot of attractive flavour, structure and balance for a modest price. Recommended.

- *Torre de Gazate Gran Reserva (red):* Rather more expensive than the above, this is still cheap by national gran reserva standards and is a superior Cabernet Sauvignon, rounded, characterful and long. Recommended.

Vinos Avilés y Alonso, S.A. (☎ 925 157 000) Founded in 1989, this large operation makes a popular range of wines under the Solmayor label. They are decent and mid-priced by La Mancha standards, and include:

◆ *Solmayor Blanco (white):* This is made from 80 per cent Macabeo and 20 per cent Airén, and is a fruity, refreshing everyday white wine, better than the La Mancha average.

◆ *Solmayor Tempranillo (red):* A tasty, fruity, young red with some bite.

Viñedos Mejorantes, S.L. (☎ 925 201 036) Founded in 1993, this small operation is another of La Mancha's best producers, making wines of some quality at competitive prices, including:

◆ *Portillejo Blanco (white):* A well made, aromatic, tasty young white from the Macabeo grape.

◆ *Portillejo Tinto Cabernet Sauvignon (red):* Young Cabernet Sauvignons can be tannic, aggressive creatures, but this avoids those pitfalls. It is notably flavoursome and soundly constructed and offers attractive drinking for a very competitive price. Recommended.

◆ *Portillejo Tinto Merlot (red):* As above, this is a rather good young wine, with lots of characterful flavours and balance for a modest price. Recommended.

◆ *Portillejo Crianza (red):* An integrated, balanced blend of fruit and oak from the Cabernet Sauvignon grape with a lot of flavour.

D.O. Méntrida

In Brief: A low-profile region making generally undistinguished wines, many of which do not travel far beyond their region of production. However, there are tentative signs of improvement.

It is open to question as to why Méntrida exists as a separate D.O.. This is not for the same reason that people query the viability of D.O.s such as Almansa and Yecla, which each have only a handful of bottling bodegas. Méntrida has 22 – and covers just over 13,000 hectares of vines, with 2,300 growers – yet its profile is almost non-existent, even in the nearby cities of Madrid and Toledo. This was not always the case. The region enjoyed some fame back in the 15th century, although this might be explained by its proximity to the aforementioned cities at a time when long-distance transportation was a time-consuming, expensive and hazardous business, and people tended to drink wine made in their local area. Things have changed. Much of Méntrida's output is sold in bulk for blending or is sent to distilleries. Of the rest, a lot becomes unlabelled, house wine in less discerning Madrid hostelries or is drunk in Méntrida itself. Thus, it is almost unknown.

Why is this the case? The answer is simple: most of the wines are not very good, while a not insignificant amount of them are poor or faulty. Méntrida's reds have traditionally been dark, thick, unstructured, tannic offerings, some containing up to 18 per cent alcohol, and many showing signs of oxidation having been made from Garnacha, a grape prone to this. The rosés have also been thick and heavy, some containing up to 14 per cent alcohol.

Authorised grape varieties are:

- **White:** Albillo, Chardonnay, Sauvignon Blanc and Viura/Macabeo.

- **Black:** Cabernet Sauvignon, Garnacha, Merlot, Syrah and Tempranillo.

Méntrida's rosés are invariably made from Garnacha and still tend to be full-bodied and sometimes over-alcoholic. The reds remain dark and full-bodied (the word 'robust' is often used) and tend to exhibit hints of over-maturity in the fruit used and, sometimes, oxidation, especially older examples made from Garnacha.

Geography, Soil and Climate

Méntrida sits in the north of the province of Toledo, to the south-west of the city of Madrid. Its vineyards are at between 400 and 600m (1,312 and 1,968ft) above sea level on sandy/muddy soils. The climate is described as 'dry, extreme continental', with long, cold winters and torrid summers. Late spring frosts are common and the scanty annual rainfall of between 300 and 450mm (12 and 18in) is distributed unevenly and erratically throughout the year.

Future Development

We have painted a rather forlorn picture of Méntrida's wines, but is there hope for the future? Yes, there are tentative signs of improvement and a discernible desire to implement changes to aid the process. Grapes are being picked earlier to avoid them becoming over-mature, over-sweet and 'jammy', while modern fermentation methods are being introduced to make the most of the grapes grown. In addition, Bobal and Tempranillo have been planted to blend with the dominant Garnacha to offer variety and improve the wines' ageing potential by counteracting oxidation. Cabernet Sauvignon, Merlot and Syrah were also authorised at the beginning of the 21st century and if Méntrida has even half of the success that the Montes de Toledo region has had with foreign black varieties, then the future is promising. Méntrida has also decided to experiment with white wines and authorised the use of four varieties accordingly.

Thus there are reasons to keep an eye on the D.O. over the coming years and the early 21st century has seen some improvement in the standard of its currently produced wines. But there is still much to do (the limited number of bodegas described below reflects the fact that not many produce wines worth investigating), and the region needs to generate a profile and attract finance to modernise installations and methods.

Selected Bodegas

Ángel Colado Pavón (☎ 925 865 278) Founded in 1934, this small bodega is improving. The following wine used to be bland with a capital 'b', but has become quite characterful:

◆ *Alariche Tempranillo (red):* A straightforward young wine with decent fruit for a modest price.

Cooperativa Nuestra Señora de la Soledad (☎ 925 784 275) Founded in 1963, this co-operative makes a good rosé but its reds display the signs of old-fashioned, sometimes faulty wine making.

◆ *Cerrolomo Rosado (rosé):* A tasty, aromatic, refreshing wine.

Juan González López (☎ 918 174 063) Founded in 1956, this small operation is showing signs of improvement with its inexpensive wines:

◆ *Viña Bispo Rosado (rosé):* This is robustly flavoursome.

◆ *Viña Bispo Tinto (red):* A reasonable young red with slightly jammy fruit.

La Cerca, S.A. (☎ 918 172 456) Founded in 1956, this operation makes a strangely sweet but drinkable young red:

◆ *El Abuelo (red):* A thick, persistent wine with lots of sweet fruit.

D.O. Mondéjar

In Brief: A recently demarcated D.O., best for young, La Mancha-like reds.

Mondéjar has only been a D.O. since 1996. The first crianzas were released only just prior to the millennium, the first reservas just after. Wine making in the region is rather older than this and there are literary references to Mondéjar wine dating back at least 400 years. However, as a D.O., Mondéjar is fledgling and wine is of course a long-term business, with vines not producing usable fruit until at least three or four years after planting, often taking rather longer to be at their best. Thus, judgements about the region are difficult to make.
Authorised grape varieties are:

● **White:** Macabeo, Malvar (which accounts for 80 per cent of white plantings) and Torrontés.

● **Black:** Cabernet Sauvignon and Tempranillo, the latter accounting for 95 per cent of black plantings.

Mondéjar's white wines can be light, fresh and fruity if the fruit is picked early and modern fermentation techniques are used, although older-style wines display the faults associated with the late picking of fruit. The rosés are agreeable enough, although they can lack freshness and aroma. As for the region's reds, these are probably its strength, the vast majority made from Tempranillo. The best are similar to La Mancha's, fresh, fruity and tasty at competitive prices, although as yet these are thin on the ground. Mondéjar presently covers 3,000 hectares, with 750 encompassed by the D.O., has 325 growers and 5 bodegas, all of which bottle their wines.

Geography, Soil and Climate

Lying between Madrid and the northern reaches of D.O. Valencia, Mondéjar's climate is subject to some coastal influences and is described as temperate Mediterranean, with warm-to-hot summers and cold winters. Annual rainfall is 500mm (20in).

Future Development

As the region develops under the D.O., standards should improve and Mondéjar will be able to compete with La Mancha in the decent, everyday red wine market. Other black grapes might be planted to encourage diversity and allow more blended wines. As with Almansa and Méntrida, Mondéjar's profile is negligible in Spain, let alone abroad, and needs developing.

Selected Bodegas

Cooperativa Santa María Magdalena (☎ 949 385 139) Founded in the '60s, this co-operative has shown itself capable of making decent, straightforward wines, but its problem is consistency. Its wines can sometimes be bland or seem past their best. The following reviews consider these inexpensive bottles when they are on form:

◆ *Señorío Jardín del Prado Blanco (white)*: This 100 per cent Malvar is light, fresh and undemanding.

◆ *Señorío Jardín del Prado Rosado (rosé)*: Rather light and not always quite fresh.

◆ *Señorío Jardinillo Tinto (red)*: In better years this can offer quite a lot of mouthfilling, mature fruit.

Mariscal, S.L. (☎ 949 385 138) Founded in 1913, this co-operative has 400 hectares of vines and produces a range of respectable wines, especially reds. The following is worth trying if you are prepared to pay the rather inflated price (when compared with La Mancha reservas):

◆ *Cueva de los Judios Reserva (red)*: This Tempranillo is soundly constructed with gentle, balanced flavours. It shows that the producer has potential.

D.O. Valdepeñas

In Brief: One of Spain's better sources of straightforward, soft, characterful red wines and light, everyday whites.

Valdepeñas lies on the undulating plains of southern Castilla-La Mancha, just to the north of Andalucía. It covers nearly 29,000 hectares of vines, has 3,810 growers and nearly 60 bodegas. The region has long been renowned for its *aloques*, red wines made with a mixture of black and white grapes. In the 16th century they were sent to the Emperor Charles 5th's troops while they were on duty in the Low Countries to keep their spirits up. Quite what they tasted like after the long, hot, arduous journey is anybody's guess.

Today, Valdepeñas is mainly associated with its smooth, oak-aged wines made with Tempranillo, but, like La Mancha, this is a region where the white grape Airén dominates, covering around 80 per cent of vineyards. There used to be more black grapes, but when phylloxera devastated the region at the end of the 19th century, much of the replanting was done with Airén, which as we saw in the section on D.O. La Mancha, has high yields and survives well in central Spain's challenging conditions, although it is bland and wines made from it do not age well.

Traditionally, Valdepeñas' reds were made with up to 80 per cent Airén (and the balance generally Tempranillo) but were ruby red in colour owing to the large quantities of extract and colour from the black grapes used. The Tempranillo did most of the work, contributing the wines' body and fruit, while the Airén did little more than bulk things out, keep the price down and contribute some gentle aroma.

The wines were matured in large clay vessels and sold young. They did not take well to oak ageing because Airén oxidises easily. Nowadays, the clay vessels have been superseded by stainless-steel tanks. Valdepeñas' better reds are now made 100 per cent from Tempranillo in the young, crianza and reserva styles. They can be fairly high in alcohol but are renowned for their rounded, smooth flavours. The region's white wines are similar to La Mancha's: light, fresh and easy-drinking for early consumption. There are many bargains to be had, but still a fair amount of poor wines produced.

Valdepeñas' wines have a ready market in Spain and they are the staples of many bars and restaurants in Madrid and Spain's southern holiday coasts. They are renowned for their attractive price/quality ratio, especially the younger reds, and there is a shortage of black grapes in the region to keep up with demand.

Authorised grape varieties are:

- **White:** Airén and Macabeo.

- **Black:** Cabernet Sauvignon, Garnacha and Tempranillo.

Valdepeñas' white wines are light and fresh, and with modern technology can be gently aromatic and flavoursome; they sometimes lack acidity. The region's rosés are straightforward, fresh wines. Valdepeñas' young reds are aromatic and fruity and can offer particular value for money. Crianzas and reservas are smooth, honest, tasty wines, as opposed to being full of subtle depths.

Geography, Soil and Climate

Valdepeñas has a continental climate with cold winters and long, hot, dry summers. Annual rainfall is scant, varying between 250 and 500mm (10 and 20in). Soils are a mix of chalk, clay and gravel, and since the name Valdepeñas means 'valley of the stones', it will come as no surprise that the vineyards are filled with stones. These are beneficial to the vines as they retain night time heat and aid water retention.

Future Development

Valdepeñas is restructuring to try to emphasise quality instead of quantity. Its vineyard hectareage is shrinking and has recently reduced from around 30,000 hectares to just under 29,000. Airén vines are being uprooted and the land replanted with black varieties or given over to other crops, the latter often financially beneficial as it attracts European Union grants. However, Valdepeñas is still Spain's second largest D.O. producer, with around 11 per cent of the market.

Black varieties are now the priority and the region needs more black grapes to keep up with demand for its 100 per cent Tempranillo wines. Quality is steadily increasing, although there is still work to be done. Some wines – both white and red – are still either poor or faulty.

Selected Bodegas

Canchollas, C.B. (☎ 926 322 357) Founded in 1889, this modest operation produces inexpensive, everyday wines of generally respectable quality. The better wines are as follows:

◆ *Joven Botija Blanco (white):* A light, fruity, young Airén at a low price.

◆ *Viejo Botija Tinto Crianza (red):* A well made, straightforward, characterful blend of fruit and oak at an attractive price.

Canuto Bodegas de Valdepeñas, S.A. (Cabovasa) (☎ 926 322 009) Founded in 1964, this is another operation making adequate, inexpensive wines, some offering decent value, including:

◆ *Monte Claro Rosado (rosé):* A well made wine with fruit and bite.

◆ *Monte Claro Tinto (red):* A clean, fruity, easy-drinking young red.

Casa de la Viña (☎ 926 696 044) Originally founded in 1857, this operation is now part of the giant Bodegas y Bebidas Group. Its wines have garnered a good reputation for affordable quality and frequently appear in 'best of' lists for Valdepeñas, especially the reds. The range includes:

◆ *Casa de la Viña Blanco (white):* A light, simple white wine.

◆ *Casa de la Viña Rosado (rosé):* A well made, aromatic, tasty rosé.

◆ *Casa de la Viña Tinto (red):* One of Valdepeñas' better young reds, aromatic, tasty and characterful for a competitive price. Recommended and representative of the region's inexpensive young Tempranillos.

◆ *Casa de la Viña Tinto Crianza (red):* Well made, straightforward and tasty.

◆ *Casa de la Viña Tinto Reserva (red):* As above.

Cooperativa La Invencible (☎ 926 322 777) Founded in 1942, this co-operative makes a range of generally respectable, everyday wines at competitive prices. Avoid the very cheapest and try the following:

◆ *Viña Lastra Rosado (rosé):* An aromatic, fruity rosé at a low price.

◆ *Viña Lastra Tinto (red):* A lively, fruity young Tempranillo. Can be a touch aggressive.

◆ *Valdeazor Crianza (red):* A well made, straightforward, inexpensive, oaked Tempranillo.

◆ *Valdeazor Reserva (red):* A well made, smooth blend of fruit and oak. Good.

Dionisos (☎ 926 313 248) Founded in 1970, this small operation stresses that all of its wines are made using the tenets of 'biological agriculture'. Its reds are recommended:

◆ *Dionisos Tinto (red):* A characterful, aromatic, tasty young Tempranillo, priced higher than the Valdepeñas average.

◆ *Dionisos Tinto Crianza (red):* A superior, powerful crianza with attractive toasty hints and personality, although more expensive than the regional norm.

Espinosa, S.A. (☎ 926 321 854) Founded in 1966, this operation's reds represent Valdepeñas' strength: decent, straightforward wines at competitive prices, especially:

◆ *Concejal Tinto Crianza (red):* A competently made blend of Tempranillo and oak at a low price.

◆ *Cencipeñas Tinto Crianza (red):* A slightly more characterful version of the above.

Félix Solís, S.A. (☎ 926 322 400) Founded in 1952, this huge producer (of around 90 million litres annually) makes a wide range of wines. Its everyday Los Molinos range and better, reliable Viña Albalis are supermarket and restaurant staples in Spain, and sometimes appear ubiquitous on Spain's holiday coast, the Costa del Sol. Most of Solís' wines are honest, everyday bottles at low prices, although at the top of the range, the producer is looking to make reds to appeal to the middle market. The wines include:

◆ *Viña Albali Blanco (white):* A respectable, young Airén.

◆ *Viña Albali Rosado (rosé):* A well made, aromatic, fruity wine.

◆ *Los Molinos Tinto (red):* A light, fruity young red at a low price. It is fine, but drink the rather better Albali instead, for not much more money.

◆ *Viña Albali Tempranillo (red):* A superior, aromatic young red at a low price.

◆ *Viña Albali Tinto Crianza (red):* A light blend of fruit and oak. The reserva is rather better, for little more money.

◆ *Viña Albali Cabernet Sauvignon Crianza (red):* 85 per cent Cabernet Sauvignon and 15 per cent Tempranillo, this is a tasty, well made, satisfying wine. It costs more than the regional average, but is worth it.

◆ *Viña Albali Reserva (red):* This very popular, inexpensive wine is one of Valdepeñas' best known reds. It is always characterful and smoothly tasty, but in some years it is slightly one-dimensional with too much oak influence. Do try it though.

◆ *Viña Albali Gran Reserva (red):* A well made, straightforward wine with soft flavours.

J.A. Megía e Hijos, S.L. (☎ 926 347 828) Founded in 1994, this modest operation's whites and rosé are unremarkable but its red crianzas are worthy. It should not be confused with Luis Megía, one of the region's larger co-operatives. JA's range includes:

◆ *Corcovo Media Crianza (red):* A well conceived, mouthfilling Tempranillo with hints of oak and lots of tasty fruit. Recommended.

◆ *Corcovo Crianza (red):* A decent, tasty crianza, slightly overshadowed by the above.

Los Llanos (Cosecheros Abastecedores, S.A.) (☎ 926 320 300) Founded in 1875, this large operation is a Valdepeñas ground-breaker: it was the first to age wines in oak and also to bottle its wines. It is most known for its light, inexpensive, aged red wines, sold under the Los Llanos and Pata Negra labels. It also makes wines called Don Opas, inexpensive, everyday bottles which are best avoided. The range includes:

◆ *Señorío de Los Llanos Crianza (red):* A light, competent, inexpensive, slightly directionless blend of fruit and oak.

◆ *Señorío de Los Llanos Gran Reserva (red):* A notably inexpensive, soft, light wine with gentle fruit and oak.

◆ *Pata Negra Gran Reserva (red):* A slightly more expensive version of the above.

Miguel Calatayud, S.A. (☎ 926 322 237) Founded in 1960, this producer makes some of Valdepeñas' better, more expensive red wines, including:

◆ *Vegaval Plata Crianza (red):* A light, smooth, easy-drinking Tempranillo crianza at a competitive price.

◆ *Vegaval Plata Reserva Tempranillo (red):* A fuller-bodied, tastier, more confident version of the above, for not much more money.

◆ *Vegaval Plata Gran Reserva (red):* A well made, lightish, flavoursome Tempranillo, drinking well at ten years old.

◆ *Vegaval Plata Reserva Cabernet Sauvignon (red):* The most expensive of the Miguel Calatayud wines reviewed, this is tasty, mouthfilling and characterful, an encouraging sign of what the grape can achieve in Valdepeñas.

Rafael López-Tello, S.L. (☎ 926 322 165) Founded in 1893, this is another Valdepeñas producer making respectable, unremarkable wines for modest prices, including:

- *López-Tello Blanco (white):* A light, vaguely characterless Airén wine.

- *López-Tello Rosado (rosé):* A decent, tasty, refreshing rosé.

- *López-Tello Tinto (red):* A light, easy-drinking young Tempranillo.

- *López-Tello Crianza (red):* A well made, straightforward blend of fruit and oak flavours for a notably low price.

Real, S.L. (☎ 914 577 588) Founded in 1989, this producer of modestly priced wines has shown with its reds that it can make wines that will appeal to the middle as well as everyday market. Its range includes:

- *Bonal Tinto (red):* A light, fruity Tempranillo for a low price. The bodega's weakest red.

- *Tinto Maceración Carbónica (red):* A tasty, aromatic, characterful young Tempranillo. Good.

- *Vega Ibor Crianza (red):* A light, flavoursome, well made blend of fruit and oak for a modest price.

- *Palacio de Ibor Crianza (red):* A more powerful version of the above. Good.

Videva, S.A. (☎ 926 322 351) Founded in 1968, this is an improving producer aiming for quality wines, especially reds. Its range includes:

- *Pago Luconer Viñas Viejas (red):* A young wine from old vines, this is powerful, characterful and fruity. Recommended.

- *Videva Crianza (red):* A well made, integrated, tasty crianza.

- *Pago Luconer Viñas Viejas Reserva (red):* A tasty, full-bodied wine with personality and some complexity. Recommended.

Viñedos y Bodegas Visán, S.L. (☎ 926 342 075) Founded in the mid-'90s, this is a producer of better-than-average reds, including:

- *Castillo de Mudela Crianza (red):* A competent, light crianza at a low price, which needs drinking soon after its release.

- *Castillo de Calatrava Cencibel Reserva (red):* A light, smooth, understated wine, drinking pleasantly at ten years old. Inexpensive.

- *Villa de Duque Reserva (red):* As above but made from Cabernet Sauvignon.

- *Castillo de Mudela Reserva (red):* Another inexpensive, aged Tempranillo, light, smooth and gentle.

- *Castillo de Calatrava Cabernet Sauvignon Reserva (red):* A lightish, flavoursome ten-year-old wine with attractive flavours. It is the bodega's most expensive wine and recommended.

D.O. Vinos de Madrid

In Brief: A low-profile region, making some decent, fresh whites and young reds, and looking to improve further.

The D.O.'s name leaves no doubt as to where it is located and also associates its wines with Spain's capital city, which might seem advantageous. However, this is not necessarily the case because some consumers find it hard to take seriously wines which are made in an urban environment. Vinos de Madrid's wines were more famous and popular in the past than they are today, with wine making in the region dating back at least to the 13th century. Their popularity surged after 1607 when the court moved from Valladolid to Madrid, but from the 19th century onwards they were overtaken by others. The region has traditionally been known for robust reds, mainly made from Garnacha and Tinto Fino (Tempranillo), but it also makes white wines, including characterful examples from the Malvar grape. Currently, the region covers nearly 11, 769 hectares of vines and has 4,170 growers and 32 bodegas.

Authorised grape varieties are:

- **White:** Airén, Albillo, Macabeo, Malvar, Parellada and Torrontés.

- **Black:** Cabernet Sauvignon, Garnacha, Merlot and Tempranillo.

Vinos de Madrid's whites made from the Malvar grape are refreshing and flavoursome, and the region also makes traditional 'sobremadre' wines – which spend around three months on their must – and barrel-fermented whites. The region's rosés, primarily made from Garnacha, are flavoursome and quite powerful. Vinos de Madrid's young Tinto Fino reds are light and fruity, in the style of La Mancha's, while the Garnachas are meaty and are sometimes noted for the maturity of the fruit and rustic feel.

Geography, Soil and Climate

The D.O. is split into three sub-regions:

- ▲ **Arganda:** This lies to the south-east of Madrid and covers 5,830 hectares, the largest sub-region. Malvar and Tempranillo are the dominant grape varieties.

- ▲ **Navalcarnero:** This lies to the south-west of Madrid and covers 2,107 hectares, the smallest sub-zone. Garnacha is the dominant grape.

- ▲ **San Martín:** This lies to the west of Navalcarnero and covers 3,821 hectares. Albillo and Garnacha are the dominant grape varieties.

Madrid has a reputation as having a particularly difficult climate, but it is no worse than the rest of the central plain, with hot and sometimes very hot summers and cold winters. Rainfall is slightly higher than other parts of central Spain, ranging from 475mm (19in) in Arganda to 650mm (26in) in San Martín.

Future Development

The wines of Vinos de Madrid are improving slowly but surely, although they need to look for more consistency. Vinos Jeromín has demonstrated that the region is capable of making bottles of good quality and with Madrid's innumerable bars and restaurants so close (some of the D.O.'s vineyards lie in the city's outlying suburbs), the D.O. has a large potential market very close by. As the quality of the region's output improves, the image problem caused by the wines being made in a capital city should diminish and with the correct marketing, the location of the zone of production could actually become an advantage. The authorities are certainly trying to raise and improve the region's profile.

Selected Bodegas

Castejón (☎ 918 943 480) Founded in 1959, this producer makes straightforward, everyday wines of varying quality, including:

◆ *Viña Rey Blanco (white):* A pleasant, light, fruity wine.

◆ *Viña Rey Tinto (red):* A smooth, tasty, young Tempranillo, sometimes a touch jammy.

Cooperativa Vinícola San Roque (☎ 918 940 230) Founded in 1958, this producer makes drinkable, everyday wines, including:

◆ *Viña Galindo Rosado (rosé):* A tasty pink wine with some bite.

◆ *Viña Galindo Tinto (red):* A straightforward, fruity, everyday wine.

Don Álvaro de Luna (☎ 918 610 272) Founded in 1963, this bodega makes a large range of wines of varying quality. The Quod wines offer simple, inexpensive, everyday drinking, while the following two stand out:

◆ *1434 Don Álvaro de Luna Albillo en Roble (white):* Aged in barrel for three months, this tasty, balanced wine is interesting and different. Recommended.

◆ *1434 Don Álvaro de Luna Tinto (red):* This young Tempranillo spends a few months in barrel and is aromatic, mouthfilling and tasty.

Francisco Casas, S.A. (☎ 918 110 207) Founded in 1942, this operation also makes (impressive) wines in D.O. Toro. Its Vinos de Madrid range is not as good, but the following are decent enough:

◆ *Tochuelo Rosado (rosé):* A fresh, tasty, fruity Garnacha rosé.

◆ *Tochuelo Tinto (red):* This inexpensive blend of Garnacha and Tempranillo is aromatic, tasty, well made, inexpensive, everyday drinking.

Hijos de Jesús Díaz (☎ 918 943 378) Founded in 1898, this small bodega is one of the region's most famous, following the success it enjoyed in the early '80s after its wines were recommended by C.L.U.V.E., the Club de Selección de Vinos. They no longer stand out particularly, although the following are respectable:

◆ *Jesús Díaz Blanco (white)*: A characterful, aromatic young white with more interest than the regional average.

◆ *Jesús Díaz Rosado (rosé)*: Respectable, tasty pink wine for drinking young.

María Idalia Rubio García (☎ 918 010 009) Founded in 1940, this small bodega makes better than average, everyday wines, including:

◆ *Viña Bayona Blanco (white)*: A tasty, refreshing, mouthfilling wine from the Malvar grape.

◆ *Viña Bayona Tinto (red)*: A blend of Malvar and Tempranillo, this is light, tasty drinking.

Orusco, S.L. (☎ 918 738 006) Founded in 1896, this bodega is known as one of the region's more reliable performers and the following wines are respectable and inexpensive, although not outstanding:

◆ *Viña Main Blanco (white)*: A simple, fruity, unremarkable Malvar.

◆ *Viña Main Rosado (rosé)*: A fruity, flavoursome Tempranillo-based wine, straightforward and honest.

◆ *Viña Main Tinto (red)*: A tasty, young Tempranillo, although possibly a little unpolished.

Peral (☎ 918 943 237) Founded in 1872, this small bodega is showing signs of being able to make wines that will raise the profile and reputation of Vinos de Madrid. Its worthy, inexpensive range includes:

◆ *Peral Sobremadre Blanco (white)*: One of the region's better whites, with mouthfilling flavours and some complexity. Inexpensive and recommended.

◆ *Peral Rosado (rosé)*: An aromatic, fruity young rosé.

◆ *Peral Tempranillo (red)*: A superior, fruity young red for a low price.

Ricardo Benito, S.L. (☎ 918 110 097) Founded in 1940, this large operation is one of the region's best, delivering wines of some quality at modest prices, including:

◆ *Castizo Blanco (white)*: This inexpensive blend of Airén and Malvar has decent fruity flavours and some bite.

◆ *Tapón de Oro Fermentado en Barrica (white)*: A mouthfilling, barrel-fermented Malvar which is a bit heavy on the oak but satisfying and characterful.

◆ *Tapón de Oro Rosado (rosé)*: A respectable, fruity pink wine.

◆ *Tapón de Oro Maceración Carbónica Tinto (red):* This aromatic Garnacha is one of the region's more characterful young reds, with powerful, mouthfilling flavours.

◆ *Madrileño Tempranillo (red):* A simple, tasty young red wine.

◆ *Tapón de Oro Tinto Crianza (red):* Mainly Tempranillo, with a small amount of Garnacha, this is a simple blend of fruit and oak.

Valle del Sol (S.A.T. 4478) (☎ 918 110 926) Founded in 1956, this bodega still makes the odd low quality wine, but generally speaking its range is decent and improving. It includes:

◆ *Antinos Macabeo (white):* A superior Vinos de Madrid white wine, with lots of characterful fruit.

◆ *Antinos Rosado (rosé):* A competent, tasty pink wine.

◆ *Antinos Tempranillo (red):* A refreshing blend of fruit and oak.

◆ *Valerius Tinto (red):* As above, with more body. Recommended.

Vinos Jeromín, S.L. (☎ 918 742 030) Founded in 1965, this is regarded by some as Vinos de Madrid's best producer. Its whites, rosés and reds are all attractive wines, although at the top end of the range, prices are quite high for a region with such a low profile.

◆ *Puerta de Alcalá Blanco (white):* A decent, fruity, inexpensive young Malvar.

◆ *Puerta del Sol Blanco Fermentado en Barrica (white):* A well made, tasty, unctuous wine, perhaps a touch pricey.

◆ *Puerta de Alcalá Rosado (rosé):* A mouthfilling, fruity wine from Malvar and Tempranillo.

◆ *Puerta del Sol Rosado Fermentado en Barrica (rosé):* This is tasty and quite powerful but rather expensive.

◆ *Vega Madroño Tinto (red):* A blend of Garnacha and Tempranillo, this inexpensive wine has lots of enjoyable fresh fruit.

◆ *Puerta de Alcalá Tinto (red):* A powerful, characterful mouthful of young Tempranillo at a low price. Good.

◆ *Puerta del Sol Cabernet Sauvignon (red):* A fair attempt at an oak-aged Cabernet, although a little rough around the edges and expensive for the region.

Selected non-D.O. Bodegas

Most of Castilla-La Mancha's best and some of its most famous wines are made by producers operating outside any of this large region's D.O.s. They include:

Dehesa del Carrizal (☎ 914 841 358) Founded in 1987, this small producer makes excellent white and red wines. Its 13 hectares of vines lie on a hunting estate and are 900m (2,952ft) above sea level; its wine maker used to work for the Marqués de Griñon (see below):

● *Dehesa del Carrizal Chardonnay (white):* This is superior barrel-fermented Chardonnay, integrated, tasty and complex. It is one of Castilla-La Mancha's best white wines, priced reasonably for its quality.

● *Dehesa del Carrizal Cabernet Sauvignon (red):* This is one of Spain's better 100 per cent Cabernet Sauvignons, a powerful, aromatic wine with length and complexity. It prides itself on having none of the harshness of some Cabernet Sauvignon wines. Recommended at four or five years old.

Manuel Manzaneque (☎ 967 585 003) Founded in 1993, Manzaneque is located at altitude in Albacete and its wines are improving annually thanks to the steady work of its French oenologist. The range includes:

● *Manuel Manzaneque Chardonnay Fermentado en Barrica (white):* A very good barrel-fermented wine, with balance, power and complexity. As good as Dehesa del Carrizal's, although a little more expensive.

● *Manuel Manzaneque Finca Elez Tinto Crianza (red):* Mainly Cabernet Sauvignon, with some Tempranillo and Merlot, this is a concentrated, characterful crianza wine.

● *Manuel Manzaneque Reserva (red):* Made from the same grapes as above, with slightly more Cabernet, this is a smooth, satisfying wine, although perhaps overpriced.

● *Manuel Manzaneque Syrah (red):* A tasty, well made wine, although again it is quite expensive and not particularly redolent of Syrah.

Marqués de Griñon (☎ 925 877 292) Carlos Falcó, the Marqués de Griñon, is one of Spain's better known wine makers, admired for both his wines and his maverick approach to the niceties of bureaucratic rules and regulations. He makes wine in Rioja, Ribera del Duero and Argentina, but is most renowned for his estate at Malpica de Tajo near Toledo, that produces some of Castilla-La Mancha's and Spain's most innovative red wines, at their best when around four years old. Falcó is famed for his innovative use of technology, being the first in Spain to utilise the canopy management technique, which lets grapes receive uniform sun exposure, meaning that they ripen at the same time. He is aided by the Australian Richard Smart and Michel Rolland from Bordeaux.

● *Dominio de Valdepusa Cabernet Sauvignon Reserva (red):* 90 per cent Cabernet with 10 per cent Merlot, this Bordeaux-style wine has changed people's attitudes to the potential of central Spain. In good years, it is a powerful, mouthfilling, balanced wine, but has been superseded by the following two.

● *Dominio de Valdepusa Syrah Reserva (red):* This grape, seemingly suited to Spain's warmer climate regions, is still little grown. Griñon's wine shows that it should be, a delicious, powerful, aromatic, complex bottle of real quality. Highly recommended.

♦ *Dominio de Valdepusa Petit Verdot Reserva (red):* Petit Verdot is very unusual in Spain and rarely used as a varietal, but this really works. It has complexity, sophistication and mouthfilling power, and is seen by some as Castilla-La Mancha's most interesting and innovative wine. Well worth hunting down.

♦ *Valdepusa Emeritus (red):* This blend of around 50 per cent Cabernet Sauvignon with Syrah and Petit Verdot spends 15 months on oak and was made for the millennium. It has been very successful, an elegant yet lively wine with notably expressive fruit and soft tannins which has garnered international plaudits. Emeritus costs around twice as much as the Syrah or the Petit Verdot.

Sánchez Muliterno (☎ 967 193 222) Founded in 1990, this small producer is making increasingly good wines in Albacete, including:

♦ *Sánchez Muliterno Chardonnay (white):* This is another superior barrel-fermented Chardonnay from central Spain, aromatic, flavoursome and interesting.

♦ *Divinus Blanco (white):* Primarily Chardonnay, with a little Sauvignon Blanc, this oaked wine is well made, tasty and unctuous, although the Chardonnay above is better and usually cheaper.

♦ *Vega Guijoso Tinto Crianza (red):* This is made from Merlot blended with Cabernet Sauvignon and Tempranillo, and is a powerful, tasty, slightly sweet wine.

Uribes Madero (☎ 969 143 020) Founded in 1990, this small bodega is yet another non-D.O. Castilla-La Mancha producer of good wines, including:

♦ *Calzadilla Crianza (red):* This blend of 50 per cent Tempranillo with Cabernet Sauvignon and Garnacha is an integrated, aromatic, flavoursome wine, although not inexpensive.

♦ *Calzadilla Syrah (red):* A mouthfilling blend of mature fruit and oak with notable length.

A castle in Castilla-León, the heart of Castilian Spain

8.

CASTILLA-LEÓN

This large region lies to the north and north-west of Madrid. It is sometimes called the traditional heart of Spain and is proud to be the originator of the Castilian Spanish language. This is a land of geographical contrasts, with a varied landscape ranging from the dominant upland plateau to mountains and river valleys. Agriculture is important and in addition to vines, wheat and cereals are grown. The climate is often harsh, with freezing winters, baking summers and scant rainfall, and some parts of Castilla-León are too challenging even for vine cultivation.

However, it produces some notable wines – and has done since Roman times – especially the reds of Ribera del Duero and the whites of Rueda, which are among Spain's best. The most important wine areas are in the middle of Castilla-León, in the region around the River Duero (which across the border in Portugal becomes the Douro). The black Tinto Fino (the local version of Tempranillo) and the white Verdejo are the most prominent grape varieties, and as with many areas of Spain the region is a mixture of co-operatives and independent producers. It has five D.O.s: Bierzo, Cigales, Ribera del Duero, Rueda and Toro, as well as significant producers of high quality wines in areas not covered by D.O. rules, as is the case in Castilla-La Mancha.

D.O. Bierzo

In Brief: A region of some potential, both for Godello-based white wines and Mencía-based reds, while the introduction of other grape varieties will add further interest.

A D.O. since the end of 1989, Bierzo covers nearly 3,700 hectares of vines, with 4,755 growers and 21 bottling bodegas. It lies in the north-west of Castilla-León, next to the border with Galicia and is a mild, green region protected by mountains, with vines planted on the terraces of the River Sil. This is an ideal environment for making good wines, although traditionally little of the region's produce was bottled, sold instead in bulk to the nearby provinces of Asturias and Galicia. Bierzo is now trying to cast off its image as a bulk producer and fulfil its undoubted potential.

The black Mencía is the region's dominant grape, accounting for 65 per cent of vineyard hectareage. Some think it is related to the Cabernet Franc grape and it makes fruity, slightly bitter, smooth wines, either in the young style or destined for oak ageing, although the latter might be better if Mencía was blended with other varieties to add complexity and tannin.

Authorised grape varieties are:

● **White:** Doña Blanca, Godello, Malvasía and Palomino.

● **Black:** Garnacha Tintorera and Mencía.

Palomino is the dominant white grape although the region's most characterful white wines often come from Godello, being fruity and balanced. Rosés are generally Mencía-based and are light and smooth. Bierzo's young reds from the Mencía grape are as described earlier and they can sometimes lack acidity due to the grape's early ripening in the region's generous climate. The crianza and reserva wines can be of decent quality and with potential changes detailed below (see **Future Development**) they should improve further.

Geography, Soil and Climate

Bierzo's climate is benevolent and transitional, lying between the continental conditions of Castilla-León and the damp, temperate weather of Galicia. The relatively low latitude and protective, encircling mountains mitigate against the late frosts which affect other parts of Castilla-León. Vines are sited at anywhere between 400 and 1,000m (1,312 and 3,280ft) above sea level, and annual rainfall is 720mm (28in).

Future Development

As things stand, given the grape varieties used and the places they are grown, Bierzo is fulfilling its potential. But if a more varied selection of high quality grapes was employed, planted in the most favourable locations, the quality of wines from this geographically favoured region could become very good indeed. The authorities in Bierzo realise that they have been slow to implement changes and are encouraging the planting of Chardonnay, Cabernet Sauvignon, Merlot and Tempranillo. Promising results from such grapes in nearby non-D.O. regions are encouraging and should help to counteract Bierzo's inertia and some growers' hostility to the idea of change. The authorities are also encouraging the planting of vines on south-facing slopes of the Sierra Cantabria, where conditions for grapes may be even more favourable than they are in the River Sil Valley.

Bierzo's future looks promising. It has distinct geographical and climatic advantages, and has already shown that it can make good wines from decent though not always top grade grape varieties. Over the coming years it should produce characterful white wines from Chardonnay and Godello, and the foreign black grapes will add variety, complexity and improved ageing potential to the region's crianza and reserva wines. Some of them are already good, although they are probably as good as they can be without changes of variety and location. This potential has been recognised by some of Spain's more prominent wine makers who are seeking to acquire land in the region.

Selected Bodegas

Antonina Álarez (☎ 987 546 725) Founded in 1996, this small producer makes a respectable, inexpensive white and red wine:

⬥ *Viña Garnelo (white):* This is mainly Godello, with small percentages of Doña Blanca and Malvasía, and offers light, fruity, everyday drinking.

⬥ *Vega del Cúa (red):* A straightforward, fruity young red wine.

Bodegas y Viñedos Luna Beberide, S.A. (☎ 987 549 002) Founded in 1986, this small, quality-driven, forward-thinking producer grows modest amounts of Cabernet

Sauvignon, Chardonnay, Gewürztraminer, Mencía and Merlot. Its wines show promise for the future, the range including:

⬥ *Viña Aralia (white):* An aromatic, flavoursome wine with some bite.

⬥ *Luna Beberide Gewürztraminer (white):* This is not a bad attempt with this distinctive grape variety and has lots of mature fruit. However, it could be more redolent of the variety.

⬥ *Luna Beberide Vendimia Seleccionada (red):* A young, aromatic wine with lots of lively fruit.

⬥ *Luna Beberide Cabernet Sauvignon (red):* This superior wine is an encouraging sign of Bierzo's potential, aromatic, flavoursome, finely structured and complex. Recommended.

Castro Ventosa (☎ 987 562 148) This small operation grows grapes on 60 hectares of its own vineyards and produces some of the region's better wines, not all of them covered by D.O. regulations.

⬥ *Airola Chardonnay (white):* A superior, unctuous Chardonnay with structure and personality. Recommended.

⬥ *Airola Gewürztraminer (white):* A flowery, refreshing example of this distinctive grape variety.

⬥ *Castro Ventosa Tinto (red):* A well made, aromatic, mouthfilling young Mencía.

⬥ *Airola Tinto (red):* This is a well conceived blend of fruit and oak flavours, with length and personality. It can be jarringly tannic when first released.

Pérez Caramés, S.A. (☎ 987 540 197) Founded in 1967, Caramés is one of Bierzo's best bodegas (although many of its wines are made outside the D.O.) producing a wide range of wines at reasonable prices, often from foreign grape varieties. The reds are much better than the whites and rosés, and include:

⬥ *Cónsules de Roma (red):* A well made Mencía red, aromatic, light and quite complex.

⬥ *Casar de Santa Inés Merlot (red):* A smooth yet characterful Merlot, aromatic and tasty.

⬥ *Casar de Santa Inés Tinto Crianza (red):* This blend of Pinot Noir, Merlot and Tempranillo offers lots of mature fruit and oak for a competitive price. Newer releases will use different grapes.

⬥ *Casar de Santa Inés Pinot Noir (red):* A decent, light, fruity example of the grape.

Prada a Tope, S.A. (☎ 902 400 101) Founded in 1989, this small operation is one of Bierzo's more reliable, making a range of decent wines from local grape varieties, including:

● *Blanco de Prada (white):* A fruity, aromatic white made from Godello. A touch expensive for a decent, everyday wine.

● *Tinto de Prada (red):* A tasty, aromatic, fruity young Mencía.

● *Prada Maceración Carbónica (red):* This wine is very aromatic, with lots of fruit on the palate. As with the white, it is expensive for a decent, everyday wine.

● *Tinto Crianza de Prada (red):* This is a well made, tasty blend of Mencía fruit and oak, but overpriced in comparison with similar quality red crianzas from other regions.

Vinos del Bierzo, Sociedad Cooperativa (☎ 987 546 150) Founded in 1963, this large co-operative makes a wide selection of wines. The whites and rosés are unremarkable, but the reds are decent and offer good value.

● *Viñas Laguas Macaración Carbónica (red):* A refreshing, flavoursome everyday young wine.

● *Viña Oro Tinto (red):* As above.

● *Guerra Tinto Crianza (red):* This is a soundly constructed blend of fruit and oak. Good.

Viñas del Bierzo, Sociedad Cooperativa (☎ 987 463 009) This sizeable co-operative was also founded in 1963, and as with the above, its reds are often better than the whites and rosés, including:

● *Naraya Tinto (red):* A straightforward, everyday red wine from the Mencía grape.

● *Gran Bierzo Tinto Crianza (red):* A competently made, easy-drinking red crianza from Mencía.

D.O. Cigales

In Brief: A well *sited region with undoubted potential, especially given the success of its neighbours, with both white and red wines. It is beginning to wake up and Cigales is to be watched, initially for young and crianza red wines.*

Cigales is currently trying to recapture the higher profile it enjoyed during Medieval times. Then it was renowned for its 'claretes', pale reds made by blending black and white grapes. The good people of the European Union – or whatever it is called at the moment – no longer allow wines to be labelled thus. Cigales was also famous for its rosés, aromatic, fruity, deeply coloured wines.

In the 21st century, the region is looking to the red wine success of its neighbours Toro and Ribera del Duero and hoping to replicate it. At the same time Cigales is considering the viability of making white wines (which would be a new departure), perhaps influenced by the success of nearby Rueda. Cigales traditionally concentrated on quantity more than quality and much of its produce was consumed locally. Almost

90 per cent of the region's output is now bottled, although exports only account for a miserly couple of per cent of output.

The previous lack of bodegas concentrating on making good quality wines explains why Cigales is Castilla-León's newest D.O.: until recently, it did not deserve to be accorded the status. It can be argued that this did not stop other regions (Almansa, Bullas and Yecla) from being denominated, but consistency is something that is often in short supply. Cigales has around 2,800 hectares of vineyards, 700 grape growers and 39 bodegas, of which 22 bottle their wines.

Authorised grape varieties are:

- **White:** Albillo, Verdejo and Viura.

- **Black:** Garnacha Gris, Garnacha Tinta and Tinta del País (the local variety of Tempranillo). The last accounts for over 50 per cent of Cigales' plantings.

The rosé wines can be well made, competitively priced, aromatic and fruity, and there are also barrel-fermented examples; however, some of them show signs of the overuse of sulphur and faulty wine making, completely unacceptable these days. Cigales' young reds are decent, fruity, everyday wines, while the crianzas have traditionally been competent but undistinguished. This is changing.

Geography, Soil and Climate

Cigales has a continental climate with moderating Atlantic influences. Summers are dry and quite hot, while winters are long and rigorous, and the region has a large annual and diurnal temperature range. Rainfall is irregular, although snow and frost are common. Vineyards are high, between 700 and 800m (2,624ft) above sea level.

Future Development

Lying close to distinguished and/or improving wine regions (Ribera del Duero, Rueda, Toro and some non-D.O. areas), Cigales has a lot to live up to, although we should point out that it is further from the beneficial influence of the Duero river than these other regions. But Cigales' geography means that it should be making good red wines. Standards are improving, although Cigales has appeared slow to develop when set against the success of its neighbours, especially Ribera del Duero and, to a lesser extent, Toro.

Frutos Villar has shown the red wine quality that the region is capable of and time will tell if Cigales' whites can approach the success of Rueda. The fact that the respected Rioja bodega Barón de Ley is setting up in Cigales is a positive sign.

Selected Bodegas

Cooperativa de Cigales (☎ 983 580 135) Founded in 1957, this modest-size co-operative concentrates on rosés, but they are of mixed quality and in some years are defective. The reds are better – try the following:

- *Torondos Tinto (red):* A very drinkable young red with lots of tasty fruit.

Emeyerio Fernández, S.L. (☎ 983 583 244) Founded in 1997, this small operation makes good quality red wines from Tinta Fina at competitive prices, including:

◆ *Valdetán Tinto (red):* This well made, inexpensive, young wine has lots of concentrated fruit flavours.

◆ *Valdetán Maceración Carbónica (red):* An attractive young red, aromatic, refreshing and fruity.

◆ *La Legua Tinto Crianza (red):* A well made, reasonably priced blend of characterful fruit and oak. Good.

Frutos Villar, S.L. (☎ 983 586 868) Founded in 1960 in Cigales, Frutos Villar is one of the region's leading lights, seekers of quality. It also makes excellent wines in D.O. Toro. The extensive range of Cigales wines includes:

◆ *Viña Calderona Rosado (rosé):* This is made primarily from Tinta del País, with Garnacha and white grapes, and is a competent, fruity pink wine.

◆ *Conde Ansúrez (red):* A competently made, fruity young red.

◆ *Calderona Tinto (red):* This is one of Cigales' better reds and shows what the region is capable of. It is balanced and mouthfilling with lots of fruit flavours and a touch of class. Recommended..

◆ *Conde Ansúrez Crianza (red):* Made primarily from Tinta del País, with some Garnacha, this is a competent blend of fruit and oak.

◆ *Calderona Crianza (red):* A well made, aromatic, powerful wine, mixing Tinta del País with oak.

González Lara, S.A. (☎ 983 587 881) Founded in 1990, this small operation makes a modest range of competent, inexpensive, everyday wines. With a few changes they could probably be good.

◆ *Viña Zapata (rosé):* This blend of Garnacha, Tinta del País and Viura is light and flavoursome, but would be better without the thinning influence of the Viura.

◆ *Fuente del Conde Rosado (rosé):* A competent pink wine, but nothing remarkable.

◆ *Fuente del Conde Tinto Crianza (red):* A straightforward, tasty, inexpensive crianza, but they might look for more depth and subtlety.

Hijos de Rufino Iglesias, S.A. (☎ 983 587 778) This small operation, founded in 1948, makes a consistently good rosé wine:

◆ *Carratravieso (rosé):* Mainly Tinta del País, with some Garnacha and white grapes, this is aromatic, fruity, balanced and as good as it could be for the modest price.

Lezcano Lacalle (☎ 983 586 697) Founded in 1991, this small operation has 14 hectares of its own vines and makes a modest range of wines. It is owned by Félix

Lezcano, who is also president of the Cigales D.O. and the first to make a reserva red in the region.

◆ *Docetañidos Rosado (rosé):* Mainly Tinto Fino, with some Verdejo, this is a characterful, full-bodied pink wine with unctuous bite.

◆ *Lezcano Reserva (red):* Made from a varying blend, but around 60 per cent Tempranillo and 40 per cent Cabernet Sauvignon, this spends 14 months in American oak and a further two years in bottle. It has structure, body and personality, a good sign for Cigales' future, but as yet it seems expensive.

Rodríguez Sanz, S.A. (☎ 983 580 006) This small operation, founded in 1931, makes a competent although unremarkable rosé and better reds:

◆ *Rosán Joven (rosé):* Light and pleasant but needs more character.

◆ *Viña Rosán (red):* Simple, tasty, everyday red wine.

◆ *Albertar Crianza (red):* Rather better than the two above, this is a characterful, well made wine with lots of fruit. Recommended.

Rosados de Castilla y León, S.L. (☎ 983 586 771) Founded in 1991, this bodega's red is better than its rosés, which sometimes display signs of faulty wine making, unfortunate given the operation's name.

◆ *Solar de Laguna (rosé):* This is usually the most reliable of the producer's rosés, commercial, fruity and well made.

◆ *Grandón Tinto Crianza (red):* An approachable, smooth blend of fruit and oak, a good sign of what Cigales can produce.

Vegapisuerga, S.L. (☎ 983 502 233) Founded in 1997, this modest operation has already shown that it is capable of making decent, reasonably priced wines, with the following being its most reliable:

◆ *Malvanegra Rosado (rosé):* A blend of four grapes, this inexpensive rosé offers characterful fruit.

◆ *Carramonte (red):* A refreshing, young red with attractive fruit.

D.O. Ribera del Duero

In Brief: *A chic D.O. that produces some of Spain's very best red wines. But quality is mixed and high prices mean that this is not a region for either those on a budget or the uninitiated.*

Ribera del Duero – which means 'banks of the Duero' – is much smaller than that other primarily red Spanish wine region, Rioja. It covers some 13,500 hectares – as opposed to Rioja's 50,000 – with around 110 producers – against Rioja's 2,500 – and 7,150 growers, but it has joined Rioja in the public consciousness as one of Spain's best red wine regions. Ribera del Duero has been known since the 19th century for the legendary red wines of the Vega Sicilia estate. But these powerful, complex wines (made from a blend of Cabernet Sauvignon, Merlot, Malbec and Tinto Fino) were seen as something of a one-off and the rest of the region's produce was little regarded.

It was demarcated as a D.O. in 1982 and began a period of steady development, but this was rapidly accelerated in the '90s when the influential American wine critic Robert Parker wrote rave reviews about the Pesquera wines made by Alejandro Fernandez and Ribera del Duero quickly became famous. Finance rushed into the region and the number of bodegas escalated rapidly.

The backbone of Ribera del Duero's wines is the Tinto Fino grape, the local variety of Tempranillo, also called Tinta del País in these parts. Because it is early-ripening, it is ideal for a region with a short ripening season and it produces red wines especially suited to long periods of ageing in oak and bottle, some of which are Spain's best and can stand comparison with reds from anywhere. Ribera reds must contain at least 75 per cent of the grape, with Cabernet Sauvignon, Garnacha and Merlot the most common other varieties employed.

Vines are grown on gentle, chalk-based, pine-covered slopes above the Duero river, 700 to 800m (2,296 to 2,624ft) above sea level. It is a difficult environment for vines and uncertain harvests lead to fluctuations in grape prices and vintage quality. Poor soils, low yields and low summer night temperatures (which allow the grapes to recuperate after the daytime heat) explain why the wines have such intense aromas and flavours and decent acidity. Unfortunately, not all of the region's wines are given enough time to develop along these lines, being sold too young. Ribera del Duero is not a region for young reds, although some bodegas will try to persuade you otherwise. There is nothing wrong with them, but they are not the region at its best and are overpriced when compared with other areas.

Authorised grape varieties are:

- **White:** Albillo.

- **Black:** Cabernet Sauvignon, Garnacha Tinta, Malbec, Merlot and Tinta del País.

Ribera del Duero is only denominated for rosé and red wines, although the former are of minor importance. Those that are made are flavoursome, but they can be a little weighty. Ribera del Duero is all about red wines. The best are powerful, delicious, structured, complex and aromatic, capable of long periods of ageing and development. Anybody who wants to be properly acquainted with Spain's, indeed the world's, better reds, needs to investigate them.

Geography, Soil and Climate

Ribera del Duero appears to the uninitiated to be a gentle environment. On a pleasant summer's day, the gentle, rolling, pine-fringed hills of the Duero river valley seem a perfect place for the easy cultivation of vines. But this is high country (700 to 800m/2,296 to 2,624ft above sea level), without much evidence of the Atlantic's benign influence and it has a continental climate, slightly moderated by the Duero river. Summers are hot and dry while winters are long and sometimes harsh. Rainfall is usually adequate in the spring and autumn, and mists originating from the river help to sustain the vines through the dry heat of summer. The region's annual precipitation varies between 450 and 500mm (18 and 20in). Hard spring frosts are not uncommon and sometimes wipe out up to half of the harvest.

The sometimes problematic climate has advantages and when conditions are just favourable, Ribera del Duero makes sublime wines. Low yields and the pronounced diurnal temperature range produce grapes with concentrated aromas and flavours and sustaining acidity. When conditions are difficult, harvests are small and sometimes of less than perfect quality, with some grapes failing to ripen properly.

Future Development

Ribera del Duero has progressed a long way very quickly. In the '80s, there were around a dozen bodegas, while in the early years of the 21st century, there are over 100. Producers have rushed to the region to try to emulate (and cash in on) the success of the likes of Vega Sicilia, Pesquera and Viña Pedrosa. But it is very difficult to move into a region and learn about its peculiarities quickly. That takes time and experimentation, especially in a region like Ribera del Duero, with its sometimes trying climate. As a result, some of the newer bodegas have found it difficult to make good wines. But after investing heavily in their new operations they have needed to recoup some of that money fairly quickly. This has meant that high Ribera del Duero prices have been charged for wines that do not always have the commensurate quality. And there has been a tendency to release wines too young. This has been noticed by consumers and has had a negative effect on the region's reputation, especially in foreign markets. Hence a period of consolidation is required. Things are already improving as growers new to the region become more experienced at handling the vagaries of Ribera del Duero's challenging climate.

Selected Bodegas

Alejandro Fernández-Tinto Pesquera, S.L. (☎ 983 870 037) Alejandro Fernández is a self-taught wine maker who used to sell agricultural machinery. He is now one of the most famous and respected Spanish wine producers, and Pesquera (named after a village near Valladolid) has become a legendary name, not just in Ribera del Duero, but globally. The bodega was founded in 1972, but it was not until the early '80s (when stainless steel tanks and new oak barrels were employed) that the wines began to show their real quality. When the former lawyer and influential wine critic Robert Parker compared Fernández's wines with Château Pétrus, they quickly became flag bearers not just for Ribera del Duero but for Spanish red wine in general. Pesquera wines invariably manage to capture the power, structure and complexity of Ribera del Duero and are one of the highest expressions of the Tempranillo grape. See also the entry for Condado de Haza, Alejandro Fernández's other bodega, on page 145.

♦ *Pesquera Crianza (red):* This is an affordable introduction to the wines of Pesquera, giving a good idea of the concentration of aroma and flavour that the wines can have. Try to find a wine from a superior year (even Pesquera has less good years) and do not drink it when first released.

● *Pesquera Reserva – (red):* A powerful, complex, flavour-filled wine with assertive tannins, yet refined. This is fruit and oak working beautifully together and thoroughly recommended.

● *Pesquera Gran Reserva (red):* An excellently assembled wine, powerful, structured and smooth.

● *Pesquera Janus Gran Reserva (red):* Only released in the very best years, this is a powerful, confident, long expression of the Ribera del Duero red wine style at its best.

Arzuaga Navarro, S.L. (☎ 983 681 146) Florentino Arzuaga's vineyards were planted in 1987, the winery was founded in 1993, and slowly but surely he has begun to make very good wines, primarily from Tinta Fina, although some contain small amounts of Cabernet Sauvignon and Merlot. As with Alejandro Fernández, Arzuaga had no family involvement in the wine industry (he owns a holiday complex in Ibiza and also produces olive oil in Toledo) but through patience and experimentation with different grape combinations and ageing methods, he has come to a position where he can compete with the region's best.

● *Arzuaga Crianza (red):* A balanced, powerful, flavoursome wine, although not as complex as some.

● *Arzuaga Reserva (red):* As above, but with complexity and extra class. Recommended.

● *Arzuaga Reserva Especial (red):* A spicy, complex wine, very well made, which can compete with the best of the region.

Balbás, S.L. (☎ 947 542 111) Founded in 1987, this bodega makes the respectable Balbás range and the more complex Ardal wines. In good years quality can be very good in both, but in difficult ones, the wines sometimes lack power and complexity.

● *Balbás Crianza (red):* In good years this is tasty, elegant and satisfying, but in weaker ones it can lack personality.

● *Balbás Reserva (red):* A better bet than the above, this offers balance, style, flavour and interest.

● *Ardal Crianza (red):* This is powerful, integrated and tasty, not to be drunk too young and 'dumb'.

● *Ardal Reserva (red):* A better version of the above.

Bodegas del Campo (☎ 947 561 034) Founded in 1989, this small bodega makes respectable rather than remarkable wines, sometimes rather rustic in feel. They are not, as yet, representative of what Ribera del Duero is really about.

● *Alfoz (red):* A decent, straightforward, fruity young wine.

● *Pagos de Quintana Roble (red):* A light wine with flavoursome fruit and up-front oak.

◆ *Pagos de Quintana Crianza (red)*: A touch rustic, without the body and flavoursome complexity required from the region.

◆ *Pagos de Quintana Reserva (red)*: Can be rustic, with hints of faulty wine making or it can also be flavoursome and soundly constructed.

Bodegas y Viñedos Alión, S.A. (☎ 983 881 236) Alión's winery was set up in 1992 by Vega Sicilia to make an alternative to their legendary Vega Sicilia wines. It was expected to be the junior partner, more accessible and less expensive, but it has quickly garnered a high reputation and the wine is nearly as sought-after as those of Vega Sicilia. The idea was to produce a high quality wine at an affordable price and this has been very successfully accomplished.

◆ *Alión Reserva (red)*: Made from Tinto Fino, aged in oak for 13 months and then for a further 2 years in bottle, this is one of Ribera del Duero's must-tastes. It offers an enticing nose, power, complexity, structure and length, and gives great drinking for at least a decade after release.

Bodegas y Viñedos Tamaral, S.L. (☎ 983 878 017) Founded only in 1997, it is rather early to judge this small bodega properly. It is new to the region and some of the vines are young and yet to develop character.

◆ *Tablares Tinto (red)*: An eminently drinkable blend of Tinta del País and oak, with flavour and structure, but lacking real Ribera class.

◆ *El Tamaral Crianza (red)*: This is smooth, tasty and well made, and future releases should have more power and complexity.

Bodegas y Viñedos Valtravieso, S.L. (☎ 983 484 030) Founded in 1994, this small bodega has quickly gained a reputation for high quality.

◆ *Valtravieso Crianza (red)*: 90 per cent Tinta Fina, with 5 per cent each of Cabernet Sauvignon and Merlot, this is powerful, smooth, concentrated and aromatic, a very satisfying wine.

◆ *Valtravieso Reserva (red)*: Made from the same blend as the crianza, this wine has all the assets of the above, with extra complexity. Recommended, although you do pay for the privilege: it costs a lot more than the crianza.

Briego (Albesa) (☎ 983 892 156) Founded in 1992, this small bodega has ably demonstrated its ability to make very good wines, including:

◆ *Briego Crianza (red)*: A tasty, well made blend of fruit and oak that needs time to integrate.

◆ *Briego Reserva (red)*: These expensive wines can be excellent, with great power, complexity and length. As is often the case in Ribera, choose a decent vintage.

Cachopa, S.A. (☎ 947 528 133) This winery was founded in 1997 and it is already showing signs that it will be capable of producing high quality wines. Its range includes:

◆ *Valdolé (red)*: A straightforward, aromatic blend of fruit and oak, well made and enjoyable.

◆ *Cachopa Crianza (red)*: This is balanced, aromatic and honest rather than remarkable.

◆ *Cachopa Reserva (red)*: Often the bodega's best wine, powerful, structured and long. Good.

Cillar de Silos (☎ 947 545 126) Founded in 1994, this small bodega uses French not American oak, giving its wines an original feel. Quality is good rather than exceptional.

◆ *Cillar de Silos Crianza (red)*: In good years, this is fruity and flavoursome, in not so good ones, rather weak.

◆ *Cillar de Silos Reserva (red)*: A tasty, powerful, toasty wine.

Condado de Haza, S.L. (☎ 947 525 254) Founded in 1993, this is Alejandro Fernández's second bodega (see the entry for Alejandro Fernández – Tinto Pesquera, S.L. on page 142). As might be expected from this master wine maker, it was an instant hit. Condado de Haza is an inexpensive introduction to Alejandro Fernández's wines, while Alenza is a more expensive, complex bottle.

◆ *Condado de Haza (red)*: An aromatic, concentrated, powerful wine, whose tannins are sometimes pronounced when it is first released.

◆ *Alenza Crianza (red)*: A notably aromatic wine with power and balance. Recommended.

Cooperativa Virgen de la Asunción (☎ 947 542 057) Founded in 1957, this co-operative's standards vary from year to year. Its wines range from the competent to the very good and include:

◆ *Viña Valera (red)*: A young Tinta del País, fruity and mouthfilling.

◆ *Vega Fina Crianza (red)*: A competent blend of fruit and oak, but can lack personality.

◆ *Viña Valera Reserva (red)*: Often the bodega's best wine, powerful and persistent.

Cooperativa Virgen de la Vega (☎ 947 540 224) Founded in 1956, this co-operative makes decent wines at modest prices, including:

◆ *Roa (red)*: A tasty, aromatic, fruity young wine, not representative of the region, but very drinkable.

◆ *Rauda Crianza (red)*: Well made, tasty and mouthfilling, and cheaper than the regional average.

Dehesa de los Canónigos, S.A. (☎ 983 484 001) Founded in 1988, the grapes from this operation's vineyards used to be bought by Vega Sicilia, a strong endorsement of their quality. They are now used for Dehesa de los Canónigos' own laudable wines.

● *Dehesa de los Canónigos Crianza (red):* Made from 85 per cent Tinto Fino, 12 per cent Cabernet Sauvignon and 3 per cent Albillo, this is a powerful, aromatic, elegant wine with lots of flavour. Recommended.

● *Dehesa de los Canónigos Reserva (red):* Made from the same blend as the crianza, this is well made, rounded and notably long. Recommended.

Dominio de Pingus, S.L. (☎ 983 680 189) Founded in 1995, and produced in tiny quantities, this wine is often cited as Ribera del Duero's and Spain's best red. Its price is vast, the country's highest, and only a few thousand bottles are made. Pingus is the brainchild of a Danish wine maker, Peter Sisseck, who is also wine maker for Monasterio (see page 150). He qualified as an oenologist at Bordeaux University and worked in France and California before moving to Spain and beginning work for Monasterio.

● *Pingus (red):* Arguably Tinto Fino's highest expression, this wine has abundant aroma, flavour, confidence and integration, and is regularly voted the country's best. Notably difficult to get hold of and Spain's ultimate 'boutique' wine.

Durón (☎ 947 541 244) Founded in 1983, this modest bodega produces well made, flavoursome wines:

● *Durón Crianza (red):* Well constructed, with flavour and personality.

● *Durón Reserva (red):* A powerful wine with balance and flavour. Recommended.

El Lagar de Isilla (☎ 947 504 316) Founded only in 1997, this small bodega is already making decent wines.

● *Zalagar (red):* An inexpensive (for Ribera del Duero) young blend of fruit and oak, pleasant rather than arresting.

● *El Lagar de Isilla Crianza (red):* A mature, fruity, well conceived crianza.

Emilio Moro, S.L. (☎ 983 457 019) Founded in 1989, this bodega makes good and very good red wines, including:

● *Finca Resalso (red):* A well made, smooth, flavoursome blend of fruit and oak, but could do with more complexity for the price.

● *Emilio Moro Crianza (red):* A more characterful, confident version of the above. Good.

● *Emilio Moro Reserva (red):* A superior (and expensive) wine, aromatic, soundly constructed and mouthfilling.

Emina, S.L. (☎ 983 485 004) Founded in 1995, this bodega, along with its sister Matarromera, makes good and very good wines, although quality is vintage-related, as is often the case in Ribera del Duero.

● *Emina Tinto (red):* A fresh, fruity, inexpensive young wine.

◆ *Emina Crianza (red):* An integrated, powerful blend of fruit and oak.

Félix Callejo, S.A. (☎ 947 532 312) Founded in 1989, this bodega has garnered a reputation for reliability, making good and very good wines in most years. Its bottles are an upmarket staple in many Spanish supermarkets, including:

◆ *Callejo Cuatro Meses en Barrica (red):* A tasty, well made 'media-crianza' (which means 'half crianza' – the wine spends four months on oak) with some bite.

◆ *Callejo Crianza (red):* This blend of 90 per cent Tinta del País and 10 per cent Cabernet Sauvignon is a well made, flavoursome wine with attractive fruit and oak tannins. It is also less expensive than the average Ribera del Duero crianza, hence its Spanish supermarket popularity.

◆ *Callejo Reserva (red):* Made from the same blend as the crianza, this is a powerful, spicy wine, which is perhaps overpriced.

Fuentespina, S.L. (☎ 947 596 002) Founded in 1960, and part of Grupo Avelino Vegas, standards appear to have slipped at Fuentespina and its wines sometimes lack character and personality. Hopefully this is a temporary blip.

◆ *Fuentespina Tinto (red):* This can be a tasty blend of fruit and oak, but in some years it is rather overcooked and one-dimensional.

◆ *Fuentespina Crianza (red):* Older releases are well conceived, satisfying wines but some of the recent ones lack power and interest.

◆ *Fuentespina Reserva (red):* As above.

García de Aranda (☎ 947 501 817) Founded in 1966, this operation makes decent, easy-to-drink wines, but they sometimes lack the power, depth and personality that we look for from Ribera del Duero. Its range includes:

◆ *Señorío de los Baldíos Rosado (rosé):* 50 per cent Tinta del País and 50 per cent Albillo, this inexpensive rosé is fresh, fruity and refreshing.

◆ *Vegaranda Tinto (red):* An aromatic, inexpensive young Tinta del País with lots of up-front fruity flavours.

◆ *Vegaranda Crianza (red):* This tends to be unpredictable and can be light, uninteresting and unsubtle.

◆ *Señorío de los Baldíos Crianza (red):* When on form, this is tasty and has attractive, fruity character, but it is sometimes one-dimensional and uninteresting.

◆ *Señorío de los Baldíos Reserva (red):* This is always well made, but sometimes lacks the aroma and power that we look for from Ribera del Duero.

Gormaz, S.C. (☎ 975 350 404) Founded in 1974, this co-operative produces correctly made wines, but they lack personality and Ribera del Duero class. They include:

- *Doce Linajes Roble (red):* Rather unsubtle and rustic.

- *Doce Linajes Crianza (red):* As above, and lacks interest.

- *Doce Linajes Reserva (red):* This can be tasty, but in some years it is unfocused and ages prematurely.

Grandes Bodegas, S.A. (☎ 947 542 166) Founded in 1985, this reliable bodega (which also makes white wines in Rueda – see page 163) produces good quality, affordable wines, including:

- *Marqués de Velilla Tinto (red):* This is a decent example of a young red wine from Ribera del Duero, aromatic, fruity and flavoursome, and less expensive than some.

- *Marqués de Velilla Barrica (red):* A mouthfilling, flavoursome, tannic blend of fruit and oak.

- *Marqués de Velilla Crianza (red):* A well made, aromatic, flavoursome wine with some sweet spice.

- *Marqués de Velilla Reserva (red):* This varies in quality from year to year. When good, it offers complex aromas, flavour, structure and interest.

- *Monte Villalobón (red):* Made from 90 per cent Tinta del País and 10 per cent Cabernet Sauvignon, from vines at least 40 years old, this is the bodega's most expensive bottle. The wine spends 250 days in barrel and a further 9 to 12 months in bottle. It first appeared on the market in 1999, an estate wine only released in very good years, and has a powerful, toasty nose with some complexity and a mouthfilling, engaging palate with long, fruity flavours and toast. Very good and priced to compete with the region's better wines.

Herederos de Doroteo San Juan (☎ 947 544 317) Founded in 1979, this operation makes modest amounts of competitively priced, good quality wines from Tinta del País, including:

- *Blasón de San Juan (red):* A meaty, tasty young blend of fruit and oak.

- *Blasón de San Juan Roble (red):* This is a more aromatic, smoother version of the above.

- *Blasón de San Juan Crianza (red):* A concentrated, integrated, mouthfilling wine at a competitive price. Good.

Hermanos Pérez Pascuas, S.L. (☎ 947 530 100) Founded in 1980, this modest-size family concern is one of the great names of Ribera del Duero, producing excellent, rich wines. The family has been in the wine business for three generations, but has been making its own wines only since 1980, having previously sold its grapes to other wine makers. It has 100 hectares of vines, 90 per cent Tinta del País and 10 per cent Cabernet Sauvignon, and produces around 400,000 bottles per year. The reassuringly expensive range includes:

- *Viña Pedrosa Crianza (red):* A rich, flavoursome, mouthfilling, persistent wine – and you pay for the privilege.

- *Viña Pedrosa Reserva (red):* At their best, these are some of Ribera del Duero's best wines, sumptuous, elegant and beautifully made. Pedrosa Reservas have become very expensive.

- *Pérez Pascuas Gran Selección (red):* Made from grapes from 60-year-old vines and aged in barrel for 26 months and a further two years in bottle, this is one of Ribera del Duero's most lauded and expensive wines, first appearing on the market in 1995. It has great elegance, structure and length, and is a wine for long keeping.

Hermanos Sastre, S.L. (☎ 947 542 108) Founded in 1992, this small family-owned bodega makes limited amounts of high quality wine from its 40 hectares of Tinta del País vines, which range in age from around 15 to 80 years.

- *Viña Sastre Crianza (red):* A lovely, powerful, aromatic wine with confident, mature tannins.

- *Viña Sastre Reserva (red):* This is smooth, integrated and unctuous. Good.

- *Viña Sastre Pago de Santa Cruz (red):* A high quality, smooth, complex, flavoursome, concentrated wine which first appeared on the market in the late '90s. It is expensive, although not especially so by Ribera del Duero standards.

Ismael Arroyo, S.L. (☎ 947 532 309) The Arroyo family has been in the wine business for many years and this winery was founded in 1979. It is much respected in Ribera del Duero, only releasing wines if they are of a high standard and thus trying to maintain standards from year to year. This does not always work (for example the 1996 crianza was superior to that from the troublesome year 1997) but the idea is a laudable one. Its range includes:

- *Mesoneros de Castilla (red):* A meaty young red with tasty, mature fruit.

- *Valsotillo Crianza (red):* When it is on form, this is a very pleasing wine, aromatic, powerful and integrated.

- *Valsotillo Reserva (red):* Made from grapes produced by 50-year-old vineyards, this has power, elegance and structure.

Lambuena, S.A. (☎ 947 540 034) Founded in 1989, this small family concern makes decent wines, mainly from Tinta del País and small amounts of Cabernet Sauvignon, including:

- *Lambuena Tinto (red):* An aromatic, characterful, fruity wine with hints of oak.

- *Lambuena Crianza (red):* A well made, fruity crianza with subtle oak influence.

- *Lambuena Reserva (red):* This is a tasty, fruity wine with confident tannins and balance.

López Cristóbal, S.L. (☎ 947 540 106) Founded in 1994, this is another small bodega turning out modest amounts of good wine, especially its reservas, made mainly from Tinta del País with small amounts of Cabernet Sauvignon and Merlot.

◆ *López Cristóbal (red)*: A tasty, fruity young wine with a hint of oak.

◆ *López Cristóbal Crianza (red)*: A powerful, complex wine with lots of flavour. Good.

◆ *López Cristóbal Reserva (red)*: A well made wine with lots of attractive flavours and length.

Matarromera, S.A. (☎ 983 485 004) Founded in 1988, this bodega makes good wines, with its Gran Reservas being very good, but the prices are perhaps high for the quality. The range includes:

◆ *Melior (red)*: A young, tannic red, well made but it can be a touch harsh.

◆ *Matarromera Crianza (red)*: A tasty, aromatic wine, but rather expensive.

◆ *Matarromera Reserva (red)*: A tasty, well made wine with decent length, but not as good as some of Ribera's other wines which sell for the same price.

◆ *Matarromera Gran Reserva (red)*: A delicious, spicy, well made wine, but very expensive.

Monasterio, S.L. (☎ 983 484 002) Founded in 1991, this bodega is one of Ribera del Duero's stars and, bearing this in mind, its wines are reasonably priced, although they are still expensive. Its wine maker is the Dane, Peter Sisseck, who also makes Spain's most expensive wine – Pingus – at his own operation (see the entry for Dominio de Pingus, S.L.).

◆ *Hacienda Monasterio Crianza (red)*: Made primarily from Tinta del País, with small amounts of Cabernet Sauvignon, Malbec and Merlot, this is one of Ribera's best crianza wines. It is full, aromatic, concentrated and flavoursome, with firm, well judged tannins. Highly recommended.

◆ *Hacienda Monasterio Reserva (red)*: Made from almost the same blend as the crianza, this is among Ribera del Duero's best wines. It is full, aromatic, concentrated, mouthfilling and has fruit and oak working beautifully together. Thoroughly recommended for a special occasion.

Montebaco (☎ 983 683 696) Founded in 1989, this is another small Ribera del Duero bodega producing modest amounts of often very good wine with an original feel, if you can find any.

◆ *Semele (red)*: Mainly Tinta Fina, with some Merlot, this is an appealing, aromatic wine with lots of fruit and toasty oak, persistence and power. Recommended and affordable.

◆ *Montebaco Crianza (red)*: One of Ribera's better crianzas, very aromatic with lots of mature fruit, toasty oak and personality. Definitely food wine.

◆ *Montebaco Selección Especial (red):* An excellent, aromatic, flavoursome wine with power and personality. Highly recommended.

Montevannos, S.L. (☎ 947 534 277) Founded in 1987, this bodega grows mainly Tinto Fino and a small amount of Merlot on its 35 hectares of vineyards, and makes lightish, approachable wines (which are sometimes too understated) including:

◆ *Montevannos Tinto (red):* A light, fruity wine, not really what Ribera del Duero is about.

◆ *Montevannos Crianza (red):* This is well made and balanced, with decent flavours, but it sometimes lacks power and punch.

Pago de Carraovejas (☎ 983 878 020) Founded in 1988, with its first harvest appearing in 1991, Pago de Carraovejas has quickly established a reputation for elegant, fruity wines at prices that are competitive in the expensive world of Ribera del Duero. Its oenologist, Tómas Postigo, worked for Protos (see the entry under that name) for four years in the '80s before founding this winery. Pago de Caraovejas is a pioneer in Ribera del Duero of estate wines, i.e. produced from the fruit of a single vineyard. The wines are made from 75 per cent Tinto Fino and 25 per cent Cabernet Sauvignon, and their quality should improve even further as the vines mature.

◆ *Pago de Carraovejas Crianza (red):* In good years, this is one of Ribera's better and most competitively priced crianzas, fruity, mouthfilling and complex. In not so good years, it is still appealing.

◆ *Pago de Carraovejas Reserva (red):* Smooth, aromatic, structured and delicious. Recommended.

Pago de los Capellanes, S.A. (☎ 947 530 068) Founded only in 1996, this modest-size bodega has quickly produced elegant red wines (in stylishly labelled bottles) at reasonable prices.

◆ *Pago de Capellanes Tinto (red):* A superior young red, with lots of mature fruit flavours.

◆ *Pago de Capellanes Crianza (red):* This blend of Tinto Fino and Cabernet Sauvignon is mature, concentrated and tasty with the Cabernet Sauvignon influence prevalent. Good.

◆ *Pago de Capellanes Reserva (red):* Made from the same grapes as the crianza, this rounded, elegant wine is very well put together. Recommended and fairly priced.

Parxet (☎ 983 870 185) As well as making very good white wines in D.O. Alella (see the relevant entry), Parxet has been making a red wine from Tinta del País in Ribera del Duero since 1985:

◆ *Tionio (red):* Very aromatic, powerful and well put together. Recommended and affordable.

Peñalba López, S.L. (☎ 947 501 381) Founded in 1903, this fair-size family firm makes a small range of good and very good wines:

◆ *Torremilanos Crianza (red):* A tasty, mouthfilling wine with length and a lighter feeling than some Ribera crianzas.

◆ *Torremilanos Reserva (red):* This is a finely structured wine with understated power.

◆ *Torre Albéniz Reserva (red):* A blend of Tempranillo, Cabernet Sauvignon and Merlot, this has everything we look for from Ribera del Duero: aroma, power, complexity and length. Recommended.

Protos, S.A. (☎ 983 878 011) Founded in 1927 and with a large output by Ribera del Duero standards, Protos is one of the region's more famous names. Its Tinto Fino wines have been much admired both in Spain and abroad, although consistency has been a problem and standards have risen and fallen as oenologists have come and gone. Thus the Protos name is not what it was. However, wines tasted recently have been better than those from the late '90s.

◆ *Protos Roble (red):* A decent, fruity, youngish red at an affordable price.

◆ *Protos Crianza (red):* Tasty and mouthfilling but can lack structure and depth.

◆ *Protos Reserva (red):* A better bet than the crianza, with aroma, power and personality, although the oak is sometimes intrusive.

◆ *Protos Gran Reserva (red):* The bodega's best wine, this is rounded, mouthfilling, tasty and long. Recommended.

Real Sitio de Ventosilla, S.A. (☎ 947 546 900) Founded in 1996, this operation is producing good wines, its Roble being one of the region's better examples of a youngish, oaked wine.

◆ *PradoRey Roble (red):* An aromatic wine with lots of mouthfilling fruit and toasty oak. Recommended and affordable.

◆ *PradoRey Crianza (red):* Well made, fruity and long, but not at the top table of Ribera crianzas.

Reyes, S.L. (☎ 983 873 015) Founded in 1994, this modest-size bodega produces a couple of high quality wines from 99 per cent Tempranillo and 1 per cent Albillo.

◆ *Teófilo Reyes Crianza (red):* This is a well conceived wine, aromatic, flavoursome and mouthfilling, but leave it a while when first released to let it knit together.

◆ *Teófilo Reyes Reserva (red):* A delicious, smooth, confident wine. Recommended.

Riberalta, S.A. (☎ 947 544 101) Founded in 1988, this bodega has recently changed its approach to wine making, introducing new barrels and ideas to produce wines for the 21st century. It should improve over the coming years as things bed down and become more consistent.

♦ *Vega Izán Tinto (red):* A mixed bag. Sometimes powerfully tasty and well made, sometimes too oaky.

♦ *Vega Izán Crianza (red):* As above. Perhaps the barrels need to settle a little.

♦ *Vega Izán Reserva (red):* A well made, flavoursome, structured wine.

Rodero, S.L. (☎ 947 530 046) Founded in 1991, this bodega, which is very much the baby and brainchild of its founder Carmelo Rodero, has quickly garnered a good reputation. Half of its production is exported and it is popular in the United States. The reserva and gran reserva are particularly well thought of, although difficult to lay your hands on.

♦ *Carmelo Rodero Tinto (red):* A tasty, fruity, persistent young Tinta del País.

♦ *Carmelo Rodero Crianza (red):* 95 per cent Tinta del País and 5 per cent Cabernet Sauvignon, this needs time after release to knit together.

♦ *Carmelo Rodero Reserva (red):* Made from 90 per cent Tinta del País and 10 per cent Cabernet Sauvignon, this is a powerful, flavoursome wine with balance and length. Recommended.

♦ *Carmelo Rodero Gran Reserva (red):* Made from the same blend of grapes as the reserva, this expensive wine (around three times the price of the reserva) is fine, smooth and flavoursome with length and structure. Recommended.

Santiago Arroyo, S.L. (☎ 947 532 444) Founded in 1960, a fair time before many Ribera del Duero bodegas, Arroyo makes reasonable, flavoursome wines, although without the depth and complexity that characterise the region's best bottles.

♦ *Viñarroyo Rosado (rosé):* Made from 70 per cent Tempranillo and 30 per cent Albillo, this is eminently drinkable but lacks the young, fruity interest we look for in pink wines.

♦ *Tinto Arroyo Joven (red):* Again drinkable, but a rather uninteresting young Tempranillo.

♦ *Tinto Arroyo Crianza (red):* This is better, with some power and length, although not as good as many of its regional competitors.

♦ *Tinto Arroyo Reserva (red):* A well made wine with flavour and body, but it perhaps lacks the depth and interest required at this price level.

S.A.T. Los Curros (☎ 983 868 097) This operation has been around since 1972 and also makes white wines in D.O. Rueda and red wines in the well known Yllera range outside the Ribera del Duero D.O. (see the entries under **D.O. Rueda** on page 164 and **Selected non-D.O. Bodegas** on page 173). In Ribera del Duero it produces a red crianza and reserva from Tempranillo, which can be very good, although quality varies from year to year (as is often the case in this region).

♦ *Bracamonte Crianza (red):* Lively and flavoursome, but not outstanding.

◆ *Bracamonte Reserva (red):* A well made, smooth, aromatic wine with some complexity.

Santa Eulalia, S.A. (☎ 947 542 054) Founded in 1950, Eulalia's Conde de Siruela range has established a firm reputation for quality and consistency in a region where the latter is sometimes lacking. Its crianza is recommended as a good introduction to Ribera del Duero's wines.

◆ *Conde de Siruela Tinto (red):* A reasonably priced, flavoursome, integrated blend of fruit and oak.

◆ *Conde de Siruela Crianza (red):* This is invariably powerful, flavoursome, integrated and persistent, and at a reasonable price. Recommended.

◆ *Conde de Siruela Reserva (red):* A powerful, mouthfilling wine with lots of flavour. Recommended.

Señorío de Nava, S.A. (☎ 947 550 003) Founded in 1986, this bodega is another of Ribera del Duero's more respected names, operating from revamped premises that used to belong to a co-operative. It grows mainly Tinto Fino, along with small amounts of Cabernet Sauvignon and Merlot from 100 hectares of vineyards. The bodega concentrates on crianza and reserva wines, but also makes rosés and sometimes young reds.

◆ *Señorío de Nava Rosado (rosé):* Made from Tinto Fino, Garnacha and Albillo, this is certainly drinkable but not very zippy.

◆ *Señorío de Nava Tinto (red):* A tasty, aromatic, fruity young red. Good.

◆ *Señorío de Nava Semi-Crianza (red):* Made from 80 per cent Tinto Fino and 20 per cent Cabernet Sauvignon, this is a mouthfilling wine and a decent example of one with limited time on oak (hence the name semi-crianza).

◆ *Señorío de Nava Crianza (red):* A well made, elegant wine, which in good years is recommended, but it can sometimes be too elegant and understated and thus lack interest.

◆ *Señorío de Nava Reserva (red):* A wine with structure, body, flavour and smoothness. Ready for drinking when released and it will also age well for up to ten years.

Tarsus (☎ 947 554 218) Founded as recently as 1998 and owned by the group Bodegas y Bebidas, this operation is producing elegantly labelled, stylish wines, which are more subtle and understated than is the Ribera del Duero norm.

◆ *Tarsus (red):* Made from 98 per cent Tinta del País and 2 per cent Cabernet Sauvignon, this aromatic wine is potent, lively and smooth. Recommended and it is 'different' to the regional standard, feeling as if it has been designed to appeal to the international market.

◆ *Quinta de Tarsus (red):* This is 100 per cent Tinta del País and, as with the Tarsus, enjoys a fine nose. It has lots of flavour and is probably more approachable when young than is the Tarsus. Again, it feels 'different', more subtle than the Ribera average.

Valdubón, S.L. (☎ 947 546 251) Founded in 1997, and owned by the giant Freixenet (see page 230), this bodega makes decent, although as yet unremarkable, wines at prices which are modest by the region's standards.

◆ *Valdubón Tinto (red)*: A tasty young wine with abundant juicy fruit. In some vintages the fruit tends towards the over-mature and jammy.

◆ *Valdubón Roble (red)*: A fruity, mouthfilling wine with light touches of oak.

◆ *Valdubón Crianza (red)*: A good, tasty, medium-bodied wine, suitable for those who find some Riberas overpowering.

Valduero, S.L. (☎ 947 545 459) Founded in 1984, Valduero's wines can be very good, but they can also exhibit over-mature fruit and weak tannins. More consistency is required.

◆ *Valduero Crianza (red)*: When good, this is a decent introduction to the pleasures of Ribera del Duero, but it can be unstructured and unfocused.

◆ *Valduero Reserva (red)*: As above, a mixed bag: sometimes tasty and balanced (although not for long ageing), sometimes mouthfilling but lacking depth and complexity.

◆ *Valduero Gran Reserva (red)*: A tasty, mouthfilling wine with power and flavour, but quite a lot of money for the quality.

Valle de Monzón, S.L. (☎ 947 545 694) Founded in 1993, this operation produces a range of decent, affordable wines, which don't ever quite raise the roof.

◆ *Gromejón Tinto (red)*: A light, fruity, slightly rustic wine for a modest price. A rare Ribera del Duero example of an everyday drinking wine.

◆ *Gromejón Crianza (red)*: An honest, well made, aromatic wine for a competitive price.

◆ *Hoyo de la Vega Crianza (red)*: As above and similarly very drinkable.

◆ *Gromejón Reserva (red)*: An enjoyable, mature wine with good honest fruit and oak. It would not claim to be the region's most sophisticated wine and if it did, it would be sadly misguided.

◆ *Hoyo de la Vega Reserva (red)*: A smoother, more structured version of the above.

Vega Sicilia, S.A. (☎ 983 680 147) Founded in 1864, and hence vastly older than the majority of Ribera del Duero's bodegas, it is no exaggeration to describe the wines of Vega Sicilia as legendary, perhaps even approaching the mythical. Within the Spanish national consciousness, Vega Sicilia sits at the pinnacle of Spain's red wine tree, although within the wine industry, Pingus (also from Ribera del Duero) and L'Ermita (from D.O. Priorato) are now sometimes voted Spain's top reds.

The term Vega Sicilia comes from 'vega', an alluvial valley, while 'Sicilia' is the name of a chapel on the bodega's land. Vega Sicilia's wines are blends of Tinto Fino with the Bordeaux varieties Cabernet Sauvignon, Malbec and Merlot, matured slowly after gentle grape crushing. There are three wines: Vega Sicilia Unico is made in the top years and is matured for seven years in oak and further in bottle, released at a minimum of ten years old; Valbuena is produced annually and released when five years old – it is at its best when Unico is not made, because then all the best fruit goes in to the Valbuena; and third, every now and again, an exceptional wine called Unico Especial is made. See also **Bodegas y Viñedos Alión** (on page 144), Vega Sicilia's other bodega in Ribera del Duero, which makes less expensive wines, also of a very high quality.

Production of Vega Sicilia is limited and top hotels, restaurants and wine merchants are rationed as to the amount of bottles they receive. Around 70 per cent of production is destined for the domestic market, 30 per cent exported, and although securing a bottle can sometimes be difficult, it is eminently worthwhile. The wines are of the highest quality and, even though prices can be very high, you are definitely left with the feeling that you have drunk something memorable; and that, for me, represents good value.

The wines are not reviewed individually since it is most helpful to say that they have all the complexity of aroma, the power and flavour associated with Ribera del Duero, along with added expressiveness, harmony and subtle complexity while also having a refined smoothness which makes them easy to drink.

Viña Mayor (☎ 983 521 011) Founded in 1876, which makes it nearly as old as Vega Sicilia, Mayor produces quite large amounts (by Ribera del Duero standards) of good and very good wine under the Viña Mayor label and also, outside the D.O., the attractive Realeza range of cheaper wines.

● *Viña Mayor Crianza (red)*: This invariably offers the nose, power and flavoursome personality required from Ribera del Duero and is both less expensive and more readily available than some of the region's wines, making it a good introduction to Ribera del Duero.

● *Viña Mayor Reserva (red)*: As above, and this is always enjoyable, although some releases could do with more complexity.

● *Viña Mayor Gran Reserva (red)*: This has a powerful, complex aroma and rounded, confident, delicious flavours. Recommended.

Viña Vilano Sociedad Cooperativa (☎ 947 530 029) Founded in 1957, this co-operative makes some of the region's better value young reds and rosés, while its crianzas and reservas are of good quality and less expensive than the Ribera norm. Unfortunately, they are not produced in large quantities.

● *Viña Vilano Rosado (rosé)*: Made from 90 per cent Tinta Fina and 10 per cent Albillo, this is a fresh, fruity, refreshing, inexpensive rosé. Good.

● *Viña Vilano Tinto (red)*: An aromatic, inexpensive Tinta Fina with lots of fruit. Not representative of Ribera del Duero, but a superior everyday red wine.

● *Viña Vilano Crianza (red)*: A powerfully aromatic wine with attractive toasty flavours and mature fruit and tannins. Recommended and reasonably priced.

◆ *Viña Vilano Reserva (red):* As above, so choose the cheaper crianza.

Viñedos y Bodegas La Cepa Alta, S.L. (☎ 983 681 010) Founded in 1992, this small operation makes modest amounts of good and very good wines from old vines.

◆ *Laveguilla Tinto Roble (red):* This is a blend of 85 per cent Tinta del País, 10 per cent Cabernet Sauvignon, with the balance made up of Malbec and Merlot, and is a well made young wine with lots of characterful fruit.

◆ *Laveguilla Crianza (red):* An aromatic Tinta del País with lots of rounded flavours and personality.

◆ *Laveguilla Reserva (red):* As above, but with more complexity.

Vizcarra-Ramos (☎ 947 540 340) Founded in 1991, this small producer makes an attractive range of good quality red wines:

◆ *Vizcarra Tinto (red):* A tasty, mouthfilling, fruity wine. Good everyday drinking.

◆ *Vizcarra Maceración Carbónica (red):* An aromatic young red with lots of characterful fruit.

◆ *Vizcarra Crianza (red):* Notable for its complexity and length, this is a superior Ribera crianza. Recommended.

Winner Wines, S.A. (☎ 915 019 042) Founded in 1986, this bodega makes good and very good wines from Tinta Fina and Cabernet Sauvignon, and sells them in distinctive, brightly labelled bottles.

◆ *Ibernoble Tinto (red):* An inexpensive, decent young blend of fruit and oak.

◆ *Ibernoble Crianza (red):* An aromatic, powerful blend of fruit and oak. At its best in better regional vintages.

◆ *Ibernoble Reserva (red):* As might be expected with a relatively young bodega, recent releases have been better than earlier ones. This is now a confident, deep, persistent wine.

D.O. Rueda

In Brief: The source of some of Spain's better and best value dry white wines, fresh, flavoursome, cold-fermented and many made from the characterful, nutty Verdejo grape.

Lying to the south-west of Valladolid and close to the north-east tip of Portugal, Rueda has been known for its white wines since the 11th century when vineyards were replanted after The Moors had been ejected from the region. Its traditional specialities were two fortified wines, containing between 15 and 17 per cent alcohol: Dorado Rueda, similar to an amontillado from Jerez, and Pálido Rueda, like a robust (some would say rough) fino sherry. These days, Rueda is known for characterful, dry table wines.

It was demarcated a D.O. in 1980 – for white wines only – and was named after the village of the same name, a local wine making centre. The region owes some of its current success to a famous wine maker from another region: it was one of Rioja's oldest, most respected bodegas – Marqués de Riscal – that kick-started Rueda along the road to modernity in the '70s, by identifying it as a promising location for the production of white wines, having decided that Rioja was not ideal for the enterprise.

Authorised grape varieties are:

- **White:** Palomino Fino, Sauvignon Blanc, Verdejo and Viura.

The characterful Verdejo, whose growth is almost entirely restricted to Rueda, is the dominant variety, accounting for around half of all plantings. Viura and Palomino Fino have just over 20 per cent each, with Sauvignon Blanc – a recent introduction – trailing the others, with only 6 per cent of vineyard hectareage. The trend is to remove Palomino vines and replace them, usually with Sauvignon Blanc and Viura.

Rueda's wines are classified as follows:

- **Rueda:** Wines carrying this title must contain a minimum of 40 per cent Verdejo and/or Sauvignon Blanc, with the balance comprising Viura and/or Palomino. They are invariably light, fresh, everyday wines with character, much of this derived from the Verdejo grape. Their Verdejo bite and flavour is obviously less pronounced than in wines containing a higher percentage of the region's star native grape variety.

  The term 'Rueda Sauvignon' applies to wines made from the distinctive, internationally popular (too popular?) Sauvignon Blanc variety. These wines are of a higher quality than the standard Ruedas, personality-filled, flavoursome expressions of the distinctive Sauvignon Blanc grape (see page 21 for further details of its particulars).

- **Rueda Superior:** Wines labelled thus must contain a minimum of 75 per cent Verdejo. They are Rueda's most characteristic wines: herbily aromatic, unctuous, slightly nutty, with body and a distinctive, attractive bittersweet bite. Verdejo is generally regarded as Spain's second best native white grape variety (Galicia's Albariño is the top dog) and its wines have a laudable price/quality ratio.

- **Rueda Espumoso:** The region's sparkling wines, which are almost as rare as hen's teeth, are made by the 'Traditional Method' (the current authorised term for The Champagne Method) and must contain a minimum of 75 per cent Verdejo. Quality is decent rather than remarkable.

- **Rueda Dorado** or **Dorado Rueda:** The modern version of the region's traditional, flor-growing, fortified wines, made with a minimum of 40 per cent Verdejo and an alcoholic strength of at least 15 per cent. These wines undergo a crianza of at least four years and the term Pálido Rueda is used for wines with a shorter time on oak. Dorado Rueda wines – as the name implies – are a golden colour and have an attractive nutty flavour from their long oxidative stay in oak. They are, however, few and far between and rarely appeal to modern drinkers; only one is listed below.

Rueda's vineyards are concentrated in a modest 6,200 hectares of land (by comparison, Rioja covers 50,000 hectares and even Ribera del Duero has 13,500) with nearly 1,300 vine growers and, as yet, only 27 bodegas. Its popularity and profile are impressive for such a compact area of land and limited number of producers.

Geography, Soil and Climate

Rueda is a flat, sometimes windswept, upland region and an important agricultural area, with its vineyards concentrated on the undulating hills to the south of the River Duero. Its climate is continental with Atlantic influences: winters are cold, summers are short and hot, and the annual precipitation of around 425mm (17in) is concentrated in the spring and autumn. The region's altitude – generally between 600 and 700m (1,968 and 2,296ft) above sea level, rising to 800m (2,624ft) in some areas – means that it enjoys all-important, marked temperature drops on summer evenings, allowing the grapes to recover after the day's heat and maintain their subtleties of aroma and flavour. Rueda's climate and calcareous clay soils produce good quality, low-yield crops of grapes.

Future Development

Rueda has come a long way in less than quarter of a century as a D.O. and is now seen as one of Spain's premier white wines regions, in terms of both quality and value. Its wines are noted for their freshness and characterful flavours, and the younger, everyday wines need only continue in this vein to maintain their popularity.

Rueda has also shown that the Verdejo grape is very suitable for barrel-fermentation, most notably with wines such as the Marqués de Riscal's Reserva Limousin. More examples of this popular style of wine will further enhance Rueda's reputation. As for its Sauvignon Blancs, Rueda is making good, reasonably priced, expressive wines from the grape, but might now look to produce wines with more complexity.

As yet, red and rosé wines are not included under the D.O.. Several of the bodegas make good quality red wines from the Tempranillo grape under the Vino de la Tierra Medina del Campo and in the near future these reds may be included within the Rueda D.O..

Another area that the region might look at is foreign markets. Exports currently account for only some 15 per cent of Rueda's production, with Holland and Germany important customers. This percentage should increase as production rises and more foreigners become aware of Verdejo's charms and Rueda's competitive prices.

Selected Bodegas

Agrícola Castellana Sociedad Cooperativa Limitada (☎ 983 816 320) Founded in 1935, this large, well equipped operation makes traditional fortified wines and fresh young whites. Quality is good and prices are competitive. It also make red wines – see page 171

- *Veliterra (white):* This blend of 40 per cent Verdejo and 60 per cent Viura is a decent, tasty, balanced, everyday Rueda wine.

- *Cuatro Rayas (white):* Made 100 per cent from Verdejo this offers lots of flavour and attractive Verdejo bittersweet bite for a competitive price. Recommended.

◆ *Pámpano Semiseco (white):* Made from 40 per cent Verdejo and 60 per cent Viura, this wine is aromatic and flavoursome, with both refreshing bite and sweetness. Well made and recommended for those who like sweetish white wines.

◆ *Azumbre (white):* 75 per cent Verdejo and 25 per cent Sauvignon Blanc, this is quite a classy, unctuous wine with good fruity character. Good and reasonably priced.

◆ *61 Solera (Rueda Dorado):* A reasonably priced introduction to the style, this golden wine offers interesting nutty touches and oaky character.

Álvarez y Díez, S.A. (☎ 983 850 136) Founded in 1941, this well respected firm employs modern facilities and production methods to make wines that are noted for their powerful aromas and more complex than some of Rueda's other offerings.

◆ *Escriño (white):* A blend of 40 per cent Verdejo and 60 per cent Viura, this inexpensive wine has lots of up-front, gutsy Rueda flavours and does not pretend to be anything more than a straightforward, tasty, everyday wine, ever so slightly rough around the edges.

◆ *Mantel Blanco Rueda Superior (white):* This blend of 75 per cent Verdejo and 25 per cent Viura has generous tropical fruit on the nose and offers a flavoursome, soundly constructed palate with signature bittersweet bite. A fair introduction to the region's wines. Recommended.

◆ *Mantel Blanco Sauvignon Blanc (white):* This has an exotic, fruit-salad nose and the palate is mouthfilling, fruitily flavoursome and refined at the same time. A superior Rueda Sauvignon for not much money.

Ángel Lorenzo Cachazo (☎ 983 822 012) Founded in 1988, this modest bodega makes a small range of good and very good wines, with the second two reviewed showing that some thought and care has gone into their manufacture.

◆ *Lorenzo Cachazo (white):* This Rueda is a straightforward, fresh, tasty, everyday wine.

◆ *Martivilli Rueda Superior (white):* Full of Verdejo character, this wine is well made and balanced with good acidity and bitter bite.

◆ *Martivilli Sauvignon Blanc (white):* The nose tends to be understated, but this is a good Sauvignon Blanc, flavoursome, long, refreshing and mouthfilling.

Antaño (☎ 983 868 533) Founded in 1989, this bodega makes a small range of Rueda's speciality: good, reasonably priced, characterful white wines. It also produces red wines – see page 172.

◆ *Viña Mocén (white):* 40 per cent Verdejo and 60 per cent Viura, this inexpensive wine is a light, fruity, everyday white.

◆ *Viña Mocén Rueda Superior (white):* A 100 per cent Verdejo, this has lots of flavour, balance, length and some complexity. Recommended.

♦ *Viña Mocén Sauvignon Blanc (white):* This wine's nose is undistinguished, but on the palate it is mouthfilling, balanced and notably fruity.

Belondrade y Lurton, S.L. (☎ 983 850 125) Founded in 1994, this small bodega, making only around 25,000 bottles per annum, is noted for the following wine, one of Rueda's most expensive and distinguished:

♦ *Belondrade y Lurton Fermentado en Barrica (white):* This wine demonstrates how well the Verdejo grape takes to barrel fermentation. It is delicious, mouthfilling and toasty, with fruit and oak working in harmony. Recommended.

Bodega de Crianza de Castilla la Vieja, S.A. (☎ 983 868 116) Founded in 1976, this is one of Rueda's most respected operations. It is innovative, having introduced barrel-fermented wines to the region and is experimenting with Chardonnay, and some of its wines are able to compete with the best in Spain. The bodega's reputation has travelled, with around 40 per cent of its output exported. Antonio Sanz is the head of the operation and he also has his own bodega – see **Vinos Sanz** on page 165.

♦ *Colagon (white):* This blend of 50 per cent Verdejo and 50 per cent Viura is the bodega's 'house' white – a fresh, fruity, inexpensive, everyday wine.

♦ *Palacio de Bornos Rueda Superior (white):* Made from 90 per cent Verdejo and 10 per cent Viura, this aromatic wine has lots of mouthfilling flavour and some complexity for a competitive price. Good.

♦ *Bornos Sauvignon Blanc (white):* Notably aromatic, this is usually fresh and fruitily flavoursome, although it can be a bit monotonous. Not the bodega's best, although this is primarily a reflection of the fact that its other wines are so strong.

♦ *Palacio de Bornos Verdejo Fermentado en Barrica (white):* A very good, reasonably priced wine, with lots of long, mouthfilling flavours and some complexity. Recommended.

♦ *Palacio de Bornos Vendimia Seleccionada (white):* This 100 per cent Verdejo is the bodega's flagship wine, much more expensive than its others and not just one of Rueda's but one of Spain's best whites. It is an aromatic, complex fruity/toasty wine with length, structure and personality. Highly recommended.

Castelo de Medina, S.A. (☎ 983 831 932) Founded in 1995, this bodega makes a range of decent, approachable, unashamedly commercial wines, including:

♦ *Real Castelo (white):* A blend of 75 per cent Verdejo, 15 per cent Viura and 10 per cent Sauvignon Blanc, this inexpensive wine is fresh, characterful and straightforward, without aspirations to greatness.

♦ *Castelo de Medina (white):* 100 per cent Verdejo, this is fresh, tasty, everyday wine for a modest price.

♦ *Castelo de Medina Sauvignon (white):* A tasty, fruity, Sauvignon, well made in a crowd-pleasing sort of way. That is not an insult.

◆ *Castelo Noble Fermentado en Barrica (white):* 80 per cent Verdejo and 20 per cent Sauvignon Blanc, this is a reasonably priced, decent, barrel-fermented wine with lots of honest character.

Cerrosol, S.A. (☎ 921 596 002) Founded in 1985, this bodega produces the well known, rightly popular Doña Beatriz range. It also makes red wines – see page 172.

◆ *Doña Beatriz Rueda Superior (white):* A worthy 100 per cent Verdejo wine with lots of fruity flavour and interest. Good.

◆ *Doña Beatriz Sauvignon (white):* A competitively priced introduction to Rueda Sauvignon Blanc, aromatic, characterfully fruity, unctuous and long. Recommended.

◆ *Doña Beatriz Fermentado en Barrica (white):* This can be a very good wine with lots of oak and fruit flavours and some class, but in some years it is rather unbalanced.

Cuevas de Castilla, S.A. (☎ 983 868 336) Founded in 1986, this bodega makes good quality, reasonably priced wines, including:

◆ *Con Class (white):* I am not sure whether to smile with or laugh at this name (probably the latter), but does it have class? In a way, yes, because this blend of 50 per cent Verdejo and 50 per cent Viura is a superior, straightforward, everyday wine with characterful flavours.

◆ *Palacio de Menade Rueda Superior (white):* Made from 90 per cent Verdejo, 8 per cent Viura and 2 per cent Sauvignon Blanc, this is a satisfying, mouthfilling wine with Verdejo's distinctive bittersweet tang.

◆ *Palacio de Menade Sauvignon Blanc (white):* This has a tropical fruit nose, bittersweet bite and balance, but the bodega's Verdejo-based wines are better.

◆ *Palacio de Menade Verdejo Fermentado en Barrica (white):* A good rather than outstanding wine, with flavour, length and hints of complexity.

Dos Victorias, C.B. (☎ 983 590 912) Founded only in 1998, this tiny, although growing, operation makes small quantities of very good wine:

◆ *José Pariente (white):* Made from 100 per cent Verdejo, this is notably aromatic, very tasty, mouthfilling and characterful, with length and style. Highly recommended.

◆ *Elias Mora Crianza (red):* As this 100 per cent Tinto de Toro is a red wine, it is not covered by the D.O., but its quality shows what the region is capable of. Powerfully aromatic, it is a full, complex blend of fruit and oak flavours with length, but perhaps overpriced for a red from a region not associated with them.

Félix Lorenzo Cachazo, S.L. (☎ 983 822 008) Founded in 1945, this bodega makes decent, reasonably priced wines rather than outstanding ones, including:

◆ *Gran Cardiel (white):* A blend of 50 per cent Verdejo and 50 per cent Viura, this is a superior, mouthfilling, everyday wine with tasty, fruity personality.

◆ *Gran Cardiel Rueda Superior (white):* A reasonably priced, fresh wine with good fruit flavours.

◆ *Carrasviñas Rueda Superior (white):* A powerful Verdejo wine with lots of flavour for a modest price. Good.

Félix Sanz (☎ 983 868 336) Founded in 1996, this bodega makes a small range of commercial, inexpensive, straightforward but decent wines:

◆ *Viña Cimbrón (white):* A lightish, fruity wine with hints of bitter bite. Good value.

◆ *Viña Cimbrón Rueda Superior (white):* A better, fuller version of the above with some complex fruit flavours. Good.

◆ *Viña Cimbrón Sauvignon (white):* This varies in quality from quite delicate and fruity to full and mouthfilling, presumably depending on the ripeness of the fruit and the time of picking. To date, the Verdejo wines are more reliable.

García y Arévalo, S.L. (☎ 983 832 914) Founded in 1991, this is another Rueda producer of decent, inexpensive, everyday wines. It also makes red wines under the name Garciarévalo – see page 172

◆ *Casamaro (white):* A blend of 60 per cent Verdejo and 40 per cent Viura, this is a light, easy-to-drink wine, although it should have more personality considering the amount of Verdejo that it contains.

◆ *Tres Olmos Rueda Superior (white):* This notably inexpensive 100 per cent Verdejo is well made and reasonably tasty.

Garcigrande, S.A. (☎ 983 868 561) Founded in 1989, this small operation makes the Rueda staple of straightforward, decent wines. It also produces reds – see page 172

◆ *Señorío de Garcigrande (white):* A competent, light, fruity wine.

◆ *Señorío de Garcigrande Rueda Superior (white):* This is rather more characterful than the above (as it should be) with lots of refreshing flavour. Good.

◆ *Señorío de Garcigrande Sauvignon (white):* A decent Rueda Sauvignon with a typical tropical fruit nose and a fruity, bittersweet palate.

Grandes Bodegas, S.A. (☎ 947 542 166) Founded in 1985, this bodega makes its red wines in Ribera del Duero (see page 148) and a small range of well made, straightforward whites in Rueda:

◆ *Viña de Mercado (white):* A blend of 50 per cent Verdejo and 50 per cent Viura, this is a decent mouthful of characterful fruit.

◆ *Viña de Mercado Rueda Superior (white):* Made from 85 per cent Verdejo and 15 per cent Viura, this is more aromatic, flavoursome and bittersweet than the above.

Hermanos del Villar, S.L. (☎ 983 868 904) Founded in 1995, this is another producer of inexpensive, decent white wines:

◆ *Oro de Castilla Rueda Superior (white)*: Made 100 per cent from Verdejo, this is fruity and refreshing rather than startlingly characterful.

◆ *Oro de Castilla Sauvignon Blanc (white)*: As above.

Hijos de Alberto Gutiérrez, S.A. (☎ 983 559 195) Founded in 1949, and thus older than many of Rueda's bodegas, this operation makes quite large quantities of reasonable wines but they sometimes lack character and are trailing the regional average standard. The Sauvignon is one of its more reliable bottles. The bodega also makes red wines – see page 172.

◆ *Viña Cascalera Sauvignon (white)*: A fair expression of Sauvignon tropical fruit, but sometimes lacks punch.

Javier Sanz (☎ 983 816 639) Founded in 1990, this bodega makes respectable wines, although they are less structured and confident than some. It also makes red wines – see page 172

◆ *Rey Santo (white)*: Made from 60 per cent Verdejo and 40 per cent Viura, this is rather good for the low price, with refreshing almondy bite.

◆ *Villa Narcisa Rueda Superior (white)*: This 100 per cent Verdejo is a more powerful version of the above but perhaps lacks complexity.

◆ *Villa Narcisa Sauvignon (white)*: Tasty and fruity, but lacks the interest of other Rueda Sauvignons at this price.

S.A.T. Los Curros (☎ 983 868 097) Founded in 1972, this bodega makes red wines in Ribera del Duero (see page 153) and a non-D.O. region of Castilla-León (see page 173) as well as the following whites in Rueda.

◆ *Tierra Buena (white)*: This blend of 50 per cent Verdejo and 50 per cent Viura is the bodega's cheapest wine and is often characterful and tasty, although it can lack subtlety.

◆ *Viña Cantosán Varietal Verdejo (white)*: Inexpensive and fruity but lacking the character and punch we expect from Verdejo.

◆ *Viña Cantosán Sauvignon Blanc (white)*: A characterful wine and a fair expression of Sauvignon's perfumes and fruit flavours. Good.

Vega de la Reina (☎ 983 868 089) Founded in 1961, this bodega has long been known for red wines (which of course are not included under the Rueda D.O. – see page 173) and it makes whites under the Rueda D.O.. Its wines are aggressively marketed in Spain and found on many supermarket shelves.

◆ *Vega de la Reina Rueda (white)*: A well made, characterful 100 per cent Verdejo for a low price with flavour and bitter bite. Good.

● *Vega de la Reina Sauvignon Blanc (white):* A mouthfilling, characterful Sauvignon, perhaps a touch expensive.

Vinos Blancos de Castilla (☎ 983 868 083) Founded in 1972 – and the operation that kick-started widespread interest in D.O. Rueda – the Marqués de Riscal's white wines are among the region's best and best known (see page 331 for its excellent red wines).

● *Marqués de Riscal Rueda Superior (white):* Made from 85 per cent Verdejo and 15 per cent Viura this elegantly presented wine is aromatic, tasty, elegant, unctuous and long. Recommended and one of the region's better known wines.

● *Marqués de Riscal Sauvignon (white):* A superior Rueda Sauvignon with lots of complex flavours, clean elegance and balance. Often voted the region's best from the grape. A milestone Rueda wine.

● *Marqués de Riscal Reserva Limousin (white):* This barrel-fermented Verdejo is one of Rueda's most characterful wines and has done much to spread the word about how good oaked Verdejo can be. It offers an inviting creamy, oaky nose and is powerful, mouthfilling, notably flavoursome, complex and long. One of Spain's most enticing whites in this price band and highly recommended.

Vinos Sanz (☎ 983 868 100) Founded in 1870, this Rueda family 'dynasty' makes its own wines under this name, but is also involved in making wines for other Rueda operations – see **Bodega de Crianza de Castilla la Vieja** on page 161. Vinos Sanz's range is decent and reasonably priced, including:

● *Sanz Rueda (white):* A light, fruity, unpretentious wine.

● *Sanz Rueda Superior (white):* A straightforward, quite characterful wine.

● *Sanz Sauvignon Blanc (white):* This is a decent, tasty Sauvignon, without setting the world on fire.

Viñedos de Nieva, S.L. (☎ 921 594 628) Founded in 1989, this bodega has shown itself capable of making characterful, reasonably priced wines, but consistency can be a problem and the fruit is sometimes overripe.

● *Blanco Nieva Rueda Superior (white):* When on form this is a tasty, mouthfilling wine with good Verdejo character.

● *Los Navales Rueda Superior (white):* As above.

● *Blanco Nieva Sauvignon Blanc (white):* On form this has attractive Sauvignon tropical fruit, but in difficult years it can be overcooked. Inexpensive.

D.O. Toro

In Brief: A fast developing red wine region, offering good value and characterful quality for those who enjoy full-bodied wines.

Lying just to the north-west of Rueda, Toro is close to Portugal's north-east border. It was Castilla-León's best known wine region in Medieval times, noted for its dark, powerful reds, which were popular in the city of Salamanca, notably among denizens of the University. But times and tastes change, and until recently its wines were seen as too dense and alcoholic (sometimes up to 16 per cent).

Toro's potential was rediscovered in the '80s and it was designated a D.O. in 1987. Progress has been steady rather than dramatic, with equipment and methods improved over time. Wine makers have looked to pick fruit earlier, reduce alcohol levels and add structure and balance to red wines based around the Tinta de Toro grape, which is the local form of Tempranillo. Toro's wines are still robust and strong, but elegance and style have been added. Some of the credit for the region's march towards success must be given to Miguel Fariña. The quality of his wines has drawn attention and other wine makers to Toro, as indeed has the difficulty and expense of finding available land in nearby Ribera del Duero.

Authorised grape varieties are:

- **White:** Malvasía and Verdejo.

- **Black:** Garnacha and Tinta de Toro.

Toro is not renowned for its whites, but they are of a decent, everyday standard, noted for bittersweet bite. The region's rosés are also often overlooked, slightly unfairly as they can be tasty and full-bodied. But it is red wines that Toro is renowned for and they are marked by their alcoholic strength (invariably 13.5 to 14 per cent), mature fruit (sometimes verging on the over-mature), power and bite. Toro currently has a modest hectareage of vineyards – around 3,400 – 850 grape growers and 10 bodegas.

Geography, Soil and Climate

Toro is a relatively flat region and lies between 600 and 750m (1,968 and 2,460ft) above sea level, making it lower and slightly hotter than Ribera del Duero. The climate is extreme continental – sometimes moderated by the Atlantic's maritime influence – with severe winters, prolonged frosts, short summers and large diurnal temperature ranges, which help to retain grape acidity. This is one of the driest parts of Spain with rainfall of sometimes only 300mm (12in) per year, sometimes rising to 400. The conditions explain Toro's low grape yields and the concentrated flavours of its wines.

Future Development

Toro's style of red wine – robust and full-bodied – is popular, as is seen by the success of other Spanish regions producing similar types of wine, e.g. Jumilla. Its profile is increasing steadily, internationally as well as in Spain, impressive for a region with only ten bodegas. This success looks set to continue because notable wine makers from nearby Rueda and Ribera del Duero are buying land and setting up shop in Toro, most notably Vega Sicilia, Pesquera, Antonio Sanz and Lurton. There are also moves to make light, easy drinking wines to offer an alternative to the traditional style.

Selected Bodegas

Covitoro (☎ 980 690 347) Founded in 1974, and formerly known as Cooperativa Vino de Toro, this operation concentrates on good quality, inexpensive wines, with its red reserva showing a lot of personality and interest for a competitive price.

◆ *Cermeño Blanco (white):* Made from Malvasía, this inexpensive wine has attractive fruit and balance. A good, everyday white.

◆ *Cermeño Rosado (rosé):* Made from 70 per cent Tinta de Toro and 30 per cent Malvasía, this is decent pink wine, aromatic, fruity and refreshing for a modest amount of money.

◆ *Cermeño Tinto (red):* A powerful, inexpensive young red with bite and robust character.

◆ *Gran Cermeño Crianza (red):* A powerful, aromatic wine with lots of mature fruit and oak flavours. Good and competitively priced.

◆ *Marqués de la Villa Reserva (red):* This has concentrated character, flavour and mature tannins. Recommended and very good with robust meat dishes.

Fariña, S.L. (☎ 980 577 673) Founded in 1942, and one of the region's driving forces, this family-owned bodega makes Toro's best known and some of its better wines, although other bodegas are now pushing it hard. The firm is run by Bordeaux-trained Manuel Fariña, one of Toro D.O.'s founders and the mover behind the bodega graduating from bulk to quality wine. He grows Tinta de Toro, Cabernet Sauvignon, Verdejo and Malvasía and has plans to extend his current 60 hectares of vines, such is the demand for his spicy, fruity wines. The following are still regarded as benchmarks for Toro:

◆ *Colegiata Blanco (white):* An attractive, inexpensive young white with good bitter bite.

◆ *Colegiata Rosado (rosé):* Made from 50 per cent Garnacha and 50 per cent Tinta de Toro, this reasonably priced wine has lots of fruity flavour. Good.

◆ *Colegiata Tinto (red):* A characterful, competitively priced young red with lively fruit and tannins.

◆ *Primero (red):* This is a notably fruity, powerful wine with confident tannins and lots of flavour. It has regularly been voted one of Spain's best young red wines.

◆ *Gran Colegiata Crianza (red):* A well made, tasty blend of spicy, mature fruit and oak. Good.

◆ *Gran Colegiata Reserva (red):* Sometimes described as a Spanish Châteauneuf-du-Pape because of its spicy character (although the comparison is rather stretched), this wine has helped to spread the message of Toro wines to a widening audience. It offers a spicy nose of mature fruit and oak and has a rounded, powerful, tasty palate with well balanced and integrated mature fruit and oak. Although the early years of the 21st century find other Toro producers making wines of at least this quality – and some are better, with more complexity – it still remains essential drinking for those exploring the wines of Toro.

Francisco Casas, S.A. (☎ 918 110 207) Founded in 1965, and with another operation in D.O. Vinos de Madrid (see page 126), Casas is making wines of real quality at notably competitive prices, being exactly the sort of bodega that has improved Toro's reputation and profile.

◆ *Camparrón (red):* This inexpensive young wine offers good value with lots of powerful fruit flavours and smooth tannins. Characterful and very drinkable.

◆ *Camparrón Crianza (red):* This has an attractive nose of mature fruit and toasty oak and a palate with lots of power and character. It can be fairly tannic when first released and should not be drunk too young. Recommended.

Frutos Villar, S.L. (☎ 980 690 795) Founded in 1920, and also an important bodega in D.O. Cigales (see page 137), Villar's Muruve range is one of Toro's best and will appeal to those who like powerful, robust red wines. It includes:

◆ *Muruve Joven (red):* A powerful, aromatic blend of Tinta de Toro and oak for a competitive price, this is indicative of how good younger Toro reds can be.

◆ *Muruve Crianza (red):* A superior crianza wine, powerful, characterful and smooth. One of Toro's best and recommended.

◆ *Gran Muruve Reserva (red):* This is a deep, balanced wine with generous fruit and oak flavours and confident tannins. A lot of wine for your money and recommended.

Toresanas, S.L. (☎ 983 868 336) Founded in its current incarnation only in 1997, this small bodega is growing in size; until recently it had only one wine on the market. It is aiming for quality and over the coming years the wines should challenge the likes of Fariña and Frutos Villar at the Toro top table.

◆ *Amant (red):* One of the region's best young wines, aromatic, powerful and full of complex fruit flavours and well judged tannins. Recommended.

◆ *Amant Novillo Maceración Carbónica (red):* This offers a powerful mouthful of mature fruit, but is not quite as good as the above.

◆ *Puerta Adalia Crianza (red):* This excellent crianza has a complex nose and flavours of mature fruit and toasty oak, and length. Very good.

Vega Saúco, S.L. (☎ 980 698 294) Founded in 1991, this operation only started to bottle wines in 1997 and has quickly established a reputation as one of the region's best producers, making traditional-style, full-bodied wines, popular not just in Spain – over 60 per cent of production is exported.

◆ *Vega Saúco Tinto de Toro (red):* This is one of Toro's best young reds, a powerful, aromatic blend of mature fruit and oak, with complexity and length. Recommended.

- *El Beybi de Vega Saúco (red):* A strange name and a 'lively' label do not hide this wine's exuberant qualities: it is a concentrated, complex mouthful of up-front fruit with organic touches. A well made, original, well regarded wine. Recommended.

- *Vega Saúco Crianza (red):* This wine has a powerful nose with some complexity and a mouthfilling palate with generous fruit and oak flavours and lively tannins. Recommended – pour into the glass at least half an hour before drinking.

- *Vega Saúco Reserva (red):* This is one of Toro's better reservas, powerful, smooth and soundly constructed. Recommended for robust meat dishes.

Viña Bajoz (☎ 980 698 023) Founded in 1962, this large operation is one of Toro's best and its top wines are some of the region's most expensive.

- *Moralinos (red):* An inexpensive, tasty, everyday young wine.

- *Viña Bajoz (red):* A reasonably priced, mouthfilling young red, powerfully fruity and mouthfilling. Good.

- *Viña Pedrera (red):* As above, perhaps slightly better.

- *Viña Bajoz Crianza (red):* One of the region's most characterful crianzas, with lots of toasty oak, mature fruit, length and confident, lively tannins. Good.

- *Viña Bajoz Reserva (red):* An integrated wine with similar qualities to the crianza. Choose the crianza first as this is rather more expensive and its price has risen over the last year or two.

- *Gran Bajoz (red):* This is the bodega's flagship wine and is priced accordingly, being one of the region's most expensive bottles by some distance. It offers lots of toasty oak and mature fruit on the nose, and is a tasty, mouthfilling wine with good length, but the price concerns me. It is perhaps too early in Toro's development to carry such price tags and the wine probably needs more complexity to justify it. I recommend that you try the crianza and reserva, and if you really like them, consider splashing out on this wine.

Selected non-D.O. Bodegas

As is the case in Castilla-La Mancha, some of the wine makers who operate outside the D.O. umbrella are of particular significance and renown in Castilla-León.

Abadía Retuerta, S.A. (☎ 983 680 314) Wine has been made in the environs of this bodega for many centuries, with the current operation dating from 1996. It has quickly established a reputation as one of Spain's most exciting, ambitious new producers, with just over 200 hectares of its own vineyards growing some 60 per cent Tempranillo, 20 per cent Cabernet Sauvignon and smaller amounts of Merlot and other varieties. The renowned French wine maker Pascal Delbeck is in charge of production, making wines different from those of nearby Ribera del Duero which he hopes will compete with some of the greats of the Bordeaux region of Médoc, including:

- *Abadía Retuerta Primicia (red):* This blend of 60 per cent Tempranillo, 20 per cent Cabernet Sauvignon and 20 per cent Merlot is a lively, fruity wine with lots of flavour. It is the logical starting point for investigating this bodega's wines, being their 'house' bottle.

- *Abadía Retuerta Rivola Crianza (red):* Made from 60 per cent Tempranillo and 40 per cent Cabernet Sauvignon, this aromatic wine has fruit flavours which contrast well with the oak and earthy touches. A good wine, although the (sometimes much more expensive) reservas are what excite most drinkers.

- *Abadía Retuerta Reserva (red):* Made from 65 per cent Tempranillo, 30 per cent Cabernet Sauvignon and 5 per cent Merlot, this affordable wine is the starting point for the bodega's top wines. It has an enticing, quite complex nose and a rounded, full-bodied palate of lively fruit, oak and earth, working harmoniously. Very good.

- *Abadía Retuerta Cuvee El Campanero Reserva (red):* Made 100 per cent from Tempranillo, this expensive wine is an excellent expression of the grape, rounded, flavoursome and engaging.

- *Abadía Retuerta El Palomar Reserva (red):* A blend of 50 per cent Cabernet Sauvignon and 50 per cent Tempranillo, this is a very flavoursome, powerful yet elegant wine with the grapes working well together and with the oak. Certain commentators have suggested that it could sometimes do with more complexity, but it is very engaging.

Alta Pavina (☎ 983 681 521) Founded in 1988, this small operation makes a modest range of wines from Pinot Noir, Cabernet Sauvignon and Tempranillo. Quality varies from year to year (most notably with the sometimes difficult to grow and vinify Pinot Noir) but this is a bodega in search of quality and its wines are worth investigating.

- *Alta Pavina Tinto Fino (red):* A blend of 70 per cent Tempranillo and 30 per cent Pinot Noir, this spends 18 months in American oak and 14 in bottle. It has quite a complex nose and palate with fruit, vanilla and rustic hints of Pinot Noir. Characterful and a bit different.

- *Alta Pavina Pinot Noir (red):* The weakest, least consistent wine, this can be spicy and characterful with animal overtones, or it can be thin and rather bland.

- *Alta Pavina Cabernet Sauvignon (red):* This medium-bodied wine spends 22 months in American oak and a further 14 in bottle, and has a nose with spicy vanilla and hints of leather. The palate has rounded flavours of the same, length and its tannins are quite pronounced when it is first released. Good.

Mauro, S.A. (☎ 983 521 439) Founded in 1980, Mauro is probably the most famous and lauded of the 'nearly but non-Ribera del Duero' producers, its reputation as strong as some of that region's most respected outfits. Mauro's general manager is Mariano García, who was technical director at Vega Sicilia until 1998. He has been involved with Mauro since its inception; indeed 'Mauro' was his father's name. The wines are designed to be full-bodied, elegant, rich expressions of fruit and native soil, and include:

● *Mauro Crianza (red):* 90 per cent Tempranillo and 10 per cent other varieties, this is a balanced, full-bodied wine with lots of integrated flavours, the fruit in no way emasculated by the oak. Very good and the most affordable bottle.

● *Mauro Vendimia Seleccionada (red):* Mainly Tempranillo, with small amounts of other varieties, this expensive wine has scored very highly at tastings with its notably full, complex, engaging palate of mature fruit and oak. Regarded by some as one of Castilla-León's – and possibly Spain's – very best wines.

Palacio de Arganza, S.A. (☎ 987 540 322) Founded in 1974, this large operation makes a wide range of popular, reasonably priced, decent quality wines, found extensively in Spanish supermarkets and on Spanish restaurant wine lists.

● *Palacio de Arganza Blanco Seco (white):* A simple, fresh, everyday, dry white wine.

● *Palacio de Arganza Blanco Semi-Seco (white):* Straightforward, fruity and sweet.

● *Palacio de Arganza Rosado (rosé):* Not the bodega's finest hour, this tends to lack fruity freshness.

● *Palacio de Arganza Tinto (red):* The bodega's most famous product, this is good value, offering lots of smooth, medium-bodied flavours of fruit and oak. Good, well made, honest wine.

Vinos de León – VILE, S.A. (☎ 987 209 712) Founded in 1966, this large, modern concern makes drinkable, everyday white, rosé and red wines, as well as other reds with more interest (see below). Its rather unfortunate (to English-speaking ears) name VILE has not stopped it from exporting at least 10 per cent of its wines, which is increasing.

● *Palacio de los Guzmanes (red):* This blend of 50 per cent Prieto Picudo, 30 per cent Tempranillo and 20 per cent Mencía (unusual in itself) is lightish, inexpensive, tasty and offers decent fruit and earthy flavours. A bit different and rather appealing.

● *Don Suero Crianza (red):* Made 100 per cent from Prieto Picudo, this attractive wine is rounded, toasty and fruity, although perhaps a touch expensive for its region.

The following wines are made under the Vinos de la Tierra Medina del Campo, which may soon be included under D.O. Rueda – see page 159.

Agrícola Castellana Sociedad Cooperativa (☎ 983 816 320) See page 159 for details and the bodega's white wines.

● *Vacceos Rosado (rosé):* Made from 50 per cent Tempranillo and 50 per cent Verdejo, this is a light, inexpensive, drinkable pink wine.

● *Vacceos Tinto (red):* 100 per cent Tempranillo, this is a decent, fruity, young wine for a modest price.

● *Vacceos Crianza (red):* A competent, tasty, straightforward blend of Tempranillo and oak, this is an everyday crianza at a low price.

Antaño, S.A. (☎ 983 868 533) See page 160 for details and the bodega's white wines.

◆ *Vega Bravía Rosado (rosé):* A blend of 50 per cent Cabernet Sauvignon and 50 per cent Tempranillo, in some years this can be full and tasty (as you would expect from the grapes) while in others it can be rather heavy, as you sometimes find with Cabernet rosés.

◆ *Vega Bravía Tinto (red):* A decent, tasty, young Tempranillo, offering fair everyday drinking.

◆ *Viña Cobranza Crianza (red):* This reasonably priced blend of 60 per cent Tempranillo and 40 per cent Cabernet Sauvignon has quite a complex nose and a palate with concentrated, mouthfilling flavours of fruit and oak. Good.

Cerrosol, S.A. (☎ 921 596 002) See page 162 for details and the bodega's white wines.

◆ *La Rivera de Castilla Crianza (red):* A decent Tempranillo crianza with a nose of spice and oak and a palate with rounded, structured flavours and length. Recommended.

Garciarévalo, S.L. (☎ 983 832 672) See **García y Arévalo** on page 163 for details and the bodega's white wines.

◆ *Latorrevieja Tinto (red):* A smooth, tasty, young wine.

◆ *Latorrevieja Crianza (red):* A tasty, characterful wine with a fair dose of oak.

Garcigrande, S.A. (☎ 983 868 561) See page 163 for details and the bodega's white wines.

◆ *Cúspide (rosé):* This is sometimes fresh, fruity and drinkable, sometimes rather overcooked.

◆ *Viña Torio (red):* A light, fruity red, but it can suffer in the same way as the rosé.

◆ *Viña Torio Crianza (red):* The producer's best red, this is a well made, tasty, fruity/toasty wine. Good.

Hijos de Alberto Gutiérrez (☎ 983 559 107) See page 164 for details and the bodega's white wines.

◆ *Valdemoya Joven (red):* A tasty, reasonably priced young Tempranillo. Good.

◆ *Valdemoya Crianza (red):* Made from 80 per cent Tempranillo and 20 per cent Cabernet Sauvignon, this is a straightforward, slightly earthy blend of fruit and oak.

Javier Sanz (☎ 983 816 639) See page 164 for details and the bodega's white wines.

◆ *Orden Tercera (rosé):* A good, fruity, flavoursome pink Tempranillo.

◆ *Nanclares (red):* An inexpensive, aromatic wine with attractive fruit and oak flavours. Good.

◆ *Nanclares Crianza (red):* A decent, straightforward Tempranillo crianza, powerful, fruity and smoothly tannic.

S.A.T. Los Curros (☎ 983 868 097) See pages 153 and 164 for details and this bodega's other red and white wines, respectively.

◆ *Yllera Crianza (red):* A rich, tasty, oaky Tempranillo with some bite.

◆ *Yllera Reserva (red):* This is a smooth and eminently drinkable Tempranillo, but perhaps a little oaky and lacking complexity for the price.

◆ *Yllera Gran Reserva (red):* This is of decent quality, with mature fruit and oak, but the price is too high for what's on offer.

Vega de la Reina, S.A. (☎ 983 868 089) See page 164 for details and this bodega's white wines. It also makes a fair range of reds, including:

◆ *Vega de la Reina Crianza (red):* A smooth, commercial, quite elegant wine with integrated fruit and oak.

Vicente Sanz (☎ 983 551 197) Founded in 1992, this small operation makes white wines in Rueda and the following red in this region:

◆ *Cañada Real (red):* Made from 85 to 90 per cent Tempranillo and 10 to 15 per cent Cabernet Sauvignon, this is a competent young red with straightforward fruit flavours.

Catalan wine makers are renowned for their use of modern technology

9.

CATALONIA

Catalonia is one of Spain's most successful and innovative regions, both culturally and commercially. Its vibrant wine industry reflects this, with numerous creative wine makers using the best of local and international grapes, ideas and expertise. The last 30 years of the 20th century saw Catalonia become one of the most technologically advanced Spanish wine regions, although production in the area dates back thousands of years.

Phoenicians, Greeks and Carthaginians all practised wine making in Catalonia, but their presence in the region was scattered and fitful, and serious vine cultivation did not begin until the Romans arrived. Progress was rapid under the new rulers, indeed too rapid, because by the 1st century of the current era the success of wine makers in the Roman provinces, especially Gaul (in modern France) and the north-east of Hispania (in modern Spain) was having a negative effect on growers in what is now Italy. As a consequence, the protectionist Romans imposed restrictions on the planting of new vines in Catalonia and France.

When Rome's influence waned, so did organised wine production, and centuries of barbarian invasions did nothing to advance Catalonia's vinous development. The period under the Moors was similarly unproductive, but after the reconquest, the church encouraged wine making, although the emphasis was heavily on quantity rather than quality. By the 17th century, Britain, Russia and America were becoming important export markets for the resurgent Catalan wine industry and as was the case in the Balearics, Catalonia took the opportunity to export a lot of wine to France in the later 19th century after that country's vines were devastated by the phylloxera louse.

After the louse ravaged Catalonia, vineyards were repopulated with vines grafted onto phylloxera-resistant American rootstocks and the industry began to recover. Unfortunately, this process was decisively halted by one of the worst periods of Spanish history: the Civil War of 1936 to 1939. Many vineyards and bodegas were damaged or destroyed by the fighting, and this terrible strife was followed by the Second World War. Although Spain was not directly involved in that conflict, it had a calamitous effect on the world's economy, including the wine industry; Catalonia's took time to recover. Indeed, it was not until the '70s and '80s that the region began to fulfil its potential to become one of Spain's most prominent and innovative wine regions. Technology played its part, with stainless steel cold fermentation used to great effect to preserve aromas, flavours and acidity in this hot part of the country. Catalonia currently has nine D.O.s: Alella, Ampurdán-Costa Brava, Conca de Barberá, Costers del Segre, Penedés, Pla de Bages, Priorato, Tarragona and Terra Alta. There have also been moves to introduce a D.O. Catalonia for areas not covered by these and/or for all Catalan wines.

D.O. Alella

In Brief: A small region noted for stylish, high quality white wines and also capable of making classy reds. Well worth investigating.

This small D.O. lies to the north of Barcelona and is hemmed in by urban development spreading from this vibrant city. It has a modest 560 hectares of vines, 160 growers and only four bodegas, yet produces some high quality wines.

Authorised grape varieties are:

- **White:** Chardonnay, Chenin Blanc, Garnacha Blanca, Macabeo, Malvasía, Pansa Blanca, Pansa Rosada, Parellada, Picapoll and Sauvignon Blanc.

- **Black:** Cabernet Sauvignon, Garnacha Negra, Merlot, Pinot Noir, Syrah and Tempranillo.

White wines dominate production, with those made from indigenous varieties being light, refreshing and easy to drink, while those made from foreign grapes have more complexity and can be notably expressive. Not much rosé is produced although Alella's limited number of pink wines are well made and flavoursome. The region's few reds demonstrate the potential it has for making high quality wines from foreign grape varieties.

Geography, Soil and Climate

Alella's climate is typically Mediterranean, with mild winters and long, hot, dry summers. Hills offer some protection to vineyards from the sometimes persistent east winds and also condense humidity. The region's whitish, granitic soils are beneficial to wine makers because they are highly permeable – helping to retain water – and they absorb solar radiation which aids the maturation of grapes.

Future Development

Some would say that survival – in the face of Barcelona's urban growth – is the region's primary objective. Trusting and hoping that this will be achieved, the D.O. will prosper by maintaining the quality of its keenly priced white wines, and also by developing and expanding the production of middle and top-end reds, wines that it has shown itself eminently capable of making. The recent addition of Sauvignon Blanc, Pinot Noir and Syrah to the gamut of authorised grape varieties will add to the range of Alella's wines.

Selected Bodegas

Alella Vinícola Can Jonc, S.L. (☎ 935 403 842) Founded in 1906, this operation has 250 hectares of its own vines and produces 375,000 litres of respectable to good wine per year. For the curious, 'Marfil' means ivory. The wines are as follows:

- *Marfil Semi-Seco (white):* Fruitily flavoursome and sweet.

- *Marfil Seco (white):* Fruity and refreshing with good acidity.

- *Marfil Rosado (rosé):* Refreshing, although can sometimes lack fruit.

- *Marfil Chardonnay Crianza (white):* Of late, the producer's best bottle, with an attractive nose and lots of toasty flavour. A well made, mouthfilling wine.

Celler J Mestre, S.L. (☎ 938 402 283) Founded in 1989, this bodega has 18 hectares of its own vines and produces 50,000 litres per year. When good, its wines are light, fresh and commercial, and this last is not a criticism. However, quality does vary from year to year and more consistency would be an asset.

◆ *Juan Mestre Chardonnay (white):* A light, rather unfocused wine.

◆ *Juan Mestre Chardonnay Fermentado en Barrica (white):* Tends to be oak-dominated.

Parxet, S.A. (☎ 933 950 811) Founded in 1920, this operation has 40 hectares of its own vines and controls over 100 hectares more, producing nearly 1 million litres per year. As well as being the D.O.'s largest bodega, it is the most prominent and makes the best whites (and some excellent Cavas – see page 234):

◆ *Marqués de Alella Seco (white):* A blend of local varieties and Chenin Blanc – an unusual grape for Spain – this is refreshing and mouthfilling with a long finish.

◆ *Marqués de Alella Clásico (white):* Made 100 per cent from Pansa Blanca, this is smooth, refreshing and flavoursome, with a hint of sweetness.

◆ *Marqués de Alella Chardonnay (white):* One of the D.O.'s best wines, this is balanced, tasty and lip-smacking – a superior, reasonably priced Chardonnay.

◆ *Marqués de Alella Allier (white):* This is another Chardonnay and is much more expensive than the above. As the name implies, it is oaked, and offers lots of unctuous, tropical flavours, structure and length. A very well made wine, but expensive – the first reviewed Chardonnay is better value.

Roura, S.A. (Tel: 933 527 456) Founded in 1987, this bodega has 45 hectares of its own vines and produces 225,000 litres annually. Its whites are of respectable and good quality, while the reds show Alella's potential:

◆ *Roura Xarel-lo (white):* Light, fresh and easy to drink.

◆ *Roura Chardonnay (white):* This is a straightforward, respectable expression of the Chardonnay grape, with more depth and interest in some years than others.

◆ *Roura Sauvignon Blanc (white):* An aromatic, fruitily flavoursome Sauvignon with body and length.

◆ *Roura Crianza (red):* This blend of Tempranillo and Cabernet Sauvignon is a competent, straightforward, fruity/oaky wine.

◆ *Roura Merlot Reserva (red):* In good years, this is one of the region's best wines, a classy, complex Merlot. The way forward? In weaker vintages, it is still good, but can lack depth and complexity.

D.O. Ampurdán-Costa Brava

In Brief: A low-profile region making competent whites and rosés, and showing definite signs that it is capable of producing red wines of high quality. One to watch.

Situated in the extreme north-east of Catalonia – and hence of Spain – this D.O., which is called Empordá-Costa Brava in Catalan, has nearly 2,500 hectares of vines, 570 grape growers and 26 bodegas.

Authorised grape varieties are:

- **White:** Chardonnay, Garnacha Blanca, Garnacha Gris, Macabeo and Xarel-lo.

- **Black:** Cabernet Sauvignon, Cariñena, Garnacha Tinta, Merlot and Tempranillo.

This is one of the lower-profile Catalan D.O.s, although as the following reviews demonstrate, it is capable of making high quality wines. Whites are generally good rather than outstanding, being in the fresh and flavoursome mould. Rosés, which account for a fair proportion of the region's output, are competent and noted for their deep colour. The D.O. makes sweet red wines from Garnacha, which are worth investigating, while table reds are divided into two basic styles: *novell* is a young, fruity style of wine made by carbonic maceration for early drinking, noted for its fruitiness and refreshing acidity; older, aged reds are spicy and mouthfilling, their reputation increasing. Vintage is of relevance because the region can be subject to damaging frosts which affect wine quantity and quality.

Geography, Soil and Climate

Ampurdán-Costa Brava is situated between the Pyrenees and, as its name indicates, Spain's most northerly, Mediterranean holiday coast. It has a fairly standard Mediterranean climate, with mild winters and hot summers, although rainfall at 600+mm (24+in) per year is higher than in more southerly areas. The dominant climatic feature is the *tramontana*, a sometimes strong north wind which can blow for anywhere up to 100 days a year. It affects all forms of agriculture – as well as the sanity of the locals – and vines are staked to counter its effects. Soils are generally of poor quality, granitic in the higher regions, alluvial on the plain and shaley closer to the coast.

Future Development

With an increasingly sophisticated drinking public, the way forward for wine makers is the pursuit of quality rather than quantity. Therefore, the D.O. might look to make more reds, from both local and foreign grape varieties, as it has shown itself capable of high standards. A fair amount of respectable although unremarkable white and rosé wine is produced, and more emphasis on quality would enhance the region's reputation and raise its understated profile.

Selected Bodegas

Cavas del Castillo de Perelada, S.A. (☎ 972 538 011) Founded in 1923, this bodega has 100 hectares of its own vines and controls another 400, producing over a million litres per year. Possibly more famous as a source of high quality, good value Cava (see page 226), Castillo de Perelada is also the D.O.'s premier table wine bodega and makes one of Spain's better reds:

- *Castillo Perelada Blanc de Blancs (white)*: A reasonably priced blend of 80 per cent Macabeo and 20 per cent Chardonnay, this is a characterful, fresh, fruity wine.

- *Castillo Perelada Chardonnay (white)*: This is a tasty, unctuous, mouthfilling Chardonnay.

- *Castillo Perelada Sauvigon Blanc (white)*: Not an authorised grape variety, but its growth can be deemed 'experimental'. Well constructed Sauvignon for easy drinking.

- *Castillo Perelada Crianza (red)*: A good value, oaked Cariñena and Garnacha blend, with flavour and interest. In some years it is lighter than in others.

- *Castillo Perelada Reserva (red)*: This superior blend of Cabernet Sauvignon, Garnacha, Merlot and Tempranillo is an aromatic, rounded, flavoursome wine with depth and complexity. Highly recommended.

- *Castillo Perelada Cabernet Sauvignon (red)*: This mouthfilling, tasty, persistent wine has toast and blackcurrants on the nose and a powerful Cabernet palate with depth and interest. A superior wine at a competitive price.

- *Castillo Perelada Gran Claustro (red)*: The D.O.'s best wine and at the top table of Spanish reds, this is a blend of 40 per cent Cabernet Sauvignon, 30 per cent Merlot, 15 per cent Garnacha and 5 per cent Cariñena. It spends 18 months in barrel and a further year in bottle, and has a complex nose, harmony, interest and a deep concentration of flavours. It sometimes needs a couple of years after release to knit together. Recommended.

Celler Cooperativa D'Espolla (☎ 972 563 049) A co-operative with 300 hectares of its own vines and an annual production of over 100,000 litres, D'Espolla's whites and rosés are unremarkable, but the following sweet red can be very good:

- *Garnacha Espolla (red)*: This has a nose of fruits and vanilla, while the palate is well made, full and sweet, with contrasting bite.

Celler Oliver Conti, S.L. (☎ 972 193 161) This small 'designer' bodega, founded in 1997 although the vineyard was planted in 1992, turns out around 40,000 litres of top quality, innovative, expensive wines from imaginative blends of grapes:

- *Oliver Conti Blanc (white)*: A surprising blend of 50 per cent Gewürztraminer and 50 per cent Sauvignon Blanc, that works. This is unusual, complex, fruity and spicy. Not for the faint-hearted.

- *Oliver Conti Negre (red)*: A blend of Bordeaux grapes – 70 per cent Cabernet Sauvignon, 20 per cent Merlot and 10 per cent Cabernet Franc – this has an engaging, complex nose and a full, complex, elegant palate. At a blind tasting you would probably not identify it as a Spanish wine.

Comercial. Vinícola del Nordest, S.A. (☎ 972 563 150) Founded in 1977, this bodega has 200 hectares of its own vines and produces 600,000 litres per year. Its whites and rosés are clean and fresh for everyday drinking, while the reds have more interest, including:

◆ *Comercial Vinícola del Nordest Ull de Llebre (red):* Ull de Llebre is the Catalan name for Tempranillo and this is a respectable young example of the grape, tasty and well made, without being remarkable.

◆ *Comercial Vinícola del Nordest Cabernet Sauvignon (red):* This is an aromatic, fruity, characterful young wine offering value for money.

◆ *Garrigal Negre Crianza (red):* Made from Garnacha and Cariñena, this is a fairly priced, decent, straightforward crianza.

◆ *Covest Garnatxa (red):* This can be very good, with a complex nose and sweet, mouthfilling, tasty, long palate.

Masía Serra, S.C. (☎ 972 335 022) Founded only in 1995, this small operation has a modest, high quality output of wines that are well worth investigating:

◆ *Masía Serra Blanco (white):* A decent, oaked Macabeo that needs time to fully integrate. Expensive.

◆ *Masía Serra Tinto Crianza (red):* A complex, flavoursome blend of 90 per cent Cabernet Sauvignon and 10 per cent Merlot, this is one of the region's finest wines, able to compete with Spain's better reds. It has a deep, complex nose and a powerful, expressive palate with well judged tannins. Highly recommended.

Pere Guardiola, S.L. (☎ 972 549 096) Founded in 1989, this bodega has 22 hectares of its own vines and produces 200,000 litres per year. Wines are respectable:

◆ *Floresta Blanco (white):* This is a light, agreeable blend of 80 per cent Macabeo and 20 per cent Chardonnay at a modest price.

◆ *Floresta Rosado (rosé):* Made from 60 per cent Garnacha and 40 per cent Cariñena, this is a decent rosé, fresh and tasty with some body.

◆ *Petit Floresta Tinto (red):* This good value blend of 50 per cent Tempranillo and 50 per cent Garnacha is a straightforward, fruity, young, commercial red wine.

◆ *Pere Guardiola Garnatxa (sweet white):* Probably the bodega's best bottle, this is a dark golden colour and has a powerful, aged nose while the palate is sweet with bitter touches. Drink in small quantities after dinner.

Soda Mas Estela (☎ 972 126 176) Founded in 1989, this tiny operation has ten hectares of vines and produces around 35,000 litres of high quality wines per year from an imaginative range of grape varieties:

◆ *Vinya Selva de Mar Mas Estela Garnacha (sweet red):* A pleasing sweet red wine with a complex nose of oak and eucalyptus, and a palate with lots of flavour, tannin and interest. Recommended.

◆ *Mas Estela (sweet red):* This is the bodega's star sweet red, concentrated, tasty, toasty and honeyed. Recommended.

◆ *Vinya Selva de Mar Mas Estela Tinto (red):* A blend of 80 per cent Garnacha and 20 per cent Syrah, this wine has a complex nose and palate with flavours of vanilla, tobacco and toast. Moreish and engaging.

◆ *Vinya Selve de Mar Mas Estela Reserva (red):* Made from 100 per cent Syrah, a grape that should be grown more in Spain, this has a complex nose while the palate is concentrated, spicy and mouthfilling. Drink when four or five years old.

Vinos Oliveda, S.A. (☎ 972 549 012) This large operation was founded in 1952 and makes a range of wines which vary in quality from respectable to good. The following hold the most interest:

◆ *Rigau Ros Fermentado en Barrica (white):* This barrel-fermented Chardonnay used to be made in the 'more oak than fruit' style, but has improved and now offers an unctuous palate of creamy oak and refreshing fruit.

◆ *Rigau Ros Gran Reserva (red):* Made from 50 per cent Garnacha, 25 per cent Cabernet Sauvignon and 25 per cent Cariñena, this well made wine has a powerful, toasty nose and a balanced, smooth, integrated palate. Recommended and competitively priced.

D.O. Conca de Barberá

In Brief: *Apart from the presence of Miguel Torres, this is a low-profile region producing decent rather than remarkable wines. It has the potential to do great things.*

Situated in the hilly centre of Catalonia, Conca de Barberá has 6,000 hectares of vines, 1,500 growers and 18 bottling bodegas, and is still often regarded as primarily a Cava grape producing region. This is because nearly 80 per cent of its vine hectarage is devoted to the production of Parellada and Macabeo, two of the standard trio of Cava grapes. However, the region also makes table wines.
   Authorised grape varieties are:

● **White:** Macabeo and Parellada.

● **Black:** Tempranillo and Trepat.

The most significant feature of Conca de Barberá's wine production is the presence of Miguel Torres, who grows grapes in the region for two of Spain's best wines, one white and one red. Aside from these two stars, the region's wines can be characterised as follows: whites: light and quaffable; rosés: fresh, flavoursome and well made; reds: light and easy drinking. Vintage can be of importance because the region has variable weather which affects wine quality.

Geography, Soil and Climate

Conca de Barberá is Catalonia's highest wine area and altitude and aspect endow it with some high quality grape-growing environments. The climate is unlike that of surrounding regions, with both Mediterranean and continental characteristics. Soils are clay-based.

Future Development

Torres has ably demonstrated that top quality white and black grapes thrive in the region. Hence Conca de Barberá could (and should) become a premier wine area. It has no excuses for not doing so and with Torres' success, interest and finance should be available.

Selected Bodegas

Cavas Sanstravé (☎ 977 892 165) Founded in 1985, this small operation produces a range of attractive wines, including:

● *Sanstravé Gasset Blanc (white):* This Chardonnay varies in quality, but when good it has a powerful, creamy nose and an unctuous palate with toasty oak and a creamy finish.

● *Sanstravé Gasset Negre Reserva (red):* A blend of Cabernet Sauvignon and Tempranillo, this is a powerful wine with some complexity, spice and lively tannins.

Concavins, S.A. (☎ 977 887 030) Founded in 1988, this bodega produces around 900,000 litres of wine per year, the reds being its strongest suit, including:

● *Vía Aurelia Merlot (red):* This has a powerful nose of mature fruit and toasty touches, while the palate is smooth and flavoursome with fruit and oak working well together. Good value.

● *Vía Aurelia Cabernet Sauvignon (red):* This is a lively, characterful wine with Cabernet personality and flavours. Not as smooth and integrated as the Merlot.

Cooperativa Vinícola de Sarral (☎ 977 890 031) Founded in 1907, this co-operative has over 1,000 hectares of its own vines, producing 4 million litres per year. Quality is mixed across its wide range of notably inexpensive wines, with the following the most reliable:

● *Portell Aguja Blanco (white):* This blend of Macabeo and Parellada is a zingy, gassy wine, just about as well made as it could be for the competitive price.

● *Portell Aguja Rosado (rosé):* As above.

● *Portell Selección (red):* A respectable, easy-drinking Tempranillo crianza.

Miguel Torres, S.A. (☎ 938 177 400) Miguel Torres is Spain's most prominent wine maker (who is based in Penedés – see **D.O. Penedés** on page 187 for further details) and he has been involved in Conca de Barberá for some years. His Chardonnay is firmly established as one of the country's best white wines, while the much more expensive Grans Muralles red is also highly regarded:

◆ *Milmanda Chardonnay (white):* This has the lot: flavour, structure, persistence, fruit and oak integration, complexity, weight and freshness. Treat yourself – despite being one of the country's best whites, the price isn't too outrageous.

◆ *Grans Muralles (red):* A fascinating cocktail of grapes – Garnacha, Monastrell, Garró and Samsó (Cariñena), which may change in future vintages – this Mediterranean wine has gamey aromas, lots of plum and blackberry fruit on the palate, complexity and length. When released, its tannins are still harsh and this is a bottle for laying down for some years before drinking.

D.O. Costers del Segre

In Brief: *A vibrant, forward-thinking, growing region – sometimes called Spain's California – making good quality, 'international-style' wines from local and foreign grape varieties at competitive prices.*

Costers del Segre consists of six small areas in arid central Catalonia. It covers just over 4,000 hectares of vineyards, has 774 grape growers and 24 bodegas, 13 of which bottle their own wines. Until recently it was seen as a one-horse D.O., with the impressive Raimat bodega dominant in terms of both size and quality. While Raimat is still the region's premier outfit, others are now making admirable wines in this seemingly unsuitable area.

Authorised grape varieties are:

● **White:** Chardonnay, Garnacha Blanca, Macabeo, Parellada, Riesling, Sauvignon Blanc and Xarel-lo.

● **Black:** Cabernet Sauvignon, Garnacha Negra, Monastrell, Pinot Noir, Samsó, Syrah, Tempranillo and Trepat.

Wine styles can be characterised as follows: whites: those made from local grape varieties are fruity, refreshing and usually straightforward; those made from foreign grapes, notably Chardonnay, are more complex, sometimes with New World characteristics; rosés: these are not an important part of the region's wine profile, but those produced are perfectly competent; and reds: these are full-bodied and flavoursome, sometimes of high quality, and often improve with further bottle ageing.

Geography, Soil and Climate

Costers del Segre sits in the arid, scorched centre of Catalonia. The climate is usually described as Mediterranean, although it is more accurate to see it as transitional-continental. Winters can be cold, reflecting the region's distance from the sea's moderating influence. Rainfall is notably scarce and soils are mainly calcareous. Although vineyard irrigation is supposedly forbidden under EU law, it is practised in Costers del Segre on an 'experimental' basis. Some would say that having friends in high places helps to smooth the introduction of such arrangements and, being owned by the giant group Codorníu, Raimat certainly has those. Whatever the case, irrigation is crucial in parts of this arid region.

Future Development

The D.O. need do no more than continue on its present course: making high quality, good value wines in most price bands. Raimat has shown what can be done and others are following suit.

Selected Bodegas

Casa Pardet (☎ 973 347 023) Founded in 1992, this bodega makes respectable wines, mainly red:

◆ *Casa Pardet Chardonnay (white):* In good years, this is fresh, fruity and eminently drinkable – although expensive – but it can have off-years.

◆ *Casa Pardet Tempranillo (red):* This is a clean, fruity, flavoursome, young Tempranillo with character. Good.

◆ *Casa Pardet Etiqueta Cerámica Cabernet Sauvignon Reserva (red):* This is spicy on the nose while the palate has mouthfilling, balanced, delicious Cabernet flavours. Recommended.

Castell del Remei, S.L. (☎ 973 580 200) Originally founded in the 19th century, but revamped in the '80s, this is the region's second most prominent bodega, behind Raimat. Quality and value are notable across a range of wines, including:

◆ *Castell del Remei Blanc Planell (white):* The 'house' white, this is now a blend of Macabeo and Sauvignon Blanc – it previously contained Parellada – and is better for the change. It is a fresh, tasty, well made wine for a modest price. Good.

◆ *Castell del Remei Sauvignon Blanc (white):* This has tropical fruit on the nose while the palate is full, unctuous and flavoursome with an attractive bittersweet bite. A wine to give similarly priced Rueda D.O. Sauvignons a run for their money. Recommended.

◆ *Castell del Remei Chardonnay (white):* Fresh, fruity, flavoursome, unctuous and reasonably priced. Good.

◆ *Castell del Remei Gotim Bru Crianza (red):* Strange name, good wine. A blend of Tempranillo, Merlot and Cabernet Sauvignon, this has flavour, complexity and body.

◆ *Castell del Remei Cabernet Sauvignon Crianza (red):* This has a potent nose of black fruits and vanilla, while the palate is spicily tasty, smooth and soundly constructed. An accomplished wine at a competitive price.

◆ *Castell del Remei Merlot Crianza (red):* This is an aromatic Merlot with body, powerful, toasty flavours and some complexity. Recommended.

◆ *Castell del Remei Cabernet Sauvignon Reserva (red):* The bodega's most lauded wine and one of Catalonia's better reds. Everything works harmoniously in this mouth-watering, persistent wine with its concentrated, complex nose and full, deep, integrated palate. Highly recommended and competitively priced.

♦ *Castell del Remei Oda (red):* A blend of Cabernet Sauvignon, Merlot and Tempranillo, this has an engaging, complex nose and a full palate with length and interest. Very good.

♦ *Castell del Remei 1780 Crianza (red):* This blend of 60 per cent Cabernet Sauvignon, 30 per cent Tempranillo and 10 per cent Garnacha is the bodega's most expensive wine, although not always quite its best. It is still admirably powerful, flavoursome and satisfying.

Celler de Cantonella, S.A. (☎ 973 580 200) Founded only in 1997, this is an example of the sort of up-and-coming operation which Costers del Segre is capable of spawning. As yet it produces only 20,000 litres per year.

♦ *Cérvoles Fermentado en Barrica (white):* This is a barrel-fermented Chardonnay and Macabeo of decent potential. As is sometimes the case with these wines, drink when two or three years old for optimum fruit/oak integration.

♦ *Cérvoles Tinto Crianza (red):* A blend of Tempranillo, Cabernet Sauvignon and Garnacha, this is a big, tasty wine with lots of flavour. Possibly a touch pricey.

L'Olivera, S.C. (☎ 973 330 276) This is another small operation, founded in 1989, and the producer of quite a wide selection of good to very good white wines:

♦ *Blanc de Serè (white):* This blend of 60 per cent Macabeo, 30 per cent Parellada and 10 per cent Chardonnay is an attractively fresh, fruity wine at the right price with apple character and bite.

♦ *Missenyora Blanco (white):* This mouthfilling, barrel-fermented Macabeo has a powerful nose of some complexity and an unctuous palate that is not too heavy on the oak and which has length and flavour. Very good.

♦ *L'Olivera Macabeo Fermentado en Barrica (white):* A respectable barrel-fermented wine with some green fruit to accompany the oak.

♦ *L'Olivera Parellada Fermentado en Barrica (white):* As above.

♦ *L'Olivera Chardonnay Fermentado en Barrica (white):* As might be expected given the grape variety, this is superior to the foregoing two, and also pricier. It is a confident wine, flavoursome, unctuous and quite complex. Good.

Raimat (☎ 973 724 000) The dominant producer of the region, one of the most respected in the country, and with a healthy international reputation, Raimat is at the top of its profession. It is renowned for its wide range of well made, flavoursome, competitively priced wines, made from both Spanish and foreign grape varieties at a high-tech winery. The techniques employed owe much to Australia and California. Owned by the huge Codorníu group (see page 228) Raimat has revolutionised wine making in a region which seemed to have given up on the grape.

♦ *Raimat Clos Casal (white):* A varying blend of Chardonnay, Xarel-lo, Sauvignon Blanc and Macabeo, this is a refreshing, flavoursome, easy-to-drink white at a fair price.

♦ *Raimat Chardonnay (white):* One of the better Spanish Chardonnays in its price range, this has balance, flavour, body and persistence.

◆ *Raimat Selección Especial (white):* A superior barrel-fermented Chardonnay offering a big mouthful of unctuous flavours with a New World feel. Powerful and well made, but not for fans of white Burgundy.

◆ *Raimat Rosado (rosé):* Made from an unusual blend – 70 per cent Pinot Noir, 17 per cent Cabernet Sauvignon and 13 per cent Chardonnay – this is superior pink wine with lots of fruity flavour. Recommended.

◆ *Raimat Clamor (red):* This is a blend of Cabernet Sauvignon, Pinot Noir and Tempranillo, a well made, mouthfilling, everyday, warm-climate red wine offering good value and interest. It benefits from being poured into the glass half an hour before drinking.

◆ *Raimat Abadía (red):* A Tempranillo/Cabernet Sauvignon blend, this is one of Spain's better reds in its price range, with smooth, concentrated, long-lived, Bordeaux-feel flavours and character. Capable of ageing and good food wine.

◆ *Raimat Tempranillo (red):* Another fine, reasonably priced wine with lots of fruit, toast and chocolate flavours and personality. Approachable and delicious.

◆ *Raimat Pinot Noir (red):* Probably the least successful of Raimat's red wines, but that is relative and it is still good. As you would expect from the grape, this wine is not as 'big' as the other reds, although it does offer lots of red fruit. Eminently drinkable.

◆ *Raimat Merlot (red):* Another success, with lots of flavour, although perhaps the second weakest red.

◆ *Raimat Cabernet Sauvignon (red):* Made from 85 per cent Cabernet Sauvignon and 15 per cent Merlot, this is full, flavoursome, balanced, persistent and with lots of interest. Drink at about five years old.

◆ *Raimat Cabernet Sauvignon El Molí/Mas Castell/Vallcorba (red):* These are three single estate Cabernets at the top of Raimat's range, with Vallcorba usually the best. They are known for flavour, subtlety, complexity and persistence. Highly recommended and drink when at least six or seven years old.

Vall de Baldomar (☎ 973 402 205) Founded in 1989, this bodega has the potential to join Costers del Segre's quality producers. Wines include:

◆ *Baldomà Blanco (white):* Fresh, fruity, drinkable Macabeo. Good value.

◆ *Baldomà Tinto (red):* Well made, quaffable red at a keen price.

D.O. Penedés

In Brief: One of Spain's most important wine regions, producing good quality wines of all hues, some very good indeed.

Lying to the south-west of Barcelona, close to the coastal resort of Sitges, Penedés is Catalonia's and one of Spain's most important wine regions. It has attained this position by embracing Catalan dynamism, showing itself to be innovative, creative, commercially minded and outward-looking. Much Cava is produced – see **Chapter 9** – but so is a good deal of laudable table wine made from a variety of local and foreign varieties. Authorised grapes are:

- **White:** Chardonnay, Chenin Blanc, Gewürztraminer, Macabeo, Moscatel of Alexandria, Parellada, Riesling and Xarel-lo.

- **Black:** Cabernet Sauvignon, Cariñena, Garnacha, Merlot, Monastrell, Pinot Noir, Syrah and Tempranillo.

As with many Catalan D.O.s, white wines are made in two basic styles: the first is produced from local grape varieties and tends to be light and refreshing for early drinking; the second uses foreign grapes, especially Chardonnay, and is more complex and increasingly fermented and/or aged in oak. Penedés makes a variety of rosé styles, depending on the grapes used.

It is difficult to generalise about the region's reds because a wide range of grapes and blends are used, but they are characterised by a concentration of fruit and medium-term ageing potential. Regarding vintage, Penedés is noted for its mild, constant climate, with little weather variation from year to year; thus its wines are generally of the same quality vintage after vintage, although this is not as set in stone as producers would like us to think. Penedés has around 27,000 hectares of vines, 5,700 growers and 162 bodegas. Some 60 per cent of production is consumed domestically, the rest exported.

Geography, Soil and Climate

Penedés is split into three sub-zones: Bajo Penedés, Penedés Central or Medio and Penedés Superior; in short, low, middle and high Penedés. The Bajo is nearest the coast, the Medio is inland from the Bajo, with vineyards at about 200m (656ft) above sea level, and the Superior lies in the hills, with vineyards sited at up to 800m (2,624ft) above sea level.

Conditions vary across the three sub-zones, but overall the region has a Mediterranean climate with mild winters and hot summers. The Bajo has the warmest weather, conditions are cooler in the Medio, and the higher parts of the Superior have a more mountainous climate with a greater annual temperature range, higher rainfall and more frosts. Soils are fairly infertile but water-retentive.

Future Development

The region will look to maintain its current commercial and critical success, although it needs to fulfil its potential to produce more red wines of the highest quality to compete with Spain's best. Their appearance has been anticipated for some years now.

Selected Bodegas

Albet i Noya (☎ 938 994 812) Founded in 1988, this superior producer makes a wide range of wines (including Cavas – see page 224 from a variety of grapes, some organically, and decorates its bottles with distinctive labels. A large proportion of its output is exported – around 80 per cent – and the bodega's wine maker was also involved in the formation of D.O. Priorato's Mas Igneus. Apart from the first three wines reviewed, prices are fairly high:

- *Albet i Noya Xarel-lo D'Anyada (white):* This 'house' white is well made and fruity for drinking young.

- *Albet i Noya Collecció Macabeu (white):* A successful, flavoursome barrel-fermented Macabeo, not too heavy on the oak.

- *Albet i Noya Collecció Chardonnay (white):* As above, but made from Chardonnay.

- *Albet i Noya Rosado (rosé):* Respectable pink wine, but since it is made from good grapes – 80 per cent Merlot and 20 per cent Pinot Noir – you might expect more personality.

- *Albet i Noya Tempranillo D'Anyada (red):* A decent mouthful of tasty, concentrated young fruit. Superior 'house' red.

- *Albet i Noya Collecció Tempranillo (red):* Well made, full, rounded and ripe, with fruit and oak working well together, although better in some years than others. Good food wine.

- *Albet i Noya Collecció Cabernet Sauvignon (red):* As above.

- *Albet i Noya Collecció Syrah (red):* Sometimes the bodega's best wine, this is an excellent Syrah – or Shiraz if you prefer – with very tasty, concentrated fruit. Drink when at least four years old.

- *Albet i Noya Martí Reserva (red):* The bodega's most expensive wine – a blend of 25 to 40 per cent Tempranillo, 25 to 35 per cent Cabernet Sauvignon, 20 to 30 per cent Merlot, 20 to 30 per cent Syrah and 5 to 10 per cent Petit Syrah – this is a pleasing, well made wine but not remarkable and quite expensive; choose the Syrah.

Alsina y Sardá (☎ 938 988 132) Founded in 1986, with 40 hectares of its own vines, this bodega makes respectable wines for everyday drinking at competitive prices, including:

- *Alsina y Sardá Blanco Selección (white):* A tasty, herby, refreshing everyday wine for drinking chilled.

- *Alsina y Sardá Blanco Fermentado en Barrica (white):* A respectable rather than remarkable barrel-fermented mouthful.

- *Alsina y Sardá Rosado Merlot (rosé):* A light, understated wine with some red fruit character.

- *Alsina y Sardá Crianza (red):* This blend of Cabernet Sauvignon and Tempranillo makes for easy drinking with barbecued food.

Can Rafols del Caus, S.L. (☎ 938 970 013) Founded in 1980, with 45 hectares of its own vines, this is a well respected, innovative producer of good wines, including Cavas (see page 225) as well as the following:

◆ *Petit Caus Blanco (white):* This varying blend of grapes – usually Xarel-lo, Macabeo, Chenin Blanc, Chardonnay and Muscat – also varies in quality: it can be a straightforward, fruity, reasonably priced everyday white, or an aromatic, complex mouthful. When on form, recommended.

◆ *Gran Caus Blanco Crianza (white):* An interesting blend of grapes, including Chardonnay and Chenin Blanc, this high quality wine is mouthfilling, complex and flavoursome.

◆ *Vinya La Calma (white):* This is a rarity in Spain, a wine made from 100 per cent Chenin Blanc. And very good it is, with a powerful, creamy nose and a flavoursome, characterful palate. But it is very expensive.

◆ *Petit Caus Rosado (rosé):* As good as pink wine gets for the price.

◆ *Gran Caus Rosado (rosé):* This Merlot is one of Spain's most expensive rosados; it offers plenty of tasty fruit, but this is a lot to pay for rosé.

◆ *Petit Caus Tinto (red):* A host of black grape varieties – currently Cabernet Franc, Monastrell, Tempranillo, Syrah and Merlot – make this notably aromatic, tasty, moreish red wine, with lots of spicy fruit and oak character. Recommended and great value for money.

◆ *Gran Caus Tinto Reserva (red):* Another interesting blend – currently Cabernet Franc, Cabernet Sauvignon and Merlot, with Tempranillo sometimes also on the menu – this is one of Catalonia's more distinguished red wines. It has an engaging nose with spice and eucalyptus, while the palate offers lots of powerful, integrated flavours and decent structure. One of Spain's better warm climate red wines and competitively priced bearing this in mind.

◆ *Caus Lubis (red):* This, the bodega's star wine, is one of Spain's best Merlots and almost certainly the most expensive. It is a subtle, complex, smooth, integrated wine, one of Catalonia's better reds, although you do pay for the privilege.

Catasús i Casanovas, S.A. (☎ 934 592 227) Founded in the early '90s this small bodega makes approachable, reasonably priced wines:

◆ *Mas Xarot Paner de Blancs (white):* Straightforward, tasty Chardonnay.

◆ *Mas Xarot Rosat Fogós (rosé):* Competent rosado from the Merlot grape with a fair amount of fruit.

◆ *Mas Xarot Gran Gresol (red):* A pleasing Cabernet Sauvignon/Merlot crianza, tasty and well put together. It offers good value.

Cavas Hill, S.A. (☎ 938 900 588) This long established producer, perhaps better known for its Cava, also makes a range of respectable table wines, including:

- *Blanc Bruc (white):* This blend of Xarel-lo, Chardonnay and Sauvignon Blanc is usually a well made, easy-drinking, fruity, everyday wine.

- *Hill Chardonnay Fermentado en Barrica (white):* Very good barrel-fermented Chardonnay, structured, flavoursome, unctuous and reasonably priced.

- *Masía Hill (rosé):* Made from 60 per cent Tempranillo and 40 per cent Garnacha, this is tasty, refreshing wine.

- *Gran Civet Hill Crianza (red):* Made from a varying blend – currently 50 per cent Tempranillo, 35 per cent Cabernet Sauvignon and 15 per cent Merlot – this has a spicy, vanilla nose and a smooth, tasty, straightforward fruit/oak palate. Well priced and do not let the name's 'catty' associations put you off.

- *Cavas Hill Cabernet Sauvignon Reserva (red):* This has an engaging nose with touches of leather and tobacco, while the palate has flavour and punch. It can be tannic when first released.

Cavas Lavernoya, S.A. (☎ 938 912 202) Founded in 1890, this bodega makes respectable, low-priced wines for the most part, but the following red stands out:

- *Lavernoya Cabernet Sauvignon (red):* Drink when at least six or seven years old for superior, reasonably priced, Mediterranean Cabernet Sauvignon.

Cavas Nadal (☎ 938 988 011) Primarily a Cava producer, but also a maker of a good quality, reasonably priced white wine:

- *Finca Boadella (white):* This blend of Macabeo, Parellada and Xarel-lo is aromatic, fruity and soundly constructed. In some years it is also quite complex and subtle.

Cavas Naverán (Sadeve, S.A.) (☎ 938 988 274) Founded in 1984, this Cava bodega (see page 227) also makes laudable table wines, including:

- *Manuela de Naverán Chardonnay (white):* Superior barrel-fermented Chardonnay, well balanced, tasty and with fruit to accompany the oak.

- *Clos Antonia (white):* An intriguing, unusual, complex, flavoursome, expensive blend of Chardonnay, Xarel-lo and Viognier, the latter little grown in Spain. Recommended, but it does cost a lot.

- *Naverán Cabernet de la Finca (red):* Tasty, inexpensive Cabernet Sauvignon. Recommended.

- *Naverán Don Pablo Reserva Cabernet Sauvignon (red):* Drink at five or six years old for an aromatic, spicy, mouthfilling wine.

Cavas Recaredo, S.A. (☎ 938 910 214) This producer of elegant Cava also makes a respectable white wine:

- *Recaredo Chardonnay (white):* This has integrated fruit and oak on the nose and an unctuous, tasty palate. Best at three years old when the fruit and oak have knitted together.

Celler Cooperativa Villafranca (☎ 938 171 035) Founded in 1933, this Cava producer also has an extensive range of respectable to good wines, with the following the most reliable:

◆ *Casteller (white):* A blend of 50 per cent Xarel-lo, 35 per cent Macabeo and 15 per cent Parellada, this is a well made, reasonably priced everyday white with green fruit and some bite.

◆ *Gran Rosat Casteller (rosé):* A soundly constructed, characterful pink wine from the Tempranillo grape.

◆ *Casteller Gran Merlot (red):* This is an engaging, confident wine with up-front personality and length. Good.

Cellers Mas Comtal (☎ 938 970 052) Founded in 1993, with 35 hectares of its own vines, this bodega produces a small range of good quality wines:

◆ *Mas Comtal Pomell de Blancs (white):* Made from 50 per cent Chardonnay and 50 per cent Xarel-lo, this has flavour and body, a superior everyday white.

◆ *Mas Comtal Rosado (rosé):* 100 per cent Merlot, this is quite elegant rosado with fruity character.

◆ *Mas Comtal Semi-Crianza (red):* A blend of 50 per cent Cabernet Sauvignon and 50 per cent Merlot, this is a powerful, tasty wine with integrated mature fruit and oak.

Cellers Puig Roca, S.A. (☎ 977 666 910) This small bodega has been producing high quality wines since 1990. The following selection is worth hunting down:

◆ *Avgvstvs Chardonnay Fermentado en Barrica (white):* A powerful, New World-style barrel-fermented Chardonnay for drinking at two or three years old. Heavy on the toasty oak and butter, but well done. Quite expensive.

◆ *Avgvstvs Cabernet Sauvignon Rosado (rosé):* This is usually excellent pink wine with lots of Cabernet flavour, one of Catalonia's best, although it does have the odd off year.

◆ *Avgvstvs Merlot (red):* This has an engaging, toasty, eucalyptus nose and a powerful, tasty palate. Recommended and competitively priced.

Cellers Can Bonastre (☎ 937 726 167) Founded in 1996, this small producer's standards are on the up and, after releasing some rather bland wines, recent vintages have been better, although there is still a lack of consistency. The following are the bodega's best wines:

◆ *Can Bonastre Chardonnay (white):* Characterful Chardonnay with unctuous flavours.

◆ *Can Bonastre Merlot (red):* A well made blend of mature, characterful fruit and oak at a competitive price.

Chandon, S.A. (☎ 938 970 900) The famous French Champagne house makes a range of excellent Cavas and also a notable white wine (see page 228):

◖ *Eclipse Chardonnay (white):* Excellent, balanced, unctuous, tasty Chardonnay at a competitive price.

Colet Cava (☎ 938 170 809) This small producer of respectable Cava also makes a worthwhile Cabernet Sauvignon/Tempranillo red:

◖ *Colet Tinto Crianza (red):* A flavoursome red wine with pleasing fruit/oak integration. Moreish and spicy.

Compañía Internaciónal de Grandes Vinos, Cigravi, S.A. (☎ 938 974 050) Decently made white wines at low prices are this producer's speciality:

◖ *Giró Ribot Blanc de Blancs (white):* The standard trio of Cava grapes makes this fresh, drinkable, uncomplicated white wine. Choose the latest release.

◖ *Giró Ribot Muscat (white):* Respectable, fruity and tasty. Good with fried fish.

◖ *Giró Ribot Chardonnay (white):* Probably as professionally made and characterful as it could be for the low price. Good.

Cooperativa Agrícola de L'Arboc (☎ 977 670 055) This fair-size co-operative has been in existence since just after the First World War. Its rosé and red wines are unremarkable, but these whites are worth investigating:

◖ *Pupitre Muscat (white):* In good years, this is a characterful dry Muscat, in poor ones it can be bland.

◖ *Pupitre Xarel-lo Fermentado en Barrica (white):* A well made barrel-fermented wine with herby character and some complexity.

◖ *Pupitre Chardonnay Fermentado en Barrica (white):* Respectable, reasonably priced and not over-oaked with some attractive green fruit.

Cooperativa Vinícola del Penedés (Covides) (☎ 938 172 552) This large operation produces a range of respectable, low-priced wines from its 3,000 hectares of vines, including:

◖ *Molí de Foc (white):* Made from 50 per cent Xarel-lo, 40 per cent Parellada and 10 per cent Macabeo, this is a straightforward, fresh, fruity, inexpensive white wine.

◖ *Duc de Foix Blanco (white):* As above.

◖ *Duc de Foix Blanco Chardonnay Fermentado en Barrica (white):* Good quality, barrel-fermented wine at a low price.

◖ *Duc de Foix Cabernet Sauvignon (red):* Young, smooth, everyday Cabernet, well conceived and commercial.

Eudald Massana Noya (☎ 938 994 124) A small, newish bodega making some decent, low-priced wines. The following are recommended:

◆ *Eudald Massana Noya Blanco (white):* A blend of 40 per cent Xarel-lo, 35 per cent Macabeo and 25 per cent Parellada, this is a well made, straightforward wine with refreshing fruity character; as good as it could be for the notably low price.

◆ *Eudald Massana Noya Chardonnay (white):* Well made, tasty, inexpensive Chardonnay.

◆ *Eudald Massana Noya Cabernet Sauvignon Crianza (red):* Concentrated, characterful Cabernet for not much money.

Finca Can Feixes (☎ 937 718 227) Founded in the 18th century, this small producer makes respected Cava and the following good quality table wines:

◆ *Can Feixes Blanc Selecció (white):* An interesting blend of grapes – Chardonnay, Macabeo, Parellada and Pinot Noir – makes this quite complex, flavoursome, low-priced wine. Recommended.

◆ *Can Feixes Negre Selecció Crianza (red):* A superior, concentrated, balanced mix of oaked Cabernet Sauvignon, Merlot and Tempranillo. Recommended.

Francisco Domínguez Cruces (☎ 938 910 182) Founded in 1988, this small producer has a varied range of wines, some rather better than others. The following stand out, both for quality and value:

◆ *Xamfrá (white):* A blend of 40 per cent Macabeo, 40 per cent Xarel-lo and 20 per cent Parellada, this is a notably fruity wine with character and bite for a modest price. Good.

◆ *Xamfrá Selección (white):* A blend of the three grapes above with Chardonnay, this is another superior young white wine with expressive fruit and personality. Recommended.

◆ *Xamfrá Cabernet Sauvignon Crianza (red):* This is a full, complex, engaging, warm-climate Cabernet at a competitive price.

Gabriel Giró Baltá (☎ 938 988 032) Founded in 1976, this small operation's wines can be very good, although when conditions are unfavourable, quality suffers.

◆ *Blanc Gorner (white):* When on form, this blend of 40 per cent Xarel-lo, 40 per cent Macabeo and 20 per cent Parellada is a powerfully fruity young white with some complexity. In some years it is rather less characterful. Notably low-priced.

◆ *Gorner Merlot Crianza (red):* A well made, straightforward, inexpensive blend of spicy fruit and oak.

Gramona, S.A. (☎ 938 910 113) Founded in 1881, this bodega makes respectable to good wines, mainly from foreign grape varieties, including:

- *Gramona Gessami (white):* This is an unusual blend of grapes – Gewürztraminer, Muscat Alejandria and Sauvignon Blanc – and a successful one. The nose has a powerful cocktail of fruit and the palate offers plenty of bittersweet flavour and bite.

- *Gramona Chardonnay (white):* A well made, characterful wine, typical of the variety and with bite.

- *Gramona Pinot Noir (red):* A tasty, characterful young wine, although not especially representative of the variety.

Heretat Vall-Ventós (☎ 937 725 251) This bodega produces a range of rather good wines at reasonable prices, which is what Penedés is all about. Try the following selection:

- *Heretat Vall-Ventós Blanc Primer (white):* A blend of Chardonnay and Macabeo, this is superior, straightforward wine, with character and punch.

- *Heretat Vall-Ventós Chardonnay (white):* Flavoursome and persistent, this is well made, characterful Chardonnay without being exceptional.

- *Heretat Vall-Ventós Chenin Blanc (white):* Well made, unctuous, interesting wine from a grape unusual in Spain.

- *Heretat Vall-Ventós Sauvignon Blanc (white):* Eminently respectable Sauvignon Blanc with flavour and bitter bite. Overpriced when compared with some of its D.O. Rueda competitors.

- *Heretat Vall-Ventós Merlot (red):* An aromatic Merlot, light and toasty.

- *Heretat Vall-Ventos Cabernet Sauvignon Crianza (red):* The bodega's best red, mouthfilling, integrated and tasty with Cabernet character. A touch expensive.

Jané Ventura, S.A. (☎ 977 660 118) Founded in the year that the First World War began, this modest-size operation, with 11 hectares of its own vines, makes one of Spain's best Cabernet Sauvignons, as well as other decent wines, including:

- *Jané Ventura Blanco (white):* This blend of mainly Xarel-lo with Parellada is a fresh, fruity, everyday wine with attractive touches of green fruit and herbs. Well priced.

- *Finca Els Camps Macabeo Fermentado en Barrica (white):* Made from 85 per cent Macabeo and 15 per cent Xarel-lo, this varies in quality. In some years it can be rather heavy-handed with the oak, in others it can be a very good – although expensive – barrel-fermented wine, with depth, balance and unctuous complexity. More consistency please.

- *Jané Ventura Rosado (rosé):* A blend of Tempranillo and Garnacha, with more of the former, this is good rosé with flavour and bite.

- *Jané Ventura Cabernet Sauvignon Crianza (red):* A well made, easy-to-drink, oaked red.

- *Jané Ventura Cabernet Sauvignon Reserva (red):* Made from 90 per cent Cabernet Sauvignon and 10 per cent Tempranillo, this spends a year in American oak and a further two years in bottle. It has a powerful, complex Cabernet nose and an elegant, concentrated palate with lots of flavour and confident tannins. One of the county's best and at a fair price, this cries, nay screams, for lamb. Highly recommended.

Jaume Serra (☎ 938 936 404) Founded in 1943, this large operation makes a range of inexpensive wines, some very good indeed. The range includes:

◆ *Jaume Serra Chardonnay (white):* A notably inexpensive barrel-fermented Chardonnay, but heavy on the oak and not the most subtle bottle around.

◆ *Jaume Serra Cabernet Sauvignon (red):* This young Cabernet, which spends four months on oak, is better than the Chardonnay, with lots of characterful fruit integrated with the oak. Recommended and inexpensive.

◆ *Jaume Serra Merlot Crianza (red):* A notably tasty, expressive blend of mature fruit and oak. Recommended and inexpensive.

Jean León, S.A. (☎ 938 177 451) One of Catalonia's, indeed Spain's, pioneer wine makers, the late Jean León's operation – founded in 1963 – is now owned by Torres. His innovation was to demonstrate how well French grape varieties could perform in Catalonian table wines. León's Chardonnay was Spain's first varietal from this now ubiquitous grape and quality remains high across the full range of wines. The bodega has done more than most to spread the gospel of Catalan wine to the west coast of the U.S.A., where León owned a restaurant.

◆ *Jean León Petit Chardonnay (white):* A powerful, elegant, reasonably priced wine, redolent of green apples, careful ageing and class. Excellent with Dover sole.

◆ *Jean León Chardonnay Crianza (white):* This was Spain's first barrel-fermented Chardonnay and is still one of the best. It is a large, confident wine with lots of flavour and complexity. Excellent, although it costs a lot more than the above. Try the Petit Chardonnay first.

◆ *Jean León Merlot (red):* Elegant and flavoursome with delicious dark fruit, tobacco and chocolate, this is an excellent Merlot, one of Spain's best. I am surprised that it does not cost more.

◆ *Jean León Cabernet Sauvignon (red):* There are several of these on the market, reservas and gran reservas from different years. They are characterised by their high quality, with concentrated, complex, Bordeaux flavours, structure and the attributes expected from top Cabernets. More recent vintages are lighter than earlier ones, which were sometimes heavy. Prices are lower than you might imagine. Highly recommended.

Joan Sardá, S.A. (☎ 937 720 900) Founded in the '20s, this bodega makes lower-priced wines, some of reasonable quality, including:

◆ *Joan Sardá Chardonnay (white):* Respectable, straightforward Chardonnay for everyday drinking. Slightly overpriced.

● *Joan Sardá Cabernet Sauvignon Rosado (rosé)*: Superior, full-bodied pink wine.

● *Joan Sardá Cabernet Sauvignon Crianza (red)*: Full-bodied, flavoursome and reasonably priced, with length and body

Josep Ferret i Mateu (☎ 938 910 105) Founded in 1949, this is another producer of straightforward, reasonably priced wines, including:

● *Vinya Sant Galderic (white)*: A blend of Macabeo and Xarel-lo, this is a straightforward, respectable, competitively priced wine with fruity, herbaceous character.

● *Ferret i Mateu Merlot Crianza (red)*: A light, tasty, characterful, oaked Merlot for not much money.

Josep María Raventós i Blanc, S.A. (☎ 938 183 262) This producer of top quality Cava is gaining a reputation for elegant, well conceived white wines, including:

● *Raventós i Blanc Xarel-lo (white)*: Richly fruity, elegant and refreshing, this is a very good example of the grape. It comes from vines over 30 years old and is a wine which will improve for a year or two after release.

● *Raventós i Blanc Chardonnay (white)*: This has balance, elegance, freshness and flavour. Delicious and a refreshing change from the oceans of barrel-fermented Chardonnay sloshing around the world.

● *Raventós i Blanc El Preludi (white)*: Fruitily mouthfilling and long. Again, delicious.

Juvé y Camps, S.A. (☎ 938 911 000) This maker of famous Cava also produces respectable table wines, including:

● *Ermita D'Espiells Blanc Flor (white)*: Made from the trio of Cava grapes, this is mouthfilling, herby and flavoursome.

● *Miranda D'Espiells Chardonnay Flor (white)*: An interesting, fruity Chardonnay with lots of mature fruit.

● *Casa Vella D'Espiells Cabernet Sauvignon (red)*: This is respectable, flavoursome, warm-climate Cabernet, better in some years than others. Drink when at least four or five years old, with food.

Manuel Sancho e Hijas, S.A. (☎ 938 918 281) This bodega produces a selection of lower-priced wines from its 40 hectares of vines, with the following recommended:

● *Mont Marçal Fermentado en Barrica (white)*: A barrel-fermented Chardonnay that varies in quality. Always unctuous and tasty, it sometimes lacks integration between the fruit and oak. Try it in years that are good regional vintages.

● *Mont Marçal Tinto Reserva (red)*: This inexpensive blend of Cabernet Sauvignon, Merlot and Tempranillo usually has a lot of flavour and structure, but has its off years. Comments as above.

◆ *Mont Marçal Cabernet Sauvignon Reserva (red)*: This powerfully aromatic wine has lots of mouthfilling flavour and character for a keen price.

Marqués de Monistrol, S.A. (☎ 938 910 276) Established in the 1880's, this bodega is now owned by Rioja's Berberana and produces some respectable, modestly priced wines, including:

◆ *Marqués de Monistrol Blanc de Blancs (white)*: A blend of Macabeo, Parellada and Xarel-lo, this is a well made, straightforward, fruity wine with some bite.

◆ *Masía Monistrol Tinto (red)*: This blend of Garnacha and Tempranillo is a characterful, smooth, tasty, everyday red wine which chills well for drinking with barbecues during the summer.

◆ *Marqués de Monistrol Cabernet Sauvignon (red)*: A well made, tasty wine with fruit and oak well integrated.

Martí Serdá, S.A. (☎ 938 974 411) A modest bodega, founded in 1987, most of whose wines are everyday offerings of mixed quality. However, one stands out:

◆ *Mare Nostrum Rosado (rosé)*: A decent, reasonably priced rosado made from Garnacha and Tempranillo with balance, fruit and a gas spritz.

Masía Bach, S.A. (☎ 937 714 052) Bach is owned by the massive Codorníu Group (see page 228) and produces decent table wines from a variety of grape varieties, including:

◆ *Masía Bach Extrísimo Seco (white)*: Respectable, unctuous, everyday white.

◆ *Masía Bach Chardonnay Crianza (white)*: Well made, characterful, oaked Chardonnay for a modest price.

◆ *Masía Bach Cabernet Sauvignon Crianza (red)*: Well priced, spicy, warm-climate Cabernet with personality. Recommended.

◆ *Masía Bach Merlot (red)*: Smooth, juicy, tasty, understated Merlot with good use of oak.

Masía Vallformosa (☎ 938 978 286) Founded in 1978, Vallformosa has 360 hectares of its own vines, producing a wide range of wines, most of good quality, especially:

◆ *Claudia de Vallformosa (white)*: A blend of 70 per cent Parellada and 30 per cent Muscat, this is clean, fruity and flavoursome with hints of sweetness and bite. Decent 'house' wine.

◆ *Vallformosa Chardonnay (white)*: When on form, this is excellent, moreish, balanced, tasty Chardonnay. Some years are better than others.

◆ *Viña Rosada (rosé)*: Admirable rosado with lots of fruit.

◆ *Vallfort Crianza (red)*: A blend of 85 per cent Tempranillo and 15 per cent Garnacha, this is a straightforward, competent crianza.

◆ *Vallformosa Cabernet Sauvignon (red):* Flavoursome, characterful, persistent warm-climate Cabernet.

Miguel Torres, S.A. (☎ 938 177 400) Generally regarded as Spain's premier wine makers, the Torres family has been in the wine business since the 17th century, with the current bodega founded in 1870. It is still family owned and the present head of the firm, Miguel A.Torres, has introduced numerous innovations to the Spanish wine scene since the '60s; he has also done as much as anyone to experiment with and make good use of foreign grape varieties. It is difficult to overestimate his influence and in many of Spain's export markets, Spanish and Torres wine are synonymous. The firm also makes wine in Conca de Barberá (see page 182), is looking to buy land in other parts of Spain (including Priorato) and has operations in California, Chile and China. Its extensive range of Penedés wines is of a good to very high standard:

◆ *Viña Sol (white):* Made from Parellada, this is a wine list mainstay in many Spanish restaurants. It is fresh and fruity with tasty green apples and lemon on the palate and sometimes quite biting acidity. Well made, commercial wine.

◆ *San Valentin Semi-Dulce (white):* A well made, sweetish, 'house', wine, with good structure and balancing acidity.

◆ *Viña Esmeralda (white):* A blend of Moscatel and Gewürztraminer, this is a fruity and flavoursome wine, with representative flavours of these distinctive grape varieties.

◆ *Gran Viña Sol (white):* Superior Chardonnay, a blend of normally fermented and barrel-fermented wine. It is mouthfilling, delicious and competitively priced.

◆ *Waltraud (white):* This is a rarity: a Spanish Riesling. It is fruity and complex and shows what can be done with this grape in suitable Spanish vineyards, although there will never be large amounts of those.

◆ *Fransola (white):* A very good Sauvignon Blanc with lots of unctuous flavour, interest, bite and character. Recommended.

◆ *De Casta (rosé):* Dark, full-bodied, moreish rosado from Garnacha and Cariñena. Good food rosé.

◆ *Sangre de Toro (red):* Made from Garnacha and Cariñena, the bodega's 'house' red is tasty and full-bodied, although sometimes a bit rough and dense when first released. It softens and opens with time.

◆ *Coronas Tempranillo (red):* A smooth, rounded, commercial mix of fruit and oak.

◆ *Gran Sangre de Toro (red):* Tasty, full-bodied, uncomplicated Garnacha and Cariñena, drinking at its best when at least five or six years old. Lacking the complexity of earlier releases and not as good as it was?

◆ *Atrium (red):* A superior, reasonably priced Merlot for drinking with food, this is tasty, finely structured and long, with laurel and leather flavours.

◆ *Mas Borrás Pinot Noir (red):* Possibly the least successful Torres red, this is reasonably characterful Mediterranean Pinot, but it can lack depth and interest – don't expect Burgundy.

- *Gran Coronas Cabernet Sauvignon (red):* This wine has done as much as any to carry the gospel of Spanish reds abroad. It is serious Cabernet for mulling over with lamb. Do not drink when it is too young.

- *Mas la Plana (red):* One of Spain's better reds and something of a legend: at a Paris tasting in 1979, the 1970 vintage was triumphant against Château Latour's vintage from the same year. This is dense, concentrated, complex Cabernet, destined for long additional bottle ageing after release and not for drinking until it is at least ten years old. It is not as expensive as you might imagine.

Molí Colomá – Cavas Sumarroca (☎ 938 911 092) Founded in 1986, this bodega makes a wide range of wines at competitive prices, with the whites rather better than the reds and rosés. The range includes:

- *Sumarroca Muscat (white):* A well made, characterful wine, aromatic, flavoursome and 'grapey', as this variety tends to be.

- *Sumarroca Chardonnay (white):* This has a fruity nose and a full, unctuous, tasty palate. Well conceived young Chardonnay.

- *Sumarroca Riesling (white):* This has tropical fruit on the nose and a fresh, fruity palate with bite. Good.

- *Sumarroca Gewürztraminer (white):* A mouthfilling, tasty wine with bite and the exotic fruit typical of the grape.

Montcau, S.L. ☎ (937 790 066) Founded in 1995, this small bodega makes some passable whites and the following red offers good value:

- *Algendaret (red):* Primarily Tempranillo, this has lots of mouthfilling, mature fruit for a low price.

Parató Vinícola, S.A. (☎ 938 988 182) Founded in 1975, with 94 hectares of its own vines, this small bodega produces low-priced, everyday wines, with the following worth seeking out:

- *Parató Blanc Coupage (white):* Made from Macabeo, Xarel-lo and Parellada, this is a light, fresh, fruity everyday white.

- *Renardes (red):* A characterful, inexpensive, everyday Cabernet Sauvignon/Tempranillo blend.

- *Parató Pinot Noir Crianza (red):* This is a decent, straightforward Mediterranean wine with lots of ripe fruit flavours, but there is not much Pinot character.

Pinord (☎ 938 903 066) Founded in 1950, Pinord produces a wide range of wines, most of them well made but none remarkable. The following are worthy:

- *Viña Mireia (white):* A characterful, dry blend of Moscatel and Gewürztraminer with bite, but quite pricey.

● *Pinord Chardonnay (white)*: A tasty, mouthfilling persistent wine with some complexity. Again, perhaps slightly overpriced.

● *Pinord Viña Chatel (rosé)*: A well made, uncomplicated, fruity rosado from Tempranillo and Garnacha.

● *Pinord Viña Chatel Tempranillo Crianza (red)*: This medium-bodied wine is a straightforward, finely structured, flavoursome blend of fruit and oak.

● *Pinord Chateldon Cabernet Sauvignon Reserva (red)*: A smooth, mouthfilling, aromatic wine with rather more oak than fruit on the palate. Superior barbecue Cabernet Sauvignon.

Ramón Canals Canals, S.A. (☎ 937 755 446) Founded in 1903, this bodega makes a small range of wines and the following stands out:

● *Masía Subirana Crianza (red)*: Smooth, tasty, inexpensive Cabernet Sauvignon crianza with decent complexity and interest considering the modest price.

René Barbier, S.A. (☎ 938 995 111) Part of the giant Freixenet group, René Barbier makes a large range of wines, some very impressive, including:

● *Kraliner (white)*: Made outside the D.O. from the standard trio of Cava grapes, this is a fresh, fruity, refreshing, reasonably priced wine.

● *Mediterráneam (white)*: Made from the same grapes as above, although in different proportions, this is an aromatic, characterful, fairly complex and mouthfilling dry white for a good price. Recommended.

● *René Barbier Chardonnay (white)*: This is aromatic, mouthfilling, powerful, unctuous and satisfying. Superior Chardonnay.

● *René Barbier Chardonnay Fermentado en Barrica (white)*: This has the classic barrel-fermented Chardonnay nose of toasty butter and a meaty palate with lots of unctuous fruit and oak for those who like the New World style.

● *Mediterráneam (rosé)*: A moreish blend of Garnacha, Tempranillo and Monastrell, this has body, balance and flavour. Good.

● *Mediterráneam Tinto (red)*: An undemanding, competently made, fruity blend of Tempranillo, Garnacha and Monastrell.

● *René Barbier Cabernet Sauvignon Reserva (red)*: Good quality, rounded, tasty food wine. Drink at five or six years old.

● *René Barbier Selección Crianza (red)*: An excellent, aromatic, warm weather Cabernet Sauvignon with body, flavour, finish and well judged tannins. Recommended.

Sabaté i Coca, S.A. (☎ 938 911 927) Founded in 1986, with 25 hectares of its own vines, this modest bodega makes a small range of reasonably priced, worthwhile wines, including:

♦ *Castellroig Blanc D'Anyada (white):* A lightish, well made, straightforward blend of 79 per cent Xarel-lo and 21 per cent Chardonnay.

♦ *Castellroig Blanc Selecció Fermentado en Barrica (white):* Made from 65 per cent Chardonnay and 35 per cent Xarel-lo, this is a decent, lightish barrel-fermented wine, without too much depth.

♦ *Castellroig Bru D'Anyada Crianza (red):* A blend of 75 per cent Tempranillo, 15 per cent Merlot and 10 per cent Cabernet Sauvignon, this is a straightforward, flavour-filled, reasonably priced wine.

♦ *Castellroig Bru Selecció Crianza (red):* A good blend of 85 per cent Cabernet Sauvignon and 15 per cent Merlot, aromatic, powerful, confident and balanced.

Segura Viudas, S.A. (☎ 938 917 070) Founded in 1954, and owned by Freixenet, Segura Viudas is renowned for its excellent Cava, but also makes some very good table wines, including:

♦ *Viña Heredad (white):* Made from the trio of Cava grapes, this is well made, characterful, fruity wine with bite.

♦ *Creu de Lavit (white):* An unusual, reasonably priced, interesting, barrel-fermented blend of Xarel-lo, Macabeo and Parellada, with complexity on the nose and a full, unctuous palate and finish. Recommended.

♦ *Viña Heredad Crianza (red):* An oaked blend of 85 per cent Tempranillo and 15 per cent Cabernet Sauvignon, this flavoursome wine has lots of well balanced, spicy personality. Good.

♦ *Mas d'Aranyó Reserva (red):* This superior, stylishly presented blend of Tempranillo, Cabernet Sauvignon and Merlot has elegance, structure and well judged tannins. Recommended.

Viladellops Vinícola, S.L. (☎ 938 188 371) Founded in1994, this small bodega can certainly make good wines, but quality is mixed across its modest range. The following is the most consistent performer:

♦ *Arteo Tinto (red):* A well made young blend of 85 per cent Merlot and 15 per cent Tempranillo, with lots of fruit. Perhaps the bodega should concentrate on reds.

Vins El Cep, S.A. (☎ 938 912 353) Founded in 1980, with 200 hectares of its own vines, this bodega's story is similar to that of Viladellops: quality is mixed, although certainly achievable. The following are the most reliable wines:

♦ *L'Alzinar Chardonnay Fermentado en Barrica (white):* Always a well made, barrel-fermented Chardonnay, which in some years has more depth and complexity than others.

♦ *L'Alzinar Gran Cubi Maceración Carbónica Tinto (red):* Inexpensive, fresh, fruity, young Tempranillo suitable for drinking slightly chilled.

D.O. Pla de Bages

In Brief: A small, low-profile region making some good wines, with the potential to make very good ones.

This small D.O., instituted in 1997, lies in central Catalonia, covering a modest 500 hectares of vines. It has 100 grape growers, only seven bodegas and a low profile in Spain, but has already shown that it can make estimable wines.
Authorised grape varieties are:

- **White:** Chardonnay, Macabeo, Parellada and Picapoll.
- **Black:** Cabernet Sauvignon, Garnacha, Merlot, Sumoll and Tempranillo.

The region's white wines follow the standard Catalan pattern: those made from local grapes are fresh, fruity and inexpensive, while those from foreign varieties – in this case Chardonnay – have more body and complexity. Rosados tend to be made from good quality varieties – Cabernet Sauvignon and Merlot – and have high colour, body and flavour. Reds are frequently made from foreign grapes – Cabernet Sauvignon and Merlot again – and are notably characteristic of these high quality varieties.

Geography, Soil and Climate

Pla de Bages lies in Catalonia's central depression, which sounds miserable for it. This is hilly country and has a Mediterranean climate with mountain influences: temperature variations are more pronounced than is normal in Catalonia and rainfall is around 550mm (22in) per year. Soils are a mixture of sand and clay.

Future Development

The D.O. should continue to make praiseworthy reds, especially from Cabernet Sauvignon and, increasingly, Merlot, and regarding whites, there are promising results from the obscure local variety Picapoll, a notably delicate grape. Pla de Bages needs to raise its profile, which will allow bodegas to increase prices and generate funds for further development; the usual chicken and egg situation.

Selected Bodegas

Cellers Cooperativa D'Artés, S.C.C.L. (☎ 938 305 325) This co-operative is designated thus because Artés was the original name for the Pla de Bages region. It was founded in 1908 and produces two interesting wines from Picapoll. Thus far, the reds are unremarkable.

- 🌢 *Artium Picapoll (white):* A delicate, fruity wine, which will appeal to a wide range of palates.

◆ *Artium Picapoll Fermentado en Barrica (white):* This shows that the delicate Picapoll is sometimes unsuited to barrel-fermentation, becoming submerged under oak if not treated carefully. It is still a tasty wine, with well judged oak flavours.

Cellers Cooperativa de Salelles (☎ 938 720 572) A small producer, whose reds are best avoided, although the following white offers notable value for money:

◆ *As de Copes (white):* Well made, fruity, everyday Macabeo.

Celler Solergibert (☎ 938 305 084) Founded in 1868, this tiny bodega makes respectable to good wines, including:

◆ *Solergibert Picapoll (white):* A well made, straightforward, oaked wine with fruit presence.

◆ *Solergibert Merlot Media-Crianza (red):* This is an aromatic, easy-to-drink blend of fruit and toasty oak.

◆ *Solergibert Cabernet Sauvignon Crianza (red):* A straightforward, well made, tasty, inexpensive wine.

Masies D'Avinyó (☎ 938 747 406) Founded in 1983, this is the region's leading bodega, making a range of decent quality, generally well priced wines. Drink the younger reds, which are better made than older ones. Wines include:

◆ *Masies D'Avinyó Picapoll (white):* Fresh, fruity, balanced and flavoursome. Possibly a touch pricey.

◆ *Masies D'Avinyó Chardonnay (white):* Decent, commercial, reasonably priced, barrel-fermented Chardonnay. The oak does not overpower the fruit.

◆ *Masies D'Avinyó Cabernet Sauvignon Rosado (rosé):* Superior, mouthfilling rosado at a good price.

◆ *Masies D'Avinyó Merlot (red):* Tasty, smooth and long, for a fair price.

D.O. Priorato

In Brief: The source of some of Spain's most lauded red wines, dark, concentrated, mineral-laced, long, expensive and sought-after.

Priorato – which means 'priory' in Castilian and is 'Priorat' in Catalan – has recently become one of the most renowned Spanish D.O.s for top quality red wines. It is a modest-size, mountainous piece of land – covering 1,100 hectares of vineyards, with 390 grape growers and 30 bottling bodegas – surrounded on all sides by the D.O. Tarragona, and was formerly known for rancio wines and 'robust' (i.e. rough), dark, sometimes over-alcoholic red wines of no real distinction.

Until the '70s, the region had only three bodegas which bottled their own wines – Cellers d'Scala Dei, De Muller and Masía Barril – and a few co-operatives which produced wine for the bulk market. In the '80s its potential for greatness was recognised and a new impulse towards quality began to permeate Priorato. Much time, investment and technology was lavished on the region – the wine making school at Falset playing a major part – and Priorato's top reds now attract some of the highest prices for any Spanish wines, both domestically and abroad.

Authorised grape varieties are:

- **White:** Garnacha Blanca, Macabeo and Pedro Ximénez.

- **Black:** Cabernet Sauvignon, Cariñena, Garnacha and Garnacha Peluda.

White wines, relatively few in number, tend to be herbaceous, with 'rural' hints. Rosados are little made and are characterised by the maturity of their fruit. Priorato's traditional rancio wines are tasty, with nutty, herby flavours. And so we come to the reds, very much the signature wines of the region. Many are made from old, miserly yielding Garnacha and Cariñena vines which produce small quantities of concentrated, dark, tannic juice. The resultant wines are a deep cherry colour and are noted for their complex nose with mineral nuances. On the palate, the best are powerful, structured, tannic and very long, and are characterised by a minerally feel, arising from the unique make-up of the region's soil (see below). Modern technology has allowed bodegas to maintain the wines' traditional robust character, while lightening formerly high alcohol levels, which occasionally approached a brain-boiling 18 per cent. Priorato's wines are sometimes for long ageing, although because of the relative youth of some of the bodegas, only time will tell if they develop as well as is predicted.

Geography, Soil and Climate

Priorato's climate is 'extreme' Mediterranean, with summers notably hot and dry and annual rainfall of around 550mm (22in). The land is hilly, with vines planted on terraces cut into the steep hillsides and the soil is volcanic with a high silica content. This unique geological profile is crucial in giving the wines the minerally feel which marks them out from all others.

Future Development

Over the last ten years Priorato has progressed so much and so quickly, easily finding ready markets even for its more expensive wines, that there might appear to be little reason for the region's producers to change what they are doing or how they are doing it. However, wine is subject to the whims of fashion as much as anything and Priorato surfed the wave of the '90s popularity for big, concentrated, tannic red wines and also – although the two often go hand in hand – for so-called 'boutique' wines. These are rare, original and difficult to find, with consequently high prices, and have found plenty of people willing to pay for them.

However, prices have kept rising and people are now wondering if the bubble will burst, especially when these prices now sometimes exceed those of wines from regions with long established reputations for quality; Priorato does not enjoy this. Thus, the region might look to produce more wines in lower price bands, possibly from foreign grapes, to offer more diversity, of both style and price. Experiments with Cabernet

Sauvignon, Merlot and Syrah, both as varietals and also blended with the region's traditional grapes, have been successful.

However, the future looks bright, despite the danger of an over-reliance on the fickle boutique market: wine impresarios are seeking to buy land in Priorato, including Miguel Torres, who is readying two estates, one of 50 hectares in Porrera, the other of 20 hectares in Lloar. Both pieces of land are typically hilly and are being terraced for the planting of Garnacha, Mandó and Syrah. Hence Priorato's 30 bottling bodegas will shortly be joined by more and it is likely that the D.O. will soon be the second Spanish region to be deemed Denominación de Origen Calificada (after Rioja).

Selected Bodegas

Álvaro Palacios, S.L. (☎ 977 839 195) This bodega was founded in 1989 at a vineyard planted with old vines by a wine maker with long experience in Rioja. He has put this to good use and the bodega is one of Priorato's leading lights, both at the cheaper end of the scale with Les Terrases, in the middle with Finca Dofí and at the luxury end with the internationally renowned, seriously expensive L'Ermita, often voted Spain's top red wine.

● *Les Terrases (red):* A blend of 50 per cent Garnacha Negra and Garnacha Lisa, 40 per cent Cariñena and 10 per cent Cabernet Sauvignon, this is often described as one of Priorato's most accessible reds, both in style and price. It is full, vigorous and character-filled with mineral nuances, and will drink well over four or five years. Recommended.

● *Finca Dofí (red):* Garnacha-based, but a blend of five grapes, this is a top quality wine, with a characteristic nose of minerals plus toast and tar, and a palate of deep, rounded flavours and smooth, powerful tannins. Its price has escalated.

● *L'Ermita (red):* This is one of Spain's most expensive wines, first appearing on the market in 1995. It is primarily Garnacha Negra, with some Cabernet Sauvignon and small proportions of Cariñena, and spends 20 months in French oak barrels. The nose is powerful with minerals, mature fruit and oak, while the palate is packed with rich complexity, which needs time to show itself when the bottle has been opened. It has already acquired legendary status in Spain.

Celler de Josep Fuentes (☎ 977 830 648) Founded only in 1995, this small bodega has already proved capable of competing with the best of the region:

● *Vinya Llisarda (white):* One of the region's better whites, this offers elegant fruit, bite and some body.

● *Gran Clos (red):* 70 per cent Garnacha, 20 per cent Cariñena and 10 per cent Cabernet Sauvignon, this is a highly rated, full-bodied, flavoursome, complex wine. Highly recommended but its price has escalated.

Cellers D'Scala-Dei, S.A. (☎ 977 827 027) Priorato received its name from the priory of Scala Dei – the first monastery on the peninsular – which was founded in 1163 and planted the region's first grapes; thus the bodega is emblematic of Priorato and its current owners took over in 1973. Codorníu bought a 25 per cent stake at the end of

2000. The bodega produces some low-priced white and rosé wines, but the reds naturally hold the most interest and include:

● *Scala dei Negre (red)*: A young wine from Garnacha Negra, this has concentrated, spicy red and black fruit on the nose while the medium-bodied palate has engaging flavours, an attractive feel and lively but not intrusive tannins. A decent, affordable introduction to the region.

● *Scala Dei Crianza (red)*: 80 per cent Garnacha and 20 per cent Cabernet Sauvignon, this is one of the region's less expensive, more approachable crianza reds, powerfully fruity on the nose and smooth and tasty on the palate, but sometimes without the depth and complexity that characterise the region's better wines.

● *Cartoixa Scala Dei (red)*: A mid-priced, i.e. expensive, Priorato reserva wine, that varies in quality. When on form it has a complex, powerful nose and a palate with lots of deep, integrated flavours, confident tannins and a long finish – but choose your vintage.

Cims de Porrera, S.L. (☎ 977 828 187) Founded in 1996, this is a joint operation between José Luis Pérez Verdú (see **Mas Martinet Viticultors** on page 209), the musician Lluís Llach and the Porrera co-operative, which has produced superior wines based on the Cariñena grape, including:

● *Solanes (red)*: This has a lovely nose of toasty oak, dark fruit and minerals, while the palate has more of the same and persistence. Recommended.

● *Cims de Porrera Classic (red)*: Made from roughly 65 per cent Cariñena and 35 per cent Garnacha, and with 15 to 18 months in oak, this is one of the region's better wines. It has a powerful, complex nose with minerals and oak, while the palate is very expressive and powerful with elegance, balance and flavour. Recommended.

Clos Mogador, S.C.C.L. (☎ 977 839 171) The Barbier family has been making wine in Priorato since 1880 and the great-grandson of the founder has been one of the driving forces behind the recent boom in the region. His first wine came to market in 1989 and René Barbier's Clos Mogador is one of Priorato's most famous and best wines, while Clos Erasmus is made by wine maker Daphne Glorian. Clos means 'enclosed', a small plot of land.

● *Clos Mogador (red)*: A blend of 40 per cent Cabernet Sauvignon, 40 per cent Garnacha and 20 per cent Syrah from old vines, this wine spends between 15 and 18 months in barrel. It is noted for its complex, mineral, toasty nose while the palate is smooth, powerful, mature and complex, requiring time and concentration to appreciate the full range of its qualities. This is a wine made to last for years. Compared with another top Priorato wine, L'Ermita (see **Álvaro Palacios** on page 206), it is inexpensive, although that is relative.

● *Clos Erasmus (red)*: A blend of 60 per cent Garnacha, 30 per cent Cabernet Sauvignon and 10 per cent Syrah, this has a remarkably complex nose and palate with power and depth. One of the region's better wines, and, as with the above, relatively inexpensive in view of its quality.

Costers del Siurana (☎ 977 839 276) This bodega was founded in 1987 by Carles Pastrana, a former politician and journalist. Along with his friend René Barbier (see **Clos Mogador** on page 207) he has been one of the leading lights of the 'Priorato revolution'. His wines include:

● *Miserere (red):* This is a blend of Garnacha, Cariñena, Cabernet Sauvignon, Merlot and Tempranillo. It has a powerful, toasty nose and a deep, fruitily flavoursome palate with subtle oak integration. Miserere is not as punchy or complex as the bodega's other wines.

● *Clos de L'Obac (red):* Made from the same grapes as above, but with Syrah replacing Tempranillo, this has more depth and length than Miserere and is very flavoursome, but it sometimes lacks the complexity of the region's greats.

● *Dolc de L'Obac (red):* A sweet wine, made from Garnacha, Cabernet Sauvignon and Syrah, this has a toasty, fruity nose and is redolent of candied fruits. Not perhaps to everyone's taste, it is well made, although expensive.

De Muller, S.A. (☎ 977 757 473) A long established firm – most famous as a leading bodega of D.O. Tarragona where it was founded in 1851 – De Muller also makes wine in D.O. Terra Alta. In Priorato it is renowned for its fortified wines and its range includes the following:

● *Priorato Legitimo de Muller (red):* A blend of Garnacha, Cariñena and Cabernet Sauvignon, this is a reasonably priced introduction to the region's reds, although in some years it lacks the distinctive, mineral feel. It is, however, very flavoursome, with a powerful nose, dark fruit and some bite. When it does have the mineral touches it is one of the region's bargains, not a word used very often in relation to Priorato.

● *Dom Berenguer Solera 1918 (fortified red):* Garnacha and Cariñena make this aromatic, sweet, toasty, sometimes slightly overcooked wine.

● *Don Juan Fort Solera 1865 (fortified red):* This blend of Garnacha Tinta and Cariñena is one of the region's star rancios and the bodega's best wine, although its pleasures do not come cheap. Amber-coloured and aromatic, it is dry, full, complex and persistent, with fruit, spices and class.

Joan Blanch, S.A. (☎ 933 074 504) Founded in 1980, this bodega makes good quality wines, affordable by Priorato standards, including:

● *Vi del Racó Dolç Crianza (sweet red):* A blend of Garnacha and Cariñena – the proportions vary – this has a honeyed, herby nose and a sweet, fruity palate with some character. Well priced by regional standards.

● *Vi del Racó Crianza (red):* A blend of 50 per cent Cariñena and 50 per cent Garnacha, this is one of the region's more affordable wines, with a characterful nose of mature fruit, oak and minerals and an unctuous palate.

● *Vi del Racó Reserva (red):* A blend of 75 per cent Garnacha and 25 per cent Cariñena, this is a characterful, tasty wine with mature fruit and oak, but sometimes lacks the Priorato feel and complexity.

Joan Sangenis Juncosa (☎ 977 828 045) Founded only in 1995, this tiny operation has already produced worthy wines:

◆ *Mas d'En Compte Blanco Media-Crianza (red):* This blend of 70 per cent Garnacha Blanca, 20 per cent Picapoll and 10 per cent Pansal is a powerful, unctuous wine with bite and rather more oak than fruit. Well made and enjoyable, but very expensive compared with similar white wines from other regions.

◆ *Mas d'En Compte Tinto Crianza (red):* A blend of 50 per cent Cariñena, 40 per cent Garnacha and 10 per cent Cabernet Sauvignon, this has an attractive, distinctive, mineral nose, while the palate has powerful, mouthfilling flavours, but it needs further time in bottle to see if it will develop the same interest as the nose.

Mas Igneus, S.L. (☎ 938 993 131) This small bodega was founded in 1919 and has a fairly extensive range of wines, with 80 per cent of its production exported. Its good to very good wines – which vary in quality somewhat from year to year – include:

◆ *Barranc dels Clossos (white):* A blend of Garnacha Blanca, Macabeo and Pedro Ximénez, this inexpensive wine varies in quality from fresh, fruity, straightforward and well made to very flavoursome with strong fruit and herb character. Recommended.

◆ *Mas Igneus FA 104 (white):* A high quality, balanced, mouthfilling, barrel-fermented Garnacha Blanca and Pedro Ximénez, this is one of Priorato's best whites, full of herby, minerally aromas and flavours. Recommended.

◆ *Barranc dels Clossos Crianza (red):* A blend of Garnacha and Cariñena, this is a superior, lower-priced Priorato red wine, which in good years has lots of mouthfilling fruit and mineral flavours integrated with elegant oak.

◆ *Mas Igneus FA 206 Crianza (red):* A blend of Garnacha, Cariñena and Cabernet Sauvignon, this is a more expensive, complex version of the above.

◆ *Mas Igneus FA 112 Reserva (red):* A blend of up to five grapes, this is over twice the price of the foregoing crianzas and, when on form, is a superior, aromatic wine with soundly constructed, concentrated flavours and interest.

Mas Martinet Viticultors, S.L. (☎ 977 830 577) This bodega's owner, José Luis Pérez Verdú, is one of those credited with the resurrection of Priorato. He has lead by example, Clos Martinet being one of the region's best wines. The bodega was founded in 1989, with the first vintage released in 1993.

◆ *Clos Martinet (red):* This is a blend of 35 per cent Garnacha, 35 per cent Merlot, 20 per cent Cabernet Sauvignon and 10 per cent Syrah, and spends 17 months in French oak. It has a lovely nose of integrated fruit and oak overlaid with minerals, while the palate is full-flavoured, elegant, expressive, complex and very long. The tannins are powerful but not intrusive and this is a wine that will last for some years. This is one of Priorato's best and at a lower price than some of the region's other top bottles. Highly recommended from about 5 years old.

Pasanau Germans, S.L. (☎ 977 827 202) Renowned for its use of the Cabernet Sauvignon grape, this small bodega produces a modest selection of wines including:

♦ *Pasanau Crianza (red)*: An aromatic wine with dark fruit and tar on the nose and a powerful, tannic, balanced and delicious palate. Recommended.

♦ *Pasanau La Morera de Montsant (red)*: A blend of 70 per cent Garnacha and 30 per cent Cabernet Sauvignon, this is a toasty, mouthfilling wine with mature fruit. Well made but lacks the depth and complexity of Priorato.

♦ *Pasanau Finca La Planeta (red)*: 80 per cent Cabernet Sauvignon and 20 per cent Garnacha, this has an engaging nose of dark fruits and elegant oak, while the palate is powerful and deep with excellent tannins. Recommended and shows what the Bordeaux grape can do in this part of the world.

Sangenís i Vaqué (☎ 977 828 238) Founded in 1982, this very small operation makes two red wines:

♦ *Sangenís i Vaqué Tinto (red)*: A young wine made from Garnacha and Cariñena, this has a powerful nose with some mineral character and a palate with lots of flavour and more mineral personality. A decent young Priorato red.

♦ *Clos Monlleó Crianza (red)*: 50 per cent Garnacha and 50 per cent Cariñena, this is a superior wine, powerfully aromatic, soundly constructed and full of depth and flavour, but it is higher priced than some of the region's very best wines.

Vinícola de Priorat, S.C.C.L. (☎ 977 839 167) Founded in the early '90s, this is a large producer by Priorato standards, making a range of lower-priced wines of reasonable quality, including:

♦ *Mas de L'Alba (white)*: This blend of 50 per cent Macabeo, 40 per cent Garnacha Blanca and 10 per cent Pedro Ximénez is well made, unremarkable and refreshing.

♦ *Onix (red)*: A flavoursome, inexpensive, fruit-driven wine from Garnacha and Cariñena. Decent everyday drinking, but not really what Priorato is about.

♦ *L'Arc Crianza (red)*: A blend of Cabernet Sauvignon, Garnacha and Cariñena, this is aromatic and well made, but it lacks depth and Priorato personality, and for this price the region offers better wines.

Vins d'Alta Qualitat, S.L. (Rotllan Torrá) (☎ 933 134 347) Founded in the early '80s, this bodega produces a range of good and improving wines, including:

♦ *Balandra Crianza (red)*: A blend of 50 per cent Garnacha, 25 per cent Cariñena and 25 per cent Cabernet Sauvignon, this has a nose of oak and minerals, while the palate has lots of flavour and power with more mineral touches.

♦ *Amadís Crianza (red)*: A blend of the three grapes above with Merlot and Syrah, this is a superior crianza, although twice the price of the Balandra. It is aromatic, powerful, integrated and elegant. Good, but quite expensive.

Viticultors del Priorat (☎ 977 262 268) Only formed in 1998, this bodega's owners include Luis Atienza Serna, a former Minister of Agriculture. Its first wine – Morlanda – came to the market in 1999 and has already proved successful.

◆ *Morlanda Blanco (white):* Made from Garnacha Blanca, this has the nutty nose of the barrel, while the palate is unctuous and mouthfilling. Well made, but the oak influence is rather pervasive.

◆ *Morlanda Crianza (red):* A blend of 60 per cent Garnacha, 30 per cent Cariñena and 10 per cent Cabernet Sauvignon, this has a nose of fruit, liquorice and minerals, while the medium-bodied palate has candied fruit, bite, personality and length.

Viticultors Mas d'En Gil, S.L. (☎ 977 830 192) Founded only in 1998, this small operation has already made its mark with high quality wines:

◆ *Coma Vella (red):* A blend of Garnacha, Cabernet Sauvignon, Cariñena and others, this has an elegant, complex nose, with vanilla and minerals, while the palate has mouthfilling, integrated flavours of same. Recommended and competitively priced by Priorato standards.

◆ *Clos Fontá (red):* A similar blend to the above, this is becoming one of the region's new stars. It has a powerful, deep, mineral nose, while the palate has unctuous flavours of mature dark fruits and smooth yet confident tannins. Very good.

D.O. Tarragona

In Brief: A fairly undeveloped region producing some good wines of all hues. With development and investment, it could make very high quality reds.

Spread over 11,000 hectares of vineyards surrounding the southern Catalan coastal city of Tarragona, D.O. Tarragona's traditional specialities were high-alcohol dessert wines, containing between 15 per cent and 23 per cent alcohol, which were sold in northern Europe as 'poor man's port', and roughish reds and whites, often sold in bulk for blending. Thankfully, times have changed, and there are signs of a new impulse towards quality in the region, with the emphasis on red wines. The fact that highly regarded Priorato is surrounded by Tarragona shows what parts of the region's land are capable of. It has over 4,700 grape growers and 144 bodegas, 32 of which bottle their wines.
  Authorised grape varieties are:

● **White:** Chardonnay, Garnacha Blanca, Macabeo, Moscatel de Alexandria, Parellada and Xarel-lo.

● **Black:** Cabernet Sauvignon, Garnacha, Merlot, Samsó and Tempranillo.

The region's whites, when well made, tend to be respectably 'Catalan': fruitily flavoursome, sometimes herby and good value. The rosés are fresh, fruity, easy-drinking wines, while the traditional fortified wines are of three types: sweet fortified, dry rancio and dry fortified. Tarragona's better reds come from the Falset sub-zone, next to Priorato, and are noted for being full-bodied and tasty, although less subtle than wines from some of the other Catalan D.O.s.

Geography, Soil and Climate

Tarragona is split into three sub-zones: El Camp, Falset and Ribera d'Ebre. El Camp has a Mediterranean climate, with annual rainfall of 500mm (20in); Falset is more temperate, with rainfall of 650mm (26in); and Ribera d'Ebre has a transitional-continental climate, with cold winters, hot summers and rainfall of only 385mm (15in) per year. The region's vineyards are situated at up to 600m (1,968ft) above sea level and soils are as follows: El Camp – light calcareous; Falset – granitic; and Ribera d'Ebre – alluvial and calcareous.

Future Development

The region lags behind other Catalan D.O.s in terms of both its table wine quality and the sophistication of its bodegas. Parts of Tarragona are suited to the production of superior reds and the presence of old Garnacha and Cariñena vines augurs well for the possibility of wines to rival those of neighbouring Priorato, perhaps without all of the mineral complexity provided by Priorato's soil. Cabernet Sauvignon and Merlot are beginning to produce encouraging results and the region is looking to grow more Syrah, which should thrive there. Much remains to be done and while the will towards improvement is there, it is now a question of generating the all-important finance.

Selected Bodegas

Agrícola Falset-Marçà, S.C.C.L. (☎ 977 830 105) Founded in 1917, this bodega makes good and improving wines, including the following:

◆ *Jovencell Blanco (white):* This is a superior, inexpensive 'house' wine, fresh, fruity, flavoursome and soundly constructed.

◆ *Martius (white):* A blend of 70 per cent Garnacha Blanca, 25 per cent Macabeo and 5 per cent Parellada, this is a characterful, well made wine with plenty of fruit and some mineral complexity. Good.

◆ *L'Antoll Rosado (rosé):* Well made, fresh and fruity rosado from 85 per cent Garnacha and 15 per cent Tempranillo.

◆ *Jovencell Tinto (red):* Well priced, full-bodied, flavoursome young Cabernet Sauvignon with bite for barbecued food.

◆ *Castell de Falset Crianza (red):* A blend of 50 per cent Garnacha, 35 per cent Cabernet Sauvignon and 15 per cent Tempranillo, this is a characterful crianza with tasty, mature fruit and oak and length, although perhaps over-priced.

◆ *Ranci (dry fortified red):* An approachable, reasonably priced introduction to this style of wine.

Celler de Capçanes (☎ 977 178 319) Founded in 1933, this worthy producer has a large selection of wines, most of fair to good quality, with some very good indeed, including:

- *Flor de Maig Blanco (white)*: A blend of 50 per cent Garnacha Blanca and 50 per cent Macabeo this is reasonably priced, herby, dry white wine with mineral hints. Good.

- *Mas Collet Blanco (white)*: A flavoursome, unctuous, oaky wine.

- *Flor de Maig Rosado (rosé)*: Made from 60 per cent Garnacha and 40 per cent Cariñena, this is reasonably priced, fruity, minerally rosado.

- *Flor de Maig Tinto (red)*: Made from 50 per cent Garnacha, 30 per cent Tempranillo and 20 per cent Cariñena, this is a young, mouthfilling, tasty red with some character for a low price.

- *Mas Donis Tinto (red)*: A lightish, aromatic, flavoursome blend of Garnacha Tinta and Syrah, better in some years than others.

- *Mas Collet Tinto Semi-Crianza (red)*: A blend of Tempranillo, Garnacha, Cabernet Sauvignon and Cariñena, this is a flavoursome, jammy, aromatic red with character and length. Good.

- *Flor de Maig Cabernet Sauvignon Crianza (red)*: Well made, aromatic, characterful, mouthfilling Cabernet for a good price. Recommended – drink at five or six years old.

- *Vall de Calás Crianza (red)*: This is a potent blend of 60 per cent Merlot and 40 per cent Garnacha Tinta, which should not be drunk before it is four years old. It has a complex nose of tobacco and minerals, while the palate has confident tannins and mature fruit and oak. Good, but the price is on the rise.

- *Costers del Gravet Crianza (red)*: A superior blend of 60 per cent Cabernet Sauvignon, 25 per cent Garnacha and 15 per cent Cariñena, this has a complex, chocolate, mineral nose and a flavoursome, elegant palate with jammy fruit and fine oak. Good, but again the price has risen somewhat.

- *Cabrida (red)*: This is one of the producer's flagship red wines, an expensive, superior Garnacha, which aspires to Priorato standards and prices. It has a deep, complex nose of dark fruits and toasty oak, while the palate is powerful, full, fruity, toasty and long. Very good.

Cooperativa Agrícola Baix Priorat Els Guiamets (☎ 977 413 018) Founded in 1913, this producer makes a small range of good to very good red wines:

- *Lóxus Negre (red)*: 50 per cent Garnacha, 30 per cent Cariñena and 20 per cent Tempranillo, this is superior, reasonably priced, young red wine, with a deep, complex nose and a tasty palate of mature fruit with tannic bite.

- *Lóxus Crianza Negre (red)*: Made from 60 per cent Tempranillo and 40 per cent Cabernet Sauvignon, this is a powerful, toasty wine with confident tannins. Recommended.

Cooperativa Agrícola Sant Isidro de Nulles, S.C.C.L. (☎ 977 602 622) Founded in 1917, the general standard of this co-operative's wines is respectable. The following are the best bottles:

◆ *Adernats Blanc de Blancs (white):* 85 per cent Macabeo and 15 per cent Chardonnay and Parellada, this is superior everyday wine, aromatic and fruity with bite.

◆ *Adernats Chardonnay (white):* A straightforward, light, refreshing, tasty blend of 85 per cent Chardonnay and 15 per cent Macabeo.

◆ *Adernats Cabernet Sauvignon (red):* A light, tasty, easy-drinking Cabernet.

De Muller, S.A. (☎ 977 757 473) Founded in 1851, De Muller is the top name in Tarragona, and also makes wine in D.O. Priorato and D.O. Terra Alta – see pages 208 and 218. It is renowned for its rancio and fortified wines and also as a supplier of altar wine to the Vatican. As yet, its table wines have not quite scaled the heights, although some are of good quality.

◆ *De Muller Chardonnay Fermentado en Barrica (white):* A superior, unctuous, balanced, flavoursome wine for a competitive price.

◆ *Solimar Rosado (rosé):* Decent, fruity rosado from the Merlot grape at the right price. Better in some years than others.

◆ *Solimar Tinto (red):* A characterful, straightforward Cabernet Sauvignon/Merlot crianza, honest and tasty for a low price. Barbecue wine.

◆ *De Muller Cabernet Sauvignon (red):* A flavoursome, characterful, easy-to-drink wine.

◆ *De Muller Merlot (red):* As above.

Josep Anguera Beyme (☎ 977 418 348) A small operation, dating back to 1830, making a small selection of good quality wines.

◆ *Joan D'Anguera Tinto (red):* A young, fresh, lively, reasonably priced young wine made from 45 per cent Syrah, 35 per cent Garnacha and 20 per cent Cabernet Sauvignon.

◆ *Joan D'Anguera Finca l'Argatá Tinto Crianza (red):* A soundly constructed, powerful wine with lots of mature fruit, made from Syrah, Cabernet Sauvignon, Garnacha and Cariñena. Drink at four or five years old. Perhaps a touch pricey.

Unió Agraria Cooperativa (☎ 977 330 055) This is a large operation, founded in the '40s. The majority of its wines are respectable, with the following worth investigating:

◆ *Viña Roureda Blanc de Blancs (white):* A light, characterful, dry, 'house' wine for a low price. In some years, it is too understated, i.e. bland.

◆ *Viña Roureda Tinto (red):* Decent, young, fruity red wine with mature fruit.

◆ *Viña Roureda Crianza (red):* A straightforward, inexpensive blend of fruit and oak. Decent, commercial, everyday wine.

Vinya Janine (☎ 977 628 305) A small operation founded in 1994, their whites are unremarkable, but it makes a couple of worthy reds which bode well for the future:

● *Vinya Janine Crianza (red):* A blend of 87 per cent Tempranillo and 13 per cent Cabernet Sauvignon, this is a decent, commercial mix of fruit and oak.

● *Vinya Janine Cabernet Sauvignon Reserva (red):* A characterful, competitively priced wine, with a distinctive Cabernet nose and a satisfying, flavoursome palate with length. Good.

D.O. Terra Alta

In Brief: An underdeveloped, growing region making some good white wines and with the potential to make very good reds. One to watch.

Terra Alta's 8,825 hectares of vines lie in south-west Catalonia. It has 2,390 grape growers and 45 bodegas, of which 22 bottle their wines. Traditionally dominated by co-operatives, with the emphasis on quantity rather than quality, the D.O. is showing definite signs of improvement, with white wines made from the Garnacha Blanca grape prominent in the drive towards better things. With regard to reds, Garnacha Tinta and Tempranillo are being planted to replace the traditional Cariñena – which sometimes produced rather jammy wines – and the results are encouraging. In fact, many of the region's vines have been judged to be past their best and there is an active programme of replanting with fresh ones. New technology and ideas are also being introduced to Terra Alta.

Authorised grape varieties are:

● **White:** Garnacha Blanca, Macabeo and Parellada.

● **Black:** Cariñena, Garnacha Tinta and Tempranillo.

The region's wine styles can be characterised as follows: whites: these are Terra Alta's strong suit, made primarily from Garnacha Blanca, with up-front, complex, fruity flavours. Garnacha, the classic Spanish rosé grape, makes most of the region's rosados, which are of fair quality. The reds are notably flavoursome, but, as yet, not always subtle, and sometimes positively robust. Terra Alta also makes several of Catalonia's better known fortified wines.

Geography, Soil and Climate

Terra Alta is remote, hilly country with a trying Mediterranean-continental climate: summers are hot and dry, winters can be very cold, and rainfall is a scanty 400mm (16in) per year; strong winds can also be a problem. The climate becomes more extreme the further east you travel in the region. Vineyards are situated at around 400m (1,312ft) above sea level and soils are calcareous.

Future Development

The D.O. needs to continue raising its profile and the production of more good quality, reasonably priced wines from Garnacha Blanca will help to achieve this. Regarding reds, in addition to promising results from Garnacha and Tempranillo, growths of Cabernet Sauvignon and Syrah should increase the region's red wine quality and variety. As with Tarragona, finance will be needed to speed the drive forward.

Selected Bodegas

Castell Bel Art, S.L. (☎ 977 420 014) Founded only in 1998, this producer is already showing signs that it is capable of making good quality, everyday wines, including:

◆ *Blanc de Bel Art (white)*: 90 per cent Garnacha Blanca and 10 per cent Macabeo, this is a fruity, characterful young white for everyday drinking.

◆ *Bel Art Cabernet/Garnacha (red)*: A smooth, balanced, tasty, everyday red wine, without pretensions to complexity or greatness (this is not a criticism).

◆ *Bel Art Merlot (red)*: Well constructed, flavoursome Merlot with touches of oak for a competitive price.

Celler Bàrbara Forés (☎ 977 420 160) Founded in 1889, this small, family operation is the most famous name in the region. Quality has been unpredictable of late.

◆ *Bàrbara Forés Blanco (white)*: This is often a superior, reasonably priced blend of 85 per cent Garnacha Blanca and 15 per cent Macabeo, aromatic, fruity, oaky and complex. However, some vintages are flat and one-dimensional.

◆ *El Quintà Bàrbara Forés (white)*: A barrel-fermented Garnacha Blanca with body and balance, but it is over-priced.

◆ *Coma d'en Pou Bàrbara Forés (red)*: This is the region's outstanding red wine, a blend of 50 per cent Cabernet Sauvignon, 25 per cent Garnacha and 25 per cent Syrah, it is aromatic, powerful, balanced and elegant. A sign of what Terra Alta is capable of.

Celler Cooperativa Gandesa (☎ 977 420 017) Founded in 1919, this co-operative makes a wide range of respectable although unremarkable wines, including:

◆ *Antic Castell Blanco (white)*: A simple blend of Garnacha and Macabeo, this is gently flavoursome, inexpensive white wine.

◆ *César Martinell (white)*: This is usually a tasty, well made, unctuous, inexpensive, oak-aged Garnacha Blanca. However, in some years it is unbalanced and monotonous.

◆ *Antic Castell Tinto (red)*: A decently made, everyday, young red from the Cariñena grape.

◆ *Garidells Tinto (red)*: Simple, tasty, reasonably priced red wine from Garnacha and Tempranillo.

◆ *Gandesa Vi Ranci (fortified)*: Flavoursome, nutty rancio from Garnacha Blanca.

Cellers Tarroné (☎ 977 430 109) Founded in 1940, this small operation produces a worthy red wine, although its others are best avoided:

◊ *Torremadrina Crianza (red):* This well made, inexpensive blend of 60 per cent Cabernet Sauvignon, 30 per cent Tempranillo and 10 per cent Garnacha is aromatic, smoothly robust, toasty and tasty. Drink when four or five years old.

Cooperativa Agrícola de Corberá d'Ebre (☎ 977 420 432) Founded in 1960, this co-operative has shown that it has the potential to join Terra Alta's better producers, although quality can vary.

◊ *Mirmil-lo (white):* Usually a respectable, fruity young wine.

◊ *Vall de Canelles Blanco Crianza (white):* A superior, oaked wine, mouthfilling, herby and flavoursome. In some years it has more depth and complexity than others.

◊ *Mirmil-lo (rosé):* This is a full-bodied rosado with lots of flavour.

◊ *Vall de Canelles Tinto Crianza (red):* A straightforward, aromatic, jammily flavoursome, oaked red.

Cooperativa Agrícola Germandat (☎ 977 438 010) Founded in 1961, this co-operative has shown itself capable of making decent wines, including:

◊ *Suprem Blanco (white):* A well made young Macabeo with body and character.

◊ *Vi de L'Alba (white):* An elegant barrel-fermented Garnacha Blanca with lots of integrated flavour. A touch expensive.

◊ *Rosalvi (rosé):* A competent, light, Garnacha rosado.

◊ *Faristol (red):* A respectable, young, light, fruity Garnacha.

◊ *Fill del Temps Crianza (red):* A decent, oaked red with body and flavour from Garnacha and Cariñena.

Cooperativa Agrícola San Josep de Bot (☎ 977 428 035) Founded in 1944, this small operation makes a wide range of wines. Quality is variable, but the following are invariably worthy:

◊ *Clot d'Encís (white):* A well made, tasty, inexpensive blend of 70 per cent Garnacha Blanca and 25 per cent Macabeo.

◊ *La Plana d'En Fonoll Blanco Crianza (white):* A straightforward, tasty, reasonably priced blend of Garnacha Blanca, Macabeo and toasty oak.

◊ *Llagrimes de Tardor Crianza (red):* A blend of Garnacha, Tempranillo, Cariñena and Cabernet Sauvignon, this is a straightforward, tasty blend of fruit and oak.

Cooperativa San Miguel de Batea (☎ 977 430 056) Founded in 1961, this is another co-operative which has shown that it can make decent wines, notably the following:

⧫ *Vallmayor Blanco (white)*: An aromatic, flavoursome, unctuous wine.

⧫ *Vivertell Crianza (red)*: A decent crianza, with lots of mature dark fruit.

De Muller (☎ 977 757 473) For further details of the bodega, see pages 208 and 214.

⧫ *Vino de Misa (sweet white)*: Vino de Misa means Mass Wine, as in religion. This blend of Garnacha Blanca and Macabeo is sweetly tasty, worth trying for its novelty value.

Vinos Piñol, S.L. (☎ 977 430 505) Founded in 1940, this is one of the region's better producers, with a worthy range of wines, including the following:

⧫ *Nuestra Señora del Portal Blanco (white)*: A superior, mouthfilling, reasonably priced blend of Garnacha, Macabeo and Moscatel, with lots of flavour and some complexity.

⧫ *L'Avi Arrufi Blanco Crianza (white)*: A powerful, tasty wine, heavier on the oak than the fruit.

⧫ *Nuestra Señora del Portal Tinto (red)*: A decent Garnacha/Cariñena blend with tasty fruit and tannins.

⧫ *L'Avi Arrufi Tinto Crianza (red)*: An aromatic, powerful, spicy blend of Cabernet Sauvignon, Tempranillo and Garnacha. One of the region's best reds, although compared with similar quality wines from other Catalan D.O.s, it is rather expensive.

Vinyes i Cellers Clúa (☎ 977 438 013) Founded in 1995, this is another producer whose wines have shown the quality of which Terra Alta is capable.

⧫ *Mas d'En Pol Blanco (white)*: A 'cocktail' of five grapes – Garnacha Blanca, Chardonnay, Macabeo, Parellada and Moscatel – this golden wine is a tasty, mouthfilling, reasonably priced mixture of fruit and oak.

⧫ *Vindemia (white)*: This oaked blend of 85 per cent Garnacha Blanca and 15 per cent Chardonnay is well made, mouthfilling and long, although not complex or classy enough to justify the elevated price.

⧫ *Mas d'En Pol Tinto (red)*: Three black grapes – Garnacha, Tempranillo and Cabernet Sauvignon – make this reasonably priced, mouthfilling, superior, everyday red wine.

⧫ *Millennium (red)*: A good Garnacha-based crianza, with interesting flavours, although as with the Vindemia, the price is too high.

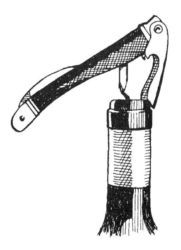

Cava production is an important and lucrative part of Spain's wine industry

10.

CAVA

European regulations decree that any new D.O. must have specific geographical boundaries. When Cava was designated thus on 27th February 1986, the D.O. had to comply and it was decided that it should encompass 159 villages spread across various parts of Spain. These villages were chosen simply because they had been making Champagne Method wines for a long time, not necessarily because they were actually good at it. Thus, D.O. Cava is not one continuous piece of land or several small parcels situated close to each other, as are the other D.O.s. It covers disparate patches of land in several parts of Spain: 63 municipalities in the province of Barcelona, 52 in Tarragona, 12 in Lleida and 5 in Girona, as well as areas of Álava, Badajoz, Navarra, Rioja, Valencia and Zaragoza.

Despite D.O. Cava's wide geographical boundaries, some 99 per cent of the wine is made in Catalonia, with 95 per cent of the total made in Penedés and 75 per cent made in and around San Sadurní de Noya, which is Santa Sadurní d' Anoia in Catalan. The D.O. covers 32,904 hectares of vines, has 7,124 grape growers and 265 bodegas. Two groups of companies – Codorníu and Freixenet – dominate Cava production, between them accounting for a colossal 80 per cent of sales.

D.O. Cava

In Brief: D.O. Cava is the source of large amounts of good value, easy-drinking sparkling wines at competitive prices – mainly from local grape varieties – and can also make high quality examples.

Don José Raventós y Fatjó was the first person in Spain to make sparkling wines using the Champagne Method – the most successful system – now called the Método Tradicional under European Union rules. His first efforts appeared in 1872 and his Catalan family firm, Codorníu, is now one of the world's largest sparkling wine manufacturers.

Cava wines used to be called Champán – the Spanish for Champagne – but after several visits to the law courts, the French won a ruling to the effect that only wines made in the Champagne region of France had the right to call themselves Champagne. This was an entirely reasonable judgement and put paid to sparkling wine manufacturers all over the world using the exalted Champagne name on their labels. Since 1st September 1994, European law has dictated that the term Método Tradicional be used for wines made by the Champagne method in places other then Champagne. Since the banning of the term *Champán*, the Champagne Method sparkling wines of Spain have been known as *Cava*. It is the Catalan word for cellar and its adoption reflects the fact that the vast majority of such wines are made in Catalonia.

Authorised grape varieties are:

- **White:** Chardonnay, Macabeo (also called Viura), Parellada, Subirat (Malvasía Riojana) and Xarel-lo.

- **Black:** Garnacha Tinta, Monastrell and Pinot Noir.

In Catalonia, the traditional trio of grapes used to make Cava is Macabeo, Parellada and Xarel-lo, and these three blended together in various proportions still make the majority of wines. Macabeo contributes freshness and fruit, Parellada offers acidity and delicate aromas, while Xarel-lo gives alcoholic strength and body. Outside Catalonia, Cava is often made 100 per cent from Macabeo.

Since being officially sanctioned in 1986, Chardonnay has increasingly been used in Catalan Cava, either as part of a blend or to make varietal wines. This has proved a controversial move: traditionalists consider that its use will compromise the Cava style and invite what will perhaps be unfavourable comparisons with Champagne, where Chardonnay is one of the primary grapes. Others point both to its undoubted qualities and to the success that it has enjoyed in Champagne as excellent reasons for its use.

Geography, Soil and Climate

Since most Cava is produced in Penedés, see **D.O. Penedés** on page 187 for details.

Future Development

Cava's commercial success, based on its attractive quality/price ratio, was a feature of the latter 20th century, both in Spain and internationally. In the early years of the 21st century annual production stood at around 200 million bottles, with half of those destined for the increasingly hungry export market. Germany, Great Britain, the United States, Switzerland, Japan and Canada are particularly important customers.

Some see this success as reason enough for continuing on the current path: 'Don't fix it if it ain't broken' is their maxim. Others disagree, feeling that no enterprise can sit on its laurels and that Cava producers should be looking to offer more variety and innovation to maintain their level of success, especially in the face of increased competition from Australia and California, among others. They think that as well as continuing to use Macabeo, Parellada and Xarel-lo, Cava houses should also offer wines from Chardonnay and the recently authorised Pinot Noir. As for the inevitable comparisons with Champagne, they maintain that Cava has carved a niche for itself as a good value, easy-to-drink sparkling wine, which, for the most part, does not aspire to compete with the much more expensive Champagne and that consumers recognise this.

This was not always the case. Some used to think that, in comparison with the wines of Champagne, Cava was aggressively frothy and sometimes too sweet; others detected 'rustic', earthy touches. While this was true of some wines, modern technology and a desire to appeal to international tastes have improved many of the wines. In addition, the differences between Cavas and Champagnes are logical when you consider the differences in grape varieties, soil, climate and ageing lengths. There is plenty of room for both and those who still decry Cava are probably only reacting to its differences from what they are used to.

Cava made from the traditional Catalan trio of grapes is probably at its best with two or three years ageing. Any less (and the *minimum* allowed is nine months) and the wines can lack the character that comes from extended lees ageing; any more, and the limitations of the grape varieties can become apparent: Macabeo, Parellada and Xarel-lo do not always make wines for long ageing. The producers who make such wines can continue to offer value while making wines which do not suffer from the blandness which some Cavas have been accused of. But Chardonnay and Pinot Noir are grapes of proven quality for sparkling wine and their use, either blended with the traditional varieties, used to make varietals or, ideally, both, should be part of Cava's future development.

Selected Bodegas

Agustí Torelló, S.A. (☎ 938 911 173) Founded in 1955, this producer has an annual turnover of some 400,000 litres and exports 30 per cent of its wine. Quality is good to very good and wines include:

● *Agustí Torello Mata Reserva (Brut)*: A high quality Cava for a competitive price, with flavour and balance. The producer's best value wine.

● *Kripta (Brut Nature)*: A full-bodied, dry wine with some complexity, made from grapes from vines over 50 years old, but it is expensive. The amphora-style bottle design is very distinctive.

Albet i Noya, S.A.T. (☎ 938 994 812) Founded in 1978, and also a producer of high quality table wines (see page 188), Albet i Noya makes a varied and admirable range of Cavas, including:

● *Albet i Noya Rosat (Brut)*: Made 100 per cent from Pinot Noir, this pink Cava s full-bodied, agreeably different and reasonably priced. Recommended.

● *Albet i Noya (Brut)*: A blend of Macabeo, Parellada, Xarel-lo and Chardonnay, this is full-bodied, flavoursome, persistent and reasonably priced. One of the better Cavas in its price range.

● *Albet i Noya (Brut Nature)*: Made from the same grapes as the Brut above, this has flavour, complexity and length. Recommended.

● *Albet i Noya 21 Reserva (Brut)*: Made from 70 per cent Chardonnay and 30 per cent Parellada, this is very good Cava, with lots of long herbaceous flavours. Recommended.

Alsina y Sardá, S.A. (☎ 938 988 132) Founded in the mid-'80s, this producer makes respectable rather than remarkable Cavas, including:

● *Alsina y Sardá (Brut)*: Fresh, fruity, respectable and reasonably priced.

● *Alsina y Sardá (Brut Nature)*: Fresh, balanced and refreshing.

Antonio Mascaró, S.L. (☎ 938 901 628) Well known for its brandy and liqueurs, this modest-size producer's Cavas are of good quality at reasonable prices. They include:

● *Mascaró (Brut Nature)*: A reasonably priced blend of 20 per cent Macabeo and 80 per cent Parellada, with flavour and some persistence.

◆ *Mascaró Monarch (Brut)*: A blend of 10 per cent Chardonnay and 90 per cent Parellada, this offers a fair amount of interest and class for the price.

Blancher-Espumosos del Cava, S.A. (☎ 938 183 286) This producer makes a modest range of adequate Cavas, with the following representative of its wares:

◆ *Blancher Especial (Brut)*: Balanced, flavoursome and reasonably priced.

Bodegas Bilbaínas, S.A. (☎ 941 310 147) Bilbaínas is a leading Rioja producer (see page 307) that also makes small amounts of Cava from Viura and Malvasía grapes. The wines are adequate rather than exceptional, generally fuller-bodied and less subtle than Catalan Cavas. Try the following:

◆ *Royal Carlton (Brut Nature)*: This is tasty and full-bodied, rather than being a shy little thing.

Can Quetu, S.L. (☎ 938 911 214) Founded in 1959, this producer's annual turnover is modest. Wines are commercial and decent but not outstanding, including:

◆ *Can Quetu (Brut)*: Made from the usual Catalan trio of Cava grapes with 10 per cent Chardonnay, this is light, fresh and inexpensive.

◆ *Can Quetu (Brut Nature)*: Fresh with a certain nutty bitterness.

Can Rafols del Caus, S.L. (☎ 938 970 013) This producer of excellent table wines (see page 190) also makes a small, high quality range of Cavas.

◆ *Gran Caus Reserva (Brut Nature)*: A superior blend of 30 per cent Chardonnay, 20 per cent Macabeo and 50 per cent Xarel-lo, this has flavour and some complexity. Recommended.

◆ *Gran Caus Rosado Reserva (Brut Nature)*: A tasty, balanced, characterful pink Cava from the Pinot Noir grape, although possibly a touch pricey.

◆ *Gran Caus Reserva Especial (Brut Nature)*: A classy, elegant, complex wine from Chardonnay, Macabeo and Xarel-lo.

Capita Vidal, S.L. (☎ 938 988 630) Founded in 1988, this Cava house is respectable rather than world-beating. Wines include:

◆ *Capita Vidal (Brut)*: Fresh, light and refreshing.

◆ *Fuchs de Vidal Cuvée Especial (Brut Nature)*: The bodega's outstanding wine, this is full-bodied, elegant, long and reasonably priced. Recommended.

Castellblanch, S.A. (☎ 938 917 025) Founded in 1908 and now part of the Freixenet Group, Castellblanch makes a range of good quality, widely available Cavas, including:

◆ *Brut Zero (Brut)*: Full-bodied, flavoursome, balanced and elegant. Recommended.

- *Brut Maritim Reserva (Brut):* Fresh, well balanced and long. Recommended.

- *Dos Lustros Reserva (Brut Nature):* This is elegant, tasty and complex, although more expensive and no better than the Brut Zero.

Castell de Vilarnau, S.A. (☎ 938 912 361) Founded in 1982 and owned by sherry giants González Byass, Castell de Vilarnau produces superior, reasonably priced Cavas, including:

- *Vilarnau Rosado (Brut):* Decent, inexpensive pink Cava from the Trepat grape.

- *Vilarnau Reserva (Brut):* A blend of 60 per cent Macabeo and 40 per cent Parellada, this has elegance, flavour and structure. Recommended.

- *Vilarnau Reserva (Brut Nature):* This is superior, reasonably priced wine, flavoursome, refreshing and quite complex. Good and recommended.

Cava Llopart (☎ 938 993 125) Founded in 1887, this Cava house has had plenty of time to attain its current level of quality. Wines include:

- *Llopart Reserva (Brut Nature):* Flavoursome, full-bodied and well made.

- *Imperial (Brut):* Fresh and fruity with some delicacy.

- *Leopardi Gran Reserva (Brut):* Made from the standard Catalan trio of grapes plus 10 per cent Chardonnay, this is balanced, tasty and long. Good.

Cavas del Castillo de Perelada, S.A. (☎ 972 538 011) Founded in 1923, this Cava house offers high quality at affordable prices from its unimaginatively labelled bottles that could do with a design makeover. Wines include:

- *Castillo Perelada Brut Reserva (Brut):* One of the best Cavas in its low price band, this is full-bodied and flavoursome, and probably as good as you can buy for the price.

- *Castillo Perelada Rosado (Brut):* A blend of Garnacha and Monastrell, this is decent pink Cava, fruity and refreshing.

- *Castillo Perelada (Brut Nature):* A superior wine, finely structured and long.

Cavas Hill, S.A. (☎ 938 900 588) A long established producer of respectable Cavas, including:

- *Cavas Hill Reserva Oro (Brut):* Delicate, flavoursome and soundly constructed.

- *Cavas Hill Reserva Oro (Brut Nature):* This is a wine for those who like dry Cavas with bite. Well made, lean and tasty.

- *Cavas Hill Gran Reserva (Brut de Brut):* Professionally made and subtly flavoursome.

Cavas Lavernoya (☎ 938 912 202) This is another decent Cava house. All of its wines are respectable, with the following standing out:

♦ *Lácrima Baccus Reserva (Brut):* Fresh, fruity and refreshing, and sometimes quite full-bodied.

♦ *Lácrima Baccus Primerísimo Reserva (Brut):* A soundly constructed wine with flavour, interest and some persistence.

Cavas Mont-Ferrant, S.A. (☎ 934 191 000) Dating back to 1848, this Cava house has built a solid reputation for its wines, which include:

♦ *Mont-Ferrant Brut Vintage (Brut):* Fresh, subtle and well made.

♦ *Mont-Ferrant Cuvée Chardonnay (Brut):* One of the better Chardonnay Cavas, with expressive flavour and interest.

Cavas Nadal (☎ 938 988 011) A family firm founded in 1943, making decent Cavas from the Catalan trio of grapes, including:

♦ *Nadal (Brut):* Aromatic and flavoursome.

♦ *Nadal Especial (Extra Brut):* Well made, rounded and tasty.

♦ *Nadal Salvatage (Extra Brut):* This has elegance and structure.

♦ *Ramón Nadal Giró (Extra Brut):* Top-drawer Cava elegance. Recommended, and reasonably priced, given its class.

Cavas Naverán (Sadeve, S.A.) (☎ 938 988 274) As well as making good table wines (see page 191) this Cava house produces a modest selection of decent, reasonably priced sparkling wines, including:

♦ *Naverán Brut Reserva (Brut):* Subtly flavoursome, refreshing and reasonably priced.

Cavas Recaredo (☎ 938 910 214) Founded in 1924, this small producer makes a modest range of Cavas that are a cut above the average, as are the prices. The following wine offers the best value:

♦ *Recaredo (Brut Nature):* The three classic Catalan Cava grapes produce this full-bodied wine with lots of interest and flavour. Recommended.

Cavas Roger Goulart, S.A. (☎ 934 191 000) Founded in 1882, this Cava house produces worthy wines, with the following recommended:

♦ *Roger Goulart (Brut Nature):* Perfumed, fruity and balanced.

♦ *Roger Goulart Gran Reserve (Brut):* Made from the classic Catalan trio of grapes plus 10 per cent Chardonnay, this has a lot of full-bodied flavour. Good with food.

Cavas Romagosa Torné (☎ 938 991 353) Dating back to 1864, this small firm makes a mixed bag of Cavas. The following is notably well made and priced:

♦ *Romagosa Torné Gran Reserva (Brut Nature):* Subtle and interesting. Recommended.

Cavas Rondel (☎ 936 560 512) Owned by the giant Codorníu group, Rondel's wines are popular Spanish supermarket staples at the everyday end of the Cava scale. Avoid the dull pink wine, but the others are professionally made, honest, simple sparkling wines. Try the following for an inexpensive introduction to Cava:

◆ *Rondel (Brut):* Fresh and fruity with some character.

◆ *Rondel Etiqueta Verde (Semi-Seco):* Well made, commercial, sweetish sparkling wine.

Cavas Torelló (☎ 938 910 793) A producer of respectable Cavas, although perhaps a touch overpriced in comparison with similar wines from other houses. Try the following:

◆ *Torelló (Brut):* The cheapest, best value wine, with expressive fruit and balance.

Celler J. Mestre, S.L. (☎ 938 402 283) This small producer makes Cavas of varying standards. The following is the least expensive and most reliable:

◆ *Juan Mestre (Brut Nature):* Well made, inexpensive Cava from 25 per cent Chardonnay and 75 per cent Xarel-lo with fruit, herbs and some class.

Celler Josep M. Ferret, S.L. (☎ 938 979 037) This firm's table wines from Penedés are wholly unremarkable but its Cavas are better. The following wine offers a light, well made, tasty mouthful:

◆ *Josep M Ferret Guasch Reserva (Brut):* Light, fruity and fairly elegant.

Chandon, S.A. (☎ 938 970 900) In addition to making one of Penedés' better white table wines (see page 193), the French Champagne house Moët et Chandon's Catalan operation also produces good Cavas, from both French and local grape varieties. Its presence in the region reflects the seriousness with which the Champagne houses regard Cava. The following medium-priced wines are particularly recommended:

◆ *Chandon Reserva (Brut):* A blend of the classic Catalan trio of grapes and Chardonnay, this has more subtlety, finesse and elegance than the average Cava. Recommended.

◆ *Chandon Cuvée Rosé (Brut):* One of the best pink Cavas, made from Pinot Noir, this is balanced, full-bodied and flavoursome.

◆ *Chandon (Brut Nature):* Made from the classic trio and 10 per cent Chardonnay, this is a superior wine with full, fresh flavours, length and structure. Recommended.

Codorníu, S.A. (☎ 938 183 232) Originally founded in 1551, Codorníu was the pioneer of the production of sparkling wine in Spain by the Champagne Method in 1872. It is now not just one of the biggest manufacturers of sparkling wines in Spain, but in the world. Codorníu and Freixenet vie for the number one Cava position and between them account for around 80 per cent of sales. Codorníu's cheaper wines are respectable rather than outstanding – with the inexpensive Codorníu Extra and

Mediterranea fresh, tasty introductions to the Cava style – but in the middle and upper brackets it produces some of the D.O.'s best wines. From its wide selection the following are particularly recommended:

◆ *Anna de Codorníu Reserva (Brut):* This well known wine is many people's first experience of the pleasures of better Cavas. Made primarily from Chardonnay it is classily flavoursome, quite powerful and elegant. Highly recommended and reasonably priced.

◆ *Non Plus Ultra (Brut):* Made from the classic Catalan trio of grapes plus 40 to 50 per cent Chardonnay, this is sold in an unusual bottle, but this does not distract from its class. An elegant, light, tasty wine. Recommended.

◆ *Gran Codorníu (Brut):* Tasty, complex and balanced.

◆ *Jaume de Codorníu (Brut):* This Chardonnay, Macabeo and Parellada blend is often regarded as one of the best Cavas. It is elegant, subtle, balanced and long. The price is reasonable considering the plaudits that it receives.

Cooperativa Agrícola i Caixa Agraria de L'Arboc, S.C.C.L. (☎ 977 670 055) Founded in 1919, this large co-operative produces a range of Cavas, two of which stand out:

◆ *Castell Gornal (Brut):* One of the better quality, cheaper Cavas, with good fruity flavours. Party wine.

◆ *Brut del Pupitre Chardonnay (Brut):* A well conceived blend of 85 per cent Chardonnay and 15 per cent Parellada, this is balanced and tasty.

Cooperativa Agrícola i Caixa Agraria Espluga, S.C.C.R.L. (☎ 977 870 105) This small co-operative makes three wines under the Francolí label, a Semi-Seco, a Brut and a Brut Nature. All are respectable and inexpensive, without being remarkable. The Brut is a good introduction to Cava:

◆ *Francolí (Brut):* A blend of Macabeo and Parellada, this is well made, straightforward and quite tasty.

Cooperativa Agrícola Sant Isidre de Nulles, S.C.C.L. (☎ 977 602 622) Founded in 1917, this modest-size co-operative produces respectable, inexpensive Cavas, including:

◆ *Adernats (Brut Nature):* Primarily Macabeo, this is full-bodied and commercial.

◆ *Adernats 1917 (Brut):* This 85 per cent Macabeo wine is gently flavoursome and refreshing.

◆ *Adernats 1917 (Brut Nature):* Another Macabeo-based wine, this is mouthfilling and fruity.

Cooperativa Vinícola de Sarral, S.C.C.L. (☎ 977 890 031) This co-operative, which makes respectable, inexpensive table wines in D.O. Conca de Barberá, also produces a range of Cavas. Most are respectable although rather bland, but the following offers flavour and value:

◆ *Portell (Semi-Seco):* A blend of Macabeo and Parellada, this is sweet, tasty and commercial.

Covides, S.C.C.L. (☎ 938 172 552) Founded in 1964, this very large co-operative produces reasonably priced, decent Cavas, including:

◆ *Duc de Foix (Brut):* A blend of the three Catalan Cava classic grapes, this is well made, tasty, commercial wine for a low price.

◆ *Xenius Reserva (Brut):* A step up from the above for only a little more money, this is well made, fruity and tasty.

Eudald Massana Noya (☎ 938 994 124) Founded in the mid-'90s, this small Cava house makes a modest range of inexpensive, commercial wines, including:

◆ *Eudald Massana Noya Familia (Semi-Seco):* Decent, tasty Cava for those who enjoy sweet wine.

◆ *Eudald Massana Noya Familia (Brut):* Well made, tasty and commercial.

◆ *Eudald Massana Noya Familia (Brut Nature):* Balanced and easy-to-drink, this is the most elegant of the three.

Freixenet, S.A. (☎ 938 917 000) Founded in 1917, Freixenet is roughly the same size as the giant Codorníu and both vie for regional supremacy. With their various brand names and acquisitions, it is sometimes difficult to work out which of the two is the bigger. Freixenet's international profile is probably higher, partly thanks to the success of its Cordón Negro range in the famous, distinctive, matt black bottles. Freixenet also has operations in Champagne, California and Mexico. Quality is generally good to very good across its wide range of Cavas, with the following wines notable:

◆ *Carta Nevada (Brut):* In its distinctive, white-frosted bottle, this is one of the world's best selling Cavas. Tasty, balanced, inexpensive and straightforward, it has done much to publicise Cava's wares.

◆ *Cordón Negro (Brut):* Eagerly drunk all over the world, this is tasty, mouthfilling wine with some persistence.

◆ *Freixenet Vintage (Brut Nature):* Superior Cava for a reasonable price, this is notably well put together. Recommended.

◆ *Cuvée D.S. (Brut):* Towards the top end of the Freixenet price scale, this is classy, subtle, complex and delicious.

◆ *Reserva Real (Brut):* Sometimes the house's most expensive wine, this is mouthfilling and balanced with attractive bitterness and notable length. One of the better Cavas.

Gabriel Giró Baltá (☎ 938 988 032) This excellent small producer, founded in 1976, makes high quality, reasonably priced table wines in Penedés and two laudable, inexpensive Cavas:

- *Gorner Reserva (Brut):* Flavoursome and herby with refreshing bite. Recommended, and one of the better Cavas in its price range.

- *Gorner Gran Reserva(Brut Nature):* A drier, slightly more delicate and expensive version of the above from the same percentages of the classic trio of grapes. Recommended.

Gramona, S.A. (☎ 938 910 113) Founded in 1921, this Cava house makes good quality wines at highish prices. They include:

- *Gramona Reserva (Brut):* A blend of Chardonnay, Macabeo and Xarel-lo, this is notably fruity and flavoursome. It is the house's cheapest wine and offers the best value for money.

- *Gramona III Lustros Gran Reserva (Brut Nature):* A blend of Macabeo and Xarel-lo, this is a classy, full, complex wine but quite expensive by Cava standards.

- *Celler Batlle Gran Reserva (Brut):* Made from the same grapes as above this, the house's most expensive wine, is aromatic, classy, flavoursome and long. However, it is very expensive and does not justify the high price.

Huguet de Can Feixes (☎ 937 718 227) Founded in 1768, this small Cava house produces two superior, reasonably priced wines:

- *Huguet Gran Reserva (Brut):* A blend of Chardonnay, Macabeo and Parellada, this is characterful and tasty with bite.

- *Huguet Gran Reserva (Brut Nature):* Made from the same blend as above, this is full-bodied, elegant and has some complexity. Only slightly more expensive than the Brut and better. Recommended.

Jané Ventura, S.A. (☎ 977 660 118) Founded in 1914, this producer of one of Catalonia's best Cabernet Sauvignons also makes some worthy Cavas. From its range, the following offer the best value:

- *Jané Ventura (Brut):* Aromatic, herbaceous, flavoursome and balanced. Recommended.

- *Jané Ventura (Brut Nature):* Refreshing and fruity with some bite.

Joan Raventós Rosell, S.L. (☎ 937 725 251) Founded in 1985, this producer of one of Penedés' better Chardonnays also makes Cavas. Quality is always decent but can vary from year to year. The following is the most reliable wine:

- *Joan Raventós Rosell Reserva (Brut Nature):* Elegant, aromatic and flavoursome. Recommended.

José María Raventós i Blanc, S.A. (☎ 938 183 262) A maker of superior white wines in Penedés, this producer is most famous for its Cavas, as befits a firm named after the man who began the Catalan sparkling wine industry. Its elegantly labelled wines are aimed at the middle and top ends of the market and are of high quality. Try the following:

- *Raventós i Blanc Reserva (Brut):* A blend of the three Catalan Cava grapes and Chardonnay, this has elegance and flavour. It offers particularly good value.

- *Raventós i Blanc Gran Reserva (Brut Nature):* The same blend as above makes a full-bodied, flavoursome wine, again distinguished by the house's elegant style and length.

- *Raventós i Blanc Gran Reserva Personal (Brut Nature):* Made from 60 per cent Macabeo, 15 per cent Chardonnay, 15 per cent Xarel-lo and 10 per cent Parellada, this is the bodega's top wine. It is quite complex on the nose and palate, very elegant and balanced. Well priced in view of the quality.

Juvé y Camps, S.A. (☎ 938 911 000) Founded in 1921, this house is noted for its classy Cavas. The following offer value at the lower and upper end of its modest range of wines:

- *Juvé y Camps Reserva de la Familia (Brut Nature):* The cheapest wine, but aimed at the middle-to-top-end market, this is famous in Spain as an introduction to the top Cavas. It was launched in 1975, and as the name implies, it was originally only drunk by the family that owns the business. The wine is aged for three years and offers substance and elegance. Recommended.

- *Gran Juvé y Camps Gran Reserva (Brut):* A long, elegant, aromatic wine near the top of the Cava tree. Recommended, although you do pay for the privilege.

Manuel Sancho e Hijas, S.A. (☎ 938 918 281) Founded in 1975, this producer of good table wines in Penedés also makes a range of Cavas. The everyday sparkling wines are uninteresting but try the following from the top of the selection:

- *Mont Marcal Gran Reserva (Brut):* This has elegance, maturity and flavour.

Marqués de Monistrol, S.A. (☎ 938 910 276) Founded in 1882, and owned by the Rioja producer Berberana, Monistrol's Cavas are of respectable to good quality and seem to be improving. Try the following from its range:

- *Gran Reserva Familia Rosé (Brut):* A blend of Monastrell and Parellada, this is an attractive, balanced, flavoursome, pink sparkling wine. Rosé Cavas are not usually very interesting and this stands out from the crowd. Good.

- *Gran Reserva Familia (Brut Nature):* Subtle and complex rather than full-bodied. Recommended.

Marrugat (☎ 938 903 066) This house produces a range of respectable Cavas and is showing signs that it could make very good ones. Try the following:

- *Marrugat (Brut):* This moreish wine has superior structure and flavours. Good.

- *Marrugat Gran Reserva (Brut Nature):* Elegant and persistent with some length. Recommended.

- *Marrugat Chardonnay Reserva (Brut):* This varies in quality. It can be rather heavy, but when on form it is a toasty, aromatic wine with structure and powerful flavour.

Mas Tinell (☎ 938 170 586) Founded in 1992, this house produces a solid range of good Cavas. The cheaper ones offer the best value, especially:

- *Mas Tinell Reserva (Brut):* An aromatic, suitably aged wine with flavour and bite. Good.

Masía Bach (☎ 937 714 052) Part of the Codorníu empire, Bach makes Cavas at the lower end of the price scale. Until recently, some of these were not worth crossing the road for, but standards are rising and the following two inexpensive wines offer value and reasonable quality:

- *Masía Bach Extrísimo (Brut Nature):* A Parellada/Xarel-lo blend, this is simple, balanced and quite flavoursome. Useful for buck's fizz, i.e. a 'cocktail' of sparkling wine and orange juice.

- *Bach Magnificat (Brut Nature):* An enjoyable, aromatic wine with green fruit flavours.

Masía Vallformosa, S.A. (☎ 938 978 286) Founded in 1978, this house makes stylish, affordable Cavas, presented in stylish bottles, including:

- *Vallformosa (Semi-Seco):* Well made, commercial and quite sweet.

- *Vallformosa (Seco):* Balanced, commercial and tasty.

- *Vallformosa (Brut):* Not as dry as some Brut wines and will hence appeal to a wide range of palates.

- *Vallformosa (Brut Nature):* Aromatic and long.

- *Vallformosa Gran Reserva (Brut):* This is herbaceous, suitably aged, light yet characterful and classy. Priced to compete with the better Cavas and it succeeds in doing so.

Molí Colomá – Cavas Sumarroca (☎ 938 911 092) Founded in 1986, this house makes good, well priced wines, the following offering the best value and interest:

- *Jordi Melendo (Brut Nature):* A blend of the classic Cava trio of grapes plus 8 per cent Chardonnay, this reasonably priced wine is well made, commercial, herbaceous and tasty.

- *Sumarroca (Brut):* A blend of the three Catalan Cava grapes with 10 per cent Chardonnay, this is a full-bodied, aromatic wine with bite. Good.

- *Sumarroca Gran Brut (Brut):* A French blend of 60 per cent Chardonnay and 40 per cent Pinot Noir, this is 50 per cent more expensive than the previous two wines. A well crafted, fruity mouthful with hints of complexity. Recommended.

Olarre, S.A. (☎ 941 235 299) Founded in 1973, this large Rioja producer makes a couple of good Cavas from the Viura grape, also known as Macabeo:

◆ *Añares (Brut):* This reasonably priced wine has some depth on the nose and a well made, commercial palate with fruit and bite.

◆ *Añares (Brut Nature):* A leaner, more elegant, drier version of the above. Good.

Parxet, S.A. (☎ 933 950 811) One of D.O. Alella's star producers of table wines (see page 178), Parxet also makes some excellent Cavas, notably:

◆ *Parxet (Brut):* A blend of Macabeo, Parellada and Pansa Blanca, this is characterful, fruity and reasonably priced. Recommended.

◆ *Parxet Cuvée Dessert Rosado (Brut):* A blend of Chardonnay and Pinot Noir, this is interesting and different, a sweet and soundly constructed dessert rosé. Recommended.

◆ *Parxet (Brut Nature):* Made from the same grapes as the Brut, this is a fine, balanced, mouthfilling wine. Recommended.

◆ *Parxet 80 Aniversario (Brut Nature):* At the top end of the Cava price scale but one of the best of its kind; complex, confident, toasty and long.

Raimat (☎ 973 724 000) Part of the Codorníu group and Costers del Segre's dominant table wine maker (see page 186) Raimat produces a range of laudable, modern Cavas:

◆ *Raimat (Brut):* A blend of Chardonnay, Macabeo and Xarel-lo, this is one of the best Cavas in its low price band. Notably characterful and well made. Recommended.

◆ *Raimat (Brut Nature):* A more subtle version of the above for more money. Good, but the Brut is better.

◆ *Raimat Chardonnay (Brut Nature):* Elegant and clean with green fruit flavours.

◆ *Raimat Gran Brut (Brut):* A blend of 75 per cent Chardonnay and 25 per cent Macabeo, this is balanced, tasty and classy. Superior, 'international-style' Cava.

Rovellats, S.A. (☎ 934 880 575) A small, impressive firm producing middle-to-top range wines, including:

◆ *Rovellats Imperial (Brut):* Mouthfilling and flavoursome, if not always the most subtle.

◆ *Rovellats Chardonnay (Brut Nature):* Characterful and moreish. Superior sparkling Chardonnay for a competitive price.

Sabaté i Coca, S.A. (☎ 938 911 927) This small firm produces good red wines in Penedés and also makes limited amounts of laudable, reasonably priced Cavas, including:

◆ *Castellroig (Brut):* Full, balanced, tasty and reasonably priced. Recommended.

◆ *Castellroig (Brut Nature)*: A blend of the classic Catalan trio of grapes plus 10 per cent Chardonnay, this is characterful, light, herby and satisfying. Recommended.

◆ *Castellroig Chardonnay (Brut Nature)*: Well made and mouthfilling with Chardonnay unctuousness. Rather less expensive than most Cavas from this grape.

Segura Viudas, S.A. (☎ 938 917 227) Part of the Freixenet Group and makers of notable table wines in Penedés, Segura Viudas also makes excellent Cavas, including:

◆ *Conde de Caralt (Brut)*: Inexpensive yet well made and characterful. One of the better everyday Cavas.

◆ *Conde de Caralt Blanc de Blancs (Brut)*: Elegant, refreshing, easy-to-drink and quite long. Good.

◆ *Aria (Brut Nature)*: Aromatic, elegant and quite complex. Recommended.

◆ *Segura Viudas Reserva (Brut)*: Notably tasty, herbaceous and persistent. One of the best in its price range.

◆ *Segura Viudas Vintage Gran Reserva (Brut)*: A blend of 67 per cent Macabeo and 33 per cent Parellada, this has quite a rich nose for a Cava and a palate with attractive, slightly unctuous flavour and length. Very good.

◆ *Reserva Heredad Gran Reserva (Brut)*: The same blend as the above, this is full-bodied, elegant and unctuous. However, it is twice the price of the preceding wine, so choose that.

Signat, S.A. (☎ 935 403 400) Founded in 1987, this small producer makes increasingly good Cavas, including:

◆ *Signat Brut (Brut)*: Made from the usual Catalan trio plus Pansa Blanca, this is aromatic, full-bodied and toasty.

◆ *Signat (Brut Nature)*: The same blend as above, this is a drier version, well made and balanced.

◆ *Signat Imperial Reserva (Brut)*: The house's top wine and by far the most expensive, this has lots of flavour and some elegance, but it is quite a lot to pay.

Torre Oria, S.L. (☎ 962 320 289) Founded in 1897 and based in Utiel-Requena near Valencia, Torre Oria makes respectable Cavas, although some of them could perhaps benefit from a lighter touch. However, the following are eminently respectable:

◆ *Torre Oria (Semi-Seco)*: Made from Macabeo, this is tasty, sweet and quite classy – a word not always used about Semi-Secos.

◆ *Torre Oria Joven (Brut)*: Another Macabeo, this is flavoursome and easy to drink.

◆ *Torre Oria Reserva (Brut)*: This comprises 90 per cent Macabeo and 10 per cent Parellada, and has fruity flavours, balance and bite. Decent commercial wine and that is not meant as a criticism.

● *Torre Oria Reserva (Brut Nature):* Made from the same grapes as above, this is a similar although slightly finer wine.

Viladellops Vinícola, S.L. (☎ 938 188 371) Founded in 1994, this small Cava house produces only one wine offering good value:

● *Arteo (Brut Nature):* A well made, pleasant wine for a modest price. It won't win any prizes, but then it is not aiming to.

Vins El Cep, S.A. (☎ 938 912 353) Founded in 1980, this producer makes respectable wines, with the following offering the best value:

● *L'Alzinar (Brut Nature):* A reasonably priced blend of the classic Catalan trio of grapes, this is straightforward, well made, fruity and flavoursome.

● *Marqués de Gelida (Brut Nature):* As above.

Viña Torreblanca, S.L. (☎ 938 915 066) Founded in 1995, this house makes a small range of reasonably priced wines. Quality can vary, with the following the most reliable wines:

● *Torreblanca (Brut):* This offers the best value, a dry, tasty wine with some bite.

● *Torreblanca Reserva Extra (Brut):* A Chardonnay-based wine, this offers lots of elegant fruit flavours. Well priced for a Chardonnay-based Cava.

Xepitus, S.L. (☎ 938 912 271) This house produces a range of around half a dozen low-priced wines which are about as good as they could be for the minimal outlay. The following are representative:

● *Xepitus (Seco):* Simple, clean, fruity and cheap.

● *Xepitus (Brut Nature):* Mouthfilling and tasty. Not the most subtle bottle, but excellent value.

In Galicia's humid, green landscape, vines are often trained off the ground to avoid rot

11.

GALICIA

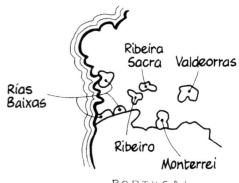

Galicia lies in the far north-west of Spain, bordered in the south by Portugal and in the west and north by the Atlantic Ocean. It looks most unlike the classic, picture-postcard image of Spain – parched landscapes, wall-to-wall sunshine and gentle Mediterranean beaches – being a green, cloudy, damp region of pine, chestnut and oak-clad hills. It resembles southern Ireland more than much of Spain, while the rías (fjord-like coastal inlets) are reminiscent of western Norway.

Although it does not sound like promising grape growing country, Galicia has produced wines for many centuries. They are mentioned in medieval literature, although not always nobly: Froissart records that in 1386 John of Gaunt's soldiers drank so much Galician wine that they were incapacitated for two days. In view of the fact that Galicia's wines are not always high in alcohol, they must have drunk amounts that are either impressive or appalling, depending upon your point of view. There was an export market for the wines to Portugal and northern Europe until the end of the 18th century, but they were not famed abroad because they did not always travel well.

By the middle of the 19th century, Galicia boasted 55,000 hectares of vines but various diseases (including phylloxera) greatly reduced this amount and when vine replanting was undertaken, growers looked to replace good quality local grape varieties with resistant, high-yielding ones to prevent future recurrences of disease, and quality obviously suffered.

The Galician wine scene changed radically during the last two decades of the 20th century. Previously, some of the region's producers were known to 'pad out' their wines with those from La Mancha, the latter's bland character taking the edge off the sometimes over-acidic Galician wine, while the Galician provided flavour and perfume. But in the '80s, Albariño, the region's great native white grape, was 'rediscovered' and found to yield Spain's best white wines. Other white grapes – Treixadura and Godello (or Verdello) – as well as the black Mencía were also reassessed. Allied to this was the march of technology, with cold fermentation and stainless steel tanks meaning that wines made from Galicia's grapes were able to express their full range of aromas and flavours. Galicia was also found to offer a wide grape variation, with at least 140 varieties known to grow in the region.

Vine growing techniques in Galicia are still traditional, with vines trained along wooden stakes or wires to keep them away from the damp ground and inhibit rot and funguses. This also means that the grapes receive less reflected sunshine than those grown low (and Galicia's sunshine levels can be inadequate anyway) and therefore do not ripen as much as they could. The resultant wines would be aggressively acidic if they did not undergo a prolonged secondary (or malolactic) fermentation.

Galicia's bodega profile has also changed, with a plethora of new, small, high quality operations producing upmarket white wines, a lot of them in D.O. Rías Baixas, Galicia's foremost wine region. Their Albariño-based wines are regarded as Spain's best whites. Previously, Galicia's white wines were bracketed with those of Vinho Verde across the border in Portugal: light, flowery, sometimes acidic and slightly fizzy, okay for throwing back with a plate of fried fish, but not to be thought about too much.

ne research in Navarra ▲
(ix Lorrio)

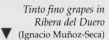

*Tinto fino grapes in
Ribera del Duero*
▼ (Ignacio Muñoz-Seca)

ality control in a bodega ▲
lo Neustadt)

▶
Castilla-León landscape
(Ulrich Hartmann)

Photographs courtesy of the Spanish Institute for Foreign Exchange (ICEX)

Stainless steel fermentation tanks
(Félix Lorrio)
◄

Processing grapes
(Carlos Navajas) ▼

▲ *Bodega and vineyards in Nava*
(Carlos Nava

▶
Historic bodega in Castilla-Léon
(Carlos Navajas)

Photographs courtesy of the Spanish Institute for Foreign Exchange (ICEX)

Vineyard of bodega Vega Sicilia
(Ignacio Nuñoz-Seca)
▶

Grape picker
▼ (Carlos Navajas)

ine aging in American oak barrels ▲
ɡnacio Nuñoz-Seca)

◀
Historic building in Valdepeñas
(Ulrick Hartmann)

Photographs courtesy of the Spanish Institute for Foreign Exchange (ICEX)

ENRIQUE·MENDOZA

Reserva
Santa Rosa
1995

L'Alfàs del Pí

A l i c a n t e

Denominación de origen

Producido y embotellado en la propiedad

14%vol. *Product of Spain* 75 cl.

MALLEOLUS

1998

Emilio Moro

RIBERA DEL DUERO

DENOMINACION DE ORIGEN

•

cl.e

ELABORADO Y EMBOTELLADO POR - BODEGAS EMILIO MORO S.L.
PESQUERA DE DUERO - VALLADOLID - ESPAÑA - Nº R.E. 6664/VA   14% vol

---

ALBA DE BRETON

1995

RIOJA

DENOMINACION DE ORIGEN CALIFICADA

SELECCION ESPECIAL DE VIÑEDOS VIEJOS
45 BARRICAS

BOTELLA: Nº 00.000

75 cl.   13,5% Vol.

EMBOTELLADO EN LA PROPIEDAD
BODEGAS BRETON Y CIA, S.A. - LOGROÑO - RIOJA ALTA - ESPAÑA

1996

ALLENDE

AVRVS

Embotellado en la Propiedad

RIOJA

DENOMINACION DE ORIGEN CALIFICADA

FINCA ALLENDE S. L.
SAN ASENSIO - ESPAÑA

R.E. Nº 4-LR   13,

PAGOS VIEJOS

1998

Rioja

DENOMINACION DE ORIGEN CALIFICADA

ARTADI

E M B O T E L L A D O   E N   L A   P R O P I E D A D

COSECHEROS ALAVESES, S.A.

LAGUARDIA · ALAVA · ESPAÑA

MALAGA VIRGEN

SIRVASE FRIO

Pedro Ximen

*Su inconfundible
sabor a uva de
Málaga se realza
al beberlo frio.
¡Disfrútelo!*

V.L.C.P.R.D.

López Hermanos, S.A.

Canadá 10 - Málaga

Alc. 17% Vol.   R.E. 410-MA   75 cl. e

19 LUSCO 99
Albariño

Rias Baixas

Denominación de Origen

Embotellado por

LUSCO DO MIÑO S.L. - Vigo
En Alxén - Salvatierra do Miño
Pontevedra - España
R.E.N. 40779-PO R.S. 3006406-PO

75 Cl.   12,5%Vol.
Lote 200

The region now has five D.O.s: Monterrei, Rías Baixas, Ribeira Sacra, Ribeiro and Valdeorras. It is mostly known for white wines, although Monterrei produces mainly reds. Indeed, Galicia's red wines are being reassessed after previously having been dismissed as inferior and too tart for all but Galician palates. Overall, Galicia probably still consumes more wine than it actually produces.

D.O. Monterrei

In Brief: *A recently formed D.O. with limited production, but its potential for both white and red wines is high. One to watch.*

Monterrei is a small wine region covering 550 hectares of vineyards in south-east Galicia, edging the Portuguese border. Indeed, the southern part of the D.O. is a 'finger', pointing down into Portugal. It is the least 'Galician' of the region's D.O.s: warmer, drier, producing more red wines and growing grapes low instead of raised clear of the ground. It has only been a D.O. since 1996 and while there are over 500 grape growers, there are only four bottling bodegas.

Currently, grape varieties employed are:

- **White:** Doña Blanca, Palomino, Treixadura and Verdello (often known as Godello).

- **Black:** Alicante, Bastardo (also known, more attractively, as María Ardoña), Gran Negro and Mencía.

Monterrei's whites can be characterful, mouthfilling wines of good quality, while the reds are made 'jóven', light, fruity and flavoursome. The region produces Galicia's strongest wines, with alcohol levels sometimes reaching 14 per cent. White wines are currently better than the reds, but quality is already evident in both.

Geography, Soil and Climate

Monterrei's climate is not typically Galician, being warmer in summer, colder in winter and drier than much of the rest of the region. It is a blend of Atlantic and continental influences, with summer temperatures reaching the high 30s Celsius and winters sometimes experiencing several degrees of frost. Conditions are promising for wine makers, with plenty of sunshine and water, and a variety of aspects on which to grow vines.

Future Development

It is still early to judge Monterrei or predict how it will develop, but the D.O. has shown that it can make characterful, inexpensive white and red wines. Whites currently lead the way, but there are moves to improve the reds by blending Tempranillo with Mencía to produce wines with more tannic backbone and ability to age.

Selected Bodegas

Bernabé Jiménez, S.A. (☎ 988 410 314) A small operation making good quality wines:

♦ *Gran Bernabé (white):* An attractive wine with a fruity, herby nose and palate. Good.

♦ *Gran Bernabé Tinto (red):* A light, fruity, tasty wine, superior everyday fare.

Gargalo, S.L. (☎ 988 590 203) Founded in 1997, this small bodega is Monterrei's leading operation, making good to very good wines at competitive prices. It is an indication of the region's potential.

♦ *Terra do Gargalo (white):* A blend of 60 per cent Treixadura, 30 per cent Godello and 10 per cent Doña Blanca, this characterful wine has pronounced fruity, herby flavours and a refreshing bittersweet bite. Recommended.

♦ *Terra do Gargalo (red):* A blend of 60 per cent Tempranillo, 30 per cent Mencía and 10 per cent Bastardo, this powerful, mouthfilling wine has some complexity and length. Recommended.

Ladairo, S.L. (☎ 988 422 757) Founded in 1990, this small operation has shown that Monterrei can make good young reds from Mencía:

♦ *Ladairo Mencía (red):* A well made, medium-bodied, fruity wine for drinking young.

D.O. Rías Baixas

In Brief: *The source of some of Spain's best white wines, invariably from the high quality Albariño grape, but vintages can be unpredictable and prices high.*

Rías Baixas – 'low rivers' – is named after the southern Galician coastline's distinctive, fjord-like inlets, found around the town of Pontevedra. It has grown rapidly since becoming a D.O. in July 1988. Then it had around 15 bodegas and 500 grape growers, while in the early 21st century there were 150 and 4,500 respectively.

Many of the region's vineyards are small and intensively cultivated by traditional methods, the vines trained off the ground to avoid contact with the damp soil. Albariño is the key grape variety, capable of making aromatic wines with a range of apple, grapefruit, peach and apricot flavours, firm acidity and a creamy richness. However, the modest amounts of wine produced and unpredictable vintages mean that prices can be high and quality variable. And prices have been pushed even higher as the wines' popularity has increased both in Spain and elsewhere.

Authorised and/or employed grape varieties are:

● **White:** Albariño, Caíño Blanco, Godello, Loureira Blanca, Treixadura and Torrontés.

● **Black:** Brancellao, Caíño Tinto, Espadeiro, Loureira Tinta, Mencía and Sousón.

The white wines are aromatic and flowery as previously described, with the better ones noted for their persistence, complexity and ability to improve in bottle for two or three years after release. The reds are much less common, characterised by light fruit and herb flavours and marked acidity.

Geography, Soil and Climate

Rías Baixas has a markedly Atlantic climate with mild winters, coolish summers, high humidity and elevated rainfall which varies between 1,300 and 1,600mm (51 and 63in) per year. This compares with the 300 to 500mm (12 to 20in) which much of central Spain receives. The inland part of Rías Baixas is drier than the coast, winters are cooler and summers warmer, although the climate is still maritime. Even though Rías Baixas has a gentle climate, conditions are not always favourable for wine makers: warm weather early in the year can induce budding of vines and frosts can then strike and kill some of the potential harvest.

Rías Baixas is currently split into five sub-zones:

▲ **Condado do Tea:** This is the most mountainous sub-zone and is situated farthest from the coast. Its wines must contain a minimum of 70 per cent of the grape varieties Albariño or Treixadura, or a blend of the two.

▲ **O Rosal:** The most southerly and warmest sub-zone, its wines must contain a minimum of 70 per cent of Albariño or Loureira, or a blend of the two.

▲ **Ribeira do Ulla:** A new sub-zone where red wines dominate.

▲ **Soutomaior:** This sub-zone only makes Albariño wines.

▲ **Val do Salnés:** This is the sub-zone with the most established reputation for making classy wines from Albariño and most of its wines are still made 100 per cent from this grape, although D.O. rules call for a minimum of 70 per cent. It is the most northerly and flattest of the sub-zones.

Future Development

In its short life as a D.O., Rías Baixas has successfully exploited its advantages, developed a strong domestic reputation for its white wines and also begun to penetrate the international market, despite high prices. Problems in the late '90s were a reminder that a hard won reputation can be undone by unpredictable wine quality and quantity in difficult vintages. Measures must be taken to try to counteract this, when possible.

A recent development has been the introduction of oak ageing for some of the white wines, which adds another dimension to the regional style and also makes wines with a longer life. But it has proved a controversial innovation: some people are critical of this approach, thinking that the flavours of the barrel not only do not enhance the wines, but actively mask their subtleties and flavours. As for its non-oaked wines, some producers think that they need to start publicising the fact that these can be wines which do not need drinking soon after production (as is the Galician tradition) but which can develop for two or three years in bottle. Moves are also afoot to experiment with different blends of the abundant selection of local grape varieties. In addition, the region might look to make more red wines and exploit the undoubted qualities of the Mencía grape, demonstrated by some of the wines of D.O. Bierzo.

Selected Bodegas

Adegas Galegas (☎ 986 657 371) Founded in 1987 as a co-operative, and in its current set-up since 1995, this well regarded bodega makes high quality wines in the traditional and barrel-fermented styles, with Pedro de Soutomayor and Veigadares two of the region's more prominent wines. Annual production is around 375,000 bottles and the range includes:

◆ *Rubines (white):* An aromatic wine with lots of unctuous flavours and complexity. Very good.

◆ *Pedro de Soutomayor (white):* A good introduction to the region's whites, this is a lightish, fresh wine with character and interest. Recommended.

◆ *Veigadares (white):* This has an exotic nose and a mouthfilling palate of refreshing, quite complex flavours with bite. Good.

◆ *Veigadares Fermentado en Barrica (white):* Made from 85 per cent Albariño, the balance being other local grapes, this is a powerful, oaky wine with flavour and elegance. It is delicious and balanced, although purists would say that the oak interferes with the fruit.

Adegas Morgadío, S.L. (☎ 986 261 212) Founded in 1984, this small operation makes the highly regarded Morgadío from Albariño:

◆ *Morgadío (white):* This is notably aromatic with a deep, balanced, fruity palate and good length. A superior wine. Recommended.

Adegas Valmiñor, S.L. (☎ 986 449 907) Founded in 1997, this small bodega makes a decent 100 per cent Albariño wine:

◆ *Valmiñor (white):* A tasty, fruity wine with length.

Agro de Bazán, S.A. (☎ 986 555 562) Founded in 1985, this is another typical Rías Baixas bodega: small and producing high quality, quite expensive white wines:

◆ *Granbazán Verde (white):* A tasty, characterful wine with some elegance.

◆ *Granbazán Ámbar (white):* A slightly more expensive, better version of the above, with more length, complexity and ageing potential. Recommended.

Bouza do Rei, S.A.T. (☎ 986 710 257) Founded in 1983, this bodega makes a notably mouthfilling 100 per cent Albariño:

◆ *Bouza do Rei (white):* A big wine, aromatic, mouthfilling and tasty, with balance and length. Will appeal to those who find some Albariños rather light and delicate.

Castro Martín, S.L. (☎ 986 710 202) Founded in 1981, this bodega makes an approachable, up-front wine, a good introduction to the region's whites, less expensive than some.

◆ *Casal Caeiro (white):* Aromatic, tasty, balanced and confident.

Gerardo Méndez Lázaro (☎ 986 747 046) A tiny operation making the following Albariño:

◆ *Do Ferreiro (white):* An elegant, fruity wine.

Granja Fillaboa, S.A. (☎ 986 437 000) Founded in 1988, this small bodega makes a good quality wine, although as with the rest of the region, it can be vintage-affected. There are plans to expand the current 30 hectares of vines and also to produce a barrel-fermented wine.

◆ *Fillaboa (white):* A tasty, unctuous wine with balance.

La Val, S.L. (☎ 986 610 728) Founded in 1985, this bodega makes a range of wines in a variety of styles:

◆ *Orballo (white):* A straightforward, delicately aromatic, tasty wine.

◆ *La Val (white):* Powerful on the nose, this is an unctuous, mouthfilling Albariño with flavour and length.

◆ *Viña Ludy (white):* Made from just over 50 per cent Albariño, with the balance Loureiro, Caíño Blanco and Treixadura, this is lightish, very fruity and character-filled.

◆ *La Val Fermentado en Barrica (white):* This Albariño is one of the region's better barrel-fermented wines, with a well judged, oaky nose and a mouthfilling, unctuous palate with length.

Lusco do Miño, S.L. (☎ 986 658 519) Founded in 1996, although the estate dates back to 1600, Lusco's wine maker José Antonio López used to work for Adegas Morgadío (see page 244) before starting his own small operation. His wines have quickly garnered a good reputation, including:

◆ *Lusco (white):* This has a complex nose and is an elegant, fruity wine with some complexity and length. It will improve in bottle for two or three years after release. Recommended.

Mar de Frades, S.L. (☎ 986 511 771) Founded in 1987, this bodega makes a range of Albariño wines:

◆ *Algareiro (white):* A light wine, inexpensive by local standards, with some character and bite. Reasonable rather than remarkable.

◆ *Casabella (white):* A fruity wine with more body than the above, and also length and structure.

◆ *Mar de Frades (white):* This can be complex and mouthfilling, but suffers in weaker years, when it can lack interest.

Marqués de Vizhoya, S.A. (☎ 986 665 825) Founded in 1966, this large (by local standards) bodega produces a range of affordable, attractively labelled and bottled wines of decent to very good quality:

◆ *Marqués de Vizhoya (white):* Made outside the D.O., this notably inexpensive (by Rías Baixas standards) wine is light, fresh and flavoursome, not typical of the region but attractive to drink.

◆ *Folla Verde (white):* This blend of 70 per cent Albariño, 15 per cent Loureiro and 15 per cent Treixadura is something of a halfway house between the bodega's other two wines. It is light, fresh and drinkable like the above, but a lot more expensive, costing the same as the Torre la Moreira below while lacking its complexity and class.

◆ *Torre la Moreira (white):* Aromatic, soundly constructed, quite complex and elegant. Good.

Martín Códax, S.A. (☎ 986 526 040) Founded in 1985, this operation used to be a co-operative and is now a joint stock company. It is one of Rías Baixas' most prominent bodegas, its wines being the most widely sold outside Galicia. The name Martín Códax comes from a medieval troubadour and the wines have been marketed very successfully, both in Spain and, increasingly, abroad, being known in the significant British and Japanese markets. The bodega is looking to broaden its range of wines to offer consumers more variety.

◆ *Martín Códax (white):* This well known Albariño is the region's most commercially successful. It is aromatic, balanced and has attractive, understated flavours. Good, and the logical starting place for learning about Rías Baixas' wines.

◆ *Burgans (white):* Priced at the same level as the above (mid-range by regional standards) this is a more mouthfilling, up-front wine with touches of complexity. Recommended.

◆ *Organistrum (white):* A high quality, expensive, barrel-fermented wine, with a powerful, oaky nose and a full, unctuous palate with flavour and personality. A good example of a barrel-fermented Albariño, but as mentioned elsewhere, some will find that the oak detracts from the fruit's elegant, complex flavours.

Pablo Padín (☎ 986 743 231) Founded in 1987, this small bodega makes low-priced (by regional standards) wines of good, commercial quality, rather than world-beaters.

◆ *Albariño Eiral (white):* This can lack aroma, but is better on the palate, with attractive fresh fruit. A modest price for an Albariño, but could do with more complexity.

◆ *Albariño Segrel (white):* Similar to the above, being light and well made, but perhaps too subtle sometimes.

Palacio de Fefiñanes, S.L. (☎ 986 542 204) Founded in 1908, this bodega is famed and respected in the region as the oldest name still on the market, and the first reviewed wine still carries the label it had in 1928, when the trademark was registered. Quality has varied over the years, but the early 21st century has seen a return to form.

◆ *Albariño de Fefiñanes (white):* A good wine, with fruit and flower aromas, and a tasty, fruity palate with hints of sweetness. Commercial rather than esoteric.

◆ *'1583' Albariño de Fefiñanes (white):* A long, very flavoursome, barrel-fermented wine – a superior example of same – and it is up to individuals to decide whether they enjoy oaked Albariño.

Pazo de Barrantes, S.A. (☎ 986 718 211) Founded in 1990, and owned by the legendary Rioja producer Marqués de Murrieta, this bodega makes modest amounts of a well regarded Albariño whose price has risen sharply over the last couple of years.

◆ *Pazo de Barrantes (white):* This has an aromatic, complex nose and is a powerful, flavoursome mouthful with length. Recommended, and improves after a couple of years in bottle, but becoming overpriced?

Pazo de Señorans, S.L. (☎ 986 715 373) Founded in 1989, this small bodega makes an Albariño reputed to be one of the most consistent, good even in difficult years:

◆ *Pazo de Señorans (white):* A fruity, fresh wine, tasty and elegant at the same time, for a reasonable price. Recommended.

Pazo San Mauro, S.A. (☎ 986 658 285) Founded in 1966, this small operation makes decent, affordable wines:

◆ *Pazo San Mauro Condado do Tea (white):* This blend of 70 per cent Albariño, 20 per cent Treixadura, 5 per cent Loureiro and 5 per cent Torrontés is a decent, inexpensive, fruity, unctuous wine, not classically Rías Baixas, but superior everyday wine.

◆ *Pazo San Mauro Albariño (white):* This has quite a complex nose and is a well made, fruity wine with some character.

Salnesur, S.A. (☎ 986 543 535) Founded in 1988, Salnesur is one of Rías Baixas' biggest producers by volume. Quality is decent.

◆ *Condes de Albarei Clásico (white):* A confident wine with aroma, flavour and body. Good.

◆ *Condes de Albarei Enxebre (white):* Similar to the above, although slightly more expensive.

◆ *Condes de Albarei Carballo Galego (white):* This barrel-fermented Albariño can be tasty, mouthfilling and delicious, or over-oaked and tiring to drink.

Santiago Ruiz (☎ 986 614 083) Founded in 1892, this modest operation makes a light, distinctively labelled wine:

◆ *Santiago Ruiz (white):* A blend of 70 per cent Albariño, 20 per cent Loureiro and 10 per cent Treixadura, this late-harvested wine has mature fruit on the nose and an agreeable, fruity palate, although without much complexity. A little overpriced perhaps.

Terras Gauda, S.A. (☎ 986 621 001) Founded in 1990, this is a fair-size operation by regional standards, making good to excellent wines:

◆ *Abadía de San Campo (white):* This is a well made, reasonably priced Albariño, aromatic, fruity and long. If you are new to the region's wines, this is another of those bottles that is a fair place to start.

◆ *Terras Gauda (white):* This blend of Albariño, Loureiro and Caíño Blanco is the bodega's best value bottle, and a notably consistent wine. It offers a powerful, quite complex nose and a personality-filled, structured palate with length. Highly recommended.

◆ *Terras Gauda Etiqueta Negra (white):* This expensive (it is one of the region's priciest bottles), barrel-fermented wine is made from the same blend of grapes as the Terras Gauda. It is one of the region's best barrel-fermented wines, integrated and with complexity rising above the expected fruit/oak integration. Recommended, but somewhat overpriced.

Valdamor, S.A. (☎ 986 747 111) Founded in 1990, this medium-size operation makes reliable, good quality wines.

◆ *Valdamor (white):* A refreshing, attractively bittersweet wine with length.

◆ *Valdamor Fermentado en Barrica (white):* A superior barrel-fermented Albariño, best at around three years old. It is integrated, flavoursome, long and quite complex. Recommended.

D.O. Ribeira Sacra

In Brief: *Beginning to be seen as a source of good young reds from the Mencía grape and some decent whites from local varieties. It also produces a fair number of average wines.*

Ribeira Sacra – named after the large number of religious establishments in the area – is a snake-like D.O. which follows part of the course of the Rivers Miño and Sil in southern central Galicia. It has a low profile, both internationally and also in Spain. Ribeira Sacra concentrates on red wines, a lot of which are sold in Galicia. In fact, around 85 per cent of output is sold locally, 13 per cent in the rest of Spain and a meagre couple of per cent abroad. The D.O. covers around 1,500 hectares of vineyards, has 2,500 grape growers and nearly 70 bodegas.
    Authorised grape varieties are:

● **White:** Albariño, Doña Branca, Godello, Loureira, Palomino, Torrontés and Treixadura.

- **Black:** Brancellao, Garnacha Tintorera, Mencía, Merenzao and Mouratón (or Negreda).

Ribeira Sacra's white wines are most commonly made from Godello and Albariño, and can be of good quality. The Albariños are fair expressions of the grape's floral and fruit qualities, while the Godellos are lighter and fresher than the better known examples from D.O. Valdeorras. Reds, especially from the Mencía grape, are the signature wines of the region, and are aromatic and fruity. Some feel that Ribeira Sacra's local Mencía clone makes wines with a French feel, not dissimilar to those made from the Bordeaux variety Cabernet Franc.

Geography, Soil and Climate

Conditions vary throughout the region: continental weather predominates along the Sil, with more Atlantic conditions along the Miño. Vineyards are planted at between 400 and 500m (1,312 and 1,640ft) above sea level – high by Galician standards – on mainly acidic soils.

Future Development

Ribeira Sacra's profile is low in Spain and almost non-existent internationally. But it finds a ready local market for its wines and is only slowly exporting them to the rest of the country and abroad. The style of its reds is appreciated locally and winning adherents elsewhere, but to appeal to a wider variety of drinkers it might be advisable to blend Mencía with Tempranillo to add structure, tannic backbone and ageing potential to some of the wines. As for whites, it could look to produce wines to rival the quality of Rías Baixas and Valdeorras. As yet, none of its wines are outstanding and too many are average. Hence the limited numbers of bodegas included below.

Selected Bodegas

Adega Don Ramón, S.L. (☎ 982 155 770) Founded in 1993, this very small bodega makes a good white and red wine:

- *Don Ramón Blanco (white):* This 100 per cent Godello has quite a complex, fruity nose and a refreshing palate with generous fruit flavours. Good.

- *Don Ramón Tinto (red):* A fruity, flavoursome Mencía with some bite for drinking young. Perhaps a touch pricey.

Adegas e Viñedos Vía Romana (☎ 982 454 005) Founded in 1998, this new operation is making one of the region's better red wines, although its price keeps rising.

- *Vía Romana (red):* This 100 per cent Mencía has a powerful, fruity nose with some depth and a palate with mouthfilling fruit flavours, balance and length. An appealing wine, but it does not come cheap.

Adegas Moure (☎ 982 452 031) Founded in 1959, this is one of Ribeira Sacra's more prominent bodegas, known throughout Spain. Its white and red wines are of good quality and have spread the message that this is a region with potential. The following are the logical starting point for an investigation of the area's wines:

◆ *Abadía Da Cova Albariño (white):* This is one of Ribera Sacra's better whites, with the aromas, flavours and elegance we look for from the grape. Priced at Rías Baixas levels, so not cheap.

◆ *Abadía da Cova (red):* One of the region's better known Mencía reds, this is fruity and mouthfilling with characteristic acidic bite.

Amedo (☎ 982 184 488) Founded in 1997, this bodega produces a respectable, straightforward white wine and a rather good red (below) with the other wines best avoided:

◆ *Donandrea (white):* Made from Godello, Treixadura and Torrontés, this is respectably aromatic and flavoursome, without scaling the heights.

◆ *Dondarío (red):* A tasty, aromatic Mencía with flavours of red fruits and mineral hints. Good.

César Enríquez Cachín (☎ 988 203 450) Founded in 1993, this small operation makes decent, reasonably priced, everyday wines:

◆ *Peza do Rei Godello (white):* Lightly aromatic and flavoursome, although it could do with a bit more punch.

◆ *Peza do Rei Mencía (red):* A tasty, fruity wine for enjoyable everyday drinking.

José Ramón Verao Pérez (☎ 982 152 981) A small operation making the Ribeira Sacra 'double' of Godello and Mencía.

◆ *Cividade Godello (white):* An aromatic wine with generous fruit flavours. Good.

◆ *Cividade (red):* A light, aromatic Mencía with enjoyable red fruit flavours.

Mario Vásquez Regal (☎ 982 171 636) Unusually for the region, this operation's white wines are better than its reds.

◆ *Viña Garoña Godello (white):* A refreshing, fruity, everyday wine.

◆ *Viña Pousa Godello (white):* As above but with more power.

◆ *Marqués de Garoña (red):* A lightly fruity, everyday red without much personality.

D.O. Ribeiro

In Brief: A source of characterful, aromatic, inexpensive white wines and some very good examples.

Wine making in Ribeiro stretches back at least to Roman times and was severely interrupted by barbarian invasions during the Dark Ages. A programme of replanting was undertaken during the 12th century and with the large number of pilgrims travelling to Galicia along the Santiago Route, there was a ready market for Ribeiro's wines and they became known throughout Europe. Thus for many centuries, Ribeiro was Galicia's most renowned wine region.

It is still regarded as thus in Spain for everyday white wines from the Palomino grape, but in the eyes of the serious wine drinker, Rías Baixas is the market leader for quality wines. The neutral Palomino still covers a lot of Ribeiro's 3,000 hectares of vineyards, but there is an active programme of replacing it with plantings of characterful, local varieties, especially Treixadura.

Authorised grape varieties are:

- **White:** Albariño, Albilla, Godello, Loureira, Macabeo, Palomino, Torrontés and Treixadura.

- **Black:** Alicante, Brancellao, Caíño, Ferrón, Mencía, Sousón and Tempranillo.

White wines are made in two styles: those made from Palomino are light and neutral, do not age well and are prone to oxidation; those made from local varieties, especially Treixadura, are aromatic, flavoursome and refreshing. For now, Ribeiro is concentrating on white wines, but it also makes reds. Those from the Alicante grape (which was planted in the region after the phylloxera epidemic) are tannic, everyday wines and rather better are those from Mencía, which are light and characterful with attractive aromas. Ribeiro is also looking to make wines from native black grapes such as Sousón and Brancellao, with early results indicating that the wines will be slightly unpolished.

Geography, Soil and Climate

Ribeiro lies around the River Avia in the west of the province of Ourense and its vineyards are planted at between 100 and 300m (328 and 984ft) above sea level on granitic, acidic soils. It is a region of gentle valleys and hills, which protect the vineyards from the prevalent westerly winds. Ribeiro has an Atlantic climate with continental influences. Temperatures are usually mild, although winters are subject to cold snaps; spring frosts are not unknown and summers can be hot. Humidity is often high and annual precipitation is between 800 and 1,000mm (31 and 39in).

Future Development

Ribeiro is Galicia's most productive vine-producing region and it is trying to substitute some of this quantity for quality. Around 70 per cent of its vineyards are still populated with the lower quality Palomino and Alicante grapes, but the active programme of replacing with good quality local varieties (usually the white Treixadura and Torrontés) is bearing fruit and the region is making better white wines, especially when cold-fermented. There are also moves to locate the superior varieties on higher hillsides, away from the overly fertile river valley. Slowly but surely Ribeiro's whites are gaining a reputation for quality and value, and sales outside the region are increasing, both to the rest of Spain and abroad.

Selected Bodegas

Alanís, S.A. (☎ 988 280 371) Founded in 1910, this operation is owned by the giant Bodegas y Bebidas group. It makes decent to good quality white wines, including:

◆ *Gran Alanís (white):* This blend of Palomino, Treixadura and Torrontés is a competent, fresh, straightforward wine.

◆ *San Trocado (white):* Made from a better blend – Treixadura and Torrontés – this is tasty, mouthfilling and unctuous. Good.

Campante, S.A. (☎ 988 261 212) Founded in 1940, this is one of Ribeiro's larger, more prominent producers, making a range of good white and red wines, including:

◆ *Campante (white):* This inexpensive Palomino is light, fruity and aromatic, a decent everyday wine for drinking young.

◆ *Viña Reboreda (white):* A blend of around 60 per cent Palomino and 40 per cent local varieties, this has good fruit and herb flavours, personality and some length. Good.

◆ *Gran Reboreda (white):* Made from local varieties, this is the bodega's most expensive white wine, offering lots of characterful fruit flavours and personality. However, it might be a little expensive in comparison with some of Rías Baixas' whites.

◆ *Viña Reboreda (red):* A straightforward, everyday red for drinking soon after it is released.

Cooperativa Vitivinícola del Ribeiro (☎ 988 470 175) Founded in 1967, this is one of Galicia's largest, most modern co-operatives, producing good red and white wines, including:

◆ *Pazo (white):* A fresh, tasty, balanced wine.

◆ *Amadeus (white):* A good wine, tasty, unctuous, quite complex and characterful. Recommended.

◆ *Pazo (red):* A fresh, fruity, superior everyday red with bite.

◆ *Alen da Historia (red):* A very aromatic and tasty young red with lots of fruit and balance.

Cunqueiro (☎ 988 489 023) Founded in 1967, this operation is best known for good white wines, including:

◆ *Viña Cunqueiro (white):* 50 per cent Palomino and 50 per cent local varieties, this is a well made, tasty white with bittersweet bite. Good and competitively priced.

◆ *Cunqueiro III Milenium (white):* Made from a blend of local varieties, this is an attractive wine, tasty, mouthfilling and balanced, but it is quite expensive.

Luis Ángel Rodríguez Vásquez (☎ 988 492 977) Founded in 1987, this tiny operation makes a characterful white and red wine:

🌢 *Viña de Martín (white):* An aromatic wine with a fruity, flavoursome palate and decent length.

🌢 *A Torna dos Pasás (red):* A tasty, fruity, characterful red with some complexity.

O'Ventosela (☎ 988 471 947) Founded in 1987, this is one of Ribeiro's larger operations, making a range of usually decent white and red wines, including:

🌢 *Viña Leiriña (white):* A blend of 60 per cent local varieties and 40 per cent Palomino, this is not the bodega's best, and is sometimes overcooked, sometimes understated.

🌢 *Gran Leiriño (white):* This is a much better bet, a 100 per cent Treixadura with unctuous flavours, balance and interest. Perhaps slightly overpriced.

🌢 *Juan Mínguez (red):* A light, fruity Mencía red for drinking young.

Portela, S.A.T. (☎ 988 480 050) Founded in 1987, this small operation makes decent white and red wines, including:

🌢 *Beade Primacia (white):* A fruity, aromatic Treixadura with unctuous hints and some interest.

🌢 *Señorío de Beade (red):* A blend of Caiño, Ferrón and Sousón, this is a decent, light, fruity everyday red wine.

Viña Mein, S.L. (☎ 988 488 400) Founded in 1988, this small operation makes one of the region's better, more interesting white wines:

🌢 *Viña Mein (white):* A blend of 70 per cent Treixadura, 15 per cent Godello, 10 per cent Loureira and the balance Albariño and Torrontés, this first came to market in 1994. It is very tasty with lots of characterful, exotic fruit flavours and is designed to improve in bottle for a couple of years after release. Recommended.

D.O. Valdeorras

In Brief: As well as making a lot of everyday wines, Valdeorras is the source of many of Galicia's better red wines and some of its Godello wines are among Spain's better whites.

Valdeorras is Galicia's most easterly D.O., lying in the hilly River Sil basin. It is endowed with the terrain and climate to make very good wines and has demonstrated that it can capitalise on this by producing high quality white wines from the Godello grape and reds from Mencía. However, as yet, the region's vineyards are still dominated by the workhouse white grape Palomino and the red Alicante, although moves are afoot to replace them with better grapes. Valdeorras' smaller wine makers are leading the way, producing the region's best wines from good local varieties.

Authorised grape varieties are:

- **White:** Doña Blanca, Godello and Palomino (the local variant is called Jerez).

- **Black:** Alicante, Grao Negro, Mencía and Merenzao.

The white wines we are interested in come from Godello and have floral aromas, good apple fruit, excellent acidity and unctuous touches; they can be of very high quality. The best reds come from the Mencía grape and are young wines with brambly aromas and fruity palates. They are probably Galicia's best. Valdeorras currently has 1,500 hectares of vineyards, 2,000 grape growers and around 35 bodegas.

Geography, Soil and Climate

Valdeorras' climate is a happy blend of Atlantic and continental conditions. It is drier than much of the rest of Galicia – although rainfall is still between 850 and 1,000mm (39in) per year – and it is very sunny, with 2,700 hours per year. Conditions are thus perfect for grapes.

Future Development

Valdeorras is a region to watch. Its conditions are wine-friendly and some producers have already shown that high quality white and red wines can be made. More will emerge as further vineyard hectareage is given over to good local grape varieties. As for red wines, there are moves to introduce Tempranillo in order to blend it with Mencía to produce wines with more tannin, structure and ageing potential. As yet, Valdeorras' profile is low and work needs to be done on marketing its wines to the rest of Spain and abroad. The logical starting place is to build on the success of A. Tapada's Guitián wines.

Selected Bodegas

A. Tapada, S.A.T. (☎ 988 324 197) Founded in 1993, this bodega's white Guitián wines are the region's flag-bearers, regarded as some of Spain's better white wines.

- *Guitián Godello (white):* Notably aromatic, this has lots of unctuous fruit flavours, length and some complexity. Highly recommended.

- *Guitián Fermentado en Barrica (white):* This barrel-fermented Godello is one of Spain's better white wines, powerfully aromatic, complex, balanced and flavoursome. Highly recommended and not too expensive for a wine with such a high reputation.

- *Viña Guitián Merenzao (red):* A light, balanced, fruity, appealing red wine.

Adegas Galegas (☎ 986 657 371) A tiny operation typifying what can be done in Valdeorras, with a very good Godello and Mencía.

◆ *Galiciano Godello (white):* A full-bodied wine with lots of flavoursome fruit and excellent acidity. Recommended.

◆ *Galiciano Mencía (red):* A fine example of how good this grape can be, with a fruity nose and lots of very flavoursome fruit. Recommended.

Concepción González Macía (☎ 988 311 659) Founded in 1991, this is another small bodega showing the region's potential. Its white wine is not very interesting but this red is worth trying:

◆ *Lavandeira (red):* An aromatic wine with lots of brambly fruit and unctuous hints. Good.

Cooperativa Jesús Nazareno, S.C.L. (☎ 988 320 262) Founded in 1963, this cooperative is by far the largest operation in Valdeorras, producing a decent to good range of inexpensive wines.

◆ *Albar Blanco (white):* A young, notably inexpensive wine made from Jerez with lots of fruity flavour.

◆ *Moza Fresca (white):* Made from 50 per cent Godello and 50 per cent Jerez, this is aromatic, mouthfilling, tasty and inexpensive. Good.

◆ *Viña Abad (white):* A decent, inexpensive Godello with honest flavour and structure.

◆ *Albar Tinto (red):* This is gentle, fruity and costs very little money. Unremarkable, except for the price.

◆ *Valdouro Crianza (red):* A blend of 50 per cent Garnacha and 50 per cent Mencía, this is a straightforward, tasty blend of mature fruit and oak for a modest price.

Godeval (☎ 988 325 309) Founded in 1986, this small operation works exclusively with the Godello grape and with some success.

◆ *Viña Godeval (white):* A rather good wine, tasty, lively and slightly unctuous.

◆ *Godeval Fermentado en Barrica (white):* Not a bad attempt to blend Godello with oak (a style of wine that is becoming increasingly popular) but it is heavy on the wood, which masks the fruit.

Joaquín Rebolledo, S.A. (☎ 988 372 307) Founded in 1982, this small bodega produces respectable wines, including:

◆ *Joaquín Rebolledo Godello (white):* A medium-bodied, tasty wine with apple fruit and herb touches.

◆ *Joaquín Rebolledo Mencía (red):* A straightforward, tasty, young red without pretensions to greatness.

The Gibraltar-like Peñón de Ifach rises above Benidorm and is also
the name of one of DO Alicante's better wines

12.

THE LEVANTE

The term 'Levante' refers to the middle and southern region of Spain's eastern Mediterranean coast. It stretches from the River Ebro delta in the north to the Cabo de Gato (east of the city of Almería) in the south. The region is closely associated with the beach holiday industry and also with agriculture: rice, citrus fruits, almonds, artichokes, dates, melons and peaches are all produced.

Vines are also important, both as a source of dessert grapes and for wine. Production of the latter in the Levante stretches back thousands of years. The region's coast has fertile soil and a mild climate (identified by The World Health Organisation as one of the healthiest in the world) which attracted several ancient peoples, and the region was colonised by Phoenicians, Greeks, Carthaginians and Romans. All brought their wine making skills with them.

When the Romans left, and as happened in other parts of Spain, the Levante's vinous development suffered during the years of barbarian invasions and the Moorish occupation. After liberation from the Moors in the 13th century, the region's wine production recovered and Valencia can lay claim to be the home of the author of one of the world's first oenological treatises, a gentleman called Arnau de Villanova.

The region's red wines were typically 'Mediterranean' in style: full-bodied, dark, spicy and sometimes overly-alcoholic. During the Middle Ages they became popular for blending, often with wines from France in years when the latter were thin and needed beefing up. Such blends were in particular demand in Britain, where the success of Port had given the populace a taste for powerful red wines.

The phylloxera vine plague hit the majority of the Levante in the late 19th century, although parts of Jumilla and Yecla were unaffected. Replanting the vineyards took time and some were planted with inferior hybrids instead of more expensive vines on grafted rootstocks. Partly because of this, throughout much of the 20th century the region languished as a bulk producer without much to offer the serious wine drinker. Its reds were too strong and rough for modern tastes, most of its dessert Moscatels too sweet, and it was only some of the rosés from higher-altitude vineyards (especially in Utiel-Requena) which were well regarded.

The last ten years have been marked by change and parts of the Levante have shown themselves to be capable of making exciting wines, especially reds. The re-evaluation of grape variety usage, earlier picking and improved fermentation technology have all contributed to the improvements. In the early years of the 21st century the region has six D.O.s: Alicante, Bullas, Jumilla, Utiel-Requena, Valencia and Yecla. All offer something to interest the discerning wine drinker.

D.O. Alicante

In Brief: Primarily a producer of competent, everyday wines, but the region has shown that it can make very good red wines, from both local and international grape varieties.

Primarily associated with the 'sun, sea, sand and sex' package holiday industry, both in Spain and internationally, Alicante also produces a wide range of wines. The D.O. covers 14,867 hectares, has 3,649 grape growers and 42 bodegas, of which 22 bottle their wines. It is divided into two zones: the maritime coastal area which concentrates on sweet Moscatel wines and the more significant region situated in the hilly interior which makes rosés, full-bodied reds, doble pasta wine and a limited amount of dry whites.

Authorised grape varieties are:

- **White:** Airén, Chardonnay, Macabeo, Merseguera, Moscatel Romano, Planta Fina and Verdil.

- **Black:** Bobal, Cabernet Sauvignon, Garnacha Tinta, Garnacha Tintorera, Merlot, Monastrell, Pinot Noir and Tempranillo.

The region's white wines are divided into three styles: the sweet Moscatels from the coast are of fair quality and characteristic of the grape's various types ('Moscatel' is a word that is often used vaguely, as a broad term for the several varieties of this grape, which are sometimes difficult to identify) with hints of honey and musk; dry whites made from local grape varieties tend to be light, fruity, everyday wines without much complexity or weight; while the dry whites made from Chardonnay are 'warm weather' wines, with ripe fruit that sometimes approaches over-maturity. Rosés are light, fruity and characterful, while the increasingly good reds are typically Mediterranean: dark, rich, full-bodied and characterful, although with a lighter touch than in the past and thus more attractive to drink. Fondillón, the traditional wine of the region, is made in a variety of styles, illustrated by some of the wine reviews which follow.

Alicante's producer profile is typical of the Levante: co-operatives and medium-quality operations dominate, while a handful of bodegas lead the way in quality and innovation, ably demonstrating what the region is capable of. In Alicante, Enrique Mendoza, Gutiérrez de la Vega and Primitivo Quiles are the torch-bearers, the first two with modern techniques and a mixture of local and foreign grape varieties, Primitivo Quiles by maintaining the traditional way and doing it well.

Geography, Soil and Climate

The coastal region enjoys a particularly mild, Mediterranean climate: winters are short, with plenty of sunshine and temperatures often reach 21°C (79°F). Summers are long and temperatures high for a coastal region: often over 35°C (95°F). Humidity is high and annual rainfall is around 400mm (16in). The interior region has a Mediterranean climate with continental influences: summers are shorter although even hotter than on the coast and winters are more severe. The diurnal temperature range is also greater throughout the year and both humidity and rainfall are lower than on the coastal strip: the latter is only around 300mm (12in) per year. The majority of the region's soils are limestone-based and low in organic content.

Future Development

Alicante's challenge is the same as that faced by other Spanish wine regions situated in areas associated with the holiday industry: to be taken seriously and not just as producers of indifferent, overpriced wines for the undiscerning, bulk tourist market. The way to do this is simply to produce good wines year after year and also to be noticed internationally and thus generate good publicity. Alicante currently exports around 40 per cent of its produce, although much of this is everyday wine. However, with the recent international popularity of the Monastrell grape (most notably under its French name of Mourvèdre), Alicante and the other Levante D.O.s have an opportunity to push their reasonably priced, tasty, full-bodied wines made from the grape. There are also plans to include the high quality, warm climate black grape Syrah in the list of authorised varieties, logical considering Alicante's weather. It is significant that one of Spain's best exponents of this grape – Agapito Rico from D.O. Jumilla – is looking to make wine in Alicante, a positive sign for the future.

Selected Bodegas

A. y M. Navarro, S.L. (☎ 965 801 486) Founded in 1956, this large producer makes a wide range of inexpensive, everyday wines, 70 per cent of which are exported. The following reds demonstrate that it is capable of making good wines:

◆ *Miguel Navarro Tempranillo Crianza (red):* A well made, characterful blend of fruit and oak for a low price.

◆ *Miguel Navarro Cabernet Sauvignon Crianza (red):* An aromatic wine with expressive fruit and bite.

B.O.C.O.P.A. Cooperativa Vinícola (☎ 966 950 489) Founded in 1987, this co-operative produces a large range of wines which vary in quality from the respectable but uninteresting to the very good, including:

◆ *Viña Alone (white):* A blend of Merseguera and Macabeo, this will cost you very little money. There is nothing actively wrong with it, but there is no real body or flavour.

◆ *Marina Alta (white):* Moscatel is the bodega's strong suit and this inexpensive example is aromatic, balanced, slightly sweet and fruity. Recommended.

◆ *Sol de Alicante (fortified white):* This is tasty, mouthfilling, satisfying Moscatel for an attractive price. Recommended.

◆ *Viña Alone (rosé):* Made from Monastrell and Tempranillo, comments are the same as for the Alone white.

◆ *Terreta Rosé (rosé):* Made from Monastrell, this is well made, fairly priced, characterful pink wine.

◆ *Viña Alone (red):* This inexpensive blend of Tempranillo, Monastrell and Merlot is a straightforward, reasonably priced, characterful young red wine for everyday drinking.

◆ *Castillo de Alicante (red):* A blend of Monastrell, Tempranillo and Cabernet Sauvignon, this is light, clean, reasonably priced, young wine.

◆ *Marqués de Alicante Crianza (red):* A blend of Monastrell, Tempranillo, Cabernet Sauvignon and Merlot, this is a straightforward, well made, commercial, aromatic wine with the fruit and oak integrated.

Cooperativa Nuestra Señora de las Virtudes (☎ 965 802 187) Founded in 1961, this large operation has nearly 2,000 hectares of vineyards. Its white and rosé wines hold little interest, but the following reds are worthwhile and show that the co-operative is capable of making decent wines:

◆ *Vinalopo (red):* A light, fruity, characterful, everyday red wine.

◆ *Vinalopo Crianza (red):* This is a competent, straightforward, mouthfilling, oak-aged red wine.

◆ *Vinalopo Reserva (red):* As above.

Enrique Mendoza, S.L. (☎ 965 888 639) Founded in 1989 – although the Mendozas began to plant vines in 1970 – this family business is one of the region's stars and the good reputation it has won in Spain is now being exported abroad. Quality is high across its wide range of reasonably priced wines, including:

◆ *Moscatel de la Marina (white):* An excellent, inexpensive, flavoursome and unctuous Moscatel.

◆ *Enrique Mendoza Chardonnay (white):* A straightforward, everyday Chardonnay.

◆ *Enrique Mendoza Chardonnay Fermentado en Barrica (white):* A better wine than the above, invariably unctuous, creamy and mouthfilling.

◆ *Savia Nova Tinto (red):* A young blend of Cabernet Sauvignon and Monastrell, this is very aromatic, with some complexity on the nose, while the palate has generous amounts of lively fruit and violets. Recommended.

◆ *Enrique Mendoza Pinot Noir (red):* A superior, Mediterranean wine from this difficult grape, with structure, concentrated spicy fruit and lots of flavour. However, it has little to identify it as Pinot Noir.

◆ *Enrique Mendoza Merlot Crianza (red):* This aromatic wine has concentrated, dark fruit flavours and body. Good.

◆ *Enrique Mendoza Cabernet Sauvignon Crianza (red):* A well made, full-bodied, warm climate Cabernet.

◆ *Enrique Mendoza Cabernet Sauvignon Reserva (red):* Rather superior to the above, this is excellent, with a complex nose, expressive palate, flavour, balance and length. A lot of wine for a modest outlay and highly recommended.

◆ *Enrique Mendoza Shiraz Crianza (red):* This is probably the wine that has convinced the authorities to add Shiraz to its list of authorised varieties. It has a powerful nose and palate with mature, spicy fruit, toasty oak and confident tannins. A very good wine that ably demonstrates how well Shiraz is suited to the Levante.

● *Enrique Mendoza Peñón de Ifach (red):* A blend of 60 per cent Cabernet Sauvignon, 20 per cent Merlot and 20 per cent Pinot Noir, this was the bodega's flagship red before the appearance of Santa Rosa. It has a moreish, concentrated nose with mature fruit and hints of eucalyptus, while the palate has abundant, structured, persistent flavours. Very good with casseroles: a wine to drink in a cold climate from a warm climate source.

● *Santa Rosa (red):* This is a blend of 70 per cent Cabernet Sauvignon, 15 per cent Merlot and 15 per cent Syrah. It spends six months in new American oak barrels followed by a year in French oak, and first appeared on the market in 1999. This is one of Spain's best Mediterranean red wines, with a deep, complex nose and a palate with power, balance, structure, length, complexity and lots of flavour. It has taken the bodega to new heights, both domestically and internationally. Thoroughly recommended and still reasonably priced given the quality, although it is on the increase.

Gutiérrez de la Vega (☎ 966 405 266) Founded in 1978, this small bodega makes modest quantities of sought-after wines with consequently high prices, which, in some cases, have begun to outstrip quality. The range includes:

● *Casta Diva Cosecha Dorada (white):* A well made, characterful, dry Moscatel for everyday drinking.

● *Casta Diva Monte Diva Fermentado en Barrica (white):* A barrel-fermented Moscatel, this is mouthfilling with some bite, but the oak submerges the fruit and the wine is expensive when compared with better barrel-fermented whites from other regions.

● *Casta Diva Cosecha Miel (sweet white):* This famous sweet Moscatel is worth its fairly elevated price. It has an engaging, complex nose with honey, flowers and toast, while the palate has power, depth, complexity and notable balance between the sweetness and bite. One of Spain's best sweet whites and highly recommended.

● *Rojo y Negro Crianza (red):* A blend of Cabernet Sauvignon, Giró and Monastrell, this is a decent, straightforward crianza with flavour and character, although not enough to justify its price.

● *Viña Ulises Crianza (red):* A blend of Cabernet Sauvignon, Garnacha and Monastrell, this has more complexity than the Rojo y Negro, but the comments are basically as above.

Primitivo Quiles, N.C.R. (☎ 965 470 099) Founded back in 1780, Primitivo Quiles has had many years to reach its current position as the region's maker par excellence of superior, traditional fortified and sweet wines. Try the following example:

● *El Abuelo Gran Fondillón (fortified):* An excellent Monastrell wine, this has a nose of vanilla, eucalyptus and sweets, while the palate is dry, full-bodied and seductive.

Salvador Poveda, S.A. (☎ 965 471 139): Founded in 1918, this respected firm makes a range of decent to good quality wines, including:

- *Salvador Poveda Riesling (white):* It is interesting to see this cool-weather grape in a warm part of the world. This example is a light, fruity, inexpensive wine, although unrepresentative of this distinctive grape variety.
- *Salvador Poveda Cabernet Sauvignon-Merlot Crianza (red):* A straightforward, well made, flavoursome red crianza at a modest price.

- *Viña Vermeta Reserva (red):* A soundly constructed, inexpensive Monastrell wine, with spicy flavour and persistence.

D.O. Bullas

In Brief: *A one-horse D.O. that should be integrated with one of its stronger, higher profile neighbours.*

Without wanting to be either negative or dismissive – which means, of course, that I am almost certain to be both – it is difficult to understand why Bullas is a separate D.O. and not part of its neighbour Jumilla. Bullas covers nearly 2,500 hectares of vineyards and has 519 grape growers, but has only seven bodegas, of which only three bottle their wines.

Authorised grape varieties are:

- **White:** Airén and Macabeo.

- **Black:** Cabernet Sauvignon, Garnacha, Merlot, Monastrell, Syrah and Tempranillo.

Bullas' white wines are simple and lightly fruity, the rosés are decent, everyday wines, while the reds are characterised by mature fruit and are lighter than those from other Levante regions.

Geography, Soil and Climate

Bullas is split into three sub-regions: the north-east at an altitude of between 400 and 500m (1,312 and 1,640ft) above sea level; the centre at 500 to 600m (1,640 to 1,968ft); and the west and north-west, at altitudes of between 500 and 800m (1,640 and 2,624ft). The last has the most vineyards and also the most potential to make good quality wines.

Weather conditions naturally vary across the three sub-zones, although overall Bullas' climate can be described as Mediterranean with continental influences. Summer temperatures can be excessive, sometimes over 40°C (104°F), while winters are subject to cold spells when temperatures fall to minus 5 or 6°C (41 or 43°F). Annual sunshine figures are high (nearly 3,000 hours) and yearly precipitation is a very modest 300mm (12in), much of that produced by short, violent thunderstorms. Soils are limestone and alluvial-based.

Future Development

As mentioned in the section on Alicante, the Levante D.O.s suffer from an image problem: they are seen as holiday regions, not wine producing areas. Wines from some of them are beginning to challenge this misconception, but there is still work to be done. Bullas' neighbour Jumilla is further along the line than most with this 'education' programme and this is a strong argument to suggest that the wine makers of Bullas would be better off as part of the increasingly successful Jumilla D.O. rather than their own low-profile one.

This will probably not happen. There are obviously 'political' reasons for Bullas' status as a separate D.O. and so we will proceed on the basis that it will remain as a separate entity. The way forward for Bullas seems to lie in focusing on the production of wines from Monastrell and recently authorised, good quality foreign black grapes in favoured, higher vineyards. It must also try to raise its profile: I doubt that any but the most wine-obsessed Spaniards have heard of it.

Selected Bodegas

Balcona, S.L. (☎ 968 652 666) Founded only in 1997, and with a modest 12 hectares of vines, this tiny operation shows what Bullas is capable of. Its small range includes:

◆ *Partal Maceración Carbónica (red):* A young Monastrell with concentrated, expressive fruit on the nose and a fruity, tangy palate with lots of lively tannins. Good.

◆ *Partal Crianza (red):* This superior blend of 60 per cent Monastrell and 40 per cent 'others' ably demonstrates what this region is capable of. It is a powerful mouthful with characterful fruit and oak, bite and some finish. The tannins are quite aggressive when first released but they soften; drink this wine at four years plus. If only it was less expensive it might draw more consumers, which is just what Bullas needs.

Cooperativa Agraria Nuestra Señora del Rosario (☎ 968 652 075) Founded in 1950, this co-operative produces a modest range of acceptable, inexpensive wines, the whites primarily from Macabeo, the rosés and reds mainly from Monastrell. The better wines are:

◆ *Las Reñas Tinto (red):* A reasonably priced, straightforward, fruity young wine.

◆ *Las Reñas Crianza (red):* Hardly subtle, but this simple, inexpensive crianza is competently made and spicy.

D.O. Jumilla

In Brief: Jumilla's stock is on the rise and it has become the source of some of Spain's more interesting and exciting red wines.

Jumilla's landscape does not look like 'classic' wine making territory: instead of meandering rivers, gentle, green hills and early morning mists on vineyards Jumilla offers bland, parched, grey-brown views. Until recently its harsh land was known mainly for powerful, dark, over-alcoholic reds, often used for blending to beef-up thin wines from elsewhere. Up to three-quarters of production was sent to Switzerland, Germany, Northern Spain, Eastern Europe and – allegedly – Bordeaux, to 'help' weak vintages.

The latter years of the 20th century saw something of a renaissance in the region. Modern techniques and technology entered Jumilla, with cooling equipment and earlier grape picking particularly significant. At the same time there was international recognition that the Monastrell grape – which accounts for at least 80 per cent of vineyard hectarage in Jumilla – was capable of making characterful wines when treated correctly. As a point of historical interest, Jumilla's Monastrell vines are ungrafted because the region's soil has a high chalk content and a consistency which inhibited the phylloxera aphids, so the plague did not hit the region too hard.

In the early 21st century, Jumilla is sometimes painted as the 'most Australian' of Spain's wine regions. This stems mainly from its increasing plantings of, and success with, Shiraz, Australia's signature black grape. However, the region can still be seen as a divided territory: between large co-operatives and bodegas making volume wine (of better quality than in the bad old days) and smaller producers who are making wines of increasingly good quality that are winning prizes not just in Spain but internationally; Agapito Rico is the best example of the latter.

Authorised grape varieties are:

- **White:** Airén, Macabeo and Pedro Ximénez.

- **Black:** Cabernet Sauvignon, Garnacha Tinta, Garnacha Tintorera, Monastrell and Tempranillo, with Merlot and Syrah soon to follow.

The region's modest amounts of white wines are generally full-bodied and flavoursome, while the rosés are similarly robust. But Jumilla is primarily red wine country and most is still made from the Monastrell grape. Until recently, older-style wines were prone to oxidation but the newer ones – which benefit from modern technology and know-how – avoid this and are characterised by their intense colour, fulsome, mouthfilling flavours of ripe, dark fruits, well judged tannins and ability to be made into a variety of styles: young wines for early drinking, wines aged in oak for short periods and those with longer periods in wood. Reds made from international varieties – primarily Shiraz, Merlot and the ubiquitous Cabernet Sauvignon – are of good to excellent quality.

Geography, Soil and Climate

Jumilla's climate is continental with Mediterranean influences. Winters can be severe with temperatures dropping below freezing, while summers are intense with temperatures often reaching 35°C (95°F), sometimes higher. This is one of Spain's more arid regions with annual precipitation of only 300 (12in), most of it restricted to the spring and autumn. As a result, limited irrigation is allowed. Vineyards are situated at between 400 and 800m (1,312 and 2,624ft) above sea level on chalk-based soils which have an all-important, high capacity for water retention.

Future Development

Jumilla's progress over the last ten years has been impressive. Of all the Levante D.O.s it has been the most successful at publicising the fact that the south-east of Spain is not just about beach holidays and rough red wines. Its future seems to lie in refining and diversifying the range of wines made from the Monastrell grape, as well as continuing to show that it can make superior wines from international varieties. Of these, Shiraz appears to be most suited to the climate and this grape's eager international fan-base can only be good for Jumilla.

Selected Bodegas

Agapito Rico, S.L. (☎ 968 757 172) Founded as recently as 1990, this small bodega is carrying the flag for the region's quality producers, both in Spain and internationally, and exports around three-quarters of its output. If you are interested in trying the best of Jumilla, the bodega's Carchelo range should be your first port of call. It includes:

- *Carchelo Tinto (red):* The bodega's young red is a reasonably priced, powerful, aromatic, fruity wine with character and interest.

- *Carchelo Merlot (red):* This young Merlot offers lots of mouthfilling flavour, structure and satisfaction for a competitive price. Recommended.

- *Carchelo Syrah (red):* Powerful, integrated, expressive and quite complex, this is a superior product which has enjoyed a lot of critical success. It is at its best three or four years after release. Recommended.

- *Carchelo Crianza (red):* A varying blend of around 30 per cent Cabernet Sauvignon, 30 per cent Monastrell and 40 per cent Tempranillo, this seductive wine is brimming with integrated fruit and oak flavours and has powerful, although not intrusive, tannins and persistence. Delicious and highly recommended.

- *Carchelo Merlot Crianza (red):* A powerful, elegant, flavour-filled, unctuous wine, the bodega's most expensive and at the top table of Spanish reds. Try hard to secure a bottle and drink at six or seven years old.

Asensio Carcelén, N.C.R. (☎ 968 780 418) Founded in 1876, this producer makes a small range of inferior to adequate wines, the following red having the most to offer:

- *Con Sello Gran Reserva (red):* A smooth, powerful, straightforward blend of fruit and oak with lots of flavour.

Bodegas Bleda, S.L. (☎ 968 780 012) Founded in the '30s, this operation makes respectable, low-priced wines which show enough promise to suggest that it can join the region's push to improve quality. The range includes:

- *Castillo Jumilla Blanco (white):* A blend of 50 per cent Airén and 50 per cent Macabeo, this is a simple, inexpensive, fruity, young wine for drinking early before its delicate fruit fades.

♦ *Castillo Jumilla Rosado (rosé):* Lighter than the average Jumilla rosé, this is clean, refreshing Monastrell for drinking when you don't want to think about anything.

♦ *Castillo Jumilla Tinto Crianza (red):* This blend of 60 per cent Monastrell and 40 per cent Tempranillo is lighter than some Jumilla reds, with good integration of fruit and oak. Respectable and inexpensive.

Bodegas 1890, S.A. (☎ 968 758 100) It doesn't take much imagination to work out that this bodega was founded in the year 1890. In the 21st century it is making a wide range of good quality wines at low prices. None of the Mayoral wines is outstanding but all are eminently drinkable and they are improving annually. The range includes:

♦ *Mayoral Rosado (rosé):* A young Monastrell that is as characterful as pink wine can be for the notably low price.

♦ *Mayoral Tinto (red):* A blend of 60 per cent Monastrell and 40 per cent Tempranillo, this is superior, reasonably priced everyday red wine, aromatic and powerful with structure and robust flavours.

♦ *Mayoral Maceración Carbónica (red):* The same blend as the above, this has lots of lively fruit on the nose, while the palate has characterful dark fruit and tannins. A good, inexpensive example of the style.

♦ *Mayoral Monastrell Selección (red):* A much praised, inexpensive wine offering lots of concentrated, mouthfilling flavours. Recommended.

♦ *Mayoral Cabernet Sauvignon (red):* A worthy, inexpensive, warm climate Cabernet Sauvignon with characteristic flavour, confident tannins and balance.

♦ *Mayoral Reserva (red):* An inexpensive blend of 60 per cent Tempranillo and 40 per cent Monastrell, this has a spicy nose and a lightish, smooth palate. A decent, straightforward, oak-aged wine for everyday drinking.

B.S.I. San Isidro (☎ 968 780 700) Founded in 1935, this is one of Spain's largest and most modern co-operatives, making both decent, low-priced wines and some superior, more expensive ones. Thus it is representative of what Jumilla is capable of, and its wines include:

♦ *Sabatacha Blanco (white):* A respectable, simple, fruity Airén white for drinking young.

♦ *Sabatacha Blanco Fermentado en Barrica (white):* Barrel-fermented Airén does not sound like a good idea: you might expect the oak to overpower the gentle fruit. However, this is not too oaky and it is quite worthy for the low price.

♦ *Sabatacha Rosado (rosé):* Straightforward yet characterful rosado from Monastrell.

♦ *Sabatacha Tinto (red):* An aromatic, flavoursome, young wine from the Monastrell grape.

♦ *Sabatacha Tinto Crianza (red):* An inexpensive, mouthfilling Monastrell with body and oaky flavour.

- *Gémina Tinto (red):* A classy, young Monastrell with body and some complexity. Good but becoming expensive.

- *Gémina Tinto Dulce (sweet red):* An elegant, fruity, sweet Monastrell. Well made and seductive but not a cheap date.

- *Gémina Tinto Reserva (red):* The bodega's flagship wine, this Monastrell has a complex nose and is full of concentrated fruit flavours. A classy, warm-climate wine. Recommended, but it is expensive and that from a region that still lacks the reputation to charge these prices.

Bodegas Huertas, S.A. (☎ 968 783 061) Founded only in the mid-'90s, Huertas is already making some good wines – especially reds – and is representative of Jumilla's drive towards quality at competitive prices. However, standards are mixed and the most reliable of its range are the following:

- *Rodrejo Blanco (white):* A blend of 50 per cent Airén and 50 per cent Macabeo, this is a simple, inexpensive, fruity wine for drinking young.

- *Rodrejo Rosado (rosé):* This is a well made Monastrell, aromatic, tasty and quite full-bodied wine. Good.

- *Rodrejo Tinto (red):* A straightforward, inexpensive, aromatic, powerful young Monastrell-based wine with lots of fruit.

- *Aranzo Crianza (red):* A well made blend of fruit and oak, usually characterful and balanced, but it is rather expensive.

Finca Luzón, S.L. (☎ 968 784 135) Founded in 1978, this producer makes quite large quantities of a small range of inexpensive, good quality wines, with the following two standing out:

- *Finca Luzón (red):* A blend of 50 per cent Monastrell, 20 per cent Merlot, 20 per cent Tempranillo and 10 per cent Cabernet Sauvignon, this is a powerfully aromatic, full-bodied, flavoursome, young wine with some complexity for a low price. Recommended.

- *Castillo de Luzón Crianza (red):* Made from the same blend of grapes as the above, this is a notably aromatic, powerful, toasty, integrated blend of oak and tasty fruit for a competitive price. Recommended and just the type of wine that Jumilla excels at.

Julia Roch e Hijos, C.B. (☎ 968 781 691) Founded in 1991, this is another Jumilla producer making increasingly good wines, especially reds, including:

- *Casa Castillo Blanco (white):* A simple, dry Viura for drinking young.

- *Casa Castillo Rosado (rosé):* A professionally made, characterful Monastrell/Tempranillo rosado.

- *Casa Castillo Maceración Carbónica (red):* A characterful, fruity, young red wine. Its price is on the increase.

- *Casa Castillo Monastrell (red)*: A blend of 85 per cent Monastrell and 15 per cent Syrah, this is aromatic, powerful and well made, and again its price is on the rise.

- *Casa Castillo Tinto Crianza (red)*: Aromatic, mouthfilling, balanced and flavoursome, this is decent crianza for a reasonable price.

- *Casa Castillo Pie Franco (red)*: This is the bodega's most expensive wine, a Monastrell designed to compete with better bottles from other regions. It has a powerful nose with mature fruit and toast, while the palate has more of the same, with lively tannins. Very good, but perhaps rather expensive.

Señorío del Condestable, S.A. (☎ 968 781 011) Founded in 1968, this operation is owned by Bodegas y Bebidas, which controls several wine concerns in Spain. Condestable makes a small range of respectable, inexpensive, everyday wines, including:

- *Vivala Monastrell (red)*: A characterful, young red with lots of ripe fruit.

- *Señorío de Robles (red)*: well made, fruity Monastrell for a notably low price.

D.O. Utiel-Requena

In Brief: Still primarily a source of large amounts of everyday wines, but it can do better and is producing more decent quality, inexpensive reds.

Utiel-Requena takes its name from the hill towns of Utiel and Requena, situated an hour or so by road from the coast at the western end of the province of Valencia. It is a high region which still has a feeling of isolation even though motorway access now means that this is no longer the case. Wine and grape juice production and related industries are the backbone of the economy and although Utiel-Requena has been making wine for many years, it became a D.O. only in 1987. It covers just over 40,000 hectares of vines, has some 6,700 grape growers and 95 bodegas.

Along with Alicante, Utiel-Requena has a long tradition of making Vino de doble pasta: grapes are briefly and lightly crushed in a vat and the resultant juice is run off and used to make light, delicate rosé wines. More crushed grapes are then added to the original vat and fermentation produces thick, dark, very alcoholic wine – up to 18 per cent – which is not intended for drinking but for blending with weaker, thinner wines, often from cooler regions. The demand for these is declining at the same time as the production of grape juice in the region is becoming more important.

The black Bobal is the dominant grape of Utiel-Requena, accounting for at least three-quarters of vineyard hectareage, although there are increasing plantings of other varieties, notably Tempranillo.

Authorised grape varieties are:

- **White:** Chardonnay, Macabeo, Merseguera and Plantanova.

- **Black:** Bobal, Cabernet Sauvignon, Garnacha, Merlot and Tempranillo.

The region's white wines are fresh and light, the rosés, made from Bobal, are fresh and very drinkable, while the reds are tasty and quite powerful, sometimes with herby nuances.

Geography, Soil and Climate

Utiel-Requena has a continental climate with Mediterranean influences. Winters are cold, with temperatures dropping below freezing, while summers can reach 38°C (100°F), although they are generally milder than in other Levante regions. There are 2,600 hours of sunshine per year and annual rainfall is low, not exceeding 400mm (16in). Soils are limestone-based, low in organic materials and have a high water retention capacity.

Future Development

Around 60 per cent of Utiel-Requena's output is exported, Switzerland and Denmark being particularly important markets. Much of this used to be bulk-shipped, although a lot more is now bottled prior to shipping, an indication of the region's improving quality. Much still remains to be done and further developments in technology and vineyard and winery expertise should continue the process of improvement. This is a region with potential, but some wines still display faults caused by wine making errors that should have been consigned to the past. Co-operatives are influential in Utiel-Requena, their size and inertia often meaning that change is slow. However, the region is gradually building a reputation for wines with an excellent price/quality ratio and can capitalise on this. There are also plans to form the so-called 'Association of the Wine Route of the D.O. Utiel-Requena' (which translates clumsily from the Spanish) intended to stimulate interest in the region's wine production.

Selected Bodegas

Asturiana de Vinos, S.A. (☎ 985 260 241) Founded in 1984, this operation makes a modest range of notably inexpensive wines:

- *Aloyón Blanco (white):* A light, undemanding, everyday Macabeo.

- *Aloyón Rosado (rosé):* A simple, competent rosé from the Bobal grape.

- *Aloyón Tinto (red):* A light, inexpensive, Tempranillo red wine.

Bodegas Schenk, S.A. (Cavas Murviedro) (☎ 962 329 003) Founded in 1927, this operation is part of a large Swiss company which has extensive interests throughout the Levante region. Its wide range is mainly composed of competent, inexpensive, everyday wines, including:

- *Las Lomas Macabeo (white):* A decent, inexpensive white wine with some bite.

- *Aldea Rosado (rosé):* A well made, fruity, pink wine from the Bobal grape for a low price.

- *Castillo Murviedro Rosado (rosé):* A tasty, fruity, balanced rosado, again from Bobal.

- *Las Lomas Tempranillo (red):* A light, inexpensive, fruity, young wine that does not have too much going on.

- *Cavas Murviedro Tinto Crianza (red):* This has lots of flavour and some balance. A decent, uncomplicated, oaked red wine.

- *Las Lomas Tinto Reserva (red):* A blend of Tempranillo, Cabernet Sauvignon and 'others', this is the bodega's most expensive wine and, in some years, shows promising flavour and structure. It is light, aromatic, balanced and persistent. An appealing wine, sometimes indicative of what Utiel-Requena is capable of, but expensive when compared with better offerings from other regions.

Compañía Vinícola del Campo de Requena (☎ 962 171 141) A small company whose whites are rather basic, but with some promising rosés and reds, including:

- *Viña Carmina (rosé):* Decent, fruity rosado from the Bobal grape.

- *Viña Mariola Tinto Crianza (red):* A straightforward, competent, inexpensive Tempranillo crianza.

- *Vera de Estenas Reserva (red):* A blend of Cabernet Sauvignon, Merlot and Tempranillo, this is an integrated, smooth, tasty, aged red wine at a fair price.

- *Martínez Bermel Merlot (red):* This barrel-fermented Merlot has subtle balance and a silky palate. Recommended.

Cooperativa Agrícola de Utiel (☎ 962 171 157) Founded in 1927, the majority of this large co-operative's wines are competent but of little interest to the serious drinker, although in some years the following red gives reason for hope:

- *Castillo de Utiel Crianza (red):* This can be aromatic, balanced and tasty with fruit and oak flavours working in harmony. If only it did not have off-years when it is submerged in oak.

Coviñas Cooperativa (☎ 962 300 680) Founded in 1965, some of the range of wines in this co-operative are eminently respectable and encouraging for the future, they include:

- *Viña Enterizo Blanco (white):* A simple, clean white for drinking young.

- *Viña Enterizo Rosado (rosé):* Competent, refreshing pink wine.

- *Viña Enterizo Tempranillo (red):* A tasty, slightly earthy red wine.

- *Peña Tejo Tinto Crianza (red):* A well made, light crianza with some structure and balance.

Latorre Agrovinícola, S.A. (☎ 962 185 028) Founded in the '60s, this operation is another whose inexpensive wines show promise, including:

● *El Parreño Blanco (white):* A simple, respectable, fruity, Macabeo.

● *El Parreño Rosado (rosé):* Light, tasty wine from Bobal.

● *El Parreño Tinto (red):* A well made, fruity, young Tempranillo.

Mas de Bazán (☎ 962 303 586) Founded in 1985, this operation produces two notably well made wines:

● *Mas de Bazán Rosado (rosé):* Aromatic, balanced and characterful, this is superior pink wine from Bobal and Garnacha, more expensive than the average rosado.

● *Mas de Bazán Tinto (red):* A worthy, young blend of 45 per cent Bobal, 45 per cent Tempranillo and 10 per cent Garnacha, this has a powerful nose, lots of flavour and length.

Proexa, S.L. (☎ 963 890 877): Founded in 1995, this producer's red wines show promise, particularly:

● *Vega Valterra (red):* A full-bodied, fruity, inexpensive Tempranillo.

● *Vega Valterra Reserva Especial (red):* A balanced, flavoursome, aromatic blend of fruit and oak. Good.

Torre Oria, S.L. (☎ 962 320 289) Founded in 1897, as well as making decent sparkling wines under the Cava D.O., this producer's table wines are increasingly well made, especially the reds. Its range includes:

● *Torre Oria Blanco (white):* A competent, fruity, everyday Macabeo.

● *Torre Oria Rosado (rosé):* Everyday, refreshing pink wine from the Bobal grape.

● *Torre Oria Tinto (red):* A respectable, straightforward young Tempranillo.

● *Marqués de Requena Crianza (red):* Made from 90 per cent Tempranillo and 10 per cent Garnacha, this has lots of robust flavours and balance. Not subtle, but willing and well made.

● *Marqués de Requena Reserva (red):* In good years, the same blend of grapes as above produces a flavoursome, aromatic wine with length. However, it can be overgenerous and unsubtle with the oak.

Vicente Gandía Pla, S.A. (☎ 962 522 443) Founded in 1885, this large operation is perhaps most famous for its Castillo de Liria range from D.O. Valencia, which consists of popular, simple wines for everyday drinking. However, it also produces an extensive range of wines in Utiel-Requena, some with aspirations to greatness, including:

● *Gandía Hoya Valley Macabeo (white):* A competent, light, undemanding white wine.

● *Gandía Hoya Valley Chardonnay (white):* A simple, respectable, inexpensive Chardonnay with decent flavour and some bite.

◆ *Gandía Hoya Valley Moscatel (white)*: A decent, dry wine which is a fair, inexpensive introduction to the grape.

◆ *Gandía Hoya Valley Tempranillo (red)*: Straightforward, inexpensive, tasty, everyday wine.

◆ *Gandía Hoya Valley Merlot (red)*: Smooth and quite characterful for a modest price.

◆ *Gandía Hoya Valley Cabernet Sauvignon (red)*: Easy-drinking and quite lavoursome.

◆ *Hoy de Cadenas Reserva (red)*: This Garnacha/Tempranillo blend is a step up in quality, with some quite complex flavours and structure for a modest price. Good.

◆ *Gandía Hoya Valley Cabernet Sauvignon Reserva (red)*: A well made, aromatic, tasty, mouthfilling wine.
◆ *Ceremonia Crianza (red)*: A finely structured, aromatic wine with attractive flavours, but too expensive. The Cabernet Sauvignon Reserva is as good and less than half the price.

D.O. Valencia

In Brief: *Still primarily a source of bulk wine and decent, everyday whites, Valencia is trying to improve the quality of its wines and some of the reds are encouraging.*

Valencia is the most northerly Levante wine region, designated a D.O. in 1987. It covers 17,355 hectares of vineyards, has 6,875 grape growers and 58 bodegas, of which 37 bottle their wines. Valencia produces more white wine than red, often from grapes of (at best) moderate quality, although the region's modern, technologically advanced bodegas make the most of the aromas and flavours that they have.

The D.O. is split into four sub-zones, with a different wine making profile in each: Alto Turia in the hilly north makes the best white wines; Valentino in the centre makes reds, whites and rosés; Moscatel de Valencia, as the name telegraphs, concentrates on the region's well regarded Moscatels; and Clariano in the south makes wines of all colours, with an emphasis on robust reds from the Monastrell grape.

Authorised grape varieties are:

● **White:** Chardonnay, Macabeo, Malvasía, Merseguera, Moscatel, Pedro Ximénez, Plantafina, Plantanova, Tortosí and Verdil.

● **Black:** Bobal, Cabernet Sauvignon, For-Cayat, Garnacha, Merlot, Monastrell, Pinot Noir, Tempranillo and Tintorera.

Valencia has traditionally been one of Spain's bigger wine exporters and over 60 per cent of its output is still sent abroad, much of it basic, everyday wine. Co-operatives have a large presence in the region and, as is generally the case with the Levante D.O.s, these large organisations have a reputation for conservatism and can sometimes slow the rate of change and progress. However, Valencia also houses some large, influential operations with foreign shareholders, notably Swiss, which have a close connection with the region.

Geography, Soil and Climate

The climate is Mediterranean, with variations caused by differences in altitude and aspect across the four sub-zones. Annual rainfall is around 500mm (20in), higher than the Levante average, much of it falling in the late summer and autumn when the region is subject to violent thunderstorms.

Alto Turia in the north of Valencia has vineyards at between 700 and 900m (2,296 and 2,952ft) above sea level; Valentino's are at between 250 and 650m (820 and 2,132ft); Moscatel's vineyards are among the lowest and it has the warmest climate; while Clariano in the south has vineyards at between 400 and 650m (1,312 and 2,132ft). Soils are generally limestone-based with good drainage.

Future Development

Apart from its historical association with Moscatel and its reputation as a significant exporter of everyday wines, Valencia does not have a high profile, especially for good quality wines. The impulse towards improvement is strong in the Levante and Valencia has recognised this. There is a programme of replanting with better grape varieties, mainly Tempranillo, but also Cabernet Sauvignon, Merlot, Syrah and Pinot Noir, this latter unlikely to be especially suited to Valencia's warm climate. There are also moves to introduce modern irrigation methods and plans to lighten the wines by reducing the time that red crianzas spend in oak from two years to six months. But the fact that bodegas from Utiel-Requena can produce wine under the Valencia D.O. – allowed because of the scarcity of black grapes in Valencia – shows how much work there is to be done.

Selected Bodegas

Bodega J. Belde (☎ 968 962 365) Founded in 1931, the quality of this bodega's wines is mixed but on the rise and the following are both encouraging and the most consistent:

◆ *Daniel Belda Verdil Fermentado en Barrica (white):* Not a bad barrel-fermented wine, with some fruit but more oak.

◆ *Daniel Belda Chardonnay Fermentado en Barrica (white):* Full-bodied, unctuous, characterful, barrel-fermented Chardonnay with fruit to balance the oak. A fair attempt at this ubiquitous international style of wine.

◆ *Eusebio la Casta Tempranillo Reserva (red):* A competent, mouthfilling, persistent wine. Could sometimes be a bit more subtle.

◆ *Eusebio la Casta Cabernet Sauvignon Reserva (red):* A full-bodied Cabernet with good flavour and length.

Bodegas Schenk, S.A. (Cavas Murviedro) (☎ 962 329 003) See also the entry under **D.O. Utiel-Requena** on page 270. Schenk's Valencian wines are competent, with the best, the Estrella Moscatel, also being one of the cheapest. The range includes:

● *Cavas Murviedro Blanco (white):* A decent, aromatic, fruity, refreshing, everyday white wine from Merseguera, Moscatel and Macabeo.

● *Estrella Vino Dulce Moscatel (sweet white):* The bodega's star buy, this is superior Moscatel for a low price. It has a complex nose, balance, unctuous flavours and length. Recommended.

● *Cavas Murviedro Rosado (rosé):* A blend of Bobal and Monastrell, this is a decent, refreshing, pink wine.

● *Los Monteros Crianza (red):* A well made Monastrell-based crianza, aromatic, balanced and attractive. It shows that Valencia can definitely make such wines.

Cooperativa Agrícola de Villar del Arzobispo (☎ 962 720 050) Founded in 1970, this fair-size co-operative makes a range of competent, inexpensive everyday wines, most of which do not merit much comment, although the following red shows the quality of which it is capable:

● *Viña Villar Crianza (red):* A well made, flavoursome Tempranillo crianza for a modest price. Recommended.

Cooperativa La Baronía de Turís (☎ 962 526 011) Founded in 1920, this large co-operative makes a range of generally decent, everyday wines at low prices, including:

● *Barón de Turis (white):* A young Malvasía, refreshing and with some bite, about as good as it could be for the low price.

● *Viñamalata (white):* Good, characterful, inexpensive Moscatel.

● *Gran Barón de Turís Crianza (red):* A decent, straightforward blend of Tempranillo and oak flavours for a low price.

● *Barón de Turis Reserva (red):* A well made, inexpensive, commercial Tempranillo with balance and flavour.

Los Pinos (☎ 962 222 090) Founded in 1990, this small operation makes a modest range of wines, better and more expensive than the regional average. The reds are especially worthy and demonstrate Valencia's potential with wines made from Monastrell blended with French grape varieties:

● *Dominio Los Pinos Selección (red):* A young blend of 45 per cent Monastrell, 30 per cent Cabernet Franc and 25 per cent Merlot, this has lots of concentrated fruit on the nose, while the palate has more of the same with fortifying tannins. Superior young wine and recommended.

● *Dominio Los Pinos 4 Meses en Barrica (red):* A blend of 40 per cent Cabernet Franc, 40 per cent Merlot and 20 per cent Cabernet Sauvignon, this has lots of lively flavour with up-front oak. Perhaps a little unsubtle.

● *Dominio Los Pinos Crianza (red):* A blend of 50 per cent Cabernet Sauvignon, 40 per cent Merlot and 10 per cent Monastrell, this is a superior crianza with lots of integrated, characterful flavours and an attractive feel. A positive sign regarding Valencia's potential, but rather expensive.

Torrevellisca (☎ 962 222 261) Founded in 1990, this is another producer of decent, notably low-priced wines, including:

● *Torrevellisca Blanco Crianza (white)*: A competently made, commercial, oak-aged white with flavour and length.

● *Torrevellisca Rosado (rosé)*: Tasty, inexpensive pink wine.

● *Torrevellisca Tinto Crianza (red)*: A Cabernet Sauvignon/Tempranillo blend, this is full-bodied and well made with bite. Good.

● *Torrevellisca Tinto Reserva (red)*: The same grapes as the above, this is a well made, aged blend of fruit and oak with balance and some length. Good.

Vicente Gandía PLA, S.A. (☎ 962 522 443) See also the entry under **D.O. Utiel-Requena** on page 272. The Castillo de Liria range of wines is known throughout Spain for offering simple, inexpensive, everyday drinking. These are two of the better wines:

● *Castillo de Liria Moscatel (white)*: A well made, moreish sweet wine for little money.

● *Castillo de Liria Tinto Reserva (red)*: A soundly constructed wine with some complexity and depth of flavour.

D.O. Yecla

In Brief: A low-profile D.O. with only one producer of note, but capable of making very good red wines.

Vines have been important in Yecla for many years because the region's soil is too poor to grow much else. It is a close neighbour of Jumilla and produces a similar style of wine: strong, full-bodied reds, many made from the Monastrell grape which accounts for around 80 per cent of vine plantings. Like Jumilla, Yecla was fortunate enough to avoid the worst of the phylloxera epidemic and at least half of its Monastrell vines are grown ungrafted.

Yecla used to export strong, heavy wines for blending but the drop in demand for these has seen exports fall over the last few years. To make up the shortfall and to move with the times and appeal to modern tastes, the region's producers have been looking to make lighter wines, with earlier fruit picking helping to make this possible.

Results are encouraging from Castaño, Yecla's only bodega of note, whose wine production is overseen by the Australian David Morrison. Castaño shows what can be achieved in Yecla, a D.O. which should be able to mimic the success of its close neighbour Jumilla. However, this is a region which has been dominated by one producer, Cooperativa La Purísima, which was so powerful that other bodegas were unable to buy grapes to supplement those that they grew themselves. This obviously stifled development and variety. Yecla still has only four bodegas, although there are over 400 vine growers, many still supplying the large co-operative.

Authorised grape varieties are:

- **White:** Airén, Macabeo and Merseguera.
- **Black:** Cabernet Sauvignon, Garnacha Tinta, Merlot, Monastrell and Tempranillo.

Yecla's white wines are fruity and aromatic but can lack acidity; the rosés are competent, the dominant reds full-bodied, sometimes meaty and flavoursome.

Geography, Soil and Climate

Yecla's climate is more continental than Mediterranean, with hot summers and cold winters. Precipitation is a lowly 320mm (13in) and as in Jumilla, a limited amount of irrigation is allowed to compensate for this. Vineyards are situated at between 400 and 700m (1,312 and 2,296ft) above sea level, on mainly limestone soils.

Future Development

As with D.O. Bullas, there seems little logic behind Yecla's existence as a separate D.O.. It might be preferable if it merged with Jumilla and benefited from the latter's better reputation and much higher profile. Yecla's name is known to few Spaniards let alone foreigners and as long as Castaño remains the only producer of note, this will continue.

Selected Bodegas

Bodegas Castaño, S.L. (☎ 968 791 115) This is Yecla's only port of call for lovers of decent wine. Founded in 1950, it did not begin to bottle its wines until the '80s and now produces a wide range of good to very good wines, most at competitive prices, including:

- *Castaño Blanco (white):* An inexpensive, aromatic, mouthfilling blend of 60 per cent Macabeo and 40 per cent Chardonnay with fruity character and bite.

- *Castaño Rosado (rosé):* Competent, inexpensive pink wine from Monastrell.

- *Castaño Tinto (red):* A well made, inexpensive young Monastrell with lots of fruity flavours and bite.

- *Castaño Merlot/Monastrell (red):* Made from 80 per cent Merlot and 20 per cent Monastrell, this has an engaging, powerful nose of mature fruit and toast, while the palate is mouthfilling, tasty, juicy and quite complex. Notably good value.

- *Castaño Cabernet Sauvignon/Monastrell (red):* A blend of 70 per cent Cabernet Sauvignon and 30 per cent Monastrell, this has attractive, peppery fruit on the nose, while the palate offers powerful, tannic flavours and length. More robust than the above and also notable value for money.

◆ *Hécula (red):* Hécula is the Latin name for Yecla and this is one of the bodega's most lauded wines. It is a blend of 95 per cent Monastrell and 5 per cent Merlot, spends four months in barrel and has a complex nose of fruit and oak, while the palate has more of the same, elegance and structure. If it wasn't from Yecla, it would cost rather more. Recommended.

◆ *Castaño Colección (red):* The bodega's flagship red is also its most expensive, a blend of 80 per cent Monastrell, 10 per cent Cabernet Sauvignon and 10 per cent Merlot. It is a superior, warm-climate red wine and is ample testimony to what can be done in unfashionable little Yecla. Aromatic, flavoursome and spicily mouthfilling.

Cooperativa del Vino de Yecla La Purísima (☎ 968 751 257) I am mentioning this large concern simply because it is Yecla's dominant producer. As for the quality of its wines, the whites are best ignored, while the inexpensive reds and rosés are generally acceptable, although they hold little interest. Thus none are reviewed here.

Navarra's ancient hills, with
modern windmills in the background

13.

NAVARRA

Until the '90s, Navarra was usually seen as Rioja's poor relation. The two regions are close neighbours, with around 15 per cent of the Rioja D.O.Ca actually lying within the province of Navarra. In fact, when the Rioja wine region was officially denominated in the '20s, it might have been expected that it would have included even more Navarran territory because Rioja producers had long secured grapes from throughout the province of Navarra.

Historically, Navarra and Rioja have strong connections: in the 11th century the Kingdom of Navarra encompassed an area which stretched from Bordeaux to coastal Catalonia and thus included the wine regions of Bordeaux, Navarra and Rioja, as well as some of the Catalan areas. Were it thus today, such a wine region would dwarf any other in importance and influence.

Navarra's wine history stretches back much further than the Middle Ages. It was known for its sturdy red wines and fresh rosés in Roman times and became an important exporter in the 13th and 14th centuries. Navarran wines were of sufficient quality and reputation to appeal to the good and the powerful: Catherine The Great of Russia enjoyed them in the 18th century. Phylloxera hit Navarra as rabidly as it did most of the rest of Europe and it took until The Second World War to rebuild the region's vineyards; as an aide to this, many growers banded together to form co-operatives.

D.O. Navarra

In Brief: One of the country's stronger wine regions, known for some of Spain's best rosés and Chardonnays, as well as increasing numbers of excellent red wines able to compete with those of neighbouring Rioja.

Co-operatives are common and influential in many parts of Spain, with increasing numbers of them modern, professional, innovative wine producers. But there can be a downside to their existence: size can mean that they are subject to inertia and find change a difficult and painful process. This is to be expected because any changes require the agreement of a majority of their participants.

Many cite the existence of co-operatives as a major reason why Navarra has only recently begun to fulfil its undoubted potential and become an exciting, high quality wine region for the 21st century. Their inertia has held up innovation and this has been more noticeable and extreme than in other wine regions that have experienced a similar problem, for two reasons: first, because Navarra's potential is greater than that of many other parts of the country; and second, because the close proximity of the exalted Rioja has further exacerbated unflattering comparisons.

The second half of the 20th century found Navarra with a reputation as a producer of good Garnacha rosés and decent, although unremarkable reds. This was a fair assessment and actually suited the majority of the co-operatives. None made much money and quite a few actively lost it, but government grants and subsidies more than made up for this, such are the vagaries and nonsensical nature of much centralised agricultural policy. This phenomenon is certainly not restricted to Spain.

There was hence little reason to change or innovate since the co-operatives were guaranteed a comfortable living without having to confront the sometimes painful process of change. Thus the wines they produced were often no more than decent. The region's reputation was at best middle-ranking, its wines could not attract high prices and therefore they were not stocked by prestigious merchants, restaurants and hotels. This meant that Navarra's wine makers' profits were low and thus money was unavailable to implement the improvements that a changing market had convinced increasing numbers of them were necessary. A vicious circle.

Throughout the '90s, Navarra's situation improved. Quality-driven wine makers like Chivite and Guelbenzu produced excellent wines that demonstrated the quality that Navarra was capable of. Gradually, consumers came to see the region as more than a producer of Garnacha rosés and it has increasingly become known for high quality red wines. Garnacha still accounts for around three-quarters of plantings, but Tempranillo and Cabernet Sauvignon are of increasing importance, and a fair amount of Navarra's success has come from wines made from blends of the three.

Much of the credit for Navarra's recent success must go to EVENA, the Estación de Viticultura y Enología de Navarra. This government-funded organisation was founded in 1981 to study all aspects of the wine making process: soil chemistry, soil texture, macro and micro-climates, vine roots, vine foliage, grapes, grape picking, wine fermentation, wine ageing, wine storage, barrels, bottles, corks – everything.

It is one of the best regarded operations of its kind in Spain and the results of the research in its state-of-the-art laboratories are available to all. Evena also holds regular lectures, conferences and other events to publicise its findings, and has actively encouraged the co-operatives to update their equipment and ideas, and all wine makers to plant varieties such as Cabernet Sauvignon, Merlot and Tempranillo, which are well suited to oak ageing and the production of long-lived wines.

But Navarra is not just a grower of black grapes and has not neglected white wines. In fact, the second half of the '90s has seen it enjoy success with that most ubiquitous white variety, Chardonnay. Not only are Navarran Chardonnays now seen as among the best in Spain, but they have also garnered prizes at international fairs and competitions. Not so long ago, to describe a wine as one of the best Spanish Chardonnays would carry as much weight as describing someone as one of the most honest politicians, but that is no longer the case.

Authorised grape varieties are:

- **White:** Chardonnay, Garnacha Blanca, Malvasía, Moscatel Grano Menudo and Viura.

- **Black:** Cabernet Sauvignon, Garnacha Tinta, Graciano, Mazuela, Merlot and Tempranillo.

White wines are still the junior partners to rosés and reds in Navarra, but the D.O. makes a variety of white wine styles. Chardonnays are made 'young' or barrel-fermented, both notable for their varietal characteristics. Some of the young Chardonnays contain proportions of Viura and these tend to be simple, everyday wines. Navarra also makes a small amount of notable sweet Moscatels, aromatic, complex and flavoursome. The top examples are among Spain's best white wines (see the entry for **Julián Chivite** on page 288).

Navarra's rosés are traditionally made from Garnacha, although some are now made from Cabernet Sauvignon and Tempranillo. They have long been renowned as some of Spain's, indeed the world's, best, noted for their intense fruitiness, balance and good value. The D.O.'s reds come in a variety of styles, depending on the grape(s) used and which of Navarra's micro-climates they are produced in: Garnacha is increasingly used to make young, lively, plummy reds; Tempranillo wines produced in Navarra's cooler regions are fresh and fruity with good acidity; but Navarra's best reds are often blends of indigenous and foreign varieties, some being elegant, subtle wines, others full-bodied and full of concentrated fruit and oak flavours. This range of styles is another of the region's strengths.

Geography, Soil and Climate

Navarra D.O. is divided into five sub-regions:

▲ **Valdizarbe**. Navarra's northernmost sub-region has an Atlantic-influenced, temperate climate. This, allied to its chalky soils, means that it enjoys the conditions to make some of the region's best wines and is increasingly fulfilling this potential.

▲ **Baja Montaña**. This is located in the north-east of Navarra and is the highest sub-region, producing some of the best rosés.

▲ **Tierra Estella**. Bordering Rioja, and to the south-west of Valdizarbe, the conditions and wines are similar to those of Valdizarbe.

▲ **Ribera Alta**. In the middle west of Navarra, this sub-region makes good reds and rosés.

▲ **Ribera Baja**. Lying in the south of Navarra, this sub-region has the largest vineyard hectareage. The hot, dry climate encourages high sugar levels in the grapes which in turn produce full-bodied, alcoholic wines.

As has been mentioned, Navarra has pronounced climatic variations. This is one of its strengths, providing a variety of environments in which to produce different styles of wine. The north is quite wet with a maritime-influenced mildness, while the south has a more Mediterranean climate with higher temperatures and less rainfall. Northern Navarra has annual precipitation of nearly 700mm (28in), while the south receives around 450mm (18in). Middle regions have climates somewhere between the two. Navarra's soils are generally chalk-based, with silt and gravel found near rivers.

Future Development

Navarra's ongoing goal is to further distance itself from its old, unwanted image as a maker of respectable but inexpensive wines. It is looking to continue producing some of the best rosés in Spain (which provide a fair amount of the region's income) but also to be seen as a maker of distinctive red wines of good quality, which will attract higher prices than some have previously been able to command. Healthy increases in the sales of red crianza, reserva and gran reserva wines are confirmation that matters are proceeding well.

Some of the region's lighter red wines need more structure and body to achieve the level of quality desired and Navarra might be advised to concentrate on more robust blends of Cabernet Sauvignon, Merlot, Tempranillo and other grapes. Regarding Navarra's Chardonnays, as the region's vines mature the fruit that they yield will become even more characterful. This should further improve the quality of the wines, produced in a variety of styles in Navarra's range of climates.

Selected Bodegas

Álvaro y Borja Marino Pérez de Rada (☎ 948 344 279) This small bodega, founded in 1991, has 30 hectares of its own vineyards growing Chardonnay, Cabernet Sauvignon, Merlot and Tempranillo. Its pricing policy puts its wines in the middle and upper brackets, with quality good or very good.

◆ *Palacio de Muruzábal Chardonnay Fermentado en Barrica (white):* This is usually a powerful, mouthfilling, finely structured wine, but in some years the oak can be rather too dominant.

◆ *A y B Marino Cosecha Particular (red):* A meaty blend of spicy fruit and oak with some complexity.

◆ *Palacio de Muruzábal Tinto Reserva (red):* This superior red reserva is priced at a level which shows that it wants to compete with the best. It is a carefully constructed, aromatic wine with well judged tannins, complexity and lots of attractive flavours. Recommended at seven or eight years old.

Ambrosio Velasco, S.A. (☎ 948 527 009) Founded in 1991, this bodega has established a reputation as one of Navarra's more solid producers, with a selection of straightforward, characterful wines, 90 per cent of which are exported. The range includes:

◆ *Palacio de la Vega Chardonnay (white):* A straightforward, everyday Chardonnay, perhaps a touch expensive.

◆ *Palacio de la Vega Rosado (rosé):* A blend of 80 per cent Garnacha and 20 per cent Cabernet Sauvignon, this is superior, inexpensive, aromatic pink wine with body and interest. Good.

◆ *Palacio de la Vega Tinto (red):* A characterful, inexpensive, young Tempranillo with lots of flavour.

◆ *Palacio de la Vega Tinto Crianza (red):* A blend of 70 per cent Cabernet Sauvignon and 30 per cent Tempranillo, this varies in quality. It can be a powerful, juicy wine with confident tannins, but occasionally it is one-dimensional and flat.

◆ *Palacio de la Vega Merlot Crianza (red):* An aromatic, well judged wine with some power and complexity. Becoming more expensive.

● *Palacio de la Vega Tempranillo Reserva (red)*: This can be very good and offer a lot of wine for the money, with sweet tannins and plenty of flavour. However, like the crianza, it has the odd off-year when it is flat.

● *Palacio de la Vega Cabernet Sauvignon Reserva (red)*: The bodega's most expensive and consistent wine, this is also usually its best. It has a deep nose with some varietal complexity, while the palate has powerful, integrated Cabernet fruit and oak. Recommended, although the price has escalated somewhat.

Bodegas Beamonte (☎ 948 811 000) Founded in 1938, this modest-size producer makes a small range of low-priced wines of decent quality, including:

● *Beamonte Blanco (white)*: A blend of Chardonnay and Viura, this is a well made wine with flavour and personality for a notably low price. Good.

● *Beamonte Rosado (rosé)*: A typically fruity Garnacha pink wine for drinking young. Good value.

● *Beamonte Crianza (red)*: This is a decent, commercial blend of Tempranillo, Garnacha and Cabernet Sauvignon, tasty and with the fruit and oak well combined.

● *Beamonte Reserva (red)*: A blend of Cabernet Sauvignon and Tempranillo, this light-to-medium-bodied wine is well made, fruity and respectable. It could perhaps do with more personality.

Bodegas y Viñedos Nekeas (☎ 948 350 296) This co-operative was founded in 1994 and produces a range of well made wines from its 225 hectares of vineyards, including:

● *Nekeas Blanco (white)*: A blend of 75 per cent Viura and 25 per cent Chardonnay, this is a superior, flavoursome, everyday wine for not much money. Good.

● *Nekeas Chardonnay Fermentado en Barrica (white)*: The bodega's best wine, this is a superior barrel-fermented Chardonnay with depth and complexity on the nose and an unctuous, balanced, tasty palate that is not over-oaked. Recommended.

● *Nekeas Rosado (rosé)*: A full-bodied, characterful rosé from 50 per cent Garnacha and 50 per cent Cabernet Sauvignon for a competitive price. Good.

● *Nekeas Tempranillo/Merlot (red)*: A straightforward, tasty, everyday red wine.

● *Nekeas Merlot (red)*: A fruity, mouthfilling wine with decent Merlot character blended with oak.

● *Nekeas Tempranillo/Cabernet Sauvignon Crianza (red)*: This is a characterful, quite complex blend of fruit and oak for a competitive price.

Camillo Castilla, S.A. (☎ 948 780 006) Founded in 1856, this operation is best known for its excellent Moscatels, but is also being lauded for its red wines. The small range includes:

● *Montecristo Blanco (white)*: An inexpensive, characterful, dryish, everyday Moscatel.

- *Montecristo (sweet white):* The producer's mid-range Moscatel, this is well made, characterful, unctuous and very tasty.

- *Capricho de Goya Gran Reserva (sweet white):* The bodega's flagship Moscatel, with lots of powerful, unctuous, satisfying flavours. Recommended.

- *Montecristo Tinto Crianza (red):* A blend of 70 per cent Tempranillo, 15 per cent Mazuelo and 15 per cent Cabernet Sauvignon, this is an aromatic, mouthfilling wine with lots of sweet fruit. It is not subtle, but is satisfying.

- *Montecristo Tinto Reserva (red):* Made from 50 per cent Tempranillo, 30 per cent Cabernet Sauvignon and 20 per cent Mazuelo, this is a superior wine with a deep, complex nose and a palate with structure, flavour, weight and length. Competitively priced for the quality and highly recommended.

Castillo de Monjardín, S.A. (☎ 948 537 412) Founded in 1988, with the first wines released in 1992, this bodega has quickly built a strong reputation for quality and innovation. Its reserva Chardonnay is one of Spain's better white wines and the reds are improving all the time. The range includes:

- *Castillo de Monjardín Chardonnay (white):* A very good Chardonnay, aromatic, unctuous, refreshing, flavour-filled and long. Recommended.

- *Castillo de Monjardín Chardonnay Crianza (white):* This is a powerful, well made, integrated, oaked Chardonnay with flavour and length. Very good.

- *Castillo de Monjardín Chardonnay Reserva (white):* This golden wine has power, elegance, structure, complexity and length. Excellent and often cited as one of Spain's better white wines. A leader in Navarra's admired range of Chardonnays.

- *Castillo de Monjardín Merlot Rosado (rosé):* This inexpensive, interesting pink wine is an oddity: a barrel-fermented rosé. And it works. Recommended.

- *Castillo de Monjardín (red):* This young, inexpensive blend of 50 per cent Merlot and 50 per cent Pinot Noir is decent, everyday drinking with tasty, characterful fruit on the palate.

- *Castillo de Monjardín Merlot Crianza (red):* A full-bodied, flavoursome wine with a complex nose, personality and well judged tannins.

- *Castillo de Monjardín Crianza (red):* A well made blend of 40 per cent Cabernet Sauvignon, 40 per cent Merlot and 20 per cent Tempranillo, this has lots of robust flavour, character and some complexity. Good.

- *Castillo de Monjardín Tinto Reserva (red):* A blend of Cabernet Sauvignon, Merlot and Tempranillo – popular with Navarra's wine makers – this is a smooth, integrated wine with some complexity. Drink at seven or eight years old.

- *Castillo de Monjardín Gran Reserva (red):* A superior Cabernet Sauvignon with full-bodied flavours of mature Cabernet fruit and toasty oak, firm but sweet tannins and length. Very good and priced accordingly.

Guelbenzu, S.L. (☎ 948 850 055) Founded in 1851, this family firm is at the forefront of Navarran red wine making. Its 42 hectares of vines produce Cabernet Sauvignon, Tempranillo, Merlot and small amounts of Garnacha which are turned into powerful, concentrated, highly recommended wines.

◆ *Guelbenzu Jardín (red):* This young Garnacha is the bodega's simplest and cheapest bottle, a straightforward, flavoursome, fruity wine, but not really what it is known for.

◆ *Guelbenzu Tinto (red):* A blend of 50 per cent Tempranillo, 35 per cent Cabernet Sauvignon and 15 per cent Merlot, this is aromatic, elegant, powerful and oak-aged with lots of flavour, smooth tannins and character. Recommended and good value.

◆ *Guelbenzu Evo Crianza (red):* Made from around 75 per cent Cabernet Sauvignon with the balance Merlot and Tempranillo, this first appeared on the market in 1992 and is one of Spain's better red wines in the price range. Its deep, fruity/toasty nose, powerful, spicy flavours, length and binding tannins have convinced many of Navarra's abilities with red wine. Highly recommended and moreish, this drinks well on release and improves over three or four years.

◆ *Guelbenzu Lautus Reserva (red):* A blend of 50 per cent Tempranillo with the balance Cabernet Sauvignon, Garnacha and Merlot, this is the bodega's flagship wine, in an elevated, although not luxury, price band. It offers deep, complex flavours that require concentration and, as with Guelbenzu's other wines (except the Jardín), it should not be drunk too young and benefits from being poured into glass an hour before drinking.

Irache, S.L. (☎ 948 551 932) Founded in 1891, Irache is a well known name in Navarra. This probably explains why some of its prices are higher than the regional norm, possibly too high. Quality ranges from decent to very good and its wines include:

◆ *Irache Chardonnay (white):* This aromatic, oaked wine has a decent amount of fruit and structure for a fair price.

◆ *Castillo de Irache Rosado (rosé):* A fruity, refreshing pink wine. Rather expensive.

◆ *Gran Irache Crianza (red):* A well made, straightforward blend of fruit and oak flavours at a fair price.

◆ *Irache Tempranillo Crianza (red):* As above.

◆ *Prado de Irache (red):* A rather good crianza with lots of interesting, integrated flavours, but too expensive.

Julián Chivite, S.L. (☎ 948 811 000) Originally founded in 1647, and still owned by the Chivite family, this is Navarra's leading bodega, renowned for its top range reds (it also makes everyday ones), Chardonnays and Moscatels, and also for its characterful, young rosé, one of Navarra's most popular and famous wines.

◆ *Gran Feudo Chardonnay (white):* A well regarded, apple-infused Chardonnay, aromatic, elegant, refreshing and flavoursome. Recommended and reasonably priced.

- *Gran Feudo Moscatel Dulce (sweet white)*: A powerful, mouthfilling wine with lots of fresh fruit. It costs about a third of the price of the following bottle, which is probably Spain's best Moscatel.

- *Chivite Colección 125 Vendimia Tardía (sweet white)*: A golden Moscatel regularly voted as among Spain's very best wines. It has real power, complexity, honey edges and 'grapeyness'. Treat yourself – for its elevated quality, it is fairly priced.

- *Chivite Colección 125 Chardonnay (white)*: One of Spain's best and most expensive Chardonnays, priced at superior white Burgundy levels. It is a fine wine, an elegant, complex, balanced blend of fruit and barrel flavours. Highly recommended.

- *Gran Feudo Rosado (rosé)*: One of Spain's better and best known rosés, this 100 per cent Garnacha has aroma, flavour, balance and subtle bite. As good as it gets for the modest price.

- *Gran Feudo Tinto Crianza (red)*: A blend of Cabernet Sauvignon, Garnacha and Tempranillo, this is a well made, lightish crianza with straightforward fruit and gentle oak flavours.

- *Gran Feudo Reserva (red)*: A blend of Cabernet Sauvignon, Merlot and Tempranillo, this is a more full-bodied, personality-filled wine than the crianza, with sweet tannins and attractive fruit/oak flavours.

- *Gran Feudo Reserva Viñas Viejas (red)*: The bodega's best non-125 Collection red wine, and arguably the red that offers the best value for money (always a difficult thing to pin down), this is a varying blend of Cabernet Sauvignon, Garnacha, Merlot and Tempranillo. It is a very satisfying, smooth, flavoursome wine, with this and Guelbenzu's Evo Crianza amply demonstrating Navarra's ability to make excellent mid-price red wines in different styles.

- *Chivite Colección 125 Reserva (red)*: A blend of around 70 per cent Tempranillo, 20 per cent Merlot and 10 per cent Cabernet Sauvignon, the 125 reservas are finely constructed, complex, concentrated wines for drinking when they have been given time to develop in bottle. They are generally regarded as Navarra's – and among Spain's – best red wines, and in view of this, are not excessively priced.

- *Chivite Colección 125 Gran Reserva (red)*: Made from 100 per cent Tempranillo and similarly priced to the reserva, this has a complex nose of toast, tobacco and leather, while the palate is medium-bodied, smooth, elegant and spicy. It is generally not as good as the reserva, although still of very high quality, and able to compete with the good and the great of Rioja and Ribera del Duero.

Luis Gurpegui Muga, S.A. (☎ 948 670 050) Founded in 1921 and with the same owners as Rioja's Bodegas Berceo, this operation makes a wide range of wines at reasonable prices, their quality varying from adequate to very good, including:

- *Monte Ory Chardonnay (white)*: An enjoyable, well made Chardonnay with decent acidity cutting through the unctuousness.

- *Monte Ory Chardonnay Barrique-Fermented (white)*: A powerful blend of fruit and toasty oak with length. Recommended and another example of Navarra's ability to make laudable examples of this type of wine. As is often the case, it is at its best at two or three years old, when the wine has settled down and knitted together.

◆ *Monty Ory Rosado (rosé)*: A decent Garnacha pink wine with tasty fruit.

◆ *Monty Ory Crianza (red)*: A light to medium-bodied blend of 70 per cent Tempranillo, 20 per cent Garnacha and 10 per cent Cabernet Sauvignon, this is well made and competent with sweetish fruit and gentle oak.

Marco Real, S.A. (☎ 948 712 193) Founded in the late '80s, this large bodega's whites and rosés are respectable, while its reds are showing increasingly high quality at competitive prices.

◆ *Homenaje (red)*: A blend of 40 per cent Tempranillo, 40 per cent Garnacha and 20 per cent Cabernet Sauvignon, this is a well made, expressive young wine.

◆ *Homenaje Crianza (red)*: A blend of Cabernet Sauvignon, Garnacha, Mazuelo, Merlot and Tempranillo, this is a characterful, competitively priced blend of fruit and oak, with lots of mouthfilling flavours.

◆ *Homenaje Reserva (red)*: A varying blend of some or all of Cabernet Sauvignon, Garnacha, Mazuelo and Tempranillo, this impressive bottle offers a lot of wine for a competitive price. It is a medium-bodied, concentrated red wine with fruit and oak beautifully combined. Thoroughly recommended.

Nuestra Señora de Ujue, Cooperativa (☎ 948 745 007) Founded in 1939, this co-operative makes a modest range of decent, everyday wines at low prices, including:

◆ *Nuestra Señora de Ujue Blanco (white)*: A light, dry, everyday white for little money from the Viura grape.

◆ *Nuestra Señora de Ujue Rosado (rosé)*: A tasty, mouthfilling Garnacha rosé.

◆ *Nuestra Señora de Ujue Tinto (red)*: A blend of 40 per cent Garnacha and 60 per cent Tempranillo, this young red offers simple, fruity drinking for a low price.

◆ *Dolomondos Tinto (red)*: A blend of 80 per cent Merlot and 20 per cent Tempranillo, this has a fair amount of concentrated fruit flavours for a modest price.

Nuestra Señora del Camino, Sociedad Cooperativa (☎ 948 816 692) Founded in 1954, this co-operative grows a range of grapes on its 230 hectares of vines and produces respectable, inexpensive wines, including:

◆ *Conde de Artoiz Rosado (rosé)*: A well made, everyday, fruity rosé from Garnacha.

◆ *Viña Riñanco Rosado (rosé)*: As above.

◆ *Conde de Artoiz Tinto (red)*: A blend of 60 per cent Garnacha and 40 per cent Tempranillo, this is a characterful, satisfying young red wine.

◆ *Montitura Maceración (red)*: An aromatic young Garnacha with lots of lively, flavoursome fruit at a modest price. Good.

Nuestra Señora del Romero, Cooperativa (☎ 948 851 411) Founded in 1951, this large co-operative has 1,100 hectares of vines and produces a range of good quality, inexpensive wines, including:

- *Malón de Echaide Rosado (rosé):* Superior pink Garnacha with lots of fruit and character.

- *Malón de Echaide Tinto Crianza (red):* Mainly Tempranillo, with some Cabernet Sauvignon and Merlot, this is a straightforward, well made blend of fruit and oak for a low price.

- *Plándenas Reserva (red):* Mainly Tempranillo, with Cabernet Sauvignon and Garnacha, the same comments as above apply.

Ochoa, S.A. (☎ 948 740 006) Originally founded in 1845, this bodega has around 105 hectares of vines and produces quite a wide range of wines for a modest-size operation. Its wine maker, Javier Ochoa, used to work for EVENA (see page 283) and is one of the most respected in the region. Quality is high although prices are on the increase across Ochoa's range of wines, which includes:

- *Ochoa Blanco (white):* Made from 70 per cent Viura and 30 per cent Chardonnay, this straightforward white wine is well made and fruity with bite. Perhaps slightly expensive.

- *Ochoa Moscatel (sweet white):* This excellent wine is at the forefront of Navarra's sweet whites. The nose is complex and elegant, while the palate has a lot of attractive flavour, some unctuousness and balancing acidic bite. It is smooth and fresh as opposed to cloying and over-sweet. Recommended.

- *Ochoa Rosado (rosé):* A superior Garnacha wine, but not inexpensive by regional standards.

- *Ochoa Rosado (rosé):* A blend of 50 per cent Garnacha and 50 per cent Cabernet Sauvignon, this is a particularly full-bodied and flavoursome wine. Recommended but as above, priced higher than many.

- *Ochoa Tempranillo Crianza (red):* A well balanced, flavoursome blend of fruit and oak flavours, enjoyable but quite expensive.

- *Ochoa Cabernet Sauvignon Crianza (red):* As above.

- *Ochoa Merlot Crianza (red):* As above.

- *Ochoa Reserva (red):* A blend of 55 per cent Tempranillo, 30 per cent Cabernet Sauvignon and 15 per cent Merlot, this is a well made reserva with spicy flavour and balance.

- *Ochoa Gran Reserva (red):* The same blend as above, this is an aromatic, balanced, powerful, soundly constructed wine. Recommended.

Orvalaiz (☎ 948 344 437) Founded in 1993, this co-operative makes a range of respectable and good quality wines at low prices, including:

- *Viña Orvalaiz Blanco (white):* A light, straightforward Viura for drinking young.

- *Orvalaiz Cabernet Sauvignon Rosado (rosé):* A satisfying, flavoursome, refreshing wine at a low price.

- *Viña Orvalaiz Tinto (red):* Made from 80 per cent Tempranillo and 20 per cent Cabernet Sauvignon, this is a decent, young, fruity wine for everyday drinking.

- *Orvalaiz Merlot (red):* A characterful, flavoursome young Merlot for a competitive price. Recommended.

- *Orvalaiz Tinto Crianza (red):* A blend of Cabernet Sauvignon and Tempranillo, this inexpensive crianza is a tasty, spicy, characterful wine with lots of fruit. Recommended.

- *Orvalaiz Tinto Reserva (red):* By far the co-operative's most expensive wine, although still inexpensive, this is a smooth, characterful blend of aged fruit and oak with touches of complexity.

Palacio de Azcona/Navayerri, S.L. (☎ 948 542 294) Founded in 1996, this small operation has a modest 37 hectares of its own vines and produces a decent range of red wines, including:

- *Palacio de Azcona Tinto (red):* Primarily Tempranillo, with small amounts of Cabernet Sauvignon and Merlot, this young, inexpensive red offers lots of concentrated, tasty fruit.

- *Palacio de Azcona Tinto Crianza (red):* A blend of 50 per cent Cabernet Sauvignon and 50 per cent Merlot, this is a straightforward, powerful, well made mixture of fruit and oak flavours for a reasonable price.

- *Palacio de Azcona Merlot Crianza (red):* A smooth, tasty crianza with well judged tannins.

- *Palacio de Azcona Cabernet Sauvignon Crianza (red):* A decent Cabernet rianza, quite characteristic of the variety.

Piedemonte (☎ 948 712 406): Founded in 1993, this co-operative offers good and very good quality at reasonable prices. Its wines include:

- *Piedemonte Chardonnay (white):* A decent barrel-fermented Chardonnay with balance, flavour and not too much oak.

- *Piedemonte Moscatel (sweet white):* A well made, tasty evocation of this distinctive grape variety.

- *Piedemonte Rosado (rosé):* A tasty, characterful pink wine from Garnacha. Good.

- *Piedemonte Oligitum Selección (red):* A blend of a third each of Cabernet Sauvignon, Merlot and Tempranillo, this has concentrated, lively fruit on the nose and palate, with lots of engaging flavour and length. Recommended and inexpensive.

◆ *Piedemonte Oligitum (red)*: An aromatic, fruity young Merlot with lots of concentrated fruit and bite for a modest outlay. Recommended.

◆ *Piedemonte Oligitum Crianza (red)*: A blend of a third each of Cabernet Sauvignon, Merlot and Tempranillo, this is a well made wine with well judged oak.

◆ *Piedemonte Oligitum Reserva (red)*: The same blend as above, this is an aromatic, balanced, flavoursome wine with depth, for an attractive price. Recommended.

Príncipe de Viana, S.A. (☎ 948 838 640) Founded in 1983, this large, well known operation makes a range of decent wines, including:

◆ *Agramont Blanco (white)*: A well made, straightforward, inexpensive Viura with flavour and interest.

◆ *Príncipe de Viana Chardonnay Fermentado en Barrica (white)*: A well made barrel-fermented wine with flavour and length.

◆ *Agramont Rosado (rosé)*: Superior Garnacha for a low price. Good.

◆ *Príncipe de Viana Cabernet Sauvignon Rosado (rosé)*: Well made but perhaps a little overpowering.

◆ *Príncipe de Viana Cabernet Sauvignon Crianza (red)*: A soundly constructed, straightforward crianza.

San Salvador (☎ 948 537 128) Founded in 1947, this co-operative makes a modest range of decent, inexpensive wines, including:

◆ *Galcibar Rosado (rosé)*: An aromatic, mouthfilling Garnacha rosé at a low price.

◆ *Galcibar Cabernet Sauvignon Crianza (red)*: An aromatic, flavoursome, straightforward blend of fruit and oak.

Sarría, S.A. (☎ 948 267 562) This bodega has been making wine in Navarra for hundreds of years and has become a respected, well known name. Indeed, the name Señorío de Sarría appears on the shirts of Osasuna football club as part of a sponsorship deal. The current set-up has been in place since the '50s and while the wines are still decent, they are no longer regarded as among the region's best. The range includes:

◆ *Señorío de Sarría Chardonnay (white)*: A tasty, unctuous, barrel-fermented Chardonnay with fruit and oak working harmoniously. Good.

◆ *Señorío de Sarría Rosado (rosé)*: A fresh, tasty pink wine at a competitive price.

◆ *Señorío de Sarría Tinto Crianza (red)*: A well made, honest crianza at a fair price.

◆ *Señorío de Sarría Cabernet Sauvignon Crianza (red)*: A decent, straightforward, powerful, flavoursome blend of Cabernet and oak.

◆ *Señorío de Sarría Cabernet Sauvignon/Merlot Crianza (red)*: A well judged wine with lots of fruit and some spicy character.

Señorío de Otazu (☎ 948 329 200) Founded in 1994, this bodega has garnered a reputation for quality and patient attention to detail. Its range of wines includes:

- *Palacio de Otazu Blanco (white):* Made 100 per cent from Chardonnay, this is aromatic, flavoursome and unctuous with some bite. Good.

- *Palacio de Otazu Chardonnay Fermentado en Barrica (white):* A very good example of the style, with balance, flavour and complexity. One of Navarra's better barrel-fermented Chardonnays.

- *Palacio de Otazu Tinto Crianza (red):* A blend of 50 per cent Cabernet Sauvignon, 40 per cent Merlot and 10 per cent Tempranillo, this reasonably priced wine is one of Navarra's better red crianzas, with flavour, structure and a smooth, elegant style. Highly recommended.

- *Palacio de Otazu Tinto Reserva (red):* Made from the same blend as above, this is superior wine at a competitive price, with power, complexity and length. Recommended.

Vicente Malumbres (☎ 948 401 920) Founded in 1940, this family concern makes a range of respectable rather than remarkable wines, including:

- *Malumbres Blanco (white):* This young blend of 70 per cent Viura and 30 per cent Chardonnay is fruitily flavoursome and well made, although perhaps a touch expensive.

- *Malumbres Rosado (rosé):* A well made Garnacha rosé, a touch more expensive than the Navarran average.

- *Malumbres Tinto (red):* A blend of 85 per cent Garnacha and 15 per cent Tempranillo, this is adequate, young, everyday red wine, but overpriced.

Viña Magaña, S.L. (☎ 948 850 034) This small operation, founded in 1968, produces limited amounts of good and very good red wines, most from the Merlot grape blended with others.

- *Dignus Crianza (red):* Made from Merlot blended with Cabernet Sauvignon, Tempranillo and 'others', this tasty crianza is full-bodied, spicy and well made, for drinking when four or five years old.

- *Barón de Magaña Crianza (red):* This is 50 per cent Merlot, with the balance Cabernet Sauvignon, Tempranillo and 'others'. It has a complex nose and offers lots of flavour, but is a little harsh when young and needs time to settle.

- *Viña Magaña Reserva (red):* A blend of 70 per cent Merlot, 15 per cent Cabernet Sauvignon and 15 per cent 'others', this is superior wine, balanced, tasty and integrated. Recommended and drinking particularly well at nine or ten years old.

- *Viña Magaña Merlot Reserva (red):* An excellent, suitably aged Merlot with flavour, balance and complexity. Highly recommended.

◆ *Viña Magaña Gran Reserva (red):* This is the same blend as the reserva, a powerful, mouthfilling wine with tannins still to the fore. The reserva is better.

Viñedos Asensio Sanz, S.L. (☎ 948 698 097) This small operation makes a modest range of good quality red wines at competitive prices, including:

◆ *Javier Asensio Crianza (red):* A blend of 58 per cent Merlot, 25 per cent Cabernet Sauvignon and 17 per cent Tempranillo, this has a powerful, complex nose and a mouthfilling, characterful palate with dark fruits and integrated oak for a competitive price. Good.

◆ *Javier Asensio Reserva (red):* A blend of 65 per cent Cabernet Sauvignon, 18 per cent Merlot and 17 per cent Tempranillo, this superior, integrated wine has power, confidence and balance, and offers value for money. Recommended.

Viñedos de Calidad, S.A. (☎ 948 782 014) Founded in 1988, and with an operation in Rioja, this producer makes a wide selection of wines of adequate and good quality. The reds are its strength and the range includes:

◆ *Alex Viura (white):* A refreshing, tasty white at a fair price.

◆ *Alex Rosado (rosé):* A mouthfilling Garnacha rosé with decent, unctuous fruit.

◆ *Alex Tinto (red):* A well made young Tempranillo with lots of fruit and some length.

◆ *Alex Tinto Crianza (red):* This is mainly Tempranillo, with some Garnacha and 10 per cent of the high quality Graciano. It is a well made, straightforward wine with generous fruit/oak flavours at a decent price.

Vinícola Navarra (☎ 948 360 131) Founded in 1864 and now owned by the giant Bodegas y Bebidas, this operation produces a wide range of solidly made wines with a traditional feel to them, including:

◆ *Las Campanas Blanco (white):* A blend of Chardonnay and Viura, this inexpensive wine offers lots of fruity flavour.

◆ *Las Campanas Rosado (rosé):* A Tempranillo wine, with a powerful nose, balance and attractive flavours. It is more expensive than the average Navarran rosé.

◆ *Castillo de Javier Rosado (rosé):* A Garnacha wine, this has characterful flavours and length, and as above, is both pricier and classier than the average pink wine.

◆ *Las Campanas Tinto (red):* Mainly Tempranillo, with some Cabernet Sauvignon and the classy Rioja rarity Graciano, this young wine has lots of fruit and balance. Good.

◆ *Las Campanas Tempranillo (red):* A tasty wine with some body and lots of fruit.

◆ *Las Campanas Cabernet Sauvignon (red):* A young, mouthfilling, flavoursome example of the grape.

◆ *Las Campanas Crianza (red):* A medium-bodied crianza with lots of attractive fruit and oak flavours. Well priced and recommended.

● *Las Campanas Reserva (red)*: A blend of 70 per cent Tempranillo and 30 per cent Cabernet Sauvignon, this inexpensive reserva is well made, balanced and tasty, without being remarkable.

Virgen Blanca (☎ 948 530 058) Founded in 1956, with 415 hectares of its own vines, this producer makes a range of good and very good wines, especially the reds, including:

● *Viña Sardasol Blanco (white)*: A blend of 40 per cent Chardonnay and 60 per cent Viura, this is competent, refreshing, everyday white wine.

● *Viña Sardasol Rosado (rosé)*: A respectable, tasty Garnacha rosé for drinking young.

● *Viña Sardasol Tinto (red)*: 90 per cent Tempranillo and 10 per cent Cabernet Sauvignon, this young red is aromatic, mouthfilling and characterfully fruity. Good.

● *Viña Sardasol Tinto Crianza (red)*: A blend of 50 per cent Cabernet Sauvignon, 40 per cent Tempranillo and 10 per cent Merlot, this is one of Navarra's better red crianzas and competitively priced. It is aromatic, balanced, mouthfilling and has lots of powerful, expressive fruit. Recommended.

● *Viña Sardasol Tinto Reserva (red)*: Made from the same blend as above, this has lots of powerful flavours, balance and length for a keen price. Recommended.

Rioja is known above all else
for its wines

14.

RIOJA

Modern Rioja – the high quality red wine region – did not begin to come into existence until the second half of the 19th century. This was as a result of misfortune elsewhere. Two outbreaks of disease in Bordeaux – of oidium or powdery mildew in 1852 and, more seriously, of phylloxera in 1867 – were crucial for Rioja. As a result, French merchants and wine makers crossed the border to the region to buy and/or make the wine that was unavailable in Bordeaux. They brought with them superior Bordeaux methods and skills, most notably the ageing of wines in 225-litre oak casks.

Many of the bodegas instituted then – including legendary names like La Rioja Alta, Marqués de Murrieta and Marqués de Riscal – are not only still in existence, but are among the region's best. And their red wines – with an oaky, vanilla nose and flavours resulting from long years in oak barrels – have become emblematic of the region.

This was Rioja's first 'boom' and it was halted in the first five years of the last century when the dreaded phylloxera virus came to visit. The First World War, Spanish Civil War and Second World War inhibited recovery and growth in the first half of the 20th century, and Rioja's next resurgence began in the '70s, when a rise in the demand for bottled table wines encouraged investment and development in the region; many large, modern bodegas were built. For 25 years Rioja's popularity flourished both in Spain and abroad, its combination of good-to-high-quality wines and competitive prices attracting and keeping customers.

The latter '90s and the early years of this century have seen changes in the region. A plethora of small bodegas has appeared, producing modest amounts of high quality wines, invariably from grapes grown in their own vineyards. And there has been a move away from ageing red wines for long periods in oak (traditionally American oak, although there is now increased use of French), with the 'new' wines being fermented at controlled temperatures in stainless steel vats prior to spending less time in barrel and receiving more bottle-ageing. The resultant wines are fruitier and more immediate than some of Rioja's traditional bottles, but many will not be destined for the long ageing that the old-style wines are capable of.

D.O.Ca Rioja

In Brief: Spain's most prominent wine region, renowned for soft, oaky, flavoursome red wines – some of exceptional quality and made in an increasing variety of styles – and also a producer of whites and rosés.

Rioja and sherry vie with each other for the title of Spain's most famous wine. Over the last twenty years, as global table wine sales have grown, easily outstripping fortified wines in popularity, Rioja has probably edged ahead. In 1926, it was the first Spanish wine region to be demarcated as a D.O. and in 1991 it was the first (and only) to achieve the status of D.O.Ca, restricted to wines of exceptional quality.

Rioja's vinous history stretches back to ancient times, with wine being made in the region before the Romans arrived. It is only recently that it has been primarily associated with red wine: throughout the medieval period and into the 17th century, Rioja produced a lot more white wine than red. And quality was not always the region's watchword, with Toro regarded as far superior well into the 18th century.

Traditional Rioja reds are made by blending different grape varieties – primarily Tempranillo and Garnacha, sometimes with smaller amounts of Graciano and Mazuelo – often grown in different parts of the region. Many of the older, larger producers have their own vineyards, but they have also always bought a lot of grapes from independent growers and the region's co-operatives.

The 'new' producers tend to rely on their own grapes and are increasingly making varietal wines, usually 100 per cent Tempranillo. Some are single estate wines – for example Contino, Finca Valpiedra and Remelluri – made from grapes grown in one specific estate or vineyard. Thus, they are seeking to express 'terroir', the specific, localised flavours and feeling produced by a particular parcel of land's micro-climate, soil-type, geology, etc.

It has been suggested that the emergence of these 'new' Rioja producers, looking to make wines that combine the best of the region's traditions with the demands of modern drinkers, was a response to the success of Ribera del Duero, which in the '80s looked set to topple Rioja from its position as Spain's premier red wine region. Priorato's progress in the '90s was also a challenge to Rioja and thus a stimulus to progress. For Spain and its wine industry, the success of all three can only be a good thing.

In the early years of the 21st century, it is thus difficult to pin down Rioja's red wine style, for there are several – a strength for any region. As a general rule, wines in which the Tempranillo grape is dominant are elegant, plummy and raspberry-scented when younger, ageing in barrel and/or bottle to develop flavours of wild strawberries, vanilla, tobacco, leather and cloves. The wines are sometimes low in acidity, but they age well. Many feel that Tempranillo is at its best when blended with other varieties, traditionally Garnacha in Rioja, although complex, complementary grapes like Graciano and Cabernet Sauvignon are probably its ideal partners. For more on the controversial question of Cabernet Sauvignon and Rioja, see **Future Development** on page 303. Rioja's Garnacha-based reds are traditionally bigger, jammier and more up-front than the Tempranillos, but without the latter's ageing potential. Wines such as Martinez Bujanda's Garnacha are beginning to challenge this view.

We must not ignore the fact that Rioja also produces white wines. And as was mentioned earlier, for many centuries they were far more significant than its reds. Until the '80s, Rioja made two styles of white: young, light, neutral wines which did not last and needed drinking soon after release, and whites aged for some time in barrel, often aggressively oaky with very little fruit in evidence, a style that had more fans in Spain than elsewhere. The current consumer's taste for light, clean, aromatic, fruity wines has penetrated Rioja over the last 20 years and modern know-how and technology – especially cold fermentation – have allowed Rioja to produce such wines and make the most of its rather average selection of white grapes. Many of the heavily over-oaked, furniture-chewing crianza whites have disappeared, but since the late '90s, there has been an increase in the production of barrel-fermented wines, which are generally more fruity and less overwhelmingly oaky than the previous generation of oak-aged whites.

Rioja currently has 50,000 hectares of vineyards, 18,000 growers and 2,575 bodegas. Around 70 per cent of output is consumed domestically, 30 per cent exported.

Authorised grape varieties are:

- **White:** Garnacha Blanca, Malvasía and Viura.

- **Black:** Garnacha, Graciano, Mazuelo and Tempranillo.

Viura is the dominant white wine grape, producing respectable, herby, fruity young whites, fruity/oaky barrel-fermented wines, and traditional crianza whites with lots of oak. Rioja's rosé wines – generally from the Garnacha grape grown in Rioja Baja – are fresh and fruity, often of good quality, although they tend to be overshadowed by those from neighbouring Navarra. However, Rioja is most famous for its red wines – see the following section for details of the different types produced in the three sub-regions.

Geography, Soil and Climate

D.O.Ca Rioja lies roughly in the middle of the northern half of Spain and is named after the River Oja, a tributary of the River Ebro. It has different boundaries from the autonomous region of Rioja. Not all of the vines that grow in the autonomous region come under the D.O.Ca, which stretches into the Basque Country and Navarra. Its vineyards extend for around 100km (62mi) on both sides of the Ebro, with the Ebro valley up to 40km (25mi) wide, bounded by hills and mountains. Rioja D.O.Ca is divided into three sub-regions:

▲ **Rioja Alavesa:** This is the smallest sub-region, covering around 11,500 hectares. Its climate is a temperate cross between the Atlantic and the Mediterranean, the southerly exposure of its vineyards making it the sunniest part of the region. Summers are short and hot, while winters are short with some frost. Spring is mild and rainy, while autumns are warm and stable. Soils are mostly calcareous clay and a lot of Tempranillo is grown. Alavesa produces some of Rioja's best reds, soft and fruity yet mouthfilling wines, although they do not tend to age as well as the reds of Rioja Alta.

▲ **Rioja Alta:** This is the largest sub-region, covering around 20,500 hectares. It has the mildest, most Atlantic climate, with the west of Alta higher and wetter than the more arid east. As a result, wines from the west tend to be more acidic and less alcoholic than those from the warmer east. Soils are a mixture of calcareous clay, ferruginous clay and alluvial silt.
   As in Alavesa, Tempranillo is the dominant grape, but there are more growths of Garnacha, Graciano and Mazuelo. Alta's wines, which are among Rioja's best, tend to have good acidity and the ability to age well for long periods.

▲ **Rioja Baja:** This sub-region covers around 18,000 hectares and has the most Mediterranean climate, characterised as semi-arid (average rainfall across the whole Rioja region is around 400mm/16in). Soils are mainly alluvial silt and ferruginous clay, while the dominant grape variety is Garnacha Tinta, which produces lively, jammy, alcoholic red wines that sometimes oxidise quickly, and fresh, fruity rosés.
   Rioja Baja's wines are usually rougher and less sophisticated than those from Alavesa and Alta, often used for blending with them. As mentioned before, because

many Riojas are blends of different grapes from different regions, it is difficult to pick out regional Rioja styles.

Future Development

The '90s was an interesting decade for Rioja, both a time of change and a sign of things to come. Excellent vintages in 1994 and 1995 (the former being the best of the century according to some experts) and a very good 1996 saw the region's reputation rise, both domestically and abroad. Prices began to climb as a result of this renewed success – which was not a problem for a couple of years because previously many wines had been under-priced and consumers recognised this – but when prices continued to rise – partly as a result of grape shortages – at the same time as wines from the weaker 1997 vintage appeared, buyers began to desert Rioja.

This was not surprising because the late '90s saw price increases of 20 to 40 per cent coinciding with the appearance of some average wines. Consumers reacted predictably and exports fell between 10 and 15 per cent. After grape prices reached crazy levels in 1999, the early 21st century has seen a return to sanity, with price stabilisations or falls and some better vintages coming onto the market. Thus the future looks better. Rioja's red wine strength lies with crianzas and reservas, offering high quality at (hopefully) reasonable prices. Its young, unaged wines can also be good, but competing wines from regions like Campo de Borja, Cariñena, Jumilla, La Mancha and parts of Catalonia have made some of them look overpriced.

Cabernet Sauvignon is a bone of contention in the region. The Marqués de Riscal has long had dispensation to use small amounts in its wines and others are allowed to grow it on an 'experimental' basis, but there is a view that its widespread use would alter or destroy the best of Rioja's qualities. The situation is not dissimilar to that which exists with Chardonnay in D.O. Cava. Some have argued that Rioja producers are actually 'frightened' of Cabernet Sauvignon, worried that if the region produced more blends or even varietals from the grape that they might not compare favourably with similar wines from Bordeaux, California and Australia.

Compromise might be the way to proceed: concentrate on Tempranillo and Garnacha, but experiment further with Cabernet in different locations and blends to offer even more choice of style of wines. The high quality (although difficult to grow) Graciano will also find many takers if more is produced. As for Rioja's whites, some have argued that their quality would be greatly improved by growing superior grape varieties, including the ubiquitous Chardonnay. This would certainly alter their character, although with so much decent white wine being produced in Galicia, Catalonia, Rueda and Navarra, Rioja will probably choose to maintain its white profile as it is, the wines always likely to be reasonably successful off the coat-tails of the reds.

Selected Bodegas

Abel Mendoza (☎ 941 308 010) Founded in 1987, this small operation makes a modest range of good and very good wines:

◆ *Jarrarte (white):* This barrel-fermented Malvasía is unctuous and mouthfilling with lots of flavour and the character of the barrel. Not subtle, but well done and enjoyable.

♦ *Jarrarte (red):* An aromatic, fruity young Tempranillo made by carbonic maceration, with typically up-front flavours. It drinks well slightly chilled, as these wines often do.

♦ *Jarrarte (red):* A superior Tempranillo crianza, richly aromatic, powerful, balanced and flavoursome. Recommended and moreish.

Age, S.A. (☎ 941 293 500) Originally founded in 1881, reorganised in the '60s and now owned by the Bodegas y Bebidas group, this large, well known producer makes a range of adequate wines, the best known being the Siglo Saco red, white and rosé in their distinctive, appealingly crude hessian bags. The range includes:

♦ *Siglo (red):* A blend of around 70 per cent Tempranillo and 30 per cent Garnacha, this is well made, straightforward red wine, honestly tasty for everyday drinking.

♦ *Siglo Crianza (red):* Primarily Tempranillo, with some Mazuelo and Graciano, this is a respectable, reasonably characterful Rioja crianza, but nothing remarkable.

♦ *Azpilicueta Crianza (red):* Roughly the same blend as above, and probably the bodega's best value wine, this is a well made crianza with some elegance, structure and decent flavours, without quite hitting the heights.

♦ *Azpilicueta Reserva (red):* The bodega's best wine, this resembles the crianza, with added spice and complexity. Enjoyable.

Alavesas, S.A. (☎ 941 600 100) Founded in 1972, and included here because of its large size rather than the quality of its wines, this operation makes a range of adequate wines, the following being the most interesting:

♦ *Solar de Samaniego Reserva (red):* A good quality, smooth, rounded, well made wine, rather than anything remarkable.

Alejos, S.A. (☎ 941 437 051) Founded in 1988, this operation has 25 hectares of its own vineyards and produces a small range of respectable and good wines, including:

♦ *Alabanza (red):* A blend of mainly Tempranillo with a small amount of Mazuelo, this is a light, everyday red wine, respectable but nothing more.

♦ *Alabanza Crianza (red):* Around 85 per cent Tempranillo, with small amounts of other grapes, this is a good crianza with tasty, integrated fruit and toasty oak. Enjoyable, competitively priced wine.

♦ *Alabanza Reserva (red):* Another enjoyable, reasonably priced wine, with characterful fruit and bite.

Amézola de la Mora, S.A. (☎ 941 454 532) Founded in 1986 at a 150-year-old estate, this small operation makes a modest range of good and very good wines, including:

♦ *Viña Amézola Crianza (red):* A blend of 90 per cent Tempranillo, 7 per cent Mazuelo and 3 per cent Graciano, this is a decent, soundly constructed crianza with tasty fruit and oak for a fair price, although it would not claim to be overly complex.

● *Señorío Amézola Reserva (red):* A rather good wine, with structure, balance and complex flavours. Recommended.

Antigua Usanza, S.A. (☎ 941 443 686) Founded in 1989, this modest-size operation makes a small range of decent and good wines, including:

● *Antigua Usanza Crianza (red):* A decent, tasty blend of mature fruit and oak.

● *Antigua Usanza Reserva (red):* An aromatic wine with lots of fruit and some oak. Good rather than remarkable and could do with more depth and complexity.

Artadi – Cosecheros Alaveses (☎ 941 600 119) Founded in 1985, with 75 hectares of vines, this modest-size operation was originally called Cosecheros Alaveses, but such has been the success of its Artadi ('home oak' in Basque) label that it has been included in the bodega's name. The bodega has developed a very good reputation for its expressive young and crianza wines, while the last two reviewed below are regarded as among Spain's better reds.

● *Artadi (red):* This is one of Rioja and Spain's more famous and best regarded young red wines, credited with making consumers take the style more seriously. Made from 85 per cent Tempranillo and 15 per cent (white) Viura, it has a complex, fruity nose, typical of a wine produced by carbonic maceration, and offers an elegant, mouthfilling palate with confident tannins and length. Its reputation has caused the price to rise quite sharply over the last couple of years.

● *Artadi Viñas de Gain Crianza (red):* An elegant, stylish, understated wine, with a slight international feel. A good introduction to the bodega's aged wines.

● *Artadi Pagos Viejos (red):* Made from 98 per cent Tempranillo and 2 per cent 'others', this has a complex, toasty, minerally, tobaccoey nose and a full, unctuous palate with confident tannins and lots of flavour. Not to be drunk too young, this is a fine wine for enjoying slowly. Highly recommended.

● *Artadi Viña El Pisón (red):* Made from the same blend as the above, this has an elegant nose of toast, fruit and herbs, while the palate is very soundly constructed with confident but unobtrusive tannins and lots of long, unctuous flavours. As above, a lovely, highly recommended wine for appreciating slowly.

Bagordi, S.L. (☎ 948 389 020) Founded in 1996, this smallish operation's wines are improving every year; it now produces a range of good and very good wines, including:

● *Bagordi Fermentado en Barrica (white):* A barrel-fermented Viura with more oak than fruit, although it is tasty and refreshing. As with some of these oaked white Riojas, it is too expensive when compared with barrel-fermented whites from other regions that are often made with superior grape varieties.

● *Bagordi (red):* A good quality, aromatic young Tempranillo with lots of lively fruit.

● *Bagordi Crianza (red):* Later releases are, unsurprisingly, better than early efforts. When on form, this Tempranillo crianza has lots of attractive, rounded fruit and toasty oak flavours for a competitive price. Recommended.

◆ *Gran Bagordi Reserva (red)*: This Tempranillo has a spicy nose and a smooth, integrated palate with interest and length. Good.

Balbino Fernández Palacios (☎ 941 607 018) Founded in 1920, this modest-size bodega has 35 hectares of vines and makes respectable wines, but they are overpriced when compared with others from the region.

◆ *Don Balbino Reserva (red)*: A tasty wine with spicy fruit and oak well integrated, but it lacks much complexity or depth, and is thus overpriced.

Barón de Ley, S.A. (☎ 948 694 303) Founded in 1985, this well regarded bodega makes stylish, approachable, mid-range wines, including:

◆ *Barón de Ley (white)*: A clean, easy drinking, everyday young white from Viura.

◆ *Barón de Ley Reserva (red)*: Some releases are 100 per cent Tempranillo, some have 10 per cent Cabernet Sauvignon. A tasty, mouthfilling wine with balance and some interest. Good.

◆ Barón de Ley Gran Reserva (red): 100 per cent Tempranillo, this is an aromatic wine with a smooth, tasty, elegant, mouthfilling palate. Good.

Berberana, S.A. (☎ 941 453 100) Founded in 1877, and now one of the region's largest concerns with 5,000 hectares of vines, Berberana has gone through several pairs of hands and incarnations in its long history. It now also owns Lagunilla and the Marqués de Griñon in Rioja (with the latter making wine in several parts of Spain) and Penedés' Marqués de Monistrol – see pages 319 and 198. Berberana itself makes reasonable quality, commercial wines which sell in huge quantities in Spain, the reds better than the whites and rosés, including:

◆ *Carta de Plata (red)*: A light, fruity, commercial crianza, honest and big-selling but nothing to think about too much.

◆ *Carta de Oro (red)*: A better version of the above, smooth and very drinkable.

◆ *Lagunilla Crianza (red)*: Made from 100 per cent Tempranillo, this is a well made, commercial although characterful blend of spicy fruit and oak.

◆ *Lagunilla Reserva (red)*: Made from 80 per cent Tempranillo and 20 per cent Garnacha, this has more complexity and interest than the crianza, with hints of Rioja's classic tobacco flavours.

◆ *Viña Alarde Reserva (red)*: A blend of 80 per cent Tempranillo and 20 per cent Garnacha, this is an up-front wine with mouthfilling fruit and toasty oak. Commercial and very drinkable.

Berceo, S.A. (☎ 941 310 744) Founded in 1872, this bodega makes a range of well made, traditional-style wines, including:

◆ *Viña Berceo Fermentado en Barrica (white)*: This is a better than average barrel-fermented Viura, flavoursome, balanced and does not make the mistake of drowning the fruit in oak.

- *Viña Berceo Rosado (rosé):* Made from a varying blend of Garnacha, Tempranillo and Viura, this is well made, fruity, tasty rosé. Good.

- *Viña Berceo Crianza (red):* Made from 80 per cent Tempranillo and 20 per cent Garnacha, this inexpensive crianza is well made, rounded and tasty without winning any prizes, but it does not intend to.

- *Gonzalo de Berceo Reserva (red):* Made from around 70 per cent Tempranillo, the rest Garnacha, Graciano and Mazuelo, this is often the bodega's best wine. In good vintages it is a very balanced, structured, flavoursome wine with personality and length. Recommended and competitively priced by regional standards.

Beronia, S.A. (☎ 941 338 000) Founded in the early '70s, and with a modest 10 hectares of its own vineyards, Beronia is a respected name producing a range of good and very good wines, especially the reds, that are light and elegant rather than big and beefy. The range includes:

- *Beronia Blanco (white):* A light, young Viura, refreshing but unremarkable. Other regions often do these wines better and more cheaply than Rioja.

- *Beronia Fermentado en Barrica (white):* This barrel-fermented Viura has a light touch, with oak and fruit well integrated without being aggressive. A better than average example and competitively priced.

- *Beronia Crianza (red):* A blend of around 85 per cent Tempranillo with the balance Garnacha and Mazuelo, this competitively priced wine is well made, medium-bodied, tasty and elegant. Decent, commercial Rioja crianza.

- *Beronia Reserva (red):* Made from around 90 per cent Tempranillo with the balance Graciano and Mazuelo, this is a good wine with lots of sweetish fruit, oak and attractive spices. More satisfying and interesting than the crianza.

Bilbaínas, S.A. (☎ 941 310 147) Founded in 1859 – with the winery built in 1901 – Bilbaínas is now owned by the giant Codorníu group (see page 225). In Zaco and Pomal it has two well established, traditional Rioja wines, while in La Vicalanda it has one of the best and most forward-looking. Its range includes:

- *Zaco Crianza (red):* A blend of 55 per cent Tempranillo, the balance Garnacha, Graciano and Mazuelo, this is a lightish blend of fruit and oak, quite tannic when first released. Good rather than very good.

- *Viña Zaco Reserva (red):* A blend of 70 per cent Tempranillo with Graciano and Mazuelo, this lightish, smooth wine is redolent of old-style Rioja oak flavours.

- *Viña Pomal Reserva (red):* Made from 85 per cent Tempranillo with Graciano and Mazuelo, this is a classic-style blend of fruit and oak, well done and enjoyable without being deep or complex.

- *La Vicalanda Reserva (red):* By far the bodega's best wine, this is a single estate, new-style Rioja of great structure, power and elegance at a remarkably affordable price. First released in 1994, it is 100 per cent Tempranillo and spends 12 months in French oak and two years in bottle. It is much more interesting and characterful than the bodega's other wines and should be compulsory drinking for anyone with an interest in Rioja wines.

Bodegas y Viñedos del Marqués de Vargas, S.A. (☎ 941 261 401) Founded in 1990 by a noble family with a long history in Rioja, this small, high quality operation only makes red reserva wines, from grapes grown in its own 60 hectares of vineyards. Its current winery is in a region known as 'Los Tres Marqueses' because of the close proximity of the Marqueses de Murrieta, de Romeral and de Vargas. The latter has quickly become highly respected, its estate wines cleverly twinning modern and traditional methods.

◆ *Marqués de Vargas Reserva (red):* Made from 70 per cent Tempranillo, 10 per cent Garnacha, 10 per cent Mazuelo and 10 per cent others – although the blend can vary – this is a notably aromatic wine with a powerful, structured, balanced palate offering lots of complex flavours of mature fruit and fine oak. An excellent wine, both classic and modern, with a long life ahead of it.

◆ *Marqués de Vargas Reserva Privada (red):* This 'special' reserva costs around twice as much as the reserva. It is a similar blend of grapes, but with slightly less Tempranillo. In some years it is regarded as one of the region's very best wines, which makes its price seem eminently competitive. It is characterised by the power and complexity of its nose and palate, and exceptional structure and balance. Highly recommended.

Bodegas y Viñedos Gómez Cruzado, S.A. (☎ 941 312 502) Founded in 1886, this smallish operation buys in grapes and wine to produce a modest range of decent and good quality wines, including:

◆ *Viña Dorana Crianza (red):* A blend of 85 to 90 per cent Tempranillo, with the balance Mazuelo, this is a decent, tasty, well made blend of fruit and oak flavours, respectable rather than remarkable, and that is not an insult Its price has risen somewhat and it needs to be careful that it does not oversell itself.

◆ *Viña Dorana Reserva (red):* A similar blend to the above, this aromatic wine has lots of flavour and is characterised by a spicy feel. Perhaps a touch expensive.

Bretón y Cía, S.A. (☎ 941 212 225) Founded in 1985, with the current winery built in 1993, this newish operation combines – like Bodegas y Viñedos del Marqués de Vargas – the best of the old and the new in Rioja. Its Loriñón wines are its 'house' bottles, while Dominio de Conte and Alba de Bretón have quickly joined the top table of Rioja's, indeed Spain's, wines.

◆ *Loriñón Fermentado en Barrica (white):* This aromatic, barrel-fermented Viura has a tasty, unctuous palate with fruit and oak flavours working well together. One of the region's better examples of the style and drinking well at two years old.

◆ *Loriñón Crianza (red):* A blend of 80 to 85 per cent Tempranillo, with the balance Garnacha, Graciano and Mazuelo, this is a good crianza with a powerful, toasty nose and a soundly constructed, flavoursome, harmonious palate with well judged tannins.

◆ *Loriñón Reserva (red):* Made from the same blend as the crianza, this is a well made wine, but the crianza is probably as enjoyable and rather cheaper, so choose that instead.

◆ *Dominio de Conte Reserva (red):* A blend of 90 per cent Tempranillo and 10 per cent Graciano, this highly regarded, delicious wine has flavour, elegance, length and bite, combining the best of the old and new Rioja. Recommended.

◆ *Alba de Bretón Reserva (red):* Around twice the price of Dominio de Conte, this is the bodega's flagship wine, first appearing on the market in 1999. It is made 100 per cent from Tempranillo produced by old vines, aged in French and American oak, and is one of Rioja's leading new-style, estate wines. Alba de Bretón has an elegant, complex nose and a beautifully structured, unctuous palate with powerful, deep fruit flavours and fine, well judged oak. One of Spain's better red wines.

C.V.N.E. (Compañía Vinícola del Norte de España) (☎ 941 304 800) Founded in 1879, and one of Rioja's oldest, most renowned names, C.V.N.E. (pronounced 'coonay') moved into a modern new winery in 1990. Some people maintain that standards slipped as a result, but the firm is back on form again, producing a range of good to excellent wines, some of which rank among Rioja's more renowned names. The range includes:

◆ *Monopole (white):* This oaked blend of 91 per cent Viura, 5 per cent Malvasía and 4 per cent Garnacha Blanca is one of the more famous white Riojas. It is a well made, tasty wine, with understated fruit and oak flavours, but new technology has helped Spain's white wines to improve quickly and it no longer stands out as it used to.

◆ *Viña Real Fermentado en Barrica (white):* One of the new generation of barrel-fermented whites, which try to taste of fruit as well as oak, this 100 per cent Viura is a powerful, mouthfilling wine with citric fruit, oak, creamy touches and length. A good example of its type.

◆ *CVNE Crianza (red):* A blend of 70 per cent Tempranillo with 25 per cent Garnacha Tinta and/or Mazuelo and 5 per cent Garnacha Blanca and/or Viura, this is a well made, lightish blend of fruit and oak. Decent everyday Rioja crianza.

◆ *Viña Real Crianza (red):* A blend of 75 per cent Tempranillo, 15 per cent Garnacha Tinta and/or Mazuelo and 10 per cent Garnacha Blanca and/or Viura, this popular supermarket and Spanish restaurant wine list bottle is a commercial introduction to Rioja crianza wines. It is a lightish, soundly constructed blend of fruit and oak at an affordable price.

◆ *CVNE Reserva (red):* A blend of 90 per cent Tempranillo, 5 per cent Graciano and 5 per cent Garnacha, we now start to get to the wines that have built the bodega's reputation: its reservas. The Viña Real, Imperial and the newish Real de Arsua are the famous wines, but this affordable bottle is a decent introduction to the bodega's reserva style. It is a rounded, mouthfilling blend of integrated and aged fruit and oak, with good length.

◆ *Viña Real Reserva (red):* A blend of 80 per cent Tempranillo, 15 per cent Garnacha and Mazuelo and 5 per cent Graciano, this is a classic Rioja wine, offering smooth, rounded, elegant flavours of fruit and oak with tobacco running through the middle. Highly recommended.

◆ *Imperial Reserva (red)*: A blend of roughly 90 per cent Tempranillo with 5 per cent Graciano and 5 per cent Mazuelo, spending three years in oak and two more in bottle, this is more full-bodied than some of the classic Riojas and has an elegant, rounded, spicy palate. A must-try wine, sometimes seen as a forerunner of the new-style of Riojas.

◆ *Real de Asúa Reserva (red)*: This blend of 80 per cent Tempranillo, 15 per cent Garnacha and 5 per cent Graciano is a newish arrival to the CVNE reserva stable and has a complex nose and an elegant, structured palate with lots of length. A superior wine, around twice the price of same vintage Viña Real and Imperial reservas.

Campillo (☎ 941 600 826) Founded in 1990 by the owners of Faustino (see page 313) Campillo has forged its own name and reputation with 50 hectares of vines and now produces a range of good and very good wines, although quality does vacillate with vintage. Reds tend to be meaty rather than soft in style and the bodega's range includes:

◆ *Campillo Fermentado en Barrica (white)*: A blend of 90 per cent Viura and 10 per cent 'others', this is a decent barrel-fermented wine, usually with an even balance between fruit and oak flavours. Given the medium quality of the majority grape, these wines struggle to be top drawer.

◆ *Campillo Rosado (rosé)*: A decent, light, everyday Tempranillo rosé, perhaps a little pricey when compared with the competition from Navarra, Cigales and Catalonia.

◆ *Campillo Crianza (red)*: A good rather than great Tempranillo crianza, with fruit and oak well integrated, this tends to be beefy rather than soft in style.

◆ *Campillo Reserva (red)*: When on form, this is very good Tempranillo, a powerful, complex, flavoursome wine, but in some years it can lack interest.

◆ *Campillo Reserva Especial (red)*: One of the bodega's most expensive bottles, this is also one of its best. Made from a varying blend of Tempranillo (the majority grape), Graciano and others, it is a powerful, complex, confident wine, although perhaps a little overpriced.

Campo Viejo, S.A. (☎ 941 279 900) Founded in 1963, and now owned by the giant group Bodegas y Bebidas, this very large operation offers a wide range of popular, well known wines, the commercial face of Rioja but also making interesting bottles. The bodega is credited with helping Rioja's success in the '60s and '70s by making wines that appealed to a wide range of tastes. In the 21st century, it is looking to respond to changing times and will soon rebrand its wines and perhaps alter production methods.

◆ *Viña Alcorta Fermentado en Barrica (white)*: This tasty, unctuous barrel-fermented Viura is a respectable example of the style.

◆ *Campo Viejo Crianza (red)*: This popular, commercial blend of Tempranillo, Garnacha and Mazuelo offers honest, straightforward, commercial flavours of fruit and oak, with the latter sometimes dominating.

◆ *Viña Alcorta Crianza (red):* Made from 100 per cent Tempranillo, this is slightly pricier than the Campo Viejo crianza and a superior product. It has more structure and complexity and is a decent introduction to the Rioja crianza style.

◆ *Campo Viejo Reserva (red):* Made from the same grapes as the crianza, this is many Spaniards' first introduction to a Rioja reserva, a popular, affordable, commercial wine. It is an integrated blend of spicy fruit and oak, rounded and with the oak sometimes dominant.

◆ *Viña Alcorta Reserva (red):* Made from Tempranillo, with comments as above.

◆ *Marqués de Villamagna Gran Reserva (red):* This is one of the bodega's top wines, made in classic Rioja style with structure, length and suitably aged, tobaccoey flavours. Recommended.

Carlos Serres, S.A. (☎ 941 310 294) Founded in 1896, this bodega makes a range of decent and good wines, including:

◆ *Carlos Serres (red):* A blend of 80 per cent Tempranillo and 20 per cent Garnacha, this young wine offers lots of attractive, lively fruit.

◆ *Carlos Serres Crianza (red):* A blend of 80 per cent Tempranillo, 10 per cent Garnacha and 10 per cent Mazuelo, this is a good rather than great blend of tasty fruit and oak.

◆ *Onomástica Reserva (red):* This is a very tasty blend of mainly Tempranillo, with Garnacha, Mazuelo and a small amount of Viura, but it sometimes lacks complexity.

Consejo de La Alta (☎ 941 455 005) Founded in 1990, this smallish operation makes respectable rather than remarkable wines, including:

◆ *Alta Río Fermentado en Barrica (white):* Not the bodega's finest hour, this barrel-fermented Viura has bite but it is rather stodgy and one-dimensionally oaky.

◆ *Alta Río (red):* A young Tempranillo with lots of tasty, straightforward fruit. Good everyday drinking and it enjoys a slight chilling on a warm day.

◆ *Alta Río Crianza (red):* A soundly constructed blend of Tempranillo and oak, with tasty fruit to the fore.

◆ *Alta Río Reserva (red):* This affordable reserva (by Rioja standards) is the bodega's most interesting and complex wine, aromatic, spicy and long with some interest. Good.

Corral, S.A. (☎ 941 440 193) Founded in 1898, this bodega's wines improve as you ascend the age and price scale. Its range includes:

◆ *Don Jacobo (white):* A young Viura, this is respectable, fruity, everyday white wine.

◆ *Don Jacobo (rosé):* Made from 60 per cent Garnacha, 20 per cent Tempranillo and 20 per cent Viura, this is decent pink wine with generous amounts of tasty fruit.

♦ *Don Jacobo Crianza (red)*: Made from 85 per cent Tempranillo and 15 per cent Garnacha, this is an aromatic wine with smooth, soundly constructed flavours. An enjoyable everyday crianza with some interest.

♦ *Don Jacobo Reserva (red)*: After some less than great wines from the later '80s and early '90s, this seems to be back on form and in good years is an attractive, soft, flavoursome wine.

♦ *Altos del Corral Single Estate (red)*: This is a big jump in both price and class, by far the bodega's best offering. Made from 100 per cent Tempranillo, it is a complex, aromatic wine with lots of smooth, long flavours. Superior Rioja and recommended.

Domecq, S.A. (☎ 941 606 001) Founded in 1973 by the large sherry firm of the same name, this operation has over 500 hectares of vines and produces a range of good and very good wines, including:

♦ *Viña Eguia Crianza (red)*: This reasonably priced blend of 95 per cent Tempranillo with 5 per cent Graciano and Mazuelo has lots of up-front, fruity, oaky flavours.

♦ *Marqués de Arienzo Crianza (red)*: Made from the same blend as the above, this is the 'senior' crianza, with a touch more complexity and fruity personality. Good.

♦ *Marqués de Arienzo Reserva (red)*: The same grapes again, this first appeared on the market in 1986 and has the feel of a classic Rioja. It is a rounded, tasty wine with structure and balance. Recommended and reasonably priced.

♦ *Marqués de Arienzo Reserva Especial (red)*: Made from 75 per cent Tempranillo and 25 per cent of the excellent Graciano, this is the bodega's best wine, expensive but probably worth the cost. It has an engaging, complex nose and a powerful, balanced, integrated palate with long-lived flavours. Highly recommended.

El Coto de Rioja, S.A. (☎ 941 122 216) Founded in 1970, this very sizeable operation makes a range of decent and good wines, well known in Spain and staples of many a supermarket shelf and restaurant wine list, especially the El Coto red crianza with its recognisable but old-fashioned stag-design label.

♦ *El Coto (white)*: A light, fresh, young Viura for everyday drinking.

♦ *El Coto Crianza (red)*: This popular, reasonably priced Tempranillo is a decent, tasty blend of fruit and oak for everyday drinking. It does not pretend to be a complex, structured mouthful.

♦ *Coto de Imaz Reserva (red)*: An aromatic wine with a rounded, soundly constructed, tasty palate. Good, everyday reserva, if there is such a thing.

Escudero, S.A. (☎ 941 398 008) Founded back in 1852, and also a producer of Cava, this bodega makes a modest range of decent and good wines, including:

♦ *Solar de Bécquer Fermentado en Barrica (white)*: A blend of 60 per cent Chardonnay (a grape which is not quite as rare in these parts as an ego-free actor, but it is on the way) and 40 per cent Viura, this is one of Rioja's better barrel-fermented whites. The Chardonnay's influence is noticeable on the nose, with good fruit as well as oak, while the palate is finely structured and tasty with bite. It is more expensive than the regional average for a barrel-fermented white, but it is also a better wine. Chardonnay's quality shines through, something that will not please those traditionalists who do not relish foreign invaders.

♦ *Bécquer Primicia (red):* This used to be made 100 per cent from Garnacha, but is now 60 per cent Garnacha and 40 per cent Tempranillo, and all the better for it. A light, attractive, fruity young wine with some elegance. Good.

♦ *Solar de Bécquer Crianza (red):* A blend of 70 per cent Tempranillo, 20 per cent Mazuelo and 10 per cent Garnacha, this is a light style of crianza with the fruit to the fore. Decent but could do with more oak influence and integration.

Faustino, S.L. (☎ 941 622 500) Founded in 1861, with the current winery built in 1971, Faustino is one of Rioja's, indeed Spain's, best known wine makers, its distinctively labelled bottles famous throughout the world. In these days of slick marketing, presentation and packaging, the bottles and labels are attractively crude, in a fake-antique style. The firm, still family-owned, is one of Rioja's biggest exporters of reserva and gran reserva wines, and its reds are noted for their limited time in oak, with fruit often to the fore. The range includes:

♦ *Faustino V (white):* A well made, fresh, tasty, young Viura, better than the average white Rioja. Good.

♦ *Faustino V Fermentado en Barrica (white):* More expensive than the above, and not as good, lacking its freshness and sometimes overcome by oak.

♦ *Faustino VII (red):* Light, fruity, decent but unremarkable wine.

♦ *Faustino de Crianza (red):* A tasty, well made wine, with more fruit than oak flavours. Could do with more depth.

♦ *Faustino V Reserva (red):* This is a well made, confident wine but it can lack depth of interest and complexity. It is nonetheless commercially successful, although as its price increased in the early 21st century, some large foreign buyers dropped it.

♦ *Faustino I Gran Reserva (red):* The bodega's top wine which, in good years, is very good indeed, despite the cheesy fake-antique bottle. Made from a varying blend of grapes – mainly Tempranillo, sometimes with small amounts of Graciano and Mazuelo – this wine spends just over two years in American oak – short by Rioja standards – and a further three in bottle. It is complex on the nose and has a full, balanced, engaging palate with smooth flavours. One of Rioja's must-trys.

Federico Paternina, S.A. (☎ 941 310 550) Founded in 1896, this sizeable operation makes large volumes of wine, some of its bottles among Rioja's most popular in Spain, especially Banda Azul. In the early and mid 20th century the bodega was famous for very classy red reservas and gran reservas, but nowadays the emphasis is on decent and good quality commercial wines. The Conde de los Andes gran reservas can be very good, a sign of what the bodega once concentrated on. Its range includes:

◆ *Paternina Banda Dorada (white):* A well made, young white Rioja with fruity personality and bite. Superior everyday wine.

◆ *Graciela Semi-Dulce (white):* An interesting wine, semi-sweet and oak-aged with sweetish fruit and nutty oak contrasting quite well. Worth trying in a group as you will probably not want to drink more than a glass of it.

◆ *Paternina Banda Azul Crianza (red):* A competent, commercial, competitively priced, medium-bodied blend of fruit and oak, without too much going on. Very popular in Spain.

◆ *Paternina Banda Oro Crianza (red):* A better, slightly pricier version of the above, with more elegance and complexity. Good.

◆ *Viña Vial Reserva (red):* A medium-bodied wine at a competitive price with straightforward, honest fruit and oak flavours. Good everyday Rioja reserva, if that is not a contradiction in terms.

◆ *Conde de los Andes Gran Reserva (red):* A big jump in price and often in quality. This is classic in style with the complex, spicy, leathery, tobaccoey flavours of carefully aged fruit and oak. It can be very good indeed and prices vary greatly according to year. Currently, your best bets are probably from the late '80s.

Fernando Remirez de Ganuza, S.A. (☎ 941 609 022) Founded in 1989, this small, 'designer' bodega's first wine did not appear on the market until 1998. The vines in its 60 hectares of vineyards are mainly Tempranillo and old – averaging 60 – and the bodega has quickly garnered a strong reputation for its expensive, high quality wines, half of which are exported.

◆ *Erre Punto (red):* A new departure for the bodega, which initially only produced reservas, this young wine is made from grapes from the bottom tip of the bunches. With the violet rim of youth, it has a powerful fruity nose, while the palate has lots of confident fruit and tannin. A superior young wine.

◆ *Remirez de Ganuza Reserva (red):* The blend varies from year to year, but this is usually around 85 to 90 per cent Tempranillo, with the balance Graciano and sometimes a touch of Garnacha. Spending 26 months in French and American oak, it has an elegant, complex nose and a powerful, balanced, expressive palate with lots of flavour, length and firm but not intrusive tannins. This wine is at the top table of Rioja's reds and in view of that, competitively priced. Highly recommended.

Finca Allende (☎ 941 322 301) Founded only in 1995 – although the owners had been making wine elsewhere since 1986 – this small operation has already established a reputation as one of Rioja's most interesting new, 'designer' producers. Its wine maker is the son of one of the senior staff at Marqués de Murrieta and previously worked at Bodegas Bretón, an enviable track record.

◆ *Allende (red):* Made from 100 per cent Tempranillo, this has a complex, toasty, fruity, herby nose and a powerful palate with excellent tannins, fruit and toasty oak beautifully integrated, and length. One of Rioja's better wines, fairly modestly priced and a must-try.

◆ *Aurus (red):* This sells for around eight times the cost of the above, putting it in very pricey territory indeed, probably appropriate for a wine which its maker hopes will compete with the world's best. Made from 85 per cent Tempranillo and 15 per cent Graciano, it has quickly attracted a lot of praise for its well judged combination of strength and elegance, with complexity and powerful yet smooth tannins, meaning that it drinks well now and will also last. Some critics have found it only slightly better than the (excellent) Allende and hence queried its elevated price. Only time will tell us how it develops in bottle.

Finca Valpiedra (☎ 941 122 188) This operation's site has been owned by the Martínez Bujanda family (see page 321) for nearly 30 years, but its first wine did not come to market until 1998. This followed a long, meticulous process of readying everything for the production of this top quality estate wine.

◆ *Finca Valpiedra Reserva (red):* Made from 90 per cent Tempranillo, 5 per cent Cabernet Sauvignon and 5 per cent Mazuelo and Graciano, this spends 16 months in new oak barrels. It is an aromatic, expressive, powerful, elegant wine at the forefront of the new Riojas. Another must-try.

Franco Españolas, S.A. (☎ 941 251 300) Founded in 1890, this large bodega has passed through several pairs of hands. It is best known in Spain for its semi-sweet white Diamante and red Rioja Bordón, and standards are respectable or good rather than earth-shattering. Its range includes:

◆ *Viña Soledad (white):* A light, young, everyday wine.

◆ *Diamante Semi-Dulce (sweetish white):* This Spanish restaurant wine list and supermarket shelf standard is a step up from the average and everyday, quite a characterful, well made, sweetish wine.

◆ *Rioja Bordón Crianza (red):* A decent, lightish, commercial wine with a bit more oak than fruit.

◆ *Rioja Bordón Reserva (red):* A spicier, slightly fuller-bodied version of the above.

◆ *Rioja Bordón Gran Reserva (red):* Twice the price of the reserva, this has more interest, with a complex nose of leather and tobacco, and a classic, rounded palate with flavour and length.

Granja Nuestra Señora de Remelluri (☎ 941 331 801) Founded in 1967, this small bodega has had an important and beneficial influence in Rioja. It began by producing classic-style, estate Riojas from its 85 hectares of high-altitude vines, before changing in the '90s to a more modern style.

◆ *Remelluri Crianza (red):* This has a complex nose of mature fruits, toast and tar and a medium-bodied palate with lots of smooth flavours and confident although not intrusive tannins. A very good Rioja crianza.

◆ *Remelluri Reserva (red):* The bodega's signature wine and notably competitively priced given its quality and renown. A blend of mainly Tempranillo, with small amounts of Garnacha and Graciano, this beautifully combines strength and elegance, with a complex nose of mature fruit, toast and minerals, and a powerful, lively, mature palate. Another must-try wine.

Heredad de Baroja, S.A. (☎ 941 604 068) Founded in 1982, this bodega makes a range of decent and good wines, including:

◆ *Cautivo Fermentado en Barrica (white):* A tasty, confident wine with more wood than fruit.

◆ *Cautivo Tempranillo (red):* A decent, everyday, young red wine with generous fruit.

◆ *Cautivo Crianza (red):* A decent, everyday blend of fruit and oak.

◆ *Cautivo Reserva (red):* A more complex wine than the crianza, but likewise decent rather than notable.

Heredad Ugarte, S.A. (☎ 945 282 844) Founded in 1988, this is another producer of respectable and good wines rather than trail-blazing world beaters. Its range includes:

◆ *Heredad Ugarte Crianza (red):* A blend of 90 per cent Tempranillo and 10 per cent 'others', in good years this is an enjoyable crianza, with a toasty nose and a tasty palate with lively fruit and well judged oak. In weaker years it can be a little bland and unfocussed.

◆ *Dominio de Ugarte Reserva (red):* Made from the same blend of grapes, this is the bodega's best wine, well made, smooth and spicy, but it is overpriced when compared with, say, Remelluri reserva (above).

La Rioja Alta, S.A. (☎ 941 310 346) Founded in 1890, this is one of Rioja's great old names and continues to produce high quality wines, very much in the classic Rioja mould. Its range is must-try for those wanting to acquaint themselves with Rioja red wines.

◆ *Viña Alberdi Crianza (red):* This is often one of Rioja's better crianzas and reasonably priced for its quality. It offers a complex nose of fruits, spices and oak, while the palate has long, elegant, mouthfilling flavours and depth of interest. Recommended.

◆ *Viña Arana Reserva (red):* A blend of Tempranillo and Graciano, this has a complex, leathery, tobaccoey nose and a rounded palate of classic, aged Rioja flavours.

◆ *Viña Ardanza Reserva (red):* The bodega's best known wine and one of Rioja's real classics, this is a blend of 75 per cent Tempranillo and 25 per cent Garnacha, aged in barrel for three years with a further 18 months in bottle. It has a classic, complex nose of tobacco, old oak and leather, and a palate with structure and powerful, smooth, rounded flavours. A must-taste wine.

◆ *904 Gran Reserva (red):* Made from 90 per cent Tempranillo and 10 per cent Graciano and Mazuelo, this has a classic Rioja nose of old leather, tobacco and cloves, and a lightish, smooth palate with long, engaging, classic flavours. It is nearly twice the price of the Ardanza, but probably no better. That is not a reflection of any deficiencies, rather of Ardanza's strengths.

◆ *890 Gran Reserva (red)*: This is the bodega's most expensive wine by a long chalk, and both its and one of Rioja's best. The nose is the definition of classic Rioja, while the palate has rounded, complex, delicious flavours from perfectly aged fruit and oak. An excellent classic Rioja, one of the best and worthy of a particularly special occasion.

Lan, S.A. (☎ 941 450 950) Founded in 1970, this bodega's fortunes have vacillated over the years. It used to enjoy a reputation for high quality wines, was then for a time seen as a producer of commercial bottles, but after management changes is again regarded as a high quality operation, most notably for its much lauded Viña Lanciano Reserva.

◆ *Lan Crianza (red)*: A blend of 85 per cent Tempranillo, 10 per cent Garnacha and 5 per cent Mazuelo, this is a good crianza, with attractive, integrated fruit and oak.

◆ *Lan Reserva (red)*: A blend of 80 per cent Tempranillo, 10 per cent Garnacha and 10 per cent Mazuelo, this superior wine has rounded, mouthfilling flavours with toasty, tobaccoey, spicy touches. Recommended.

◆ *Lan Gran Reserva (red)*: A blend of 85 per cent Tempranillo, 10 per cent Mazuelo and 5 per cent Garnacha, this is an elegant, spicy wine with unctuous complexity. Delicious.

◆ *Viña Lanciano Reserva (red)*: A blend of 85 per cent Tempranillo and 15 per cent Mazuelo, with 18 months in barrel and a further 20 in bottle, this is the bodega's flagship bottle. It is an estate wine that combines the best of the old and new Rioja, with excellent, elegant, spicy fruit and oak, complexity, length and a lovely feel. Highly recommended.

López Heredia – Viña Tondonia (☎ 941 310 244) Founded in 1877, this is one of Rioja's oldest and most traditional establishments. Methods – and indeed some of the label designs – have not changed for 100 years and some of the wines are 'classic' Riojas in the deepest sense of the word.

◆ *Viña Tondonia Reserva (white)*: Made from 85 per cent Viura and 15 per cent Malvasía, this wine is something of a curiosity, a non-sweet white built to last for 10, 15 or even 20 years. The nose is of toasty oak, while the palate has powerful, mouthfilling, quite complex flavours of nuts and ageing, and acidic bite. An unusual, interesting and increasingly expensive experience.

◆ *López de Heredia Reserva (rosé)*: Made from 85 per cent Garnacha and 15 per cent Viura, this is even more of a curiosity, a pink reserva, often not drunk until 10 or 15 years old. Oak dominates the nose while the palate has surprising balance and smoothness. Around half the price of the white but still an expensive curiosity.

◆ *Viña Bosconia Crianza (red)*: A blend of 80 per cent Tempranillo, 15 per cent Garnacha, with the balance Graciano and Mazuelo, this has a nose of old wood, toast and fruits, while the palate is soft, smooth and rounded with classic old wood to the fore.

◆ *Viña Tondonia Reserva (red):* Made from 75 per cent Tempranillo, 15 per cent Garnacha, 5 per cent Graciano and 5 per cent Mazuelo, this is the bodega's most famous wine, and one of Rioja's most traditional, classic reds. In good years it is lovely, with a spicy, tobaccoey nose and a soft yet powerful and mouthfilling palate of classic, beautifully integrated Rioja flavours, thanks to its traditional production, including four years in oak and a further two in bottle. Compulsory drinking and often competitively priced given its name and quality.

Luberri (☎ 941 606 010) Founded in 1991, this modest-size bodega produces a young red and red crianza wine of good or very good quality. Success has seen prices rise.

◆ *Luberri (red):* Made from 90 per cent Tempranillo and 10 per cent Viura, this is one of Rioja's most characterful young red wines, with a powerful nose of mature fruits and a concentrated, fruity palate with flavour and bite. Good.

◆ *Altun Crianza (red):* This used to be made 100 per cent from Tempranillo but now sometimes contains 10 per cent Cabernet Sauvignon. It has a full nose of toasty, mature fruit and oak, while the palate has lots of concentrated, quite complex flavours of integrated fruit and oak, and good length. Recommended, but no longer the bargain that it was in the later '90s.

Luis Alegre (☎ 941 600 089) Founded in 1968, this small bodega makes a modest range of respectable and good wines, including:

◆ *Luis Alegre Crianza (red):* 100 per cent Tempranillo, this is a well made, straightforward, lightish wine at a competitive price.

◆ *Luis Alegre Reserva (red):* Again made 100 per cent from Tempranillo, this has more nose, body and complexity than the crianza, a good wine but probably overpriced for its quality.

Luis Cañas, S.A. (☎ 941 123 373) Founded in 1970, although the family has been in the wine industry for hundreds of years, this bodega is in the ascendancy. Throughout the '90s the production of good quality, aged wines became more important at Cañas and it has recently shown itself capable of making some top quality bottles. With Amaren it has moved into designer territory and the range includes:

◆ *Luis Cañas (white):* A light, fresh, everyday Viura with some bite.

◆ *Luis Cañas Fermentado en Barrica (white):* This is establishing a reputation as one of Rioja's better barrel-fermented Viuras and is cheaper than some of the competition. It has decent fruit as well as wood on the nose, while the palate offers lots of flavour, balance, integration and length. Recommended.

◆ *Luis Cañas (rosé):* An aromatic, fruity pink wine, with flavour and balance. The grape varieties used vary from year to year.

◆ *Luis Cañas Tinto (red):* Made from 90 per cent Tempranillo and 10 per cent Viura, this is an aromatic, tasty, well made young wine. Good.

- *Luis Cañas Crianza (red):* Made from 98 per cent Tempranillo and 2 per cent 'others', this is a decent, inexpensive crianza with characterful fruit and oak flavours.

- *Luis Cañas Reserva (red):* Made from 95 per cent Tempranillo and 5 per cent 'others', this is a fair step up in quality from the crianza, with more depth, complexity and structure. Good.

- *Luis Cañas Selección de la Familia (red):* A blend of 95 per cent Tempranillo, 3 per cent Graciano and 2 per cent Garnacha, this is a superior red Rioja, aromatic, mature and integrated at around six or seven years old. Recommended and competitively priced in view of its quality.

- *Amaren Reserva (red):* Made from 100 per cent Tempranillo, this is the bodega's flagship wine. First released in 1999, its grapes come from 70-year-old vines and spend 18 months in French oak and a further six months in American oak. It has an engaging nose while the palate is both powerful and elegant, with depth and interest, and it should develop beautifully over a decade. Highly recommended – although you pay for the privilege – and a clarion call that this bodega is aiming high.

Luis Gurpegui Muga, S.A. (☎ 948 670 050) Founded in 1921, this producer traditionally concentrates on quantity rather than quality. Its range of straightforward, inexpensive wines includes:

- *Viñadrian (white):* A straightforward, refreshing, young Viura.

- *Viñadrian (rosé):* A fresh, everyday rosé.

- *Viñadrian (red):* A simple, everyday, young red, mainly Tempranillo with some Garnacha.

Marqués de Griñon (☎ 941 453 100) Founded in 1994, and now owned by Berberana, the Marqués de Griñon is one of Spain's more interesting wine makers (see page 130 for further details), most famous for the excellent varietal wines that he produces in the Montes de Toledo near Madrid.

- *Marqués de Griñon Tempranillo (red):* A decent, straightforward blend of fruit and oak, well made, tasty and easy to drink.

- *Marqués de Griñon Reserva Privada (red):* A superior Tempranillo reserva, this is by far the Marqués' most distinguished Rioja wine. It has a powerful, spicy nose and a palate with personality, flavour, structure and balance. Recommended.

Marqués de Murrieta, S.A. (☎ 941 271 370) Founded in 1852, this bodega, along with Marqués de Riscal, is the most famous Rioja producer, the pair seen as the region's most distinguished aristocrats. Its wines are must-trys for anyone wishing to become acquainted with Rioja's wines, their style very traditional, with most spending long periods in oak and noted for their acidity. During the '80s there was a feeling that quality was beginning to slip but this has been arrested and Murrieta's wines are back on form, with a slightly more modern feel to some of them.

◆ *El Dorado de Murrieta Reserva (white)*: This is *the* classic, oaked white Rioja, something of a legend in the canon of Spain's wines. It attracts strong reactions and people tend to either love or loathe it. The nose has powerful oak influence with vanilla and toasty hints to the fore, while the palate is very much oak too, with toasty, nutty, bitter touches and some acidic fruit. It is one of the best, most famous expressions of oaked white Rioja, but it is a style of wine that some modern drinkers do not enjoy. Drink it in a group as more than a glass can be overpowering.

◆ *Marqués de Murrieta Reserva (red)*: This is many people's first introduction to superior, classic red Rioja. It has a spicy, vanilla and leather nose, while the palate offers smooth tannins, suitably aged and integrated spicy flavours and personality. Considering the reputation of the bodega, it is competitively priced.

◆ *Castillo de Ygay Gran Reserva Especial (red)*: Sitting at the top table of Rioja wines, this is only released in exceptional years, and prices – which can be very high indeed – vary according to vintage. Noted for its complex Rioja nose and palate – tobacco, cloves, leather, aged wood – this wine has excellent structure and depth. Another must-drink.

◆ Dalmau Reserva (red): This is the bodega's latest departure, first appearing in 1998. Made of 85 per cent Tempranillo, 10 per cent Cabernet Sauvignon and 5 per cent Graciano, and priced to compete with the best bottles from anywhere, it is a contemporary wine from one of the most traditional bodegas. Dalmau does not spend years in wood or have high acidity, but has a complex nose and a palate that is powerful, smooth and elegant, a clever mix of classic and modern Rioja flavours. Highly recommended, although you pay for the privilege.

Marqués de Vitoria, S.A. (☎ 941 122 134) Founded in 1988, this bodega makes a range of decent and good wines at competitive prices which do not quite hit the heights, including:

◆ *Marqués de Vitoria (white)*: A decent, lightish, fruity young Viura for not much money.

◆ *Marqués de Vitoria (rosé)*: Made from Tempranillo, this is a tasty, characterful pink wine at a good price. One of the region's better rosés.

◆ *Marqués de Vitoria Crianza (red)*: A decent, straightforward, inexpensive crianza, quite full-bodied.

◆ *Marqués de Vitoria Reserva (red)*: As above, with a touch more complexity.

Marqués del Puerto, S.A. (☎ 941 450 001) Founded in 1972 as López Agos, this French-owned bodega's name was changed in 1981. It produces a range of good and very good wines, some aspiring to sit at Rioja's top table, including:

◆ *Marqués del Puerto (white)*: A fruity, flavoursome young Viura with more body and personality than average.

◆ *Marqués del Puerto (rosé)*: Made from 50 per cent Garnacha and 50 per cent Tempranillo, this is a tasty, refreshing rosé with good fruity character.

◆ *Marqués del Puerto Crianza (red):* Made from 95 per cent Tempranillo and 5 per cent Mazuelo, this is an aromatic wine with aged hints on the nose reminiscent of a reserva. The palate is a meaty, balanced blend of fruit and oak.

◆ *Marqués del Puerto Reserva (red):* Made from 90 per cent Tempranillo, 8 per cent Mazuelo and 2 per cent Graciano, this is a jump in elegance and quality, with a quite complex, toasty nose and a rounded, tasty, elegant, integrated palate. Recommended.

◆ *Marqués del Puerto Selección Especial Reserva (red):* A blend of 90 per cent Tempranillo and 10 per cent Mazuelo, this wine first appeared in 2000 with the 1994 vintage. It is another jump in quality and price for the bodega and shows its intention to compete with the region's best. It has an elegant, complex nose and is smooth, structured and balanced on the palate with a lovely feel. A high quality wine, as it needs to be when priced at this level.

Martínez Bujanda, S.A. (☎ 941 122 188) Founded in 1889, and still family owned, this operation produces a range of good and very good wines – although standards vary and some recent crianzas and reservas are not as good as they could be – successful both in Spain and abroad. It exports around 60 per cent of production – high by Rioja standards (see also the entry for **Finca Valpiedra** on page 315). Bujanda's range includes:

◆ *Conde de Valdemar Fermentado en Barrica (white):* This barrel-fermented Viura has a powerful, oak-dominated nose, while the unctuous palate has more of the same and also some fruit and refreshing acidity. It is enjoyable, although not the region's most subtle example of the style.

◆ *Conde de Valdemar (red):* A superior young red with lots of fruity personality.

◆ *Conde de Valdemar Crianza (red):* A blend of 85 per cent Tempranillo and 15 per cent Mazuelo, this reasonably priced wine seems to have lost its way a little, a rather one-dimensional blend of very mature fruit and oak, decent and tasty but without much contrast.

◆ *Conde de Valdemar Reserva (red):* As above – and also reasonably priced – in that there is plenty of spicy flavour but it sometimes lacks elegance and complexity. Better than the crianza.

◆ *Conde de Valdemar Gran Reserva (red):* Quite a lot better than the previous two, with rather more complexity on both the nose and the palate, and classic Rioja tobacco and spice flavours. As with the crianza and reserva the fruit is very mature and the wine is sometimes fairly full-bodied and meaty.

◆ *Martínez Bujanda Garnacha Reserva (red):* This is a well known wine, partly for its quality and partly because it challenges the idea that it is not possible to make aged 100 per cent Garnacha wines because the grape is too prone to oxidation. Quality varies, but when on form this is a superior wine with a fine, quite complex nose and a very tasty, rounded palate with fruit and oak working well together. It is not as good as some of the reverential reviews written about it suggest, but then it couldn't be.

Martínez Lacuesta, S.A. (☎ 941 310 050) Founded in 1895, this sizeable firm buys in wine and turns out a small range of good bottles, which do not quite hit the heights, including:

- *Martínez Lacuesta Crianza (red)*: A light-bodied, characterful wine with classic, aged Rioja hints and aromas.

- *Martínez Lacuesta Reserva (red)*: The crianza is probably a better bet because recent releases of this, while tasty and drinkable, need longer in bottle to settle down and integrate.

- *Campeador Reserva (red)*: A meatier wine than the above, this is respectable with mouthfilling, spicy flavours more than complex depths.

Montecillo, S.A. (☎ 941 440 125) Founded in 1874 and now owned by Osborne (see page 34) Montecillo is a large concern producing a range of good and very good wines. Its reputation is solid rather than astral, but this is increasingly inaccurate as from the late '90s it has shown that it can make very good red wines, especially gran reservas. Nearly half of the bodega's output is exported and its range includes:

- *Montecillo Crianza (red)*: A superior Tempranillo crianza, medium-bodied, integrated, tasty and juicy. Recommended.

- *Montecillo Reserva (red)*: A good wine with some complexity on the nose and a rounded, tasty palate, but the crianza offers better value for money.

- *Montecillo Gran Reserva (red)*: These increasingly expensive wines are often excellent, with complex, smooth, integrated flavours, length and style. Recommended.

- *Montecillo Gran Reserva Selección Especial (red)*: These 15 to 20-year-old wines are lasting very well, with comments as above. Highly recommended and ample evidence of the high quality that the bodega is capable of.

Muga, S.A. (☎ 941 311 825) Founded in 1932 and still family owned, Muga is currently one of Rioja's leading bodegas, especially for its reserva and gran reserva wines. This is another bodega producing wines that are compulsory drinking for those wishing a knowledge of Rioja's better bottles, combining tradition with innovation.

- *Muga Fermentado en Barrica (white)*: One of the better barrel-fermented white Riojas, mouthfilling, unctuous and refreshing with oak expression more to the fore than fruit, as is often the case with these wines.

- *Muga (rosé)*: Made from 60 per cent Garnacha, 30 per cent Viura and 10 per cent Tempranillo, this is a superior pink wine with characterful, mouthfilling fruit. One of the region's better rosés.

- *Muga Crianza (red)*: Made from 70 per cent Tempranillo, 20 per cent Garnacha and 10 per cent Graciano and Mazuelo, this spends only six months in oak and a further two years in bottle. It has quite a complex nose and a well made, tasty palate which sometimes has more fruit than oak, sometimes the other way round. Its price has risen quite sharply.

● *Muga Reserva (red):* Made from the same blend of grapes as the crianza, this has also seen its price rise and is now quite expensive. Fortunately it is of high quality, with a toasty, tobaccoey nose and a full, balanced, long palate with some complexity. Recommended.

● *Torre Muga Reserva (red):* Made from 75 per cent Tempranillo, 15 per cent Mazuelo and 10 per cent Graciano, this is the bodega's most expensive wine, priced to compete with the region's best, although not as expensive as some wines with a lower reputation, for this has received a lot of plaudits. It is not the most aromatic Rioja and its qualities come through on the palate with full, long, mouthfilling, mature, toasty flavours very much to the fore. A must-taste wine.

● *Prado Enea Gran Reserva (red):* The bodega's other signature wine, this is generally as good as the above, but only two-thirds of the price. It has great elegance and style, while also being full-bodied and deep. Another must-taste.

Murua, S.A. (☎ 941 606 260) Founded in 1974, this small bodega makes a modest range of good quality, full-bodied wines.

● *Murua Fermentado en Barrica (white):* Made from 70 per cent Viura and 30 per cent traditional local varieties, this is unctuous, mouthfilling and flavoursome, with more wood than fruit, as is usually the case with these wines. Well made and competitively priced.

● *Murua Reserva (red):* Made from 75 per cent Tempranillo, 15 per cent Graciano and 10 per cent 'others', this is mouthfilling and finely structured with flavours of mature, spicy fruit. It is an enjoyable, approachable wine at a competitive price, rather than a complex trail-blazer.

● *Veguin de Murua Reserva (red):* This is a big jump in price, perhaps too much. Made from the same blend as the above, it is a powerful, well made wine with flavour and interest, but at this price it is up against better bottles.

Olarra, S.A. (☎ 941 235 299) Founded in 1973, this large, modern winery – which also makes Cava – produces a range of wines which vary in quality from the respectable to the very good. Its reputation looks to be on the up, mainly thanks to the fashionably labelled Summa Añares reserva. The range includes:

● *Reciente (white):* A fresh, fruity, young Viura with some bite.

● *Añares (rosé):* Made from 80 per cent Garnacha, 10 per cent Tempranillo and 10 per cent Viura, this is tasty, fruity rosé.

● *Otoñal (red):* A blend of 60 per cent Tempranillo, 30 per cent Garnacha and the balance Graciano and Mazuelo, this is a decent, fruity, young red for everyday drinking. Its price has risen rather steeply.

● *Añares Crianza (red):* 75 per cent Tempranillo with the balance made up of Garnacha, Graciano and Mazuelo, this is quite an elegant, balanced, flavoursome wine.

● *Añares Reserva (red):* A better version of the above. Good rather than remarkable.

◆ *Summa Añares Reserva (red):* The bodega's best wine, this recent release has a powerful nose with some complexity and a similar palate with length and personality. Recommended and reasonably priced, this is a good sign for the bodega's future.

◆ *Cerro Añón Reserva (red):* The bodega's most expensive wine – although not excessive by regional standards – this is aromatic with some complexity on the nose and a palate with smooth, spicy flavours. Good.

Ondarre, S.A. (☎ 948 645 300) Founded in 1984, this bodega produces a small range of good and very good wines, including:

◆ *Ondarre Crianza (white):* Made from 90 per cent Viura and 10 per cent 'others', this is a superior, oak-aged white Rioja, with decent fruit as well as oak and a balanced, tasty, expressive palate. Good and cheaper than some.

◆ *Ondarre Reserva (red):* This varies in style and quality from year to year, sometimes quite light, other times more powerful. It is always flavoursome and well put together.

◆ *Mayor de Ondarre Reserva (red):* This is the bodega's best and priciest wine, twice as expensive as the above. It is a superior 100 per cent Tempranillo with a complex, concentrated nose and a very flavoursome, structured palate with length. Recommended, although not cheap.

Ostatu, S.C. (☎ 941 609 133) Founded in 1970, this small bodega has shown itself capable of making white and red wines of good quality. Its range includes:

◆ *Ostatu Fermentado en Barrica (white):* A blend of 90 per cent Viura and 10 per cent Malvasía, this is a superior barrel-fermented white Rioja at a competitive price. It has a powerful nose with oak to the fore, but also citrus fruits. The palate has unctuous flavour, good balance and acidic bite.

◆ *Ostatu (red):* An inexpensive, everyday, young red with precocious fruit.

◆ *Ostatu Crianza (red):* Made from 90 per cent Tempranillo and 10 per cent Graciano, this is a well made, confident blend of suitably aged fruit and oak with some interest. Its price has risen quite sharply.

Palacio, S.A. (☎ 941 600 057) Founded in 1894, this firm has been through several pairs of hands, with quality and reputation vacillating as a result. The last decade of the 20th century saw things stabilise and the wines become better and more consistent. Its wide range includes:

◆ *Cosme Palacios y Hermanos Crianza (white):* A superior oak-aged white Rioja with fruit as well as oak to the fore and lots of powerful flavour and bite.

◆ *Regio Reserva (white):* A rarity – a white reserva – this maintains fruit character as well as oak and is a soundly constructed mouthful of integrated flavour, although it is expensive.

◆ *Glorioso (rosé):* A well made, fresh, tasty rosé. Good.

◆ *Milflores (red)*: A popular young Tempranillo in a distinctive bottle with flower patterns painted on the glass, this is a well made, commercial red with fruity character.

◆ *Castillo Rioja (red)*: A straightforward blend of fruit and oak, this semi-crianza has personality and flavour, with the oak influence to the fore.

◆ *Glorioso Crianza (red)*: A well made, commercial Tempranillo crianza with balance and fruit/oak integration, but it can lack depth and complexity.

◆ *Cosme Palacio y Hermanos Crianza (red)*: Twice the price of the above and a rather better wine with more finesse and interest, although it is quite expensive for what it offers.

◆ *Glorioso Reserva (red)*: A well made, integrated wine with a good finish. Worthy, but could perhaps do with a touch more complexity.

◆ *Bodegas Palacios Reserva Especial (red)*: Priced to compete with the region's big guns, this has spicy character and some mouthfilling complexity, but it lacks the quality to justify its elevated price.

Palacios Remondo, S.A. (☎ 941 237 177) Founded in 1948, although the family has been in the wine business since at least the 17th century, this operation is unusual in Rioja in that it has recently garnered as much attention for one of its white wines as its reds – Plácet, a barrel-fermented Viura. Its wide range of good and excellent wines includes:

◆ *Placet (white)*: First released in 1999, the bodega produced this wine to demonstrate that Viura has more qualities than is commonly supposed. It is one of Rioja's better barrel-fermented whites, with a herby nose and a palate offering balance, interest and flavour, in which the fruit is not buried under oak. Recommended.

◆ *Herencia Remondo (rosé)*: A good, fresh, fruity rosé from Garnacha.

◆ *Herencia Remondo (red)*: A superior, young Tempranillo with lots of fruity flavour. Good.

◆ *Herencia Remondo Crianza (red)*: Made from around 70 per cent Tempranillo with the balance Mazuelo, Graciano and Garnacha, this is a decent, straightforward blend of fruit and oak for a competitive price.

◆ *Herencia Remondo Reserva (red)*: A better version of the above, with more depth and interest, again at a fair price.

◆ *Dos Viñedos Reserva (red)*: This is a huge jump in price, but is a very classy creature, made from a changing blend of grapes. It is both powerful and elegant with lots of flavour and interest and has been garnering plaudits, although you do pay for the privilege.

Primicia, S.A. (☎ 941 600 296) Founded in 1985, this bodega has quickly proved itself capable of making good and very good wines, including:

◆ *Viña Diezmo Crianza (red):* Made from 100 per cent Tempranillo, this is a good, straightforward crianza with mature fruit and oak in abundance.

◆ *Gran Diezmo Mazuelo Crianza (red):* This is a novelty – a 100 per cent Mazuelo – and it works, a tasty, structured, balanced wine with bite. Good.

◆ *Gran Diezmo Reserva (red):* Made 100 per cent from Tempranillo, this has lively fruit and toasty oak flavours which should settle and develop as it ages.

◆ *Viña Carravalseca (red):* The bodega's most expensive wine by some distance is also its best, with a complex nose and a full, integrated, characterful palate with length. Recommended.

Ramón Bilbao, S.A. (☎ 941 310 295) Founded in 1924, this fair-size operation makes a range of decent and good wines, including:

◆ *Ramón Bilbao Fermentado en Barrica (white):* This is a decent barrel-fermented Viura with some fruit and bite to keep the oak in check.

◆ *Ramón Bilbao Crianza (red):* Made 100 per cent from Tempranillo, this is a good crianza with unctuous flavours of mature fruit and toasty oak and some length.

◆ *Ramón Bilbao Reserva (red):* Made from 90 per cent Tempranillo and 10 per cent 'others', this has some complexity on the nose and a balanced, structured, long palate. Good, but perhaps a touch expensive for what's on offer.

Real Divisa, S.A. (☎ 941 258 133) Founded in 1969, this small bodega produces limited amounts of good and very good red wines, including:

◆ *Marqués de Legarda Crianza (red):* A good crianza, with elegant yet mouthfilling flavours.

◆ *Marqués de Legarda Reserva (red):* A smoother, more complex version of the above. Recommended.

◆ *Marqués de Legarda Gran Reserva (red):* At around 15 years old this has classic flavours of leather, tobacco and earth. Well done but not for fans of up-front, lively fruit.

Riojanos, S.A. (☎ 941 454 050) Founded in 1890, this large operation makes a wide range of wines, which vary in quality from average to excellent, including:

◆ *Cancheles (white):* A light, fresh, everyday Viura without much to say for itself.

◆ *Monte Real Crianza (white):* A blend of 95 per cent Viura and 5 per cent Malvasía, this is a pretty good oak-aged wine, with balance, flavour and bite.

◆ *Viña Albina Fermentado en Barrica (white):* A better than average barrel-fermented Viura with good fruit/oak balance, flavour and bite. Good.

◆ *Puerta Vieja Crianza (red):* Made from 80 per cent Tempranillo, 15 per cent Mazuelo and 5 per cent Graciano, this is a light, commercial, relatively inexpensive crianza.

◆ *Viña Albina Reserva (red):* Made from the same grapes as above, this is a large jump in quality, a superior wine with flavour, elegance and character. Recommended and reasonably priced, although quality can vary from year to year.

◆ *Monte Real Reserva (red):* Again the same blend of grapes, this is another superior wine, spicy, tobaccoey and mouthfilling with length and character. Recommended.

◆ *Monte Real Gran Reserva (red):* This offers smooth, integrated, classic Rioja flavours of tobacco and old wood. Good rather than outstanding.

Roda, S.A. (☎ 941 303 001) Founded in 1991, this small operation has quickly garnered a stellar reputation and is seen as making some of Spain's very best red wines in the new Rioja style. Its first wine came on the market only in 1992 and Roda's approach is to blend the new with elements of the traditional, especially the use of oak, producing wines that are ready for drinking now but can be kept for many years. The name Roda comes from the first two letters of the two owners' surnames.

◆ *Roda II Reserva (red):* Made from 77 per cent Tempranillo and 23 per cent Garnacha this is the logical place to start, the bodega's least expensive and most approachable bottle. It is a high quality wine, powerful, mature, elegant and complex, drinking well at five years old and with the ability to integrate further.

◆ *Roda I Reserva (red):* Made 100 per cent from Tempranillo – the grapes coming from vines over 30 years old – and nearly twice the price of Roda II, this spends 2 years in oak and a further year in bottle. Seen as a trailblazer in Rioja, it combines elegance and strength, fruit and oak, and has complex, unctuous flavours, balance and length. One of Spain's very best wines and in view of that, reasonably priced. An absolute must-taste.

◆ *Cirsión (red):* Another 100 per cent Tempranillo, this is Roda's highest expression and at around four times the price of Roda I so it should be. It looks set to become one of Spain's top reds, a complex, exotic, unctuously rich wine, beautifully combining high quality, mature fruit and fine toasty oak with hints of minerals and soil. Wonderful, but costly.

Sáenz de Santa María, S.L. (☎ 941 454 008) Founded in 1993, this is a producer of straightforward, decent to good quality wines at competitive prices, including:

◆ *Rondan Blanco Crianza (white):* An aromatic, barrel-fermented Viura with lots of toasty flavours. It has more oak than fruit but is not overpowering and has refreshing bite. Less expensive than some.

◆ *Rondan Tinto Crianza (red):* Made from 90 per cent Tempranillo and 10 per cent 'others', this is a smooth, characterful wine with some complexity. Good and reasonably priced.

◆ *Rondan Reserva (red):* Made from the same grapes, this is not always as good as the crianza, sometimes being unbalanced.

San Pedro, S.C. (☎ 941 121 204) Founded in 1987, this operation's crianza and reserva reds can be of good quality:

◆ *Vallobera Crianza (red):* Made from 97 per cent Tempranillo and 3 per cent Graciano, this is a superior Rioja crianza, with powerful, characterful, integrated fruit and oak. Recommended.

◆ *Vallobera Reserva (red):* An older, more traditional version of the above.

Santa María López, S.L. (☎ 941 121 212) Founded in 1937, this is primarily a producer of decent, straightforward wines, with one standing out. Its range includes:

◆ *Solar Viejo Crianza (white):* A good, oaked white Rioja, with nutty, oaky flavours, refreshing acidity and some fruit peeping through the oak. Enjoyable and reasonably priced.

◆ *Solar Viejo Reserva (red):* This varies in quality. It can be complex, smooth, balanced and elegant, but in some years it is rather unfocused and one-dimensional.

◆ *Angel SantaMaría Selección Especial (red):* This is the wine that stands out, an aromatic, mouthfilling red with character and spicy oak, combining old and new Rioja flavours. Good.

Señorío de Arana, S.A. (☎ 941 331 150) Founded in 1905, this is a producer of a range of respectable and good, everyday wines at competitive prices. It has 10 hectares of its own vines and buys in grapes and wine from elsewhere. The following are generally its best bottles:

◆ *Viña del Oja Crianza (red):* Made from 80 per cent Tempranillo, 10 per cent Garnacha and 10 per cent Mazuelo, this straightforward, inexpensive blend of fruit and oak is an honest, decent, everyday wine.

◆ *Viña del Oja Reserva (red):* A blend of 80 per cent Tempranillo, 15 per cent Mazuelo and 5 per cent Graciano, this is a suitably aged, straightforward, quite elegant wine, enjoyable and modestly priced.

Señorío de San Vicente (☎ 941 308 040) This very small bodega is run by a family that has been involved in the wine business since the late 19th century. The current operation's first wine came on the market in 1991 and its 18 hectares of vines are planted with the low-yielding Tempranillo Peludo, this being a bodega very much after quality not quantity.

◆ *San Vicente (red):* A lovely, complex blend of mature fruit and toasty oak, expressive, vigorous, structured and elegant. Highly recommended.

Sierra Cantabria, S.A. (☎ 941 334 080) Founded in 1979, this bodega is run by the same family as Señorío de San Vicente above. It produces a range of wines varying in quality from respectable to excellent.

◆ *Sierra Cantabria (white):* A clean, fruity, young white with some character.

◆ Murmurón (red): A young Tempranillo made by carbonic maceration, this has lots of aromatic fruity flavour and character, although its price has escalated.

◆ *Sierra Cantabria Crianza (red):* Made from 100 per cent Tempranillo, this is a straightforward, tasty crianza, but lacks the interest of the reservas.

◆ *Sierra Cantabria Reserva (red):* A superior, reasonably priced Rioja reserva, mouthfilling, flavoursome and persistent. Recommended.

◆ *Sierra Cantabria Colección Privada (red):* The bodega's top wine and its most expensive, this is Sierra Cantabria's bid to sit at the top table and has garnered many plaudits. Made 100 per cent from Tempranillo, it has a powerful nose and palate with unctuous, mouthfilling flavours. Very good and it will be interesting to see how it develops in bottle.

Solar de Carrión (☎ 941 322 246) Founded in 1950, this large operation produces a range of decent, reasonably priced wines, with the following probably the best combination of quality and price:

◆ *Marqués de Carrión Crianza (red):* A blend of 80 per cent Tempranillo and 20 per cent Garnacha, this is a well made, characterful, suitably aged blend of mature fruit and oak. Good.

Sonsierra (☎ 941 334 031) Founded in 1962, this large co-operative has 750 hectares of its own vines and makes a range of respectable to good quality wines at fair prices, with the following worth seeking out:

◆ *Sonsierra Rosado (rosé):* A tasty, aromatic rosé from Tempranillo.

◆ *Sonsierra Tinto (red):* A tasty, aromatic young Tempranillo with character. Good.

◆ *Viña Mindiarte Reserva (red):* A competitively priced 100 per cent Tempranillo, this is a well made, tasty wine, integrated and balanced. Good rather than great.

Tobía (☎ 941 457 425) Founded in 1982, this small bodega treads its own path, producing among other things a barrel-fermented rosé. Its range of reasonably priced wines is worth investigating, especially:

◆ *Viña Tobía Fermentado en Barrica (white):* A barrel-fermented Viura and Malvasía, this is a well made, tasty wine, integrated and characterful, less expensive than some. Good.

◆ *Viña Tobía Fermentado en Barrica (rosé):* Made from 100 per cent Tempranillo, this works, being mouthfilling, refreshing and flavoursome. Recommended.

◆ *Alma de Tobía (red):* A blend of Tempranillo, Garnacha and Mazuelo, this spends nine months in barrel, short by Rioja standards but the oak still manages to dominate the fruit in this powerful, tasty wine. Unfortunately it is rather expensive.

Torre de Oña (☎ 941 121 154) Founded in 1987, this small bodega makes a tasty, moreish red reserva, popular on the export market as well as in Spain.

◆ *Barón de Oña Reserva (red):* A blend of around 90 per cent Tempranillo with Cabernet Sauvignon and Mazuelo, this is an aromatic wine with flavour, balance and length. Recommended, although its price has risen quite sharply. Do not drink too young.

Unión de Cosecheros de Labastida (☎ 941 331 161) Founded in 1964, this co-operative has around 170 members and 500 hectares of vines. This might lead one to believe that it concentrates on quantity rather than quality. In fact, its wines are of respectable and good standards, the following being the most interesting:

◆ *Montebuena (red):* A fruity, aromatic young Tempranillo.

◆ *Solagüen Crianza (red):* A decent, commercial blend of fruit and oak.

◆ *Manuel Quintano Reserva (red):* This is by far the bodega's most expensive wine, a recent addition to its range designed and priced to sit with the region's best. Made 100 per cent from Tempranillo, it spends nearly four years in American oak. It is an engaging wine, powerful and unctuous with mature fruit and oak that does not overpower the whole. However, it is priced to compete with some noble, complex wines and probably falls short as yet. Might this change with longer bottle ageing?

Unión Vitivinícola, S.A. Marqués de Cáceres (☎ 941 454 000) Founded in 1970, and designed along Bordeaux lines with advice from the University of Bordeaux, this is far from being a typical Rioja operation. It has no vineyards but buys in grapes from local growers and its wines are more 'international' in style than the regional average, less oaky than many Riojas. The cleverly designed bottle labels are also non-country specific, as well as being slick and neutrally stylish. Thus it is ironic that this foreign-influenced, relatively new bodega should be so popular, both in Spain and abroad, and thus strongly associated with the region. Its wines range in quality from good to very good indeed.

◆ *Marqués de Cáceres (white):* This young, unoaked Viura is credited as being Rioja's first wine in this fresh, fruity style. It is a well made, tasty, fruity wine, a Spanish supermarket and restaurant wine list staple.

◆ *Satinela Semi-Dulce (semi-sweet white):* A well made, aromatic wine from the Malvasía grape, unctuous, balanced, quite sweet and long.

◆ *Marqués de Cáceres Blanco Crianza (white):* A tasty, oak-aged Viura, with more oak than fruit, but nicely unctuous.

◆ *Antea Fermentado en Barrica (white):* A good barrel-fermented white Rioja, unctuous, mouthfilling and with fruit and oak working well together.

◆ *Marqués de Cáceres (rosé):* A blend of 80 per cent Tempranillo and 20 per cent Garnacha, this is decent, fresh wine but perhaps a touch pricey.

◆ *Marqués de Cáceres Crianza (red):* Made from 85 per cent Tempranillo, the balance Garnacha and Graciano, this is a well made, competitively priced wine, with understated yet characterful fruit and oak. It is not a typical Rioja, more international in style.

◆ *Marqués de Cáceres Reserva (red):* The bodega's reservas can be very good indeed and in strong vintages are powerful and complex wines, cleverly combining the old

Rioja flavours of tobacco and leather with the new Rioja fruit. Recommended and some of them are very reasonably priced.

◆ *Marqués de Cáceres Gran Reserva (red):* As above.

◆ *Gaudium Reserva (red):* A recent release, this is the bodega's flagship wine, much pricier than any of its other bottles. It has quickly received many plaudits, an elegant, complex, international wine with powerful flavours. Very good indeed, but also very expensive.

Vinícola Riojana de Alcanadre Sociedad Cooperativa (☎ 941 165 036) Founded in 1957, this co-operative draws grapes from 700 hectares of vineyards and makes a wide range of wines. Prices are notably low by Rioja standards and quality varies from adequate to good. The following wines are the best bet:

◆ *Aradón (red):* A blend of 50 per cent Tempranillo and 50 per cent Garnacha, this is a notably aromatic young wine with a lively, tasty palate. Good.

◆ *Silval Tempranillo (red):* An aromatic, fruity young wine with character. Good.

◆ *Barzagoso Crianza (red):* A blend of 70 per cent Tempranillo, 15 per cent Garnacha and 15 per cent Mazuelo, this is an engaging, inexpensive wine, medium-bodied, balanced and flavoursome.

◆ *Barzagoso Reserva (red):* Made from nearly the same blend as the crianza, this has a complex, classic Rioja nose and a tasty, balanced palate with fruit and oak working well together. In good vintages it is something of a Rioja bargain.

Vinos de los Herederos del Marqués de Riscal (☎ 941 606 000) Founded in 1860, and along with Marqués de Murrieta the most frequently mentioned Rioja 'aristocrat', Riscal has a noble history of making excellent wines, with more of a French feel than some in the region. It was founded along the lines of a Bordeaux château and has long had dispensation to use small amounts of Cabernet Sauvignon in its wines. The bodega has had its ups and downs over the years but has been performing well for some time now and sits at Rioja's top table. The following are must-taste wines:

◆ *Marqués de Riscal Reserva (red):* Made from 90 per cent Tempranillo and 10 per cent Graciano and Mazuelo, this is one of the region's more reliable reservas. It has an engaging nose of characterful fruit and oak, while the palate is powerful yet elegant with complex flavours and a lovely feel. Highly recommended.

◆ *Marqués de Riscal Gran Reserva (red):* A suitably aged wine, with classic flavours of mature fruit, oak, tobacco and leather, and length. Recommended, although it costs quite a lot more than the reserva, so choose that first.

◆ *Barón de Chirel Reserva (red):* The bodega's top wine, this is something of a legend in Rioja, made from around 50 per cent Tempranillo and just under 50 per cent Cabernet Sauvignon, with some Graciano. First appearing on the market in 1991, it broke the mould with its Cabernet content and price, and pushed consumers into paying elevated prices for high quality, modern Riojas. It has a complex nose of fruits, spices, tar and tobacco, and a palate with superb power, elegance, interest, structure and balance. The price has escalated, but this is a must-have bottle.

Viña Herminia (☎ 941 144 169) Founded in its current form in 1997, this outward-looking bodega – it exports half of its production – makes a range of wines which vary in quality from decent to very good:

● *Viña Herminia Crianza (red)*: A blend of 85 per cent Tempranillo and 15 per cent Garnacha, this is a well made, competitively priced, medium-bodied wine with flavour and balance, elegant rather than mouthfilling.

● *Viña Herminia Reserva (red)*: Made from the same blend of grapes as the crianza, this is similarly elegant and well made. Good rather than outstanding.

● *Duque de Huéscar Reserva (red)*: A blend of 80 per cent Tempranillo, 10 per cent Graciano and 10 per cent Garnacha, this is the bodega's best and most expensive wine, priced to compete with the middle range of Rioja's top bottles. It is very good, with a complex, tobaccoey nose and a medium-bodied palate with expressive flavours and elegance. Recommended.

Viña Ijalba (☎ 941 261 100) Founded in 1991, with 70 hectares of its own vines and exporting half of its output, this operation makes a range of wines that vary in quality from respectable to very good. The following are the best:

● *Aloque (rosé)*: A blend of 50 per cent Garnacha and 50 per cent Tempranillo, this is a tasty, characterful wine, but rather expensive in comparison to similar quality competitors from Navarra, Cigales and Catalonia.

● *Solferino Maceración Carbónica (red)*: This is not the usual exuberantly fruity, in-your-face, carbonic maceration wine, but a more subtle creature. The nose is fruity but not excessively so, while the palate is medium-bodied and flavoursome, soundly constructed and enjoyable. Recommended, but price increases have made it expensive for a young red.

● *Ijalba Reserva (red)*: Made from 90 per cent Tempranillo and 10 per cent Graciano, this is the bodega's most reliable aged red. It is a well made wine, tasty and balanced with well judged tannins.

Viña Salceda (☎ 941 606 125) Founded in 1969, this bodega is well worth investigating for its attractively priced, good and very good red wines. Its profile deserves to be higher.

● *Viña Salceda Crianza (red)*: Made from 85 to 90 per cent Tempranillo, with the balance Mazuelo and/or Graciano, this is a characterful, reasonably priced, mouthfilling wine with confident, enjoyable fruit and oak flavours, rather than a deeply complex, elegant bottle for mulling over. Recommended.

● *Viña Salceda Reserva (red)*: Made from roughly the same blend as the crianza, this is a rather more complex, rounded, mature and satisfying wine. Delicious, confident and recommended.

Viña Valoria (☎ 941 204 059) Founded in 1860, making it one of the region's oldest operations, this is a solid rather than remarkable producer, with a range of decent to good quality wines, including:

◆ *Viña Valoria (red)*: Made from 70 per cent Tempranillo, 20 per cent Graciano and 10 per cent Mazuelo, this is a well made, aromatic wine with fruity character and bite.

◆ *Viña Valoria Crianza (red)*: Made from the same blend of grapes as the above, this is a lightish, straightforward blend of gentle fruit and oak.

◆ *Viña Valoria Reserva (red)*: The same blend again, this is the bodega's best wine, with rounded, spicy flavours and more structure and elegance than the crianza.

Viña Villabuena, S.A. (☎ 941 609 086) Founded in 1987, this operation has shown that it can make high quality wines, including:

◆ *Izadi Fermentado en Barrica (white)*: Made from 80 per cent Viura and 20 per cent Malvasía, this is a superior barrel-fermented white Rioja, unctuous, mouthfilling and long. As with many of these wines, oak dominates fruit, but it is elegant, toasty oak.

◆ *Viña Izadi Crianza (red)*: A blend of 90 per cent Tempranillo, with the balance Graciano and Mazuelo, this is a tasty crianza with fruity character. Not always especially representative of the region but an enjoyable wine.

◆ *Viña Izadi Reserva (red)*: This blend of 90 per cent Tempranillo, with the balance Graciano and Mazuelo, is a powerful, integrated, flavoursome wine, which can be very good indeed. Recommended.

Viñedos de Aldeanueva, Sociedad Cooperativa (☎ 941 163 039) Founded in 1956, this very large operation has access to 2,800 hectares of vineyards and it might be expected that its strength would be quantity rather than quality. However, its wines are of good and very good quality, and include:

◆ *Viña Azabache Tempranillo (red)*: A well made, reasonably priced, concentrated, flavoursome young wine.

◆ *Azabache Crianza (red)*: This is a soundly constructed, straightforward blend of fruit and oak, in some years with touches of complexity.

◆ *Azabache Reserva (red)*: The bodega's best wine, this is well made, confident, mouthfilling and balanced. Appealing, reasonably priced and recommended.

Viñedos del Contino, S.A. (☎ 941 600 201) Founded in 1974, and belonging to C.V.N.E. (see page 309), this is a much praised, high quality operation and an important exponent of modern Riojas and estate wines. Its Tempranillo-based bottles can be among Rioja's best and are compulsory drinking for those wanting to understand the region.

◆ *Contino Crianza (red)*: A superior, balanced, mouthfilling yet elegant crianza, whose price has risen quite steeply. It can be one of the region's best. Recommended.

◆ *Contino Reserva (red)*: Powerful and complex on the nose, this has body, mature tannins, unctuous flavours and complexity. An excellent wine, highly recommended. Considering its renown and quality, the price is reasonable.

◆ *Contino Graciano Reserva (red):* An important wine, which has done as much as any to showcase the delights of this high quality, difficult-to-grow grape. It has a powerful, complex, toasty, peppery and leathery nose, with a mouthfilling, unctuous, toasty, fruity palate, very expressive and long. Highly recommended, although the price has risen steeply over the last few years.

Viñedos y Bodegas de la Marquesa (☎ 941 609 085) Founded in 1880, this bodega makes a range of wines most of which are good and combine the best of the old and new Rioja. The following are worth investigating:

◆ *Valserrano Fermentado en Barrica (white):* This is an enjoyable barrel-fermented white Rioja, with fruit to partner the oak and unctuous flavours and bite.

◆ *Valserrano Crianza (red):* A well made, balanced wine with lively fruit and fine oak.

◆ *Valserrano Reserva (red):* Made from 90 per cent Tempranillo and 10 per cent Graciano, this has a complex nose and a smooth, concentrated palate with balance, integration and length. Recommended.

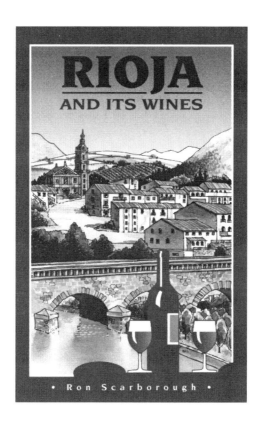

This book is required reading for lovers of fine wines and beautiful, unspoilt countryside. Rioja is much more than one of the world's great wine-producing areas and is a fascinating region with a rich and colourful history, stunning scenery and picturesque villages.

Some of the topics covered are: Details of 200 of Rioja's Best Known Bodegas; The History of Rioja Wine and the Region; Wine Production, Classification & Quality Control; Tasting, Storing & Buying Rioja Wines; Glossary of Spanish Wine and Food Terms; Wine Routes for Touring Wine Lovers.

Rioja and its Wines is the most comprehensive and up-to-date source of information available about Rioja wines and the region. In addition to introducing you to the delights of Rioja wine, the author will take you on a guided tour through this charming region, its history, architecture, villages, wildlife and warm-hearted, friendly people. So fill your glass, sit back and enjoy a journey through time with *Rioja and its Wines*. Salud!

Order your copies today by phone, fax, mail or e-mail from: Survival Books, PO Box 146, Wetherby, West Yorks. LS23 6XZ, United Kingdom (☎/▭ +44 (0)1937-843523, ✉ orders@survivalbooks.net, ▨ www.survivalbooks.net).

APPENDICES

Appendix A – Wine Terminology

Acid: Mention of this in the context of wine may seem negative, but the opposite is generally true. Various acids are crucial to wine, both as preservatives and to give it refreshing, tangy bite. This is especially true of whites. An excess, of course, is a defect and makes the wine overly tart. As with many things in wine production, balance is essential.

Aftertaste: See Finish.

Aggressive: Self-explanatory and invariably the result of too much acidity, tannin or both.

Alcoholic Strength: Important in giving wine body and flavour. For the great majority of table wines it varies between 9% and 15%, with most in the 11.5% to 13.5% range. As a general rule, higher alcohol wines come from warmer climates because grapes become riper and hence contain more sugar which can turn into alcohol.

Amontillado: A fino sherry aged to become darker, stronger and more aromatic.

Año: Year, often of production.

Aroma: This, along with Bouquet and Nose, tend to be interchangeable these days. Traditionally, aroma describes the primary, fruity, flowery smells of a wine, bouquet the smells arising from ageing and nose is a combination of the two.

Balance: For a wine to be balanced, a very desirable quality, all of its elements – acid, alcohol, fruit, possibly oak and tannin – must work harmoniously and none should be overly dominant.

Barrica: Barrel.

Blanco: White.

Blend: Mixing grapes from different regions to make one wine, or mixing different grape varieties to make a wine.

Bodega: A flexible term, which can refer to a wine retailer; a cellar; or a business which makes, blends or distributes wine, perhaps all three.

Body: This refers to the weight of the wine. The more body a wine has, the less watery it is and the more alcohol and flavours it tends to have.

Botella: Bottle.

Bouquet: See Aroma.

Brut: Very dry sparkling wine.

Carbonic Maceration: A wine making technique whereby whole bunches of grapes are put in sealed fermentation tanks along with carbon dioxide. Fermentation occurs within individual grapes, causing them to swell and burst. The resulting juice gives fruity, vibrant, low-tannin wines for drinking young. The best known example of a wine made in this way is probably Beaujolais Nouveau.

Cava: Has three meanings: a business making sparkling wine, as in Cava House; the sparkling wine itself, made by the Champagne method, also called the Método Tradicional; the D.O. covering the areas where the wine is made.

Cepa: A vague one this. It actually means a vine, but is sometimes used to mean a grape. **Uva** is the usual word for grape.

Clarete: Something of an anachronism, this is a term for a light red or dark rosé, a style of wine little made now. This is fortunate, as the word has been banned by the good folk of the European Union.

Cold Fermentation: Fermentation of wine in stainless steel vats at carefully controlled low temperatures. It maintains freshness and crispness in wines.

Commercial: Invariably used to describe lighter, inexpensive, simple wines – or gluggers – designed to appeal to a wide range of people. It is not a criticism.

Complex: Refers to wines with a wide range of flavours and nuances, which often develop and deepen in the mouth and on the finish. See Deep/Depth.

Consejo Regulador: The governing body of a Denominación de Origen, or D.O..

Cosecha: Vintage, harvest or crop.

Criado y embotellado por: Grown/matured and bottled by.

Crianza: This literally means 'nursing' and is the term used for the process of ageing a wine, as well as being the name of the youngest officially recognised category of aged/matured wine. Red, white and rosé crianzas are released for sale in their third year, after a minimum of two years ageing, of which at least six months must have been in oak barrels, longer in some regions.

Crisp: Oft-used term to describe white wines. It refers to those with well judged acidity and freshness. See Fresh.

Deep/Depth: This refers to wines with layers of flavours which develop in the mouth after the initial 'attack', i.e. first impressions. See Complex.

Denominación de Origen: Commonly shortened to D.O., this refers to an official wine region, with the Consejo Regulador deciding and overseeing the region's boundary, permitted grape varieties, vineyard management techniques, minimum quality levels, etc. See also Consejo Regulador, Vino de la Tierra and Vino de Mesa.

Denominación de Origen Calificada: D.O.Ca is the classification for wines of the very highest quality. Currently only Rioja enjoys this honour and has done so since 1991, but it may be awarded to a couple of other regions soon.

Dulce: Sweet.

Espumoso: Sparkling.

Etiqueta: Label.

Farmyardy: An unlikely sounding description of the nose of some wines made from the Pinot Noir grape. Surprisingly, it is not unpleasant.

Finish: The aromas and flavours which remain after a wine has been swallowed. Also called Length. Generally speaking, the longer the finish, the better the wine.

Fino: Pale, dry, tangy sherry or Montilla.

Fresh: Almost the same as Crisp, but also indicates cleanliness, a good quality.

Generoso: A fortified aperitif or dessert wine.

Gran Reserva: The top tier of aged wines, with reds spending at least two years in oak and a further three in bottle before release, although sometimes much longer. White and rosé gran reservas, which are incredibly rare, are aged for four years before release, of which at least six months must be in oak.

Jammy: Another self-explanatory term, referring to red wines which smell and sometimes taste like jam. They usually hail from warm or hot climates and are often made from very mature grapes.

Joven: Literally 'young', this refers to young, unoaked wines which emphasise their fruitiness and are designed to be drunk soon after release.

Length: See Finish.

Madera: Wood, invariably oak. See Roble.

Manzanilla: A type of fino sherry made at coastal Sanlúcar de Barrameda, especially fine with a tangy, maritime bite.

Meaty: A word much used for describing 'big', concentrated wines, usually red, but it is also appropriate for some barrel-fermented Chardonnays.

Media-Crianza: A non-official wine category, somewhere between Joven and Crianza. Wines are aged in oak for short periods, usually three or four months.

Método Tradicional: The best method of making sparkling wine. It used to be known as the Méthode Champenoise, but that is no longer the 'official' term. See Cava.

Oaky/Oaked: A commonly used term referring to the aromas and flavours of wines which have been fermented and/or aged in oak barrels. New oak imparts colour, flavours and tannin to wines, and oak also allows them to breathe because small amounts of oxygen permeate the barrels. High quality wines destined for bottle-ageing benefit from prior oak ageing, but oak flavours can be overdone. See Balance.

Nose: See Aroma.

Oloroso: A dark, pungent, matured sherry or Montilla.

Reserva: To qualify as a reserva, the second highest quality designation, red wine must be aged for a minimum of three years, although the period is often far longer, with at least one year in oak barrel. White and rosé reservas have to age for at least two years, of which at least six months must be in oak.

Roble: Oak.

Rosado: Rosé.

Seco: Dry.

Semi-Dulce: Semi-sweet.

Semi-Seco: Semi-dry.

Sin Crianza: Wines which have not been aged in oak. Often the same as Joven, but can also mean older wines which have not been oak-aged.

Tannin: Associated mainly with red wine, tannins are chemical compounds found in grape skins, pips, stems and oak . In younger wines which require further bottle ageing, the tannins can be aggressive, leaving a 'film' in the mouth, rather as strong tea does. As the wine ages, the tannins soften and sometimes become sweet. Reds made for ageing require tannins, but they must not overpower the other elements in the wine. See Balance.

Tinto: Red, as in wine. Rojo is the usual Spanish word for the colour red when used in any other context.

Uva: Grape.

Vendimia: Vintage.

Vid: Vine.

Viejo: Old, often in the context of aged.

Viña: Vineyard. If used on wine labels, it does not necessarily mean that the grapes used in the wine are all from the same vineyard.

Vino: Wine.

Vino de Aguja: Wine which is naturally slightly sparkling, characteristic of some of Galicia's whites.

Vino de la Tierra: A step up from Vino de Mesa, i.e. superior table wine. See also D.O. and Vino de Mesa.

Vino de Mesa: Table wine. See also D.O. and Vino de la Tierra.

Appendix B – Vintage Chart 1990 to 1999

	'90	'91	'92	'93	'94	'95	'96	'97	'98	'99
Alella	VG	E	G	E	VG	VG	VG	E	VG	VG
Alicante	VG	G	G	G	G	E	G	G	G	VG
Binissalem	–	G	G	G	E	G	G	VG	VG	VG
Campo de Borga	G	VG	VG	G	G	G	G	G	VG	G
Cariñena	VG	VG	VG	VG	G	G	VG	R	VG	G
Cigales	G	VG	R	G	G	G	G	G	G	VG
Costers del Segre	G	VG	VG	VG	R	G	G	G	VG	VG
Jumilla	G	VG	G	VG	G	G	VG	VG	VG	VG
La Mancha	G	G	VG	E	VG	G	VG	VG	E	VG
Navarra	G	G	G	G	VG	E	VG	G	VG	VG
Penedés	G	VG	G	VG	G	G	VG	VG	VG	VG
Priorato	G	G	VG	E	VG	E	VG	G	VG	VG
Rías Baixas	VG	G	G	G	VG	VG	VG	VG	G	G
Ribera del Duero	VG	VG	G	R	VG	E	E	G	VG	E
Rioja	VG	VG	G	R	E	E	VG	G	VG	G
Rueda	G	G	G	G	G	G	VG	VG	VG	VG
Somontano	G	VG	VG	E	E	VG	VG	G	E	VG
Tacoronte-Acentejo	–	–	–	G	G	VG	VG	VG	VG	G
Toro	E	E	VG	VG	E	VG	VG	G	VG	E
Valencia	G	G	G	VG	VG	G	VG	G	VG	VG

R – Regular   G – Good   VG – Very Good   E – Excellent

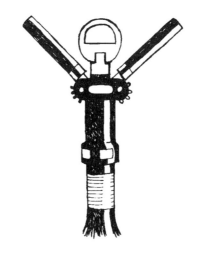

INDEX